A HISTORY OF
LITERARY AESTHETICS
IN AMERICA

A HISTORY OF
LITERARY AESTHETICS
IN AMERICA

Max I. Baym

Frederick Ungar Publishing Co.

NEW YORK

To Ide,

my wife and tireless collaborator
in all my work

PREFACE

Literary aesthetics is primarily concerned with the criteria of beauty and pleasure in the creation and in the appreciation of literary works of art. My point of view is that the aesthetic quest is itself a thing of beauty. To trace the fluctuations in that quest in America through more than two centuries, I have combed the works of writers who have dealt explicitly with the problem of aesthetic definition and those in whose writings a considered point of view is implicit. This work presents a survey of literary aesthetics in America from Jonathan Edwards to recent "scientific" criticism. This study is not to be interpreted as a history of *solutions* but rather of *efforts* to grasp and express the meaning of that elusive entity which, since the time of the early Greeks, has been called beauty and, since Plato and Aristotle, has been called art. I have tried to avoid the tumult of opinion and of opinionated doctrine that so often accompanies this subject. Since literature is one of the fine arts, it follows that the aesthetics of it can be most richly grasped in the context of principles that apply to artistic expression generally. Hence it seemed fitting to treat the history of literary aesthetics in the context of the history of general aesthetics.

Throughout, I have kept the European heritage in mind. Wherever possible I have analyzed the ways in which American critics and writers adapted ideas from both modern Europe and antiquity.

Among the aesthetic questions I shall examine are the relationship of sensibility to knowledge, the nature of poetic creativity, the roles of symbolism and metaphor, the differentiae of poetry and prose, the tension between poetry and science, feeling and reason as forms of cognition, the literary applications of metaphysics and science, and the nature of sentimentality.

It is of course true that the responses that thoughtful men have recorded in works of inquiry, analysis, and historical résumé do help to enrich one's own experience of beauty in art and in nature. But anyone who feels he must formulate a rigorous definition of beauty before he is free to respond to works of art will be in the pitiable state of the man looking on while others feast. He who does respond spontaneously to a Mozart symphony, to a Titian painting, or to a Goethe poem will inevitably begin to wonder about the nature of his response and of the stimuli that call it forth.

For the man endowed with intellectual curiosity and an analytical turn of mind, this wonderment will be the initial step in a lifelong exploration of the study known as aesthetics. Such a man will turn to the history of the subject to find out how people who have devoted considerable effort to this area of experience have analyzed and interpreted it.

For spirited dialogue on the controversial problems of the tension between poetry and science and the possible relation between the humanities and the sciences in a unified aesthetic, I offer my thanks to two distinguished friends: Leonard S. Schwartz, communication systems expert and theoretician, member of the New York Academy of Science; and John Pappas, outstanding scholar in the literature of the enlightenment and a professor at the Graduate School of Fordham University. A long delayed expression of gratitude is also due to my lifelong friend Meyer Ross, M. D., whose honors in the medical profession are matched by his keen interest in the humanities, and whose insistence that I persevere in writing this book expressed a sincere concern for the successful completion of a long-term project.

I wish to express my indebtedness to a number of people who have generously extended their help during the writing of this book. Alex Preminger, head of the Humanities Division of the Brooklyn College library, has offered many useful suggestions and has been a constant source of encouragement. Minerva Katz, a member of his staff, put her bibliographical expertise and scholarly insights at my service and enthusiastically entered into the spirit of my work; I am greatly indebted to her. Other members of the library staff who deserve my thanks are Oscar P. Dickinson, Daniel L. Levy, Blanche Vitrogan, and James Gibson. To Mr. Gibson, I am especially grateful for his untiring efforts in securing books and documents on inter-library loan. Charles Hill of Brooklyn College often helped me in obtaining books in foreign languages. The Harvard and Yale library staffs were prompt in replying to my inquiries. For their care in typing the manuscript in its various stages, my gratitude goes to Terry Segal and to Muriel Paster. Finally, I offer my warm thanks to my two editors, Lina Mainiero and Leonard Klein. Their sympathetic guidance has helped me to overcome many a dilemma in the course of writing this book.

MAX I. BAYM

CONTENTS

EARLY INTIMATIONS OF AESTHETIC SENSIBILITY

Jonathan Edwards (1703–1758)

Among the gifts bequeathed to the world by the Renaissance was the American continent. The discovery of this new region was the result, at least in part, of an aesthetic affection for the remote and the exotic, as well as of the desire for riches and power. It was also the result of the quest for freedom that inspired such earlier settlers as the Pilgrims. Plymouth Rock itself, in its Atlantic setting, is a kind of monument to man's sense of the sea, in which all life originated, and to his continuing search for a vast and terrible beauty, which bewilders him with its awesomeness and sublimity.

The Pilgrims, of course, did not include aestheticians in their company, and the books that John Harvard contributed to the college named after him contained little that could illuminate the nature of beauty. Indeed, Harvard University did not offer courses in aesthetics for more than two centuries. The "sense of beauty," however, was present in the colonies long before this phrase was used as the title of a famous book (*The Sense of Beauty* by George Santayana, 1896), and the yearning for the aesthetic considerably antedated scholarly dissertations on the subject. Findings at the beginning of this century, moreover, contradicted the prevailing belief that the Puritans

were opposed to art.[1] Indeed, despite the lack of imaginative literature in the New England colonies, a certain amount of aesthetic
imagination was occasionally expressed.[2]

Certain elements of an early aesthetic theory may be found, for
example, in the works of the clergyman and theologian Jonathan
Edwards. His youthful "Notes on Natural Science" indicated the
direction of his thought. Influenced by Locke's *Essay on Human
Understanding*, he became aware of the distinction between wit
and judgment. The first combines

> . . . ideas with pleasing variety, discovering their similarities
> and relations and thus grouping them into beautiful pictures
> which divert and strike the imagination; the latter [judgment
> or intellect] seeks dissimilarities, guided by the criterion of
> truth.
>
> Further: The mind, without looking any further, rests satis-
> fied with the agreeableness of the picture, and the gaiety of
> the fancy; and it is a kind of an affront to go about to examine
> it by the severe rules of truth and good reason; whereby it
> appears that it consists in something that is not perfectly con-
> formable to them.[3]

For young Edwards, who as a boy doted on balloon spiders and
rainbows, these words meant much more than an addition to his
erudition.

At Yale, Edwards studied under the noted early American educator
Samuel Johnson (1696–1772), whose *Elementa Philosophica* introduced American readers to the thought of George Berkeley as well
as of Nicholas Malebranche and Francis Hutcheson. Edwards was
also familiar with the writings of Hutcheson and Shaftesbury (An-
thony Ashley Cooper). In Shaftesbury's *Characteristics*, Edwards
encountered the analogy between beauty and virtue, and in his
"Notes on Natural Science" he referred to the Earl of Shaftesbury.[4]
According to Arthur Cushman McGiffert, Edwards's definition of
virtue in terms of beauty (in his *Dissertations on the Nature of True
Virtue*) owed much not only to Shaftesbury and Hutcheson but also
to Ralph Cudworth.

Edwards's perception of beauty included, in Pythagorean fashion, mathematical forms, since for him being itself illustrated the aesthetic principles of proportion and balance of parts, symbolized by numbers. Beauty was a quality of the world; it inhered in the structure of the cosmos. In the moral realm beauty becomes goodness, which is a quality of the disposition of the will. The apperception of spiritual beauty is a divine gift. For Edwards, the universe, existing "nowhere but in the divine mind," was an aesthetic construct, the expression of a will to shape and dominate matter.[5]

Edwards followed Hutcheson in the belief that God implanted in man an internal sense that enabled his mind to discern natural beauty. Although he was under a pietistic mandate not to confuse spiritual with physical beauty, Edwards's enthusiasm and wonder in the presence of nature brought him close to a romantic approach to it. He was sensitive not only to the architectonics of the spider, the blandishment of the rainbow, and the shape of flowers, but even to the beauty of man's body (the mores did not permit him to comment on the beauty of a woman's body).

His intellectual extrapolation of equalities from correspondence, symmetry, regularity, and the like, was intimately associated with his sensitivity to the beauty of the shapes and motions of things, the apperception of which was sharpened by his love of music. He spoke of the pleasures of the senses, which result from equality: "Thus in music, not only in the proportion which the several notes of a tune bear, one among another, but in merely two notes there is harmony."

He understood that the "proportion is in the particular vibrations of the air, which strike on the ear." Similarly, the pleasantness of light, color, taste, smell, and touch "all arise from proportion of motion. The organs are so contrived that upon the touch of such and such particles, there shall be a regular and harmonious motion of the animal spirits." His universal definition of "excellency" as "the Consent of Being to Being, or Being's Consent to Entity" suggests an overall notion of a universal harmony, an aesthetic of equalities applicable to spiritual as well as to physical entities.[6]

Granted that Edwards was first and last a man of God, his responses to natural phenomena were nevertheless such as to lead him to crystallize his impressions in an aesthetic that sought to relate the physical and the spiritual in a framework of harmony and musicality. In the very story of his conversion we find the realization of the element that Ethel Dench Puffer was to call aesthetic balance or stabilization, as shown in the rhythm of his prose:

> The appearance of everything was altered; there seemed to be . . . a calm, sweet cast, an appearance of divine glory . . . in the sun, moon, and stars; in the clouds, and blue sky; in the grass, flowers, trees; in the water and all nature. . . .[7]

Here, nature becomes a metaphor of the mind, as it did later for Emerson.

Benjamin Franklin (1706–1790)

Franklin represented a turn from the implicit aesthetic of a divine to that of a man of the world and of science. Surprisingly, the author of "The Way to Wealth," who became the symbol of the self-made man and who, for all his flair for science, was more interested in its applicability than its theoretical aspects, did engage in aesthetic speculation for its own sake. In 1752, he printed Samuel Johnson's *Elementa Philosophica*, which had so influenced Edwards, and he may well have favored the quotation in which mathematics was extoled as revealing "that inimitable beauty, that Harmony, that inimitable Order . . . in the Formation and Government of the Universe,"[8] suggesting Franklin's own humanistic approach to science.

Influenced by Defoe's *Essays* and the *Spectator*, Franklin's aesthetic theory of literary style called for precision and clarity, and was related to "mathematical plainness" and to the scientific procedure of generalizing from the known to the unknown. He believed that the written word should be "as near as possible to the spoken," producing a "beautiful simplicity." Mere poetasters, he cautioned, needed instruction on how to govern fancy and imagination with judgment.[9] In *A Dissertation on Liberty and Necessity, Pleasure and Pain* (1725), he declared that pleasure and pain were "constant yoke fellows"[10]—an idea that was to become a dominant factor in the aesthetic theory of the nineteenth century. A negative attitude toward aesthetics, however, appeared in the *Preface to Poor Richard* (1735):

> Whatever may be the Musick of the Spheres, how great soever the Harmony of the Stars, it is certain there is no Harmony among the Stargazers; but they are perpetually growling and snarling at one another like strange curs.[11]

In the Newtonian system that dominated Franklin's thought as well as that of the philosophers (some of whom he met in France), the "prime mover" was reason, not sensibility—logic and not the dictates of imagination and desire. The center of gravity of the aesthetic that arose in this system was in exterior nature, not in the inner world of man. Behind this aesthetic was not only a reason that calculates but a *calculated* reason. Metaphysics would be condemned in the manner of Voltaire because it questioned the dominance of reason and suggested the expansiveness of the human imagination. Franklin's aesthetic, therefore, could consider love, for example, primarily in terms of prudence, just as his science could find its fullest expression in lightning rods and other immediate applications. He scarcely recognized the imaginative faculty of man or the free play of the emotions in a metaphysical context.

Despite such attitudes, however, Franklin was not entirely devoid of a poetic sense. His predominantly rationalistic view of the universe was accompanied by a sense of the unresolved contradiction between pain and pleasure, which must also be considered in any theory of human existence. His speculation on these issues in the *Dissertation* may be categorized as follows:

1. At birth a creature receives the capacity for the sensation of uneasiness or pain.

2. This uneasiness produces the desire to be rid of it; the desire is in proportion to the uneasiness.

3. The desire to escape from uneasiness expresses itself in such means of expelling it as fame, wealth, power, and an infinite number of other escapes. Unlike the others, the *final* escape is death.

4. The satisfaction of this desire produces the sensation of pleasure

in exact proportion to the desire that is wholly caused by pain and is accomplished by the desire to escape from pain.

5. Accordingly, *the sensation of pleasure is equal, or in exact proportion, to the sensation of pain.*[12]

Franklin further reflected in the *Dissertation* that the quantity of pleasure and pain is not to be measured by its duration any more than the quantity of matter by its extension. As one cubic inch may be made to contain, by condensation, as much matter as would fill ten thousand cubic feet, so one single moment of pleasure may outweigh and compensate for an age of pain.

This discussion, and the two dialogues that Franklin composed when he was twenty-four, suggest that a consideration of the conflict between pleasure and pain produced in him a sensitivity to the dialectic of the spirit and with it an implicit aesthetic that was not as aridly rationalistic as many of his other works would suggest. His emotional depth was further indicated by his study of Plato and by his profound response to the poetry of James Thomson.

Thomas Jefferson (1743–1826)

Psychoanalysis has shown that human behavior is motivated both by sexual drives and by the so-called death wish, and that both may form the basis of aesthetic sensibility. Franklin was responsive to these "twin yokes" in the form of pain and pleasure. Jefferson, also primarily a man of reason, was nonetheless a "sensibilitist" (to use Frost's description of himself). Indeed, the same sensibility that predisposed Jefferson against political schismatizing may have led him to aesthetic discrimination in the arts.

His quotations from the works of various authors suggest his preoccupation with the fundamental themes of love and death, pleasure and pain, as in the passage that he copied from Cicero:

> *Non enim silice nati sumus; sed est, natura in animis tenerum quiddam, atque molle, quod aegritudine, quasi tempestate, quaeritur.*

(We are not the offspring of flint; but we have by nature something soft and tender in our souls that may be tempest-tossed by grief.)[13]

The disease of ennui, which plagued Pascal and later Leopardi, Vigny, Byron, and all the Romantics, is precisely expressed in the passage that Jefferson copied from Horace:

> . . . *Adde, quod idem*
> *Non horam tecum esse potes, non otia recte*
> *Ponere, teque ipsum vitas fugitivus et [ut] erro,*
> *Jam vino quaerens, jam somno fallere Curam;*
> *Frustra: nam comes atra permit, sequiturque fugacem.*

(And, again, you cannot yourself bear to be in your own company for an hour, you cannot employ your leisure aright, you shun yourself, a runaway vagabond, seeking now with wine, and now with sleep, to escape anxiety. In vain: that black consort dogs and follows your flight.)[14]

These quotations as well as other passages copied from Ovid and from Mark Akenside's *Pleasures of Imagination* should prevent an overemphasis on the utilitarian elements in Jefferson's interests at the expense of his concern with aesthetic essence and the sense of beauty.

Philosophically, Jefferson apparently leaned toward the ideologist Destutt de Tracy, who associated metaphysical speculation with emotive rather than cognitive intent and classified it with the imaginative arts. Jefferson's thought suggested the conflict between science and the humanities that began to gather momentum among some of the philosophers and that manifested itself among the ideologists. Adrienne Koch correctly regarded their metaphor of a chain of ideas as an apology for the incompleteness of ideology as a system.[15] In many respects an "idea" is a romantic construct, and psychology is a romantic science par excellence. The ideational climate of Jefferson, as he approached the nineteenth century, was thus tinged with romanticism.

Did Jefferson have a philosophy of art? He has himself declared:

> I have always very much despised the artificial canons of
> criticism. When I have read a work in prose or poetry or seen
> a painting. . . . I have only asked myself whether it is animating,
> interesting, attractive? If it is, it is good for these reasons.[16]

Yet he had sustained thoughts and tastes regarding the arts, as in
his views on English prosody, which he initially considered a matter
of the arrangement of long and short syllables, but later adopted the
idea that it was primarily a function of accent. Verse, he maintained,
does not depend on its visual appearance, but on its sound quality.
In any rhythmical composition:

> . . . the ear is pleased to find at certain regular intervals a
> pause where it may rest, by which it may divide the composi-
> tion into parts, as a piece of music is divided into bars. . . . The
> interval between these regular pauses constitutes a verse.

He also suggested that a person who is insensible to these pauses

> . . . like him who is insensible to the charm of music, who is
> insensible to love or gratitude, is an unfavored son of nature
> to whom she has given a faculty fewer than to others of her
> children, one source of pleasure the less in a world where there
> are none to spare.[17]

Eleanor Davidson Berman noted that Lord Kames (Henry Home),
Edmund Burke, and William Hogarth were central to the formation
of Jefferson's aesthetic. Like Franklin, Jefferson composed a dialogue;
his was entitled "Dialogue between My Heart and My Head." In
this dialogue, like Kames and Shaftesbury, he expressed the hope
that the arts might be used to promote altruism and refinement among
the people. In Kames he found the connecting link between fiction
and social usefulness: "Fiction, by means of language, has the command of our sympathies for the good of others." Jefferson appealed
"to every reader of feeling and sentiment [to see] whether the ficti-
tious murder of Duncan by Macbeth . . . does not excite in him as
great a horror of villainy as the real one of Henry IV by Ravaillac
as related by Davila?"[18]

On the other hand, Burke, also one of Jefferson's sources, rejected Hogarth's identification of beauty with fitness and use: "In beauty, the effect is previous to any knowledge of use." Burke separated beauty from reason, from calculation and geometry, and from goodness. For him, "beauty is, for the greater part, some quality in bodies acting mechanically upon the human mind by the interaction of the senses."[19] Jefferson admired Burke's aesthetics, however much he abhorred his Toryism, and was particularly attracted by Burke's ideas on the sublime. As Berman suggested, Jefferson himself used the word "sublime" for David's description of the good men in the Fifteenth Psalm, for Homer's measures, the poetry of Ossian, and for Cleanthes's *Hymn to Zeus*. The soil worked upon by man elicited an aesthetic response:

> The plough is to the farmer what the wand is to the sorcerer. We now plough horizontally, following the curvatures of the hills and hollows. . . . In point of beauty nothing can exceed that of the waving lines and rows winding along the face of the hills and valleys.[20]

Jefferson linked the sublimity of nature—clouds, rain, thunder, dawn—with the sublimity of suffering—bereavement, sickness, want.[21] With his espousal of these sublimities, again anticipating romanticism, and with his love for music as "the favorite passion of my soul," he indicated that his rationalistic and libertarian thinking was motivated by intuition, imagination, and the vision of beauty.

Philip Freneau (1752–1832)

Jefferson, who encouraged Joel Barlow in his literary work, offered Freneau, in his need, a position as a secretary who could use clerkship for foreign languages. At Princeton, Freneau had voraciously read the major English writers as well as the Latin and French classics. His reading also included Barlow, Franklin, Irving, and

Cotton Mather. His translation of Horace is still regarded as excellent. In one instance (Ode 20, Book II) Horace boasts of the poet's superiority to all mundane things—a sentiment with which the translator agreed. In his own poetry, as Lewis Leary indicated, the melancholy strain was shown in such themes as change, decay, and death,[22] as in "The Power of Fancy":

> Wakeful, vagrant, restless thing,
> Ever wandering on the wing,
> Who thy wondrous source can find,
> Fancy, regent of the mind;
> Come, O come—perceived by none,
> You and I will walk alone.

This suggestion of an aesthetic of creative solitude may be taken as a response to Newtonian thought. The lyric poet needed to balance physics with metaphysics in order to make allowance for the aesthetic dimension, without which the universe would seem empty of meaning, leading to a profound sense of alienation. Man, haunted by death and constantly in quest of life's meaning, cannot find his balance in technology and science alone:

> Thus, skill and science both must fall
> And ruin is the lot of all. . . .
> Where shall I go, what Lethe shall I find,
> To drive these dark ideas from my mind!

The elements themselves became a source of wisdom for Freneau. He found "the sea . . . the best school for philosophy" and thought it capable of teaching more in a short time than "could be gained in half a century on shore." His allegorical suggestions of man's pilgrim spirit—venturesome and stormy, constantly battered by its own bodily limitations, like sea against shore[23]—were balanced by his belief that mind would survive matter, the "vast machine" that "scorns to change her wonted course."[24]

In an early poem, "The Wild Honey Suckle" (1786), he uttered a "tone of muted wonder" and lamented the "frail duration" of "beauty amid American swamplands."²⁵ Unfortunately, the development of a meaningful aesthetic in Freneau's work was hindered by the effort that he devoted to composing abortive propaganda against the British, and little of a vital literary aesthetic remained in his own work.

John Quincy Adams (1767–1848)

The creative imagination in America at the end of the eighteenth century began to be dominated by a concern for accomplishments beyond material success and territorial exploration. "I see a Homer and a Milton rise," Freneau and Hugh Brackenridge wrote in their joint *Poem on the Rising Glory of America* (1772).²⁶ To be sure, the Congregationalist clergy continued to maintain a rigid standard of personal morality in which little consideration was given to aesthetic matters. As Henry Adams pointed out, however, in the course of less than two decades such Americans as Bryant and Irving achieved distinction in literature, and Washington Allston and Edward Greene Melbone became prominent painters. Form and style began to mean something quite apart from English models in literature and oratory and Italian models in painting.²⁷

John Quincy Adams, having been installed as first Boylston Professor of Rhetoric and Oratory at Harvard in 1806, created a school of oratory through the lectures delivered to juniors and seniors; these lectures were published in 1810. Adams may be truly regarded as a transitional figure between the eighteenth and the nineteenth centuries. His memoirs reveal early signs of romanticism, while some of his ideas on the role of literature recall eighteenth-century thought. His reading for the lectures was extensive, including works that touched on aesthetics directly, as in the writings of Aristotle, Plato, and Longinus, Burke's *On the Sublime and Beautiful*, René Rapin's *Réflexions sur l'éloquence,* Hugh Blair's *Lectures on Rhetoric* and *Belles Lettres,* Kames's *Elements of Criticism,* and the *Traité des Tropes* of César Chesneau Dumarsais.²⁸

Adams also studied Johann J. Winckelmann's *Geschichte der*

Kunst des Alterthums and, curiously, Hogarth's works in *German* translation. In addition, Adams maintained personal contact with several artists, as suggested by the Petrarchan sonnet he addressed in 1837 to the sculptor Hiram Powers.[29]

The advice that Adams gave his students was aesthetic in nature, as in his admonition "never to indulge a looseness of imagery, which would dissolve the texture of the sentiment."[30] This advice suggested the necessity of balancing the power of passion with the power of expression. Such statements recall Aristotle's *Rhetoric*, which was devoted to the passions and which Adams considered "one of the profoundest and most ingenious treatises upon human nature that ever issued from the pen of man."[31]

Following Aristotle, Adams believed that the orator himself should feel the passion he proposes to excite, and he referred his students to Horace: *Si vis me flere, dolendum est primum tibi esse* ("If you would have me weep, you must first feel grief yourself"), recalling the problem raised in *Paradoxe sur le comédien* by Diderot, whom the Adamses read and annotated.[32]

In general, Adams reflected late eighteenth- and early nineteenth-century preoccupation with the nature and function of language. He had read the *Diversions of Purley*, a philological work by John Horne Tooke in which the question of metaphor and the value of words in every systematic art was raised. His associationism reflected eighteenth-century thought and rhetoric.[33]

Certain aspects of this associationism are still of great interest to us, especially that phase which concerns the relationship between the humanities and science:

> The great foundation of figurative language rests on the association of ideas. When a word has in the first instance been appropriated to any particular thing, and is afterwards turned or converted to the representation of some other thing, its new signification must arise from some association with the old. . . . The most abundant of all the sources of figurative association is the analogy between matter and spirit. For as ideas of reflection can be communicated only by material images, nothing that relates to spiritual nature can be expressed but by figures.[34]

Here the psychology of association, aided by metaphor and analogy, carried intimations of a monistic approach to reality. Later Adams said that it is impossible to grasp abstract ideas otherwise than by means of images borrowed from the senses. When these abstractions are clothed anew, "the relations between spiritual and material existence are so multiplied and hence the faculty of discovering new relations of that sort forms perhaps the first characteristic of genius."[35]

Three kinds of association may be described: (1) figurative language; (2) the analogy between one material substance and another (the resemblances between animate and inanimate objects); and (3) sound, which is superficial because it comes from the immediate report of the senses:

> Sometimes these three kinds of association are all united in the composition of a figure. For example, Virgil calls the two Scipios *"duo fulmina belli,"* two thunderbolts of war. Here is a striking analogy between the effects of their warlike talents and a natural phenomenon. The association is between physical and intellectual nature.

Adams continued:

> Such is the general doctrine of figurative language, which originated first from the necessity of communicating images of sensation; founded upon a natural association of ideas, and upon the analogies between the properties of spirit, of matter, and sounds; and afterwards greatly multiplied by the charm, which the discovery and display of these analogies possess over the minds of men.[36]

This passage provided a structural account of the aesthetics of metaphor, with more than a hint that metaphor may be at the heart of aesthetics.

As for figurative speech, its purpose, according to Adams, was "to address the eye through the medium of the imagination. . . . As an inlet of ideas to the mind, its capacities [of sight] are greater than those of all other senses together." The powers of the imagination, however, extend beyond sight into forms different from any of the combinations of nature. The mind is therefore capable of new creation.[37]

Of all the tropes—metaphor, metonymy, synecdoche, and irony—Adams considered metaphor the most beautiful as well as the most frequent. Whereas the simile is the equivalent of a portrait, the metaphor is an image reflected by a mirror.[38] Allegory, founded on similitude, is considered by some as an extended metaphor.

Such remarks by Adams indicate that he saw aesthetic problems in the context of tension between the humanities and the sciences. Indeed, he suggested this conflict even in his famous report to Congress on weights and measures:

> It has been remarked, of a very distinguished character of France, D'Alembert, that there was too much poetry in his mathematics, and too much mathematics in his poetry. Of the poetical and philosophical explanation of memory something similar might perhaps be said. The one is just as figurative as the other. I have brought them here together to show you how much they are alike.[39]

The aesthetic of composition, as Adams expressed it, is a composite of four closely interrelated aspects: the natural, the grammatical, the metaphysical, and the musical, which are variously combined. The natural corresponds with the feelings of the speaker or writer. The grammatical accords with the relationship of words to one another. The metaphysical is an order of abstract ideas. The musical rests on the agreeableness of sound. This categorization was reminiscent of Aristotle's poetics and anticipated such writers as Jules Laforgue, Rimbaud, and Pound, and the aesthetic classification of language forms as logopoetic, phanopoetic, and melopoetic.[40]

Some of Adams's general observations on taste and beauty reflected his adherence either to the ancients or to late eighteenth-century thinkers, as in his remark "A good man, or a beautiful woman is perceptible to the eye and to the reason of us all; but the qualities themselves we cannot readily discern, without the aid of imagination."[41]

We can see that long before the word was used in America, the figures whom I have presented in this chapter were preoccupied with "aesthetic" questions. These questions arose in the context of European thought from the ancients through the thinkers of the eighteenth century.

Although literary aesthetics was related by all of them to religion, ethics, science, and a rationalistic view generally, there is evidence of an early burgeoning sensibility in America to beauty as separate from all such relationships and of a rising concern with the tension between exterior nature and man's inner world. This concern manifested itself in an inquiry into the nature of pleasure and pain and in a romantic response to ennui, love, and death, all in a chain of interrelated ideas.

This connection also involved the struggle between the heart and the head, cognition and feeling, and the nature of imagination. Newtonian thought had to contend with lyricism and called for a balance between physics and metaphysics, between passion and expression as well as for an enriched understanding of the role of figures of speech, especially metaphor, in that expression. In all these respects we find a glimmer of future development, if not a full anticipation of nineteenth- and twentieth-century literary aesthetics.

THE CURRENT OF IDEAS:
FOREIGN SOURCES AND THE
AESTHETICS OF CRITICISM

Although literary aesthetic ideas in America, such as they were during the early decades of the nineteenth century, were gathered from English periodicals and Scottish rhetoricians, after the War of 1812, as William Charvat[1] pointed out, some American critics turned to Germany for enlightenment about aesthetics. Charvat enumerated the following lessons that American critics learned from Schlegel's *Lectures on Dramatic Art and Literature*, which was characterized in the *Portfolio* for 1817 as "an epoch in the history of criticism": (1) Man must learn to perceive the beauties of alien literatures. (2) Beauty exists in the literature of all periods and countries, even in the barbarous periods. (3) The literature of the ancients has been perverted by modern, especially French, interpretation; men must return to classical art itself to understand its spirit.

The critics, however, were apt to be impatient with the metaphysics of romanticism—"an infinite longing after the absolute and the infinite. . . . The antique is the infinite realized in a positive shape."[2]

Aside from critical response to A. W. Schlegel in the *North American Review*, in the *American Quarterly*, and in the *Portfolio*

—with Longfellow, R. H. Dana, William H. Prescott, and A. H. Everett as the respondents—American dramatic criticism generally was under the influence of A. W. and Friedrich Schlegel after 1815.

GERMAN PHILOSOPHY AND MADAME DE STAËL

Ideas originating in Germany first became known in America, as George Ticknor indicated, largely through Madame de Staël's *Germany*, which appeared in England in 1813 and was reprinted in New York in 1814.[3] Henry Adams declared some seventy-five years later that while a few Bostonians could possibly read and speak French, Germany was nearly "as unknown as China, until Madame de Staël published her famous work."[4] Early in 1815 John Quincy Adams renewed acquaintance with Madame de Staël in Paris, and he may very well have discussed aesthetic matters with her. Many French and German ideas were also transmitted through England, as Henry Crabb Robinson indicated when he recorded a remark of Madame de Staël in his diary: "The English mind is in the middle between the German and the French, and is a medium of communication between them."[5]

Madame de Staël's work on Germany became the subject of conversation in both Europe and America, leading to widespread recognition of her idea that romantic literature is the true expression of the soul, as suggested in her earlier book, *On Literature*.[6] Man recognizes beauty, she said, as the outward images of the ideal type existing in his intellect. She thus followed the course of German idealism, with its emphasis on feeling as the primary fact of mind.

Kant assigned to sentiment the first rank of human nature and made conscience the innate principle of moral existence, indicating the need for a philosophy that confirmed by reason the truth that feeling revealed. Even though the mystery of the universe is beyond the reach of human understanding, the study of that mystery expands the human intellect and enables man to comprehend truths that would otherwise have remained unknown to him.[7] Precisely this sentiment was later expressed by Einstein. James Marsh (1794–1842), who made Coleridge the thinker known in America by publishing *Aids to Reflection* with an introductory essay, began to consult Kant's *Critique of Pure Reason* with the aid of Coleridge and Madame de Staël.[8]

Through the reading of Madame de Staël's *Germany* Sarah Helen Power Whitman (1803–1878), Margaret Fuller (1810–1850), and Elizabeth Fries Lummis Ellet (1818–1877) became interested in Goethe and Schiller.[9] In 1845 Emerson's friend Samuel Gray Ward (1817–1907) published a translation of Goethe's *Essays on Art* in Boston. In his preface, Ward said that with Goethe art was not a single side of humanity, but a medium for viewing all mankind, a core around which all experience—the scientific, the ideal, the practical—arranges itself into one harmonious whole.[10] Ward's translation included such essays from the artistic periodical *Propylaeum* as "Upon the Laocoön," "Truth and Probability in Works of Art," "Landscape Painting," "Hints to Young Artists," and "Upon Dilettantism."

Among the most influential of Goethe's dicta were the following: Man is the highest, indeed the proper object of plastic art. Form is an idea of the general operations of nature. The moment an artist lays hold on an object in nature, that object no longer belongs to nature. A true work of art, like a work of nature, never ceases to open boundlessly before the mind; it can never be completely comprehended. Poetizers, showmen, phantomists, phantasmists, nebulists lack artistic truth and real beauty. A mere operation of the understanding is not satisfactory in art. Style rests on the deepest foundations of knowledge, on the essence of things. He who would write or dispute about art ought to have some notion of what philosophy has accomplished and is still accomplishing. He who would reproach an author with obscurity ought first to make an examination of himself, to be sure that he is inwardly clear; a very clear hand may not be legible by twilight. When artists speak of nature, the idea is always understood, without their being clearly conscious of it. Nature and idea cannot be separated, without destroying art as well as life.[11]

A detailed comparison of Allston's dicta and Goethe's aphorisms would further indicate the extent of Goethe's influence on American aesthetics. Ward interjected a note of warning on Goethe's discussion of dilettantism:

> Whether it be good or evil, we are too busy a people to anticipate its having any deep hold among us. . . . [The] subject has the strongest possible bearing on our present condition, and that in fact, with rare exceptions, all our literature falls inevitably within his definition of dilettantism [that is, the false approach to art].[12]

Goethe figured prominently in Emerson's *Representative Men* (1850), and his influence is suggested in "Thoughts on Modern Literature" (*Dial*, I), where Emerson noted that the "new love of the vast, always native in Germany, was imported into France by de Staël, appeared in England in Coleridge, Wordsworth, Byron, Shelley, Felicia Hemans, and finds a most genial climate in the American mind." He called the second part of *Faust* "a philosophy of history set in poetry."[13]

The influence of Schiller was noted in Elizabeth F. M. Ellet's *Characters of Schiller* (1839), regarded as one of the earliest large specimens of American literary criticism, and clearly modeled on the work of Madame de Staël. Schiller's mind was called intuitively "romantic," according to the distinctions of classic and romantic poetry as formulated by Madame de Staël as well as by Schlegel. Schiller's objective of "art becoming a second nature" is realized, according to Ellet, in *Wilhelm Tell*.[14]

Six years after Ellet's book, John Weiss (1818–1879) published a translation, with an introduction, of Schiller's *The Aesthetic Letters, Essays and the Philosophical Letters*. The title page contained this quotation from Schiller's *Album*:

> *Schön zu leben ist wahre Kunst,*
> *Kunst im Leben das schöne Wahre,*
> *Leben der Kunst das wahre Schöne,*
> *Wahres Leben die schöne Kunst.*
>
> (To live beauty is real art,
> Art in life is beautiful truth,

> The life of art is true beauty,
> True life is beautiful art.)

Weiss found in Gervinus the following statement on the relation of Schiller to Goethe, both of whom lived in Weimar: "They exhibit to us a common whole in the shape of a coalescence."[15] Weiss called Schiller the best German aesthetician. Schiller felt that in a time of crisis and under a barbarous polity, men must seek an instrument that is independent of the state. This instrument consists of the fine arts. The artist may secede from his age and elevate himself above it. Weiss indicated that the success of America depended on its acceptance of the principles enunciated by Schiller. According to Gervinus, whom Weiss followed throughout his own introduction, Schiller did not carry out his idea of the relation between aesthetic and political culture, but left it a fragment.[16]

Because the problem of the relation of subject to object is of aesthetic as well as general philosophic interest, it is important to note that in this respect Schiller in *The Aesthetic Letters* tried to maintain a position between Hume and Kant, which consisted of an appreciation of both subject and object.[17]

Kant separated art from all the demands of exigency and utility. A free beauty is distinct from dependent beauty and makes the essential of art to consist in the form. For Kant, beauty was the symbol of moral goodness, and the fine arts the embodiment of moral ideas. The development of moral feeling was for him the true preliminary for the establishment of taste. These principles attracted Schiller. Kant's chance word that art compared with labor might be considered as a play excited numerous ideas in Schiller. That chance word was the origin of Schiller's "play impulse," a term nowhere used by Kant.

The *Critique of Judgment*, however, did contain such remarks as these:

> Every form of objects of sense (both of the external and, mediately, of the internal) is either Shape or Play; in the latter case, either play of shapes (in Space, posture and dance) or play of perceptions (in Time).

Play is that which in itself is agreeable. Labor is that which is agreeable only for its pay:

> Oratory is the art which carries on a business of the intellect as a free play of the imagination: Poetry, that which conducts a free play of the imagination as a business of the intellect.

Schiller elevated the play idea into a theory: the play impulse is the basis of his aesthetic system. The aesthetic art impulse will never unfold itself if the play impulse has not first become active.[18]

Weiss's introduction did not stop at a mere exposition of Schiller but attempted to measure American national life by Schiller's aesthetic standards. He remarked that as far as the sports of a people are indicative of its aesthetic culture and the development of its play impulse, the sons of the Puritans may be judged to be still in a state of nature. With them life is still "all work and no play."

Weiss noted that the oscillation to the subjective extreme has just begun. We are not self-poised, our center of gravity is not removed far enough from the surface: "*We are not yet Persons, but we only represent conditions*" (my italics). Tried by Schiller's aesthetic rules, we are not so enormously removed from the savages whom we have just dispossessed. So long as in our search, "fiery-red with haste," we seek definite results, we shall never apprehend that golden mean between person and condition, freedom and nature. In short, Weiss suggested to his fellow Americans that many of the characteristics of Schiller's age mentioned in his earlier letters could describe his own as well. In his fifth letter Schiller said: "Civilization, far from placing us in freedom, only unfolds a new want with every power that it educates within us.[19]

FRENCH INFLUENCES

The influence of French thought on American aestheticians was shown in the *Portfolio*, which carried translations from J. C. L. Sismonde de Sismondi's *History of the Literature of the South of Europe*, as well as excerpts from Madame de Staël and Chateaubriand. Alexander Hill Everett (1791–1847) criticized Madame de Staël for not studying Kant adequately, and he wrote on Marie-Joseph de Gerando's *Histoire comparée des systèmes de philosophie*. His article on Madame de Staël revealed his dislike of mysticism; in an address delivered at Brown University, he attacked Rousseau as a harmful influence on German, French, and English literature,[20] anticipating Irving Babbitt's attacks on Rousseau.

Jesse Cato Daniel, in the introduction to his translation of Victor Cousin's *The Philosophy of the Beautiful*, described the difference between the ideas emanating from Germany and France and those originating in England and Scotland. Cousin attempted to reduce Kant's categories to two fundamental ideas: cause and being. German philosophers thought the idea of cause evolved from the *I*. Cousin distinguished two moments in the development of the I: the moment of spontaneity and the moment of reflection. The first is primitive and confused. All the elements of intellectual life first exist in this primitive state of the mind. We might say that reason emanates from spontaneity and is ultimately a broken-up, arrested spontaneity, which imagination tries to recapture in the interest of creative reason, which, in turn, is not merely a fixed set of categories. Life is a continual transition from darkness (spontaneity) to light (reflection), from the spontaneous activity of the infancy of the human mind to the intelligent and reflective activity of the manhood of the mind.

Cousin's whole philosophic structure rested on the idea that the beautiful is not to be separated from the good and the true—that the beautiful encloses a *moral* idea that has its source in God. Daniel suggested that the theory of beauty set forth in Cousin's lectures should be studied not only by the artist but by all for whom he labors, because every man requires culture:

> It is surprising how few persons seem to be aware of the aesthetic forces which are pressing upon them; and yet must we not conceive of every man as a centre towards which silent and invisible influences converge as they are darted evermore from a myriad objects? There is a sense in which it may be said that the objective universal exists for man.[21]

Daniel therefore insisted on the relevance of aesthetics not only for aestheticians and philosophers but for every man.

In his introduction, Daniel reminded those who had religious scruples about the blandishments of beauty that the Bible interprets, and is in perfect harmony with, nature. The study of the beautiful is not only our duty, but is eminently beneficial both speculatively, as a philosophical exercise, and practically, as a catalyst to our own moral improvement. Daniel emphasized his idea with a quotation from Archibald Alison's *Essays on Taste* (Essay II, Chapter 6, Section 6):

> Amid the magnificent system of material signs in which we reside, it [the study and contemplation of beauty] gives us the mighty key which can interpret them; and it makes us look upon the universe which we inhabit, not as the abode only of human cares, or human joys, but as the temple of the Living God, in which praise is due, and where service is to be performed.[22]

Thus, more than a century ago Cousin presented the aesthetic problem of beauty in the context of a chain of being in which *outward* and *inward, simple* and *complex, finite* and *infinite, natural* and *ideal, subject* and *object* were all inextricably enfolded in each other. He also suggested the now well-known polarity of reason and desire and drew it into the framework of a philosophy of knowledge. He was fully aware of the problem of the dissociation of sensibility from thought and of the so-called objective correlative before the expression came into use. He was committed to an idealistic monism that would accommodate the individual and the universal in a balanced tonality or fusion. For Cousin, the loftiest aim of art was to arouse the sentiment of the infinite.[23]

Coming closer to the aesthetics of literary creativity, Cousin suggested that the creative faculty of a poet is neither a wild outpouring of passion without form to give it shape and meaning beyond the poet's self-indulgence, nor merely the expression that a twentieth-century poet was to call a "mechanical operandum." *To produce the beautiful,* he thought, *the will must work with love according to the rules of reason.*[24]

Cousin linked the *expressive* and the beautiful. He affirmed that the face of nature is expressive like the face of man. All is symbolic in nature. Form is not form only; it is the form of something and it unfolds something inward. Beauty, then, is expression; art is the seeking after expression. According to Daniel, Alison's work on taste maintained that the forms themselves are beautiful and that their beauty is bestowed on them by arbitrary associations. Cousin, on the other hand, maintained that the simple absolute idea of the beautiful irradiates the various forms in nature and is followed by them.[25]

Cousin held that poetry, because of the mysterious power of language to excite the profoundest emotions, is the best reflection of universal beauty. He referred to Burke's admirable chapter on this subject.[26] In a hierarchy of the arts that Cousin set up, he placed poetry first, above music, painting, sculpture, architecture, and landscape gardening.[27] His statement, *Emotion and pleasure are not arguments*,[28] is worth pondering. A modern critic might say that no one can argue with the libido.

All the arts excite the same emotions, but by different symbols. Because of the vagueness of the meaning of music, it can comply and unite with the dispositions of all men, and men can, as the melody proceeds, delight and deceive themselves with the favorite ideas of their imagination.[29] The very vagueness in both music and poetry provides a latitude for the free play of the imagination in the reader or the listener.

In a sense, music is the art of the vague, the art of stimulating and releasing a flow of emotional energy characterized by freedom and occasional choice of concretion. And this choice is itself contingent on unconscious strivings and reveries. Thus men find a dreamlike quality in music and poetry, which, in its suggestibility, approaches music.

The nearer poetry moves to speech, the more limited becomes the latitude of vagueness, of reverie, of dream. Music, in the most limited definition, is mere sound, but poetry to remain itself cannot be mere speech: "Heard melodies are sweet, but those unheard are sweeter." The quality of unheard melodies permits us to say that thought itself may be "mood thought" and that the arts are instruments that give a musical quality to experience. For Cousin, language is at once thought and matter, objective and subjective. Thought is the most definite and exact of forms; it scarcely belongs to the physical world. Thus poetry in itself is nearly equal to all the arts combined and excels each separate one.[30]

In Chapter 11, in which Cousin brought together the various parts of his doctrine, he said that the artist resembles the mathematician and the philosopher. In every beautiful object two elements exist: the general and the particular. If the general is disengaged from the particular, the absolute in art, the ideal, will be achieved. Art is a perfected nature that conceives of unity beneath variety, of the general within the particular, the moral within the physical, the absolute within the relative, the ideal within the real. In this sense, it surpasses nature.[31]

The vogue of Cousin and of his pupil Théodore Jouffroy in America[32] was contemporary with the vogue of German idealism, which Madame de Staël was practically the first to introduce to France and, through France, to America as well. Cousin, the principal exponent of French idealism of the early part of the nineteenth century, was the most noteworthy precursor of New England transcendentalism.[33] He said that one can neither abide by idealism or sensualism nor escape from them.[34] For him, "spontaneity is the point of departure, reflection the point of return; the entire circumference is the intellectual life; the center is absolute Intelligence which governs and explains the whole."[35] His eclecticism was overtly expressed when he declared: "Without empiricism, we should never have all that was contained in the bosom of sensation; and without idealism we should never have known the power properly belonging to thought.[36]

In the preface to his *Philosophical Fragments*, Cousin came close, at one point, to being a precursor of Freud's notion of the unconscious:

> In the recesses of Consciousness, and at a depth to which
> Kant did not penetrate . . . I detected and unfolded the fact
> . . . of the spontaneous perception of truth . . . in the interior

of consciousness . . . which, at a subsequent period, in a logical form and in the hands of reflection, becomes a necessary
conception.[37]

In its origin, the intuitive process is related to "the interior of consciousness." Further, "every man, if he knows himself, knows all the
rest."[38] Heavily indebted to a brilliant line of philosophic precursors
from Plato to Friedrich Heinrich Jacobi, Cousin rendered a positive
service to America by alerting it to the possibility of an aesthetic
envisioning of a harmony between forms of thought and forms of
feeling. He was strongly instrumental in making aesthetic thought
current in an America dominated by moralism, theological caveats,
and financial pursuits. The influence of Cousin was further seen in
1841, when the *North American Review*[39] praised him for treating
profound subjects without the pomposity of the German metaphysicians and with clarity, although the philosopher's superficiality was
not overlooked.

Cousin's dicta on art, taste, genius, imagination, and beauty included the following: Art is the free representation of the beautiful.
Art should have only one aim, the sentiment of the beautiful. The
loftiest aim of art is to arouse the sentiment of the infinite. The three
conditions of taste are the sentiment of the beautiful, reason, and
the representative faculty. Genius is taste in action. Genius is the
vivid and rapid perception of the proportion in which the ideal and
the natural should be united. The imagination is the association of
sentiment; it is love combined with memory and reason and will.
Imagination is neither sensation nor reason taken exclusively. To
imagine is to seize the representations, either when they are before
us or when they are not in our presence. Beauty is a reality adorned
by the ideal. The beautiful is the true and the good manifested to
man under sensory forms. The beautiful lifts us out of ourselves,
and carries us toward action and external life; its influence is such
as to develop our nature.

With regard to the artist himself, Cousin suggested that the man
who can discover in the external symbol the idea with which it is
filled is beautiful. Whenever we apprehend beauty from without,

it is because we have it within us.[40] All these insights Cousin shared with Plotinus. They throw light on the organic and dynamic relations between the creator and his object and between the re-creator (the appreciative participant) and the work of art.

Cousin's insights reveal art as a continuum or process in which the artist (as well as the participant) imbues the object with the idea of beauty and in which the object in turn reflects the idea. Accordingly, the failure to respond to beauty is not so much a failure to respond to objects of art as a manifestation of a lack of the idea (or sentiment) of beauty within oneself. Nothing can exist without that is not already within.

The provocation to beauty exists in the object only when the artist or participant is subject to such provocation because of a principle of beauty resident within him, as suggested by Plotinus.[41] This idea recalls the comment that Goethe himself was a great work of art.

Daniel, the translator of Cousin's *Philosophy of Beauty*, was among the first in America to use the term "aesthetic" and to urge the study of aesthetics for the understanding of the nature and function of beauty. He recognized aesthetics as an important aspect of philosophy and accordingly attempted to commend such study to those who had religious scruples or reservations on the subject.[42]

American Aestheticians

Although American students were helped to a knowledge of German literature by Madame de Staël, most of the transcendentalists read (or were certainly aware of) De Gerando's *Histoire comparée des systèmes de philosophie*, which delighted Emerson and fascinated both Margaret Fuller and Elizabeth Palmer Peabody.[43] The *North American Review* for April, 1824, called attention to that volume, and its influence is suggested in Fuller's papers on art and literature in the *Dial*, and in Peabody's editing of *Aesthetic Papers*. In the prospectus of this collection (May, 1849) Peabody stated that she wished "to assemble upon the high aesthetic ground," away from all regions of strife, writers of different schools and to effect a synthesis of different and even "antagonistic views among the various divisions of the Church, and of the scientific and literary world." In that way she hoped to "cultivate an harmonious and moral life in our country." Among the contributors and their contributions were Samuel Gray Ward (1817–1907), "Criticism"; John Sullivan Dwight (1813–1893), "Music"; Sampson Reed, "Genius"; and the editor, "The Dorian Measure, with a Modern Application" and "Language."

Finally, Peabody considered the word *aesthetic* difficult to define, "because it is the watchword of a whole revolution in criticism."[44] In a metaphor resembling those of Emerson, Peabody drew an analogy between chemicophysical facts (like the composition of water and air) and a psychological fact, the nature of the aesthetic element. Both terms of the metaphor deal not with disparate but with component elements. Just as air and water do not represent simple substances but chemical combinations, so the aesthetic represents a component and indivisible part of human creativity. From this another insight followed—the place of the aesthetic in a large ideational frame, in which it is distinguished from appetite.

Again, Peabody saw the aesthetic at the heart of a dialectic in which contraries (subject-object, personal-impersonal, *Me-Not-Me*) live in each other and refer to "the central fact of the constant relation of the individual to the universal," kept in balance by constantly uniting and separating. Finally, she showed an acute recognition of a break with authoritarian criticism, in which willfulness usurped the rights of analysis and intuitive insights.

Literary criticism in America did not begin to reflect a philosophy or aesthetic of literature until the 1820s. The clash between the individual and the social was echoed in American poetics, as in the influence of Schlegel, who helped to break down the neoclassical idea of poetry as a mechanical metrical arrangement, establishing it as the product of genius, and thereby influencing the work of Edgar Allan Poe.

Thomas Campbell's (1777–1844) opinion that poetry teaches truth through sympathy corresponded to the new dynamic moralism in American criticism. His ideas on versification and diction found favor in several liberal journals: "In prose we enjoy the harmony of periods only as they pass; in verse, we not only enjoy the recollection of cadences that are past but agreeably anticipate those which are coming." The whole world of words ought to be at the poet's command; no special poetic diction exists. Campbell's ideas were echoed after 1821 in many American magazines. His defense of Pope in the Pope-Bowles controversy was applauded by the more conservative American critics.[45]

In its judgments on the philosophy of literature, American criticism was generally guided by Scottish philosophy and rhetoric. What the high points of these were, William Charvat helped us to see.

In the Scotch Common Sense School, founded by Thomas Reid (1710–1796), rhetoric and aesthetics were closely allied. Scotch aesthetics was rooted in human experience, and in so-called native faculties. Literature was to be enjoyed through analysis, while literary enthusiasm was to be frowned upon. American rhetoricians based themselves, in part, on Shaftesbury (1671–1713) and Francis Hutcheson (1694–1746). The former believed that the *sense of beauty* and the *moral sense* were fundamentally allied and inherent in man (compare with Cousin).

Carrying this doctrine further, Hutcheson proposed a theory of association that became the basis of Scotch aesthetics. This theory held that the sense of beauty is activated when objects become connected in our minds with emotions. Freud's *cathexis* comes to mind, as well as the objective correlative. In the same manner, Lord Kames, in his *Elements of Criticism* (1762), tried to relate the pleasurable emotions to their sources in the human mind. In spite of his declaration that the standard of reason and taste is universal, he actually believed that the standard was to be set by the educated and privileged classes. The individual artist was to yield to that society as the arbiter of taste.

With this, Charvat pointed out, the English and American quarterlies were in agreement. Less philosophical than Kames's work, Hugh Blair's *Lectures on Rhetoric and Belles Lettres* reached a twelfth edition by 1812 and constituted a summary of neoclassical opinion. In Lecture 4 Blair declared that in all good writing the sublime resides in the thought, not in the words: "When the thought is noble, the language will be dignified." In Charvat's opinion, Blair did a disservice to literature when he insisted that the familiarity of common words degraded style. He was also guilty of encouraging the erroneous idea that rhythm is a matter of the artificial arrangement of syllables.

A new departure in Scottish aesthetics took place with Archibald Alison's application of the principle of association of ideas to aesthetics. The idea of the intrinsic beauty of objects gave way to the conception of subjectivity, which is of the very essence of romanticism. Alison's *Essays on the Nature and Principles of Taste* (1790) was dedicated to Dugald Stewart, who believed that *the mind not only perceives but creates in the apprehension of the beautiful*.

Alison declared: "The poet addresses the understanding only as a vehicle of pleasure." Good poetry is not abstract but concrete and poetic pleasure comes from the contemplation of images. This idea not only points to Coleridge, as Oliver Elton thought, but to the New Critics' emphasis on concrete images.

In determining whether aesthetic experience was social rather than individual, both Alison and Francis Jeffrey (who, in his review of 1810, called attention to Alison's work) described two kinds of association: universal and individual. By 1835, however, intellectual homogeneity could no longer be assumed. The romantic movement revealed a double awareness, that of a societal structure with attendant folk memories and that of the private world of the individual. The tension involved in such a dual awareness was only another aspect of one of the persistent problems in philosophy, the dialectic of the one and the many.

At any rate, through all the changes in Scottish criticism and its correlative aesthetic, one critical principle prevailed: literature is primarily social, and the artist must conform to the dictates of established society. This made it clear to Charvat why early nineteenth-century romanticism rejected Godwin, Shelley, and Keats, partially accepted Byron, Wordsworth, and Coleridge, and completely accepted Scott. It also accounted for the similar history, in this respect, of romanticism in America. Yet Charvat felt that the chemistry of our national character was opposed to European romanticism and tended toward a romanticism of its own.[46] After 1830 America began to appreciate in Coleridge the admixture of poetry and philosophy out-side Scottish dogma, although an abortive effort was made to apply to Coleridge's poetry the associative principles of Scottish aesthetics.[47]

In the main, critical thought in America in the first third of the nineteenth century allowed for a polite obeisance to poetry and phi-losophy, provided that one never lost sight of the reality of the sober fact. In general, few critics understood the nature of the lyric. Like Blair and Kames, William Cullen Bryant insisted on the necessary connection between imagery and emotion. Figures were considered natural to the language of passion; they should never be introduced for their own sake.

Before Poe, Bryant discussed the length of a poem in relation to its ability to sustain itself on the wing, as it were. A long poem, Bryant maintained, was as impossible as a long ecstasy. His own *Lectures on Poetry* (1825) was influenced by Burke, Alison, and Wordsworth. Burke's influence appeared in the first lecture, "On the Nature of Poetry," in which Bryant noted that words suggest both the object and the association—that poetry is a suggestive art. His discussion of the necessity of passion in imagery was a reflection of both the rhetoricians and Wordsworth, and he differentiated be-tween abstract reasoning and the subtle suggestion of truth in poetry.

In the aesthetics of prose, the style encouraged by Hugh Blair, one of the main forces abroad, was artificial and impersonal, an unidiomatic precision called by Oliver Wendell Holmes "Blairing it." Encouraging a Latinity of diction, this style neglected the elements of emotion and sensibility. The first change came about partly through a study of Rousseau, the "sensibility" of whose style was universally praised, and partly through Washington Irving, whose *Sketchbook* (1819) demonstrated Addisonian correctness combined with sensi-bility. William Hickling Prescott, who wrote the best essay on Irving's style, urged: "Put life in the narrative, if you would have it take. . . . In fine, be engrossed with the thought, and not with the fashion of expressing it."[48]

Surveying, then, the early decades of the nineteenth century, one can see that before America could attain a literary aesthetic of its own, it was subject to foreign influences. Among these, first and last, was the impact of Scottish aesthetics and criticism, stemming in a common-sense philosophy that was most congenial to a practical, pioneer society. Madame de Staël's *Germany*, however, helped turn attention to the aesthetic ideas of Schlegel, Goethe, and Schiller, among others. American translations of Cousin's works served to promote an interest in French aesthetics. Added to this was the fascination, particularly among the transcendentalists, for De Gerando's *Histoire comparée des systèmes de philosophie.*

ALLSTON'S POETICS AND

THE AESTHETIC

OF HIS TIME

Washington Allston (1779–1843)

The aesthetic ideals prevailing in the United States between 1800 and 1840 were exemplified by the American painter and poet Washington Allston, who attracted the attention of Elizabeth Peabody and Margaret Fuller and of the English art critic Mrs. Anna Murphy Jameson (1794–1860). No one can discuss Allston without being heavily indebted to Edgar Preston Richardson's authoritative and fascinating book on this subject.[1]

Coleridge, whom the young Allston met in England, described him as a "high and rare genius, whether I contemplate him in the character of a Poet, a Painter, or a philosophic analyst."[2] As one who was to reflect in America the opening phase of the romantic movement, Allston helped to change "the America of Benjamin Franklin and Jonathan Edwards into that of Emerson and Hawthorne."[3]

Like Hawthorne and like other romantics, Allston was haunted by the opposition of appearance and reality, thought and feeling. His confrontation of the mystery of man and "the vastness of the universe"[4] recalls Pascal.

Like most painters of the romantic movement, Allston was interested in literary subjects. While at Harvard, Allston painted subjects from Schiller's *The Robbers* and Mrs. Radcliffe's *The Mysteries of Udolpho,* as well as Satan rallying his hosts from Milton's *Paradise Lost.* Allston identified his own creativity with what he called "those intuitive powers which are above and beyond both the senses and the understanding."[5]

For Richardson, Allston was important because he was "our first full-scale romantic artist." As such, he could exert an influence on American art and enlarge its horizon. He began to develop his theory of art sometime after 1830. Chapters of his work on the subject were read aloud to his friends, Professors Cornelius Conway Felton and Henry Wadsworth Longfellow of Harvard, in the winter of 1842–43. These chapters were published in 1850 as *Lectures on Art and Poems,* which crystallized forty years of thought and artistic activity.[6]

Early in his volume, Allston declared:

> [There] can be but one rule by which to determine the proper rank of any object or pursuit, and that is by its nearer or more remote relation to our inward nature. Every system, therefore, which tends to degrade a mental pleasure to the subordinate or superfluous, is both narrow and false, as virtually reversing its natural order.[7]

Here Allston touched deftly on the intimate relationship between value, intuitive process, and—at least by implication—the role of the aesthetic. Allston pointed here to the reductive process of thought itself when it separates feeling from ideation and thus fragments the mind: "Nothing in nature can be fragmentary, except in the seeming, and then, too, to the understanding only—to the feeling never."

In the creative process the artist deals with wholes, not with parts. He must therefore lend harmony to details in his work of art in conformity with his feeling and through this harmony reflect the interdependence of elements in the world.[8] "This power of infusing one's own life . . . into that which is feigned" appeared to Allston as "the sole prerogative of genius."[9]

The visions of Allston's generation, Richardson pointed out so astutely, were those of Coleridge, Shelley, and Keats. They were "visions of the supernatural, tragic and the fabulous"—"shapes of delight, of mystery, and fear," which Keats saw, in the vision of the Charioteer, as the meaning of poetry ("Sleep and Poetry," 1817). These visions, Richardson added, included "Death on a Pale Horse" by Benjamin West (1738–1820). They also included Allston's "The Dead Man Revived by Touching the Bones of the Prophet Elisha."[10] In the prologue to *The Sylphs of the Seasons and Other Poems*, Allston asserted that the poet's work in the world is to create a dream.[11]

The dream work agitated Allston's soul in his own paintings as well as in his contemplation of the creations of the masters, especially those exhibited at the Louvre. As William Dunlap said, Allston "saw objects with a poet's as well as a painter's eye—indeed they are the same." In a letter quoted by Dunlap, Allston related:

> Titian, Tintoret, and Paul Veronese absolutely enchanted me, for they took away all sense of subject. When I stood before the "Peter Martyr," the "Miracle of the Slave," and the "Marriage of Cana," I thought of nothing but of the *gorgeous concert* of *colors*, or rather of the indefinite forms (I cannot call them sensations) of pleasure with which they filled the imagination. It was the poetry of color which I felt; procreative in its nature, giving birth to a thousand things which the eye cannot see, and distinct from their cause. I did not, however, stop to analyze my feelings—perhaps at that time I could not have done it. I was content with my pleasure without seeking the cause. But I now understand it, and think I understand *why* so many great colorists, especially Tintoret and Paul Veronese, gave so little heed to the ostensible *stories* of their compositions. . . . They addressed themselves not to the senses merely, as some have supposed, but rather through them to that region (if I may so speak) of the imagination which is supposed to be under the exclusive dominion of music, and which, by similar excitement, they caused to teem with visions that "lap the soul in Elysium." In other words, they leave the subject to be made by the spectator, provided he possesses the imaginative faculty—otherwise they will have little more meaning to him than a calico counterpane.[12]

This passage anticipated symbolism with its essential idea of art as a means of providing musical expression for the soul—music above all; it was certainly a premonition of Pater's idea of the arts aspiring to the condition of music.

Allston's *Lectures on Art* reflected his experience of philosophical idealism, which he derived to some extent from Coleridge. For Allston, an object that delighted the eye or the ear was not so much the cause as the occasion of the pleasure that emanated from the mind. He placed the source of the pleasure of art in the mind, not in the object of art. His so-called inborn idea (that is, the capacity to feel that pleasure) was really *intuition*, a faculty that all men share but that, in the power of apprehension, varies from individual to individual. Allston called this principle the "law of mental pleasures." The agency that produces the effect of beauty is the single living, intuitive universal principle of harmony. This pleasure is free from personal desire.[13]

The artist is able to reproduce images or feelings precisely as they exist within himself. To the extent that he can do this he is an originator. His invention is of two types: the *natural* and the *ideal*. The natural consists of new combinations of known forms; the ideal, of the transformation of the known and the fragmentary into the possible or unknown. The test of truth, Allston maintained, is not in things but in feeling: "It is enough to know that there is that within man which is ever answering to that without, as life to life —which must be life and which must be true."[14] Again, "the several characteristics, Originality, Poetic Truth, Invention, each imply a something not inherent in the objects imitated [that is, represented] but which must emanate alone from the mind of the Artist."[15] Richardson found it remarkable that in 1840 Allston could set aside the old theories of art as imitation and that of beauty as a quality of the object contemplated.[16]

Allston believed that the language of art may be learned from tradition, but he held that the thoughts expressed must be those of the individual artist; they must come to him from nature: "Every original work becomes such from the infusion, so to speak, of the mind of the author; and of this the fresh materials of nature alone seem susceptible."[17] He noted further: "The only competition worthy of a wise man is with himself," and "Discussion is the consequence, never the object, of a great mind."[18]

In her "Last Evening with Allston" (1839), Elizabeth Peabody recalled that Allston said that he had taken several subjects from Spenser's *The Faerie Queene*. More importantly, the discussion involved several aesthetic ideas, as when Peabody portrayed to Allston her vision of Sir Artigal's career of victory being turned into defeat by the beauty of Britomartis. Peabody spoke of the lady's beauty reflecting a lively mind, and of the gentleman as tall and slender, with a pale face, through which "his intellectual soul shone like a light through an alabaster vase."

Allston was charmed with Peabody's description and said he should be glad "to see such beings with his own eyes, as well as through my imagination." To which she retorted: ". . . not of the creation of my imagination but of what was visible to the senses." He, in turn, responded:

> In a certain strict sense . . . imagination does not create, it only sees the spiritual creation of God. It was not your senses, but your imagination that saw what you have described to me, but the visual object was unquestionably there. It can be transferred to the canvas, so as to satisfy you, however, only if the painter sees what transcended your senses.

She countered with this question: "Then you think you would do it better, perhaps, if you do not see them?" To which he replied:

> That does not follow . . . for I know you have eyes as well as imagination. A model helps, not hinders, the artist who knows how to use it. But the object of sense must be his servant, not his master. This is the secret of ideal art.

Allston then recited some lines from a poem he had inscribed to Mrs. Jameson:

> Who loves thee, Nature, loves thee not apart
> From his own kind; for in thy humblest work

There lives an echo to some unborn thought,
Akin to man, his Maker, or his lot.

Nay, who has found not in his bosom lurk
Some Stranger feeling, far remote from earth,
That still, through earthly things, awaits a birth?

This conversation clearly revealed a serious concern with fundamental questions in aesthetics: Does beauty inhere in objects or in
the creative (and re-creative) mind? What is the role of the imagination in the creation of ideal beauty? This dialogue of Allston and
Peabody revealed responsiveness to aesthetic ideas stemming from
Victor Cousin, Coleridge, and German philosophy. This dialogue
also raised the question of the role of memory in the creative imagination. Peabody recalled that for Allston the question took the following form: "Is the memory our spiritual body?"[19]

Elizabeth Peabody (1804–1894) and
William Ellery Channing (1780–1842)

During the period that Elizabeth Peabody was in touch with Allston,
she was even more so with the noted clergyman William Ellery
Channing. To her, he seemed "a fixed centre around which was
much revolution of thought in Massachusetts." In the preface to her
Reminiscences of Channing she quoted from Eckermann's *Reminiscences of Goethe*—"I dare give the world my Goethe"—and she
went on to declare in turn, "I offer my Channing."[20] She recalled
that Allston once said that he valued no man's judgment of a work
of art so much as Channing's and that he had an unerring eye for
beauty. Of course, his judgment was determined by moral sentiment.
Channing was Allston's brother-in-law and like Allston he fell under
the spell of Coleridge, whom he saw in Europe in 1821. Coleridge's
Biographia Literaria and Madame de Staël's *Germany* stimulated in
him an interest in the German philosophers.[21]

Channing, having returned from Europe—where, as he put it, "the
revelation of the divine perfection made by the great masterpieces

[of art] seemed to fall upon blind eyes"—determined to do his share in educating American sensibility: "Everything is crude enough around us. But everything is in a state of fluidity, in great contrast to the petrified condition of the Old World." He believed, coming closer to home, that the best cure for New England intemperance would be to promote the fine arts.[22] He despised the effeminate rich who in the selfish cultivation of "their own aesthetic tastes and intellect" failed to consider that "it is the highest office of beauty and culture to minister to the general happiness of society."[23]

Elizabeth Peabody first heard Channing preach in 1825. When he asked her what philosophy she had read, she replied: "Reid, Stuart, Alison on Taste and the volumes of Brown." In the circle of Channing (Charles Follen, Jonathan Phillips, among others), she was exposed to some significant considerations on the tension between language and what it tried to express. She quoted Phillips's remark: "The sensitive who cannot disport themselves with imagination suffer too much from real life."[24]

In her journal she recorded that in 1826–27 Channing published his "great article" on Milton. Channing asked her how she understood the lines "The cherub contemplation/Guiding her fiery-wheeled car." Why "fiery-wheeled" to express the act of contemplation? She took this question to be an attempt to develop her understanding: "Perhaps he thought I had more imagination than understanding; but I know he thought *imagination is the supreme act of intuitive reason set on fire by the heart*" (italics added).[25] The young Elizabeth Peabody reflected simultaneously Kantian and romantic ideas, especially when she remarked that "a great deal of truth is shadowy, veiled in material forms, whose light gleams and fades."[26]

As a close follower of Channing, Peabody shared many of his insights and cherished many of his remarks. He noted that "Jean Paul said music was a prophecy of immortality," and he asked, in connection with Jean Paul's dictum:

> What would the sense of beauty be without immortality? How inconceivable that God should mock us with glimpses of such enjoyment never to be realized! Music does not cheer those who do not believe in immortality,—it makes them sad;

but they covet this sadness beyond all gross enjoyments. Beauty
is sometimes described as a vain longing,—it is a longing, but
not vain![27]

Such ideas now bring to mind Poe's and Lafcadio Hearn's ideas on
sadness in art and Schopenhauer's and Pater's reflections on the role
of music in the human psyche.

Margaret Fuller (1810–1850)

Margaret Fuller's ideas on aesthetics, especially on literature, were
expressed in her *Papers on Literature and Art*,[28] as suggested in her
preface: "I feel with satisfaction that I have done a great deal to
extend the influence of the great minds of Germany and Italy among
my compatriots." This influence was clear in her own thought and
writing.

In "A Short Essay on Critics" she noted: "An essay on Criticism
were a serious matter; for, though this age be emphatically critical,
the writer would still find it necessary *to investigate the laws of
criticism as science, to settle its conditions as art*" (italics added). For
her, the value of impressionistic criticism was "merely reflex"; it characterized the critic. Then she proceeded to talk like Taine: "They
[the impressionistic critics] give an idea of certain influences on a
certain act of men in a certain time or place." Such writers are content to tell what they feel, "to praise or denounce without needing
to convince us or themselves. They sought not the divine truths of
philosophy, and she proffers not if unsought."[29]

Her morphology of critics included, first, the subjective, then the
"apprehensive," now called the *empathetic*—those who "can go out
of themselves and enter fully into a foreign existence." Next were
the "comprehensive" critics, who also had to be apprehensive. They
could enter into the nature of another being and judge his work by
its own law: "The critic is not a base caviller, but the younger brother
of genius. Next to invention is the power of interpreting invention;
next to beauty is the power of apprehending beauty" (italics added)
and of making others appreciate it.[30]

As a transcendentalist, Fuller saw criticism as a step in the Plotinian ladder: "Nature is the literature and art the divine mind; human literature and art the criticism on that; and they, too, find their criticism in their own sphere." The critic, she maintained, should be tempered of all three: the poet, the philosopher, and the observer. The true critic will not let the part blind him to the whole. She was generally against all those who would impose ready-made opinions.[31]

In "A Dialogue" Fuller pursued further her line of thought on the relationship between the poet and the critic. She had the critic say to the poet: "I am the rock which gives you back the echo. . . . Who would speak, if no one heard, nay, if no mind knew what the ear heard?" The critic must understand the poet, who too frequently does not understand himself. The poet objects to hearing in prose the meaning of his melody, and he regards the critic as an excrescence of his own life.

The critic presents a catenation of transmutations from religion into philosophy, from poetry into criticism, from life into science, from love into law, from lyric into the review of the critic. The poet wonders: "What is gained by looking again at what has already been seen?" To which the critic counters: "What is gained by living at all?" To this the poet retorts: "Beauty loving itself—Happiness! True communion of thought is worship, not criticism."[32]

In the midst of the argument, the poet disappears on a floating cloud, leaving the impression that Fuller opted for the poet because she regarded his craft as holy and beyond the vulgar touch of the critic. Her adulation was made vocal in her apostrophe to Shelley, where she quoted the lines in which Shelley saw himself as

> . . . A frail form,
> A phantom among men, companionless,
> As the last cloud of an expiring storm. . . .
> With feeble steps o'er the world's wilderness,
> And his own thoughts. . . . A pard-like
>   Spirit, beautiful and swift—
> Alone in desolation masked. . . .
> A herd-abandoned deer, struck by
>   the hunter's dart.[33]

Of Coleridge, Fuller said: "Give Coleridge a canvas, and he will paint a single mood as if his colors were made of the mind's own atoms," thus anticipating the early twentieth-century revival of interest in Coleridge and the resulting so-called New Criticism. She expressed "a conviction that the benefits conferred by him [Coleridge] on this and future ages are as yet incalculable." She pointed to his power of infinite suggestibility and his power to *inform* as well: "To the unprepared he is nothing, to the prepared everything. Of him may be said what he said of Nature: 'We receive but what we give,/ In kind though not in measure.' "[34]

She declined to "explain" "Christabel" and "The Ancient Mariner." A discrepancy must exist "between those minds which are commonly styled *rational* (as the received definition of *common sense* is insensibility to *uncommon sense*) and that of Coleridge." Her own greatest admiration for Coleridge was "for his suggestive power."

In her evaluation of Wordsworth she seems to have followed the advice that Coleridge gave to Allston: never judge a work of art by its faults. "Where there is such beauty and strength, we can afford to be silent about slight defects. . . . [We] refine our tastes more effectually by venerating the grand and lovely, than by detecting the little and the mean."[35]

Spontaneity was a categorical imperative of the poetic process in Fuller's theory. No form of art, she maintained, will succeed if it is the object of deliberate choice. It must emanate from the artist's nature: "It must be no garment taken from the shining store to be worn at a banquet, but a real body gradually woven and assimilated from the earth and sky which environed the poet in his youthful years."[36] Poetry is neither a superhuman nor a superficial gift. It is the most completely natural expression of the human:

> All the poets are the priests of Nature, though the greatest are also the prophets of the manhood of man. . . . For, when fully grown, the life of man must be all poetry; each of his thoughts will be a key to the treasure of the universe; each of his acts a revelation of beauty, his language will be music, and his habitual presence will overflow with more energy and inspire with a nobler rapture than do the fullest strains of lyric poetry now.[37]

Fuller called for poets with genuine vision and spontaneous expression rather than men who merely know the rules of versification —the rhyme jinglers "who do not feel obliged to relieve themselves of the swelling thought within" but who look upon poetry "as an elegant exercise which may win them rank and reputation above the crowd. Their lamp is not lit by sacred and inevitable lightning from above, but carefully fed by their own will to be seen of men."[38] She placed Longfellow between the jinglers and the genuine poets.

In her own attempt to translate Goethe's *Torquato Tasso*, Fuller confronted the problem of the aesthetics of language in a practical situation. She realized the advantages of the great variety of compound words in German for the achievement of precision and delicacy of shades of meaning in the original, not available in the terse, dignified, but by no means flexible English idiom. She sought support from Coleridge for her somewhat paraphrastical translation, not because she presumed to compare her translation with Coleridge's rendering of Schiller's *Wallenstein* but because she knew that Coleridge favored translations that, while not always literal, successfully evoked the spirit of the original.

Despite her concern over her inability to reproduce the richness of Goethe's verse, Fuller hoped that the harmony of plot, the nicely adjusted contrasts between the characters, and the beauty of the composition would be left intact. She was fascinated, moreover, by the dramatic situation, in which one great poet is whipped into creativity by another: "For we too," says Leonora to Princess Leonora in Goethe's play, "love/Not Tasso, not the man, but the embodying/ Of the soaring and impassioned in our nature."[39]

In discussing drama, Fuller described the power that effective acting can exert on both poet or playwright as well as on the audience. Accordingly, she exhorted the actor to be proud of his art and to consider it on a par with other arts. Macready's portrayal of Hamlet caused certain points in the play to appear to her with a new prominence. Fuller also indicated the power of music in binding individuals to one another: "We meet our friend in a melody as in a glance of the eye, far beyond where words have strength to clinch." Fuller should be credited with an early use of the word "nuance" in critical writing. She contrasted the earlier style of writing in music, which was simple and direct and drew no inferences, with the brilliance of statement and infinite "nuances" of the present style of writing on such subjects.[40]

As a transcendentalist, she was naturally attracted by the idea of a symbolic correspondence among man, nature, and art. For her, Haydn was the untouched green forest in the fullness of a June day; Handel, the illuminated garden. With Mozart the nightingale sang, and the lonely heron waved his wings; Bach was the towering, snowy mountain: "Earth and heaven are no longer lonely while such men live to answer their meaning."

On originality, Fuller noted the French distinction between *une savante originalité* and *une rayonnante originalité*. We might say that the first is satisfied with the originality of facts; the second, with their infinite implications. Thus, for example, she held that a document, if read poetically, will not be less true for being inaccurate. She believed that the intuitive faculty speaks clearly in those devoted to the worship of beauty. The philosopher seeks the thought through the symbol, but the artist is happy at the implication of the thought in his work.[41]

Turning from music to painting, Fuller produced "A Record of Impressions," which was inspired by an exhibition of Washington Allston's paintings in the summer of 1839, although she herself said that this record did not aspire to the dignity of criticism. In her opinion, the grand historical style did not afford the scope most proper to Allston's genius. His excellence appeared in such paintings as "The Italian Shepherd Boy," with the atmosphere of the forest caught in greens and browns, and in his realistic landscapes. On Allston in general, Fuller marveled that "the poetical mind can live and work in peace and good faith! How it may unfold to its due perfection in an unpoetical society!"[42]

In her essay "American Literature" Fuller's tone anticipated Whitman's. She spoke of an American literature independent of English tradition—a literature as "wide and full as our rivers, flowering, luxuriant and impassioned as our vast prairies, rooted in strength as the rocks on which the Puritan fathers landed." To produce such a literature, she warned, Americans must prize moral and intellectual freedom no less than political freedom. Truth to oneself and the eschewing of cant and compromise all accompany originality. There is, she declared, "in every creature a fountain of life which, if not choked back by stones and other dead rubbish, will create a fresh atmosphere, and bring to life fresh beauty. And it is the same with the nation as with the individual man."[43]

Fuller singled out William H. Prescott, George Bancroft, Channing, Emerson, Irving, Cooper. In discussing Cooper, she cited the remarks of William Gilmore Simms (1806–1870) in his *Views and Reviews*, in which he explained the powerful interest excited by Hawk Eye and Pilot:

> They both think and feel with a highly individual nature, that has been taught by constant contemplation in scenes of solitude. The vast unbroken ranges of forest to its one lonely occupant press upon the mind with the same sort of solemnity which one feels condemned to a life of partial isolation upon the ocean. The very isolation to which, in the most successful of his stories, Mr. Cooper subjects his favorite personages, is alone a proof of his strength and genius. While the ordinary writer, the man of mere talent, is compelled to look around him among masses for his material, he contents himself with one man, and flings him upon the wilderness. The picture, then, which follows, must be one of intense individuality. Out of this one man's nature, his moods and fortunes, he spins his story. . . . This mode of performance is highly dramatic. . . .

This significant quotation was the quintessence of a *primitive aesthetic of loneliness* in literature. Fuller appreciated Simms's exposition of aesthetic sensibility in the psychological atmosphere of solitude and his insight into the sublime as it reverberates in the solitary mind in confrontation with the vastness and inscrutability of forest and ocean.

Cooper's baldness and shallowness of thought, both noted by Fuller, seemed almost the deliberate choice of an artist who conjures up great effects with notable economy of means. Simms suggested an adumbration of Rousseauistic primitivism without the rhetoric of sentimentality, indicating an aesthetic of the ineffable of which Fuller was undoubtedly aware.[44]

This awareness was further registered in Fuller's reviews of Charles

Brockden Brown's *Ormond and Wieland,* where she described the self-sustaining force of which a lonely mind is capable and noted Brown's ability to portray it. He took one person, made him brood like the bee, and extracted from the common life before him all its sweetness, bitterness, and nourishment. Fuller's metaphor of the bee revealed not only her rhetorical skill but, more importantly, her own attitudes. She reprimanded her country for neglecting Brown and hoped that when it achieved spiritual maturity it would return to his novels.[45]

Horatio Greenough (1805–1852) *and*
James Moffat (1811–1890)

A number of aesthetic ideas were discussed by the sculptor Horatio Greenough in his *Form and Function: Remarks on Art, Design and Architecture.*[46] The chapter titles suggest his interests: "Aesthetics at Washington," "Remarks on American Art," "American Architecture," "Relative and Independent Beauty," "Burke on the Beautiful," "Criticism in Search of Beauty," "Structure and Organization," "Fashion in Relation to Progress." Greenough presented a catenation of ideas in which one link is enmeshed in the other. He defined beauty as the promise of function; action as the presence of function; character as the record of function. Accordingly, beauty, character, and action are bound together in function.[47]

Greenough found that Hogarth's ingenious plea for his *line of beauty,* the graceful serpentine line, is valid for the spinal column and the necks of long-necked birds and beasts, and that it is the line of moving water, of flowing drapes, and of many attractive plants. Greenough recalled that the beautiful had been defined as the result of the combination of uniformity with variety.

For him, art was not a thing but a form, a development of man: "Your art [work] is, so to speak, the grandchild of God."[48] He saw the problems of art, beauty, and form as a process in which "organization and dissolution . . . are the two poles of the divine magnet," and he affirmed that to "the pure intelligence the one is as har-

monious a speech as the other, since it is correlative."[49] This statement
recalls Hegelian dialectic.

James C. Moffat (1811–1890), in his *Introduction to the Study of
Aesthetics*, attempted to define that portion of philosophy which per-
tains to art. For him, the aesthetic was "that faculty of our spiritual
nature whereby we combine the similar and set it aside from the
dissimilar," which is our guide "to the highest achievements of science
and to every excellence in the domain of art." The objective of aesthetics, then, is "to unfold the native working of that faculty and to
direct its application to the productions of genius."[50]

Moffat indicated that within the previous 150 years (that is, from
1700 to 1850) attention had been given to inquiring into the nature
and sources of beauty, and that this effort was regarded as a branch
of philosophy. He sought to elucidate the following points: the peculiar nature of the emotion called beauty, its immediate intellectual
antecedent, and its relationship to a variety of objects.[51]

His definition of beauty was as follows: The beautiful—that is, the
invariable intellectual antecedent of the emotion of beauty—*is the
mind's conformity in objects to its own nature.*[52] Moffat here attempted to express two ideas: (1) a concordance between "inner"
and "outer," and (2) a plastic principle of the mind, which "im-
proves," so to speak, on nature by making objects conform to the
mind's own inner plan. He spoke of sensation in relation to intel-
lection and emotion:

> Sensation may be said . . . to be the mind's apprehension
> of the different affections of the body, while emotion always
> follows an act of intellection; the operation of sense lying be-
> tween the mind and external things; the intercourse of intel-
> lection and emotion being entirely within the mind.[53]

The world that extended from Allston to Moffat was characterized
by the aesthetic ideas, in art and literature, of Shelley, Keats, and
Coleridge (with Plato and Kant as their background). Their philosophic idealism involved the opposition of appearance and reality.
The ultimate goal of the poet's work was envisioned as the creation
of a dream out of the supernatural, the tragic, and the mythical. The

artist's mission was to find new combinations in known forms and to transmute these into the possible or unknown.

Truth was not in the objects that the artist confronted but emanated from his mind; and the test of truth was not in things but in feeling. The nature of the creative act formed the substance of many inquiries of Allston, Peabody, and Channing. Over all of them— Allston, Peabody, Channing, and Fuller—was the spell of Coleridge. They were all attracted by the idea of symbolic correspondence among man, nature, and art. Moffat's definition of beauty, taking in the concordance of the "inner" and the "outer," had as its background a period of 150 years (1700–1850) of thought.

TOWARD A POETIC
PRINCIPLE

Edgar Allan Poe (1809-1849)

As part of the continuing attempt to develop an aesthetic of literary criticism in America, Poe's critical articles were notable for their indebtedness to Coleridge and to such German romanticists as the Schlegels, De la Motte Fouqué, and Ernst Theodor Hoffmann.[1] Albert J. Lubell suggested that Poe's theory of beauty as the source of all poetic creation was inspired by Schlegel's statements in *Lectures on Dramatic Art and Literature*, on "the sense of the beautiful which at once calls the fine arts into existence" and on poetry as "the power of creating the beautiful." The mystic notion of a beauty beyond all earthly beauties may also have been derived from the *Lectures*.[2] Poe indicated that he used the term "mystic" in the sense given it by Schlegel and most of the German critics: "It is applied by them to that class of compositions in which there was beneath the transparent upper current of meaning an under or suggestive one."[3]

In *The Poetic Principle, The Philosophy of Composition*, and *The Rationale of Verse*, Poe not only antedated modern aestheticians by some seventy-five years but even surpassed some of them. Summerfield Baldwin maintained that in *The Poetic Principle* Poe came

closer than any one before him to reconciling Plato with Aristotle.[4]
The poet, said Poe, provides pleasure not merely by imitating reality
and repeating the forms of life before him but by creating another
reality, which yields an escape from routine. Poetry, moreover, must
transcend reality through the sheer beauty of sound:

> It is in music . . . that the soul most nearly attains the great
> end for which, when inspired by the Poetic Sentiment, it
> struggles—the creation of supernal Beauty. It *may* be, indeed,
> that here this sublime end is . . . attained *in fact.* We are often
> made to feel, with a shivering delight, that from an earthly
> harp are stricken notes which *cannot* have been unfamiliar to
> the angels. And thus there can be little doubt that in the
> union of Poetry with Music in its popular sense, we shall find
> the widest field for the Poetic development.

For Poe, then, "the Poetry of words" is "the Rhythmical Creation
of Beauty." In his view, a poem has little, if anything, to do with
duty and truth: "Its sole arbiter is Taste. With the Intellect or with
the Conscience, it has only collateral relations. . . ." A "poem is a
poem and nothing more—this poem written solely for the poem's
sake."[5]

This claim raises the complex issue of the function of poetry. A
poem converts emotional chaos into a rhythmic, musical pattern,
sublimating desire through expressive form. By releasing repression
it becomes therapeutic, as Aristotle recognized. Poe remarked: "Let
me remind you that (how or why we know not) this certain taint
of sadness [in a poem] is inseparably connected with all higher manifestations of true Beauty."[6]

As a pre-Freudian man, Poe could not consciously articulate the
close bond between Thanatos and Eros, between pleasure and pain,
although he did use the phrase "pleasurable sadness." He could not
fully grasp the dialectic dynamism of beauty (the promise of happiness) as being always accompanied by the sinister reminder of its
transitory nature—of its death.[7] He was unable, moreover, to describe
the subtle connection between poetry and religion, in which the
sorrow of the religious mystic arises from his knowledge that his

desire for perfect union with the universal cannot be fulfilled on earth. Poetry thus becomes a way of seeking that union.

Poe's term for "aesthetic emotion" was "elevation of soul," suggesting a transcendence of reality and a reconciliation of imitation and illusion (the Aristotelian and the Platonic). In *The Philosophy of Composition*, Poe asserted that the poet should allow the public (and, presumably, the critic) to "take a peep behind the scenes" of the spectacle that the poet has supposedly created "by a species of fine frenzy—an ecstatic intuition." He should not object to an examination of

> the elaborate and vacillating crudities of thought . . . the true purposes seized only at the last moment . . . the fully matured fancies discarded in despair as unmanageable . . . the painful erasures and interpolations . . . the wheels and pinions— the tackle for scene-shifting—the step-ladders and demon-traps —the cock's feathers, the red paint and the black patches, which, in ninety-nine cases out of the hundred, constitute the properties of the literary *histrio*.[8]

Such labor forms the foundation of any significant writing. The poet's inspiration, moreover, is limited in time. Poe therefore suggested that a long poem does not exist, and that " 'a long poem' is simply a flat contradiction in terms":

> What we term a long poem is, in fact, merely a succession of brief ones—that is to say, of brief poetical effects. . . . A poem is such, only inasmuch as it intensely excites, by elevating the soul; and all intense excitements are, through a psychical necessity, brief.[9]

This statement is also true for a story. Indeed, "there is a distinct limit, as regards length, to all works of literary art—the limit of a single sitting."[10] In his *Rationale of Verse* Poe studied the rhythmic aspect of poetry. He failed, however, to distinguish clearly between quantitative and accentual systems. He considered verse "an inferior and less capable music." Furthermore, "music, when combined with a pleasurable idea, is poetry; music without the idea is simply music; the idea without the music is prose from its very definitiveness." Rhyme he related (in *Marginalia*) to the human delight in the sense of equality, that is, the similarity between two sounds.[11]

At the heart of Poe's aesthetic was the philosophy of monism. This belief involved a catenation and assimilation of several categories: in philosophy itself, a unified view of mind and matter is envisioned; in religion, the universe as God's perfect plot; in mathematics, equality as "the root of all beauty"; and in literature—on the analogy of scientific unity—the ideal plot, in which "no part can be displaced without ruin to the whole." In a discussion of a unitary approach to art and science, one later writer suggested:

> One wonders how Science and Art will achieve the great harmony on which the future depends. Pascal, Balzac, Edgar Poe, Villiers de l'Isle Adam knew the answer. Art will touch Science with its foot in order to ascertain within it a solid foothold or foundation, and will, with one certain swoop, clear it on the wings of intuition.[12]

Poe's aesthetic was compounded of the complementary ideas of poetry as knowledge and knowledge as poetry—the dream revealing the aspirations of the waking mind and the latter seeking the substance of the dream: reality as a poem of the mind.[13] His *Eureka: An Essay on the Material and Spiritual Universe* should therefore be considered not as a handbook in factual cosmology but as a stimulus for contemplation of the universe. As Poe noted: "It is as a Poem only that I wish this work to be judged after I am dead."[14]

Like Novalis and other romantics in quest of a unified approach to an aesthetic of sensibility, Poe wished to overcome the divisions between fable and truth, past and present, not by confusing them but by transcending them in an all embracing I-Am. As Paul Valéry has written:

> In Poe's system, *consistency* is at once the means of discovery and discovery itself. Here we have an admirable design, an example and operandum of appropriative reciprocity. The uni-

verse is constructed according to a plan whose profound symmetry is somehow present in the intimate structure of our spirit (or mind). Poetic instinct ought to lead us blindly to truth.[15]

T. S. Eliot echoes Valéry when he maintains that Poe, like Mallarmé, made use of metaphysical speculation to refine and develop his own power of sensibility and emotion.[16] By studying Poe through the interpretations of Baudelaire, Mallarmé, and especially Valéry, Eliot became more thoroughly convinced of the importance of Poe's work as a whole.[17]

With Poe, American literary aesthetics seemed to depart for the first time from its theological foundation. Whereas, before him, literary insights of a philosophical and aesthetic nature looked backward, his perceptions looked forward, as shown in his influence on such figures as Baudelaire, Mallarmé, and Valéry; on the symbolists in general; and even on a philosopher of science like Gaston Bachelard. The great service Poe rendered literary aesthetics came not so much directly through his dicta and formulations as through his awakening of literary criticism to a search for the forces underlying artistic expression.

Poe considered reason an intermediary in the communication of a poem to the reader. He therefore attempted to bring reason and imagination together (because "the mind is a unity in its operations"), while emphasizing the importance of metaphysical acumen in the poet. A poem, he maintained, "is not the Poetic faculty, but the means of exciting it in mankind." He thus suggested that the poetic enterprise is a metaphysical act propelled by a socially oriented aesthetic. The *engagement* of the poet depends on a close relationship between the poet and the reader.[18]

Poe's aesthetic also involved him in the question of the relationship of poetry and science, and in analogies between the physical universe and the psychological realm. In both realms the forces of gravitation, attraction, and repulsion are equally operative. The replacement of a speck of dust alters the nature of the universe, as does a change of thought or feeling. Poetics is a sort of subtle physics, although the one defies the kind of measurement that might be applied to the other. Poe's theory of poetry was clearly influenced by his reading of such writers as Newton, Pierre Simon Laplace, James Ferguson, Alexander von Humboldt, Thomas Dick, and Coleridge.[19] The notion of a universal analogy (scientific unity and literary structure) had great repercussions in Baudelaire, Emerson, and present-day thinkers.

Like Baudelaire, Emerson, and Carlyle, Poe was attracted by the idea of synesthesia, an affinity among different orders of sensation. The artist, through his powers of evocation and incantation, has access to a transcendental reality, which is symbolized by sensory objects. In Baudelaire's phrase, creativity is a *sorcellerie évocatoire*, and for Poe certain words have an "incantatory" power.[20] Such elements also appear in the poetry of Mallarmé and Valéry, largely through the influence of Poe.[21]

Poe's stories are characterized by an unusual atmosphere, sometimes described as a pattern of "black and white." According to Leo Spitzer,[22] the poet's concept of atmosphere is derived from the ideas of such thinkers as Geoffrey Saint-Hilaire, who studied the effect of the environment on psychological processes. Thus in "The Fall of the House of Usher" (1839) Roderick described the "effect" of the gray walls on his emotions, suggesting a determinism that has been called *"le réalisme des romantiques,"* or "romantic realism." Baudelaire was particularly attracted by this type of realism in Poe.[23]

As we have seen, then, at the center of Poe's poetic principle is the lyrical, the indefinite (the elusive), the musical. This principle, however, has its matrix in a unitary view of knowledge that envisions poetry as an integral part of a universal mathesis engaged in the study of the cosmos and man's place in it.

Ralph Waldo Emerson (1803–1882)

Emerson never devoted himself directly to a concerted treatment of aesthetic theory.[24] His views are best understood in terms of a monism, a universe without contradictions, in which thought and

sensibility are, if not thoroughly assimilated and fused, at least reconciled, as described in his important work *Nature* (1836).[25] The background of Emerson's idealism may be found in Plato and Plotinus
and, in modern times, in Marie-Joseph de Gerando, Victor Cousin,
Coleridge, as well as in the German metaphysicians. Swedenborg
was also a major influence, with his reflection on the mysterious
analogy between the physical and the moral world.[26]

For Emerson, "nature, in the common sense, refers to essences
unchanged by man, space, the air, the river, the leaf. Art is applied
to the mixture of his will with the same things, as in a house, a canal,
a statue, a picture." In the mind, however, nature has "a distinct
but most poetical sense." Although nature, in man's use of it, is
related to commodity, "a nobler want of man is served by nature,
namely, the love of Beauty." The great term for the world, cosmos
(in Greek, "beauty"), suggests the importance that men have always
attached to "the plastic power of the human eye." Even the "simple
perception of natural forms" is a delight: "The health of the eye
seems to demand a horizon." The beauty of nature, however, has an
elusive quality: "Go forth to find it and it is gone."

The first aspect of beauty, then, is simple perception. The second
is "the spiritual element [that] is essential to its perfection." Beauty
accompanies all great or significant actions. Nature itself becomes
"ancillary" to a man of powerful character. Beauty may also be an
object of the intellect: "The beauty of nature re-forms itself in the
mind, and not for barren contemplation, but for new creation."

Emerson equated the delight that some take in "the face of the
world" with taste: "This love of beauty is Taste. . . . The creation
of beauty is Art." For Emerson, however, art is far more than merely
the product of an artist. It "throws light upon the mystery of humanity," while it is "an abstract or epitome of the world. . . . The
standard of beauty is the entire circuit of natural forms." A single
object is beautiful insofar as "it suggests universal grace."

The artist concentrates this universal radiance on one point: *"Thus
is Art a nature passed through the alembic of man"* (italics added).
To satisfy man's desire for beauty is, for Emerson, the ultimate end
of the world. Except that beauty is, "in its largest and profoundest

sense . . . one expression of the universe," no reason "can be asked or given why the soul seeks beauty."

Emerson's aesthetic was presented in a unified symbology. The consideration of the use and nature of language was therefore extremely pertinent to it: "The world is emblematic. Parts of speech are metaphors, because *the whole of nature is a metaphor of the human mind. The laws of moral nature answer* to those of matter as face to face in a glass."

Emerson defined the imagination as "the use which the Reason makes of the material world." Taking Shakespeare as an example, he described that poet "tossing the creation like a bauble from hand to hand," with all objects shrinking and expanding to serve the passion of the poet. Although the poet and the philosopher may differ in their emphasis, in that one has beauty as his principal objective and the other truth, for Emerson they had a common purpose, because a "beauty which is truth, and a truth which is beauty, is the aim of both."

Ideas are themselves beautiful. Thus the physicist creates beauty when he formulates a law that transcends the "cumbrous catalogues of particulars, and carves centuries of observation in a single formula." Emerson clearly placed the *true* scientist in the company of the true philosopher and the true poet:

> I cannot greatly honor minuteness in details, so long as there is no hint to explain the relation between things and thoughts; no ray upon the metaphysics of conchology, of botany, of the arts, to show the relation of the forms of flowers, shells, animals, architecture, to the mind, and build science upon ideas.

Science dare not overlook—lest it be charged with inhumanity—

> that wonderful congruity which subsists between man and the world; of which he is lord, not because he is the most subtile inhabitant, but because he is its head and heart and finds something of himself in every great and small thing, in every mountain stratum, in every new law of color, fact of astronomy, or atmospheric influence which observation or analysis lays open.[27]

In his essay "The Poet" Emerson described the literary artist as the representative who "stands alone among partial men for the complete man. . . ." Men are only half themselves when they lack the power of expression. Poets "are natural sayers, sent into the world to the end of expression. . . ." A poem is not made significant by meter but by "a metre-making argument . . . a thought so passionate and alive, that, like the spirit of a planet or an animal, it has an architecture of its own, and adorns nature with a new thing."

Associating with poetry "the magic of liberty, which puts the world like a ball in our hands," Emerson conceived of the poet as acquainted with the various sciences but not losing himself in the facts. He merely "employs them as signs." He serves the higher end of nature, which is "ascension." In art "the path of things is silent" and resists spying, but "a lover, a poet is the transcendency of their own nature —him they will suffer."

The poet resigns himself "to the divine *aura* which breathes through forms." He helps men to a new sense by giving them a vision of new worlds in an endless metamorphosis: "If the imagination intoxicates the poet, it is not inactive in other men. The metamorphosis excites in the beholder an emotion of joy." The poet reads the meanings of colors and forms, but he will often make the same sensations or objects "exponents" to his changing thought. The poet's power is electric and causes a motion and a vision in others, although the "dream-power" is his own.[28]

Emerson did not overlook—in fact, he stressed—the disparity he felt between sensibility and the means available for the expression of it. He regarded the genius of expression as a sort of alchemy.[29] In "The Poet" he described the discrepancy between intuition and expression and the ensuing struggle to overcome this discrepancy:

> He hears a voice, he sees a beckoning. Then he is apprised with wonder, what herds of daemons hem him in. He can no more rest; he says . . . "By God it is in me and must go forth of me." He pursues a beauty, half seen, which flies before him. . . . What a little of all we know is said!

In apostrophizing the poet, Emerson indicated the creator's inner frustrations:

> Stand there, balked and dumb, stuttering and stammering, hissed and hooted. Stand and strive, until at last rage draw out of thee that *dream-power* which every night shows thee is thine own; a power transcending all limit and privacy, and by virtue of which a man is the conductor of the whole river of electricity.

Vivian C. Hopkins maintained that Emerson's theory resembled Croce's in assigning the source of creative activity to spirit rather than to matter and in displaying a relative indifference to external form.[30] I cannot agree with Hopkins that Emerson disregarded the role of passion in creativity as well as the importance of technique. His images of fire and electricity, for example, significantly point to the passion that fills the poet's work. His rebuke of those who have "lost the perception of the instant dependence of form upon soul" is not a denial of technique but, in line with his organicism, a logical assignment of it to a secondary role.

As Adams has noted,[31] Emerson's organicism recalls Pepper's definition of the principle as "the world hypothesis that stresses the internal relatedness or coherence of things." In art, organicism involves the integration of feelings.[32] Its objective is the organization of all things in a unified and harmonious relationship of human experience with all the processes of nature or the universe.[33]

Emerson's basic metaphor was the living plant. When he declared, however, that "the methodizing mind meets no resistance in its attempts," he contradicted his other statements on the frustrations encountered by the mind in the course of its creativity. When he asserted further that "every hose in nature fits every hydrant," he failed to recognize the fundamental difference between deterministic mechanism and pliant organicism.

The unconscious shift from the metaphor of the tree or the plant to a hose or a hydrant was unfortunate for Emerson's image of the poet and the nature of poetry. Poetry is an unfolding in the course of natural growth, not a product of a mechanical system.

Emerson's organic metaphor did encompass contraries in a dynamic balance, as Hopkins pointed out,[34] but that balance was threatened by a sudden shift in metaphor, indicating the importance of language in all discussions of aesthetic theory.

Emerson held that rhythm and rhyme issue directly from human nature and that rhythm is related to the human pulse. Length of line is related to breathing: inhalation and exhalation. Rhythm, Emerson found, ascends in power according to the sense, the "metre-making argument." Unlike Poe, Emerson did not define poetic rhythm in terms of music, but he was fond of "rhythms of a faery and dream-like music."

The most striking characteristic of Emerson's aesthetic thought was his wonderment and even bewilderment at the nature of poetic creativity: "The statue is then beautiful when it begins to be incomprehensible." The poet's activity, in his struggle with the ineffable, reaches out to the infinite. In this striving, memory, dreams, wonderment, and musical ecstasy are commingled. The poet takes one to spiritual Alps where "the traveller sometimes beholds his own shadow magnified to a giant. . . ." He "melts away all resistance . . . turns everything like fire to its own nature."[35]

Henry David Thoreau (1817–1862)

Emerson admired Thoreau greatly. Indeed, F. O. Matthiessen called his tribute to Thoreau "one of the finest, briefest biographies in the language."[36] Although Emerson said of Thoreau that "he no doubt wanted a lyric facility," Thoreau's aesthetic ideas were nonetheless suggested in his statement: "A man's life should be a stately march to an unheard music."[37] This idea, as Matthiessen noted, had a compelling power for Thoreau, and he used it repeatedly: "It is not so much the music as the marching to the music that I feel." In the conclusion to *Walden* he wrote: "Let him step to the music which he hears, however measured or far away."[38]

Thoreau's deep affinity for the woods and the elements allowed him to regard rhythm as a primary experience and to see body and spirit wedded to each other in an organic harmony. Words had meaning only when they were palpitant with the circulation of the blood. He felt that "hard and steady and engrossing labor with the hands, especially out of doors, is valuable to the literary man and serves him directly. . . ."[39]

In his attempt to unite the literary fact with an actual experience ("Let not your life be wholly without an object, though it be only to ascertain the flavor of a cranberry."), Thoreau anticipated Eliot's objective correlative, in which every emotion may be referred to a symbolic object. When the symbol is seen or remembered, it will recall the emotions associated with it.

On the other hand, Thoreau led the way to an aesthetic of the senses in which sensory objects generate images, feelings, and emotions beyond the physical fact that occasioned them. His ideas thus anticipated Santayana's "animal faith." Thoreau also prefigured Whitman's "body electric": "My body is all sentient. . . . As I go here and there, I am tickled by this or that I come in contact with, as if I touched the wires of a battery."

With Thoreau, sensibility and sensuousness went together, although his sensuousness seems to have been predominant:

> In our lonely chambers at night we are thrilled by some far-off serenade within the mind, and seem to hear the clarion sound and clang of corselet and buckler from many a silent hamlet of the soul, though actually it may be but the rattling of some farmer's waggon rolling to market against the morrow.

This passage suggests a metaphorical assimilation of the outer-world sensation and stimuli to inner-world images and dreams—the aesthetics of the dream. Although Matthiessen seemed anxious to *save* Thoreau "from gliding away into a romantic reverie of escape,"[40] *Walden* nevertheless provides an escape from a world that has little patience or use for those who place their thoughts and sensations above purely materialistic considerations.

For Thoreau, body and mind were not two separate entities, but formed a partnership. He dealt with "facts which the mind perceived" and "thoughts which the body thought." Apparently fascinated by a relationship between physics and psychology, Thoreau copied the following passage from Sir Thomas Browne's *Religio Medici*:

> We carry with us the wonders we seek without us. . . . We are that bold and adventurous piece of Nature, which he that studies wisely learns in a *compendium* what others labor at in a divided piece and endless volume.[41]

Thoreau's aesthetic, then, was based on his sense of an organic relationship between natural creations and the works of man: "As naturally as the oak bears an acorn, and the vine a gourd, man bears a poem . . . since his song is a vital function like breathing, and an integral result like weight."[42] Nothing in composition

> goes by luck. . . . The best that you can write will be the best you are. . . . [If] one has anything to say, it drops from him simply and directly as stones fall to the ground. . . . The art of composition is as simple as the discharge of a bullet from a rifle, and its masterpieces imply an infinitely greater force behind them.[43]

In the metaphors based on the laws of physics—gravitational pull, initial momentum—the problem of the relationship between poetry and science becomes apparent:

> Man cannot afford to be a naturalist, to look at Nature directly, but only with the side of the eye. He must look through and beyond her. To look at her is as fatal as to look at the head of Medusa. It turns the man of science to stone.

The ultimate expression or fruit of any created thing "is a fine effluence which only the most ingenious worshiper perceives at a reverent distance."[44] According to Burroughs, such a mystic reverence for nature was the objective of Thoreau's aesthetic aspirations.[45]

In addition, however, he maintained an intellectual approach to creative processes, as Joseph J. Kwiat suggested in "Thoreau's Philosophical Apprenticeship."[46] Thoreau's fragmentary essay "Imagination as an Element of Happiness" cited a line from Dugald Stewart's *Elements of the Philosophy of the Human Mind*: "The Imagination is the power that gives birth to the productions of the poet and the painter." In the same essay Kwiat found an allusion to Burke's concept of terror as the ruling principle of the sublime.[47] Thoreau's recognition of the genetic roots of imagination in the child showed the influence of Locke. Thoreau also followed the Scottish philosophers in much of his aesthetic and ethical thought.

The predominant question of the sublime Thoreau discussed in one of his college essays, "The Sublimity of Death" (1837):

> Burke has said that "terror is in all cases whatsoever, either more openly or latently, the ruling principle of the sublime." Alison says as much, but Stewart advances a very different theory. The first would trace the emotion in question to the influence of pain, and of terror, which is but an apprehension of pain. I would make that ruling principle an inherent respect or reverence, which certain objects are fitted to command; which reverence, as it is altogether distinct from, so shall it outlive that terror to which he refers, and operate to exalt and distinguish us, when fear shall be no more.

Kwiat suggested that as the essay advances, the influence of Emerson's *Nature* may be seen: ". . . fear may be overcome, death may be despised; but the Infinite, the Sublime, seize upon the soul and disarm it."[48]

Both Emerson and Thoreau, in reaching out for beauty and a viable theory of it, tried to emancipate themselves from Scottish dourness and theological respectability. Thoreau had the path prepared for him by transcendentalism. Emerson had to struggle against puritan orthodoxy.[49]

For Thoreau, the poet was, in the last analysis, a person whose life was worth recording, and a poem was the record of that life.[50] True verses were "not counted on the poet's fingers but on his heart strings." The creation of nuance and atmosphere was the distinguishing mark of creativity. Thus "a true poem is distinguished not so much by a felicitous expression, or any thought it suggests, as by the atmosphere which surrounds it." The writer is "the scribe of all nature; he is the corn and the grass and the atmosphere writing."[51]

One recalls that Emerson had said that "Centrality is all." Thoreau's whole being was centered in the idea that freedom and beauty and natural impulse were intricately and inextricably bound together. Like Poe, he sought to establish a poetic principle that would recognize the inner, and often hidden, impulses of man. The poet, in speaking from his heart and the depth of natural experience—whether in verse or prose—would thereby create the very atmosphere of beauty.

TONALITIES OF AN IMPLICIT
LITERARY AESTHETICS

Nathaniel Hawthorne (1804–1864): The Aesthetics of Evil

Hawthorne's problems as a literary artist were far more complex than those of Emerson and Thoreau, because he worked "from within his own mind out toward the world of actual fact."[1] Like Baudelaire, he examined the nature of evil and its moral effects, while distilling from it a sense of beauty. Poe found a preestablished design in each of Hawthorne's tales, which had "a certain unique or single *effect*" in view—a characteristic that Gates also found in Hawthorne's novels. Avoiding simple realism, Hawthorne sought to present character in an atmosphere of spiritual emotion, "vaporous, unaccountable, forlorn of light"—the atmosphere of a dreamland.[2] His symbolism, however, was sometimes excessive, as in the display of the letter "A" in the heavens during the scaffold scene of *The Scarlet Letter*.

Hawthorne's general objective was the communication of a sense of tenderness rather than the display of intellectual pride. In seeking to realize this objective he frequently engaged in a Pascalian struggle between head and heart, mechanism and organism. Millicent Bell,[3] following F. O. Matthiessen and Malcolm Cowley, noted that Hawthorne often imagined that he saw in mirrors and in reflections of all sorts the realm of the ideal. This activity recalls Emerson's

metaphor of the mirror: "The laws of moral nature answer those of
matter face to face in a glass."

Bell further noted Hawthorne's observation that reflection is more
beautiful than so-called reality—"the real thing which Nature imperfectly images to our grosser sense. . . . At all events, the disembodied
shadow is nearest to the soul.[5] By way of comparison, Bell quoted
Shelley's remark that "poetry is a mirror which makes beautiful that
which is distorted." This beauty is deepened by the sense of remote-
ness of the object mirrored and its being bathed, as it were, in a
sky of vision, or, better still, in a visionary sky.

Hawthorne's expression of evil, anticipating Baudelaire's, may be
found in the story "Rappacini's Daughter." Dr. Rappacini distills
potent medicines from rare herbs in his garden. A ruined fountain
in the center of the garden cheers the young student Giovanni, who
has taken lodgings in the gloomy old mansion. Here beauty appears
in the midst of ruin and gloom and evil. The mingling of good and
evil is repeated in the plant, in the garden as a whole, in Beatrice.
The plant, set in a marble vase, is poisonous; yet, with its profusion
of purple blossoms, it "seemed to illuminate the garden," in an
atmosphere suggestive of Baudelaire's *Flowers of Evil.*[6] Although
Thanatos and Eros are engaged in an embrace of struggle and death,
the shimmer of beauty hovers over them.

Hawthorne's aesthetic was derived from the gothic novel, with its
emphasis on dark and mysterious elements in symbolic representation
of the dark areas of the human psyche. Thus, Hawthorne's aesthetic,
like Poe's, is a product of "the power of darkness," with beauty ever
accompanied by Satan and Death.[7]

The exploration of the "dark cavern of the mind" can be both a
fascinating and a terrifying process. An aesthetic arising from such
a conflicting experience allows the artist to examine the areas of
human thought lying between dream and reality, even between sanity
and insanity. The experience of beauty therefore comes to mean far
more than the experience of something tangential to the substance
of life. It appears as an important part of the substance itself. As
Hawthorne noted, beauty is diametrically opposed to a moralistic
puritanism, which was "sinister to the intellect and sinister to the

heart."[8] Indeed, beauty, as interpreted by Hawthorne, reveals new areas of intellectual and emotional activity.[9]

Many years ago, when I found myself walking in the Stockbridge Bowl area, not far from Lenox, with some of the Tanglewood music still in my ear and mind, I suddenly recalled that it was in this environment that Hawthorne and Melville had peripatetic reckoning with the cosmos as they touched on the nature of tragedy. They wrote about each other: the one, an essay on the author of *The Scarlet Letter* and *The House of the Seven Gables*; the other, on the writer of *Typee*. With considerable insight, Matthiessen pointed out that the discoveries Melville made about Hawthorne were equally illuminating about himself.

Many elements of Hawthorne's literary aesthetic were illuminated by Melville, who noted that Hawthorne "sent few thoughts into circulation, except they be arterialized at his large warm lungs and expanded in his honest heart." His great power of blackness derived its force, Melville thought, "from its appeal to the Calvinistic sense of innate Depravity and Original Sin."[10] In this regard, the sketch "The Haunted Mind" (1834) suggests an aesthetic based on the spontaneous response of the artist to the dictates of the unconscious. Thus Hawthorne's aesthetics went beyond formal beauty into the heart of form itself.

Melville's dedication of *Moby Dick* to Hawthorne was like the salute of the majesty of the ocean to the genius of darkness. It was a recognition of the affinity of the outer elements for the inner. If both creators had anything to do with Coleridge, it was with the poet of "Kubla Khan" and *The Ancient Mariner*, not with the writer who played ineffectually with the distinction between fancy and imagination—"a distinction without a difference." Melville and Hawthorne were two great symbolists who saw through the mask of things and the desires of the mind behind them.[11] They were both professors of the aesthetics of evil. Over their stories, one could truly inscribe: "Of us these stories are told."

Many elements of Hawthorne's aesthetics may be found in the story "The Chimaera." Here Hawthorne portrayed the travail of poetic genius in a society beset by the ugliness of materialism and vulgarity. A handsome young man, Bellerophon, holding a bridle studded with brilliant gems and a golden bit, comes to the Fountain of Pirene, named after a beautiful woman who melted into tears when her son was killed by the huntress Diana. Bellerophon is searching for the peerless winged horse, Pegasus. No one at the fountain has heard of such a horse, and some even chide the young man as a useless idler. Only a fair, bright-eyed maiden and a child who comes to the fountain to sail little boats seem to have any memory of having seen such a horse.

Bellerophon needs the winged horse because he has promised King Isobates of Asia that he would annihilate the terrible monster Chimaera, whose blasts of fire have destroyed forests and villages. After Bellerophon has lingered at the fountain, encouraged by the child, who had once seen Pegasus mirrored in the water, the winged horse appears. Bellerophon mounts, but before he can slip the magic bit into the horse's mouth, Pegasus flies to his abode on Mount Helicon.

Bellerophon is then overtaken by a generous impulse to free Pegasus by removing the bit, which he has succeeded in slipping into the horse's mouth in the course of the flight. "Leave, Pegasus— Either leave me, or love me," says the adventurous youth. The winged animal bolts out of sight, but soon returns. Bellerophon and Pegasus become great friends. The vision of conquering the Chimaera, however, haunts the youth, and he finally accomplishes the deed with the aid of Pegasus. Together they return to the Fountain of Pirene and the child, who never wearies of gazing into its waters.

Again Bellerophon offers Pegasus his freedom, but the latter refuses. They become inseparable:

> Then Bellerophon embraced the gentle child, and promised to come to him again, and departed. But, in after years, that child took higher flights upon the aerial steed than ever did Bellerophon, and achieved more honourable deeds than his friend's victory over the Chimaera. For, gentle and tender as he was, he grew to be a mighty poet![12]

All this has a dreamlike quality. The dream, as Hawthorne described it, was told by Eustace Bright, a student at Williams College,

to a spellbound audience "beneath the porch of the country-seat called
Tanglewood." Primrose, one of the rapt listeners, twined a wreath
of mountain laurel and placed it on the brow of Eustace, who wished
he had the use of Pegasus to make literary calls on his brother-authors.
He mentions Longfellow and Melville. The latter, he says, sits on
the hither side of Pittsfield, "shaping out the gigantic conception of
his 'white whale.' "[13]

Certain elements emerge symbolically from this tale: the fight of
the poet with his own demon; his struggle with a society encrusted
with vulgarity and insensitivity; the embodiment of genius and creativity in youth; the freedom that the imagination must have to roam
between heaven and earth if it is to be truly productive; the necessity of love as an atmosphere in which creativity could come to frui-
tion. These principles constitute the foundation of Hawthorne's
aesthetic. It envisions evil, articulated by the artist, as a source of
beauty.

Herman Melville (1819–1891): The Aesthetics of the Oceanic

Hawthorne, Shakespeare, and the sea were mixed in Melville, whose
thought was oceanic in the vastness of its conceptions. The power of
Melville's cosmic intuitions united the three into a family, one of
whose members (the sea) was not human but was an emblem of
the human mind in its vastness, its wildness, and its vacillation between storm and calm. Melville, of course, also gathered ideas from
his purely intellectual sources, as *The Melville Log* composed by
Jay Leyda amply testifies.[14] But his most important insights were
derived from the emotional attitudes that formed the basis of *Moby
Dick*.

Thus Melville's aesthetic arises from his imaginative power and
cannot be fully understood apart from it. *Moby Dick*, moreover,
furnishes the fundamental text for the study of the quest for beauty
that involved Melville in an exploration of the relationship of the
self to the elements that confront it. In Hawthorne's story, Bellero-

phon wishes to mount the winged horse to rise above the vulgarity characterized by the Chimaera. Melville (under the persona of Ishmael), concerned with "whales in paint; in teeth; in wood; in sheet-iron; in stone; in mountains; in stars," wished that "with a frigate's anchors for [his] bridle-bitts and fasces of harpoons for spurs, [he] could mount that whale [that he had chased round and round the Pole] and leap the topmost skies, to see whether the fabled heavens with all their countless tents really lie encamped beyond [his] mortal sight!"[15]

Dread and beauty go together in this cosmic matrix. The reader is asked to "consider the subtleness of the sea," the treachery hidden "beneath the loveliest tints of azure," the devilish "brilliance and beauty of many of its most remorseless tribes":

> . . . then turn to this green, gentle and most docile earth; consider them both, the sea and the land; and do you not find a strange analogy to something in yourself? For as this appalling ocean surrounds the verdant land, so in the soul of man there lies one insular Tahiti, full of peace and joy, but encompassed by all the horrors of the half known life.[16]

The universal analogy suggested here recalls similar observations in Emerson, Poe, Baudelaire, and others. In this view, the natural world is the reproduction of the spiritual world. The poetic genius must interpret this analogy.[17] Melville, however, was not content with a mere "counting-room philosophy." He was fully aware that profound knowledge could be "discouraging knowledge."[18] In his account of the whale, he equated beauty with strength, symbolized by him in the great animal's tail. Here "the confluent measureless force of the whole seems concentrated to a point. Could annihilation occur to matter, this were the thing to do it." This amazing strength, far from crippling the graceful flexion of the whales' movements, allows them to "derive their most appalling beauty from it. Real strength never impairs beauty or harmony, but it often bestows it."[19]

The assimilation of the elements of nature and the human in a symphonic beauty appears throughout Melville's work:

It was a clear steel-blue day. The firmaments of air and sea
were hardly separable in that all-pervading azure; only, the
pensive air was transparently pure and soft, with a woman's
look, and the robust and man-like sea heaved with long, strong,
lingering swells, as Samson's chest in his sleep.[20]

Disregarding the so-called pathetic fallacy, Melville suggested an
aesthetic derived from man's response to the elements:

Ahab stood forth in the clearness of the morn, lifting his
splintered helmet of a brow to the fair girl's forehead of heaven.
. . . Sweet childhood of air and sky! How oblivious were ye of
old Ahab's close-coiled woe! . . . Ahab leaned over the side,
and watched how his shadow in the water sank . . . the more
and more that he strove to pierce the profundity. But the lovely
aromas in the enchanted air did at last seem to dispel, for a
moment, the cankerous thing in his soul. The glad, happy air,
the winsome sky, did at last stroke and caress him; the step-
mother world, so long cruel—forbidding—now threw affectionate
arms round his stubborn neck. . . . From beneath his slouched
hat Ahab dropped a tear into the sea; nor did all the Pacific
contain such wealth as that one wee drop.

For Melville, beauty was the product of the collisions of man with
the elements and of man with himself—the classic tragic conflict.
Like Ahab, man would cheerily "bowl on [his] way to see old Nan-
tucket again . . . [with] such mild blue eyes . . ." if it were not for
the fierce compulsion within to "give chase to the hated fish!"[21]

This conflict between man and nature is suggested by such details
as the watch ticking in dead Pynchon's hand—merciless time indifferent to mortality—or the stump taking the place of one of Captain
Ahab's legs. These striking images are indicative of the constructive
power of the imagination, which can combine elements of hatred
and cruelty to form a strange and inscrutable beauty.[22] Further, as
in Hawthorne's concern with mirrors, man finds himself reflected in
the mystery of nature, as when Ahab exclaims: "O Nature, and
O soul of man! how far beyond all utterance are your linked
analogies."[23]

Walt Whitman (1819–1892): The Aesthetics of Unanimism

A universal unanimism (a poetic ideal of collective life), marked by grandeur and beauty, related Melville to Whitman. The two were united by an imagery of the elements, especially of the sea and the sky. Both used the symbol of the voyage, as in Whitman's "In Cabin'd Ships at Sea": "The boundless blue on every side expanding,/With whistling winds and music of the wave. . . ."[24] As a unanimist, Whitman proposed "not [to] make poems with reference to parts,/ But [to] make poems, songs, thoughts, with reference to ensemble." He saw himself in all people: "It is you talking just as much as myself." Anyone torn apart by inner divisiveness also "felt the curious abrupt questionings stir within" him. He "too knitted the old knot of contrariety."[25]

Closely related to "the old knot of contrariety" was an element that might be called the aesthetics of perturbation. It echoed the medieval *Timor mortis conturbat animan meam* ("The fear of death disturbs my soul") with obsessive passion and even sexuality. Artistic expression is the struggle with, and the effort toward, an orderly articulation of these perturbations—the urges of desire, the striving for fame, and the fear of death—as shown in Whitman's *Leaves of Grass*. In Whitman, too, "The order of becoming [was] simultaneously the becoming of an order."[26] For him, the body was the true philosopher and the real aesthetician. All "subtle analogies and other theories" were related to theories of earth and body,[27] as in Emerson and Melville.

Whitman's metaphors associated the physical and the mental. He did not differentiate between inner and outer knowing and doing, reason and feeling, waking and dreaming. His work was a continuum in which cosmos, poet, and poem were combined. At the same time, Whitman was aware of the elusive nature of the poetic articulation of experience. The desired expression "flies away like an always uncaught bird."[28]

Among other characteristics of Whitman's "fundamental aesthetics," as noted by Roger Asselineau,[29] was a belief that nature is "the only complete, actual poem." The soul, "buoyant, indestructible, [sails] space for ever, visiting every region, as a ship the sea." Poems are as "total and irresistible as those [forces] which make the sea flow or the globe revolve."[30] Thus the principal objective of Whitman's poems was to be a centrality and totality of observation and expression.[31]

Aesthetic unanimism, which we associate with Whitman, had been gathering momentum in France from Hugo to Émile Verhaeren, in both poetry and prose—a situation that may account for the enthusiastic reception of Whitman in France.[32] According to this movement, the poet's sensibility was activated by his relationship with the masses and, beyond them, with the cosmos. This inclusive aesthetic also calls on poetry to transcend the limitations of space and time, to embrace "Something far away from a puny and pious life!/ Something unproved! something in a trance!/ Something escaped from the anchorage and driving free."

In his reaching out for a higher goal, Whitman joined Melville in the savage joy of pursuing "far out in the ocean the wounded whales." The yearning for immensity ("O to realize space—To emerge and be of the sky, of the sun and moon and flying clouds, as one with them")[33] suggests a sense of the sublime. Whitman's so-called "catalogues" were so many efforts at describing an endless journey of the poet's imagination across infinity. His travail and his goals complemented each other. He declared his belief in "wing'd purposes" and regarded "Agonies [as] one of [his] changes of garments."[34]

The word "aesthetic" occurred several times in Whitman's writings. In "A Backward Glance O'er Travel'd Roads" he described an intimacy between the objects of nature, the explorations of the mind, the qualities of a given point of view, and "the themes of aestheticism." He stated: "The time has come to reflect all themes and things, old and new, in the lights thrown on them by the advent of America and democracy."

For him, "the question of Nature, largely considered, involves the question of the aesthetic" as well as "the emotional and the religious —and . . . happiness."[35] He called for an enlarged idea of nature that would serve as "the pervading atmosphere to poems" and would meet "the test of all high literary and aesthetic compositions." He hastened to add that by this he did not mean "smooth walks . . . poseys and nightingales," but the whole "Kosmos."[36]

The perception of the beauty of "dumb real objects" is open to all men. They expect the poet to "indicate the path between reality and their souls."[37] Aware of this expectation, Whitman desired a partnership between the poet and the nation. Both were to be involved in an aesthetic enterprise: "The soul of the largest and wealthiest and proudest nation may well go half-way to meet that of its poets." Thus Whitman realized that his real goal was

> . . . to articulate and faithfully express in literary or poetic form, and uncompromisingly, my own physical, emotional, moral, intellectual, and aesthetic Personality, in the midst . . . of current America . . . in a far more candid and comprehensive sense than any hitherto poem or book.[38]

As for the nature of poetry itself, he would "not dare . . . to attempt the definition of [it]. . . . The Poetic area is very spacious—has room for all—has so many mansions."[39] In any event, its main task, in line with a "genuine aesthetics," was the equalization in America of the materialistic and spiritual forces.[40] Such a view called for "a new Metaphysics, certainly a new Poetry," which would be the speech of nature. It involved aesthetic, emotional, religious questions as well as that of happiness itself.[41] It certainly would not be an expression of mere "aestheticism."[42] Furthermore, such poetry would be free of the strictly measured and the ornamental. It would have the organic unity and beauty of nature.

In this context, one questions Asselineau's suggestion that Whitman elaborated ideas first expressed in prose into genuine poetry. At best, the idea could be embodied in a prose poem. Prose never becomes poetry unless the poetic quality or spirit—rhythm, image, intensity, dramatic tension, and a certain "quickness" either resident in words or in their combinations—is already present in the prose, in which case the work is already a prose poem.

Most of Whitman's verse is of this type. In "When Lilacs Last in the Door-Yard Bloom'd" the prose is charged with lyrical intensity. In certain poems, however, the verse, lacking true lyricism, virtually becomes prose, as in the "Song of the Answerer": "Divine instinct, breadth of vision, the law of reason, health, rudeness of body, withdrawness/Gayety, sun-tan, air-sweetness, such are some of the words of poems."

Clearly, none of these words, in the combinations in which they appear (with the possible exception of "air-sweetness"), are "words of poems." This poem, in fact, is cluttered prose, as is attested by the unfortunate word "withdrawness." The situation is not altered, nor in any critical sense redeemed, by saying (as Asselineau does) that Whitman's poems were composed like mosaics.

More to the point is Whitman's own confession:

> The first thing necessary is the thought. . . . The two things being equal I should prefer to have the lilt present with the idea, but if I got down my thought and the rhythm was not there I should not work to secure it. [Frost has said that you cannot worry a poem into being.] I take a good deal of trouble with words . . . but what I am after is the content not the music of words. Perhaps the music happens—it does not harm: I do not go in search of it.

Whitman's remarks here seem shockingly philistine. A poem is not *sewed* together of bits of thought (content) and strands of music (form). Both are there as organically one, or no poem exists! The poet of "When Lilacs Last in the Door-Yard Bloom'd" surely must have known this and felt it. The following passage, apparently an apologia for looseness of form on the ground of freedom and masculinity of expression, is actually a denial of looseness of form:

> I have not so much emulated the birds that musically sing,
> I have abandoned myself to flights, broad circles.
> The hawk, the seagull, have far more possessed me than the
>   canary or mocking-bird,
> I have not felt to warble and trill, however sweetly,
> I have felt to soar in freedom and in the fullness of power,
>   joy, volition.[43]

Out of the welter of Whitman's reflections ("melanged cogitations" is his own phrase), certain ideas did emerge. To be sure, some of them stemmed from the authors he read, including Goethe, Jean Paul Richter, the Schlegels, Coleridge, Carlyle, Arnold, and others. He was principally inspired, however, by organic nature. Thus power was obviously associated with maleness, and delicacy with femininity (in Jungian terms, *animus* and *anima*). The ocean impressed him with its two opposite qualities; grim power and subtle delicacy (as Asselineau indicates)—qualities he emphasized both in nature and art. This aesthetic, then, was based on a dialectic of opposites. On the one hand, he hailed the oceanic, intense practical energy.[44] On the other, he courted the diffuse, the enigmatic, which approached Poe's dogma of the indefinite and the atmospheric—the so-called alchemy of lyricism.[45]

Like Baudelaire, Whitman was fascinated by Poe, although Whitman was presumably of utterly different, if not opposed, temperament from Poe. On the question of how far Whitman was preoccupied with Poe, Matthiessen quoted Whitman:

> In a dream I once had, I saw a vessel on the sea, at midnight in a storm. It was no great full-rigg'd ship, nor majestic steamer, steering firmly through the gale, but seemed one of those superb little schooner yachts I had often seen lying anchored, rocking so jauntily, in the waters around New York, or up Long Island sound—now flying uncontrolled with torn sails and broken spars through the wild sleet and winds and waves of the night. On the deck was a slender, slight, beautiful figure, a dim man, apparently enjoying all the terror, the murk, and the dislocation of which he was the centre and the victim. That figure of my lurid dream might stand for Edgar Poe, his spirit, his fortunes, and his poems—themselves all lurid dreams.[46]

To the extent that poetry, in its effect, is more an infection than an imposition, Whitman is most memorable for his "When Lilacs Last in the Door-Yard Bloom'd." The musicality of this poem, orchestrating a dream of life, a memory of love, and the imperiousness of death, allies him to Poe, despite his strictures. Thus both writers joined the poets who followed the words of Verlaine: "Music above all—and all the rest is literature." Whitman, however, differed radically from Poe in his lyrical unanimism, which relates the individual to the collective as rivers are related to the ocean.

James Russell Lowell (1819–1891): The Aesthetics of the Established Norm

No aesthetician himself, Lowell was in practice an eclectic. To evaluate a literary work he resorted to impressionism, historical insight, and aesthetic principle in turn, or all at once. Although he gravitated toward a norm between classic and romantic, he frequently indulged in delightful impressionistic divagations. As Herman Foerster pointed out, however, Lowell held subjective criticism to be "as untrustworthy as it is fascinating."[47] He sought objective standards in the historical, aesthetic, and didactic approaches.

Foerster differentiated Lowell from Poe and Emerson. Poe lacked the learning and the flexibility implied in the historical approach to literary judgment; Emerson sensed only in a general way the relation of an author to his times. Lowell was the first American critic-scholar to assess properly the combination of knowledge and sympathy, historical understanding and vivid impressions. His attitude was undoubtedly influenced by Goethe and Taine, who enabled him to see through Pope's artificial style, for example, as a way of expressing an artificial state of society with artificial modes of thinking.[48]

For the fundamentals of aesthetics—unity, design, proportion, clarity, economy, power, control, repose, sanity, impersonality—he was indebted to the Greeks. Foerster, who gave this enumeration, stopped short of the consideration of genius, the psychology of creativity, the nature of lyricism, and the principle of musicality—elements without which no full ontology of art can be established. Lowell himself fell short of exploring these elements in depth. Perhaps he was too much preoccupied with mere "decorum."

In his essay on Lessing, Lowell spoke of "the dark forest of aesthetics.[49] As a Dante scholar, he understandably thinks of "the dark forest," but why "of aesthetics"? Unless he felt lost in it! As the teacher of Henry Adams at Harvard, he directed his student to seek advanced learning from the German scholars. Rather surprisingly, however, he also criticized such scholars (for example, Gervinus) for offering "to be our guide into an obscurity of [their] own contriving." He attacked Friedrich Theodor von Vischer's *Aesthetik*, which he admitted to be "the best treatise on the subject, ancient or modern," but which he called a book that

> none but a German could write. . . . The abstracts of its sections are sometimes nearly as long as the sections themselves, and it is hard to make out which head belongs to which tail, as in a knot of snakes thawing themselves into sluggish individuality under a spring sun.

He added later, however: "And yet the admirable thoroughness of the German intellect!" Lowell maintained the work was too heavy and lacked French *esprit*. For all its German thoroughness, it lacked lucidity as well as the ability to entertain. The German always shows "the professional grind" and the tendency "to bear on too heavily, where a French critic could touch and go with such exquisite measure."[50] Lowell's suspicion that a good deal of this German heaviness stems from the language itself recalls the simple person who returned from a visit to Germany with the verdict: "The German people are a fine folk, but the language kills them."

Goethe himself, in Lowell's estimate, "limpidly perfect as are many of his shorter poems, often fails in giving artistic coherence to his longer works." *Wilhelm Meister*, for example, seems "a mere aggregation of episode if compared with such a masterpiece as *Paul and Virginia*, or even with a happy improvisation like the *Vicar of Wakefield*." So also with Part II of *Faust* and even with many of Schiller's lyrical poems, which are much too long in parts.[51]

By contrast, he found the character of Lessing unimpeachable: "He was the first German who had any conception of style, and who could be full without spilling over on all sides." Lowell found fault with Adolf Stahr's biography of Lessing because it furnished little material for a comparative estimate "or for judging of the foreign influences which helped from time to time in making him what he was." He was "little actuated by an inward creative energy, was commonly stirred to motion by the impulse of other minds, and struck out its brightest flashes by collision with them."[52]

Lowell remarked of Lessing's purely imaginative works that they were all written "not to satisfy the craving of a poetic instinct, nor *to rid head and heart of troublous guests by building them a lodging outside himself,* as Goethe used to do, but to prove some thesis of criticism or morals by which Truth could be served."[53] The words I have italicized suggest both the Freudian conception of art as sublimation and the Aristotelian concept of catharsis. Lowell, however, clearly favored a less therapeutic approach to art.

Other elements of his rather fragmentary aesthetic may be found in the following dicta:

> Words, to hold fire, must first catch it from vehement heat of thought, while no artificial fervors of phrase can make the charm work backward to kindle the mind of writer or reader.[54]
>
> Originality, eloquence, sense, imagination, not one of them is enough by itself, but only in some happy mixture and proportion.
>
> Comparative criticism teaches us that moral and aesthetic defects are more nearly related than is commonly supposed.[55]
>
> The idea and the form in which it naturally embodies itself, mutually sustaining and invigorating each other, cannot be divided without endangering the lives of both.[56]
>
> Talent is that which is in a man's power; genius is that in whose power a man is.
>
> [The] same genius that mastered him who wrote the poem masters us in reading it, and we care for nothing outside the poem itself.
>
> The very susceptibility that makes him [the sentimentalist] quick to feel, makes him also incapable of deep and durable feeling.
>
> Originality does not consist in a fidgeting assertion of self-hood, but in the faculty of getting rid of it altogether.

Fabulists always endow their animals with the passions and desires of men.

[We] must not be hasty to condemn a sentimentalism which we do our best to foster.[57]

Lowell deplored the drift of romanticism because he saw in it a tendency to sentimentalism rather than to true passion.[58] Sentimentalism, however, may be a species of passion, and life itself may be a sentimental episode. Indeed, sentimentalism partakes of varying degrees of passion, and is closely related to mood or *Stimmung*. Passion is a function of the organism; sentimentality is a function of education and environment. Despite Lowell's strictures, no civilized person escapes the sentimental mood.

Lowell was a highly accomplished man whose thought was marked by a continuing conflict between instinct and reflection—a divisiveness that Lowell himself found in Dryden. In Lowell, as Foerster noted, head and heart, reason and imagination, aristocracy and democracy, religion and science were engaged in inconclusive warfare.[59] From such divisiveness no concerted aesthetic could be expected. Like his pupil Henry Adams after him, he took refuge in irony, always a sign of unresolved conflict—the irony that is at the heart of romanticism, which Lowell decried.[60]

Despite his concern with decorum, Lowell elaborated a theory of the imagination, derived in part from Coleridge.[61] Its tripartite structure involved the spiritual (intuitive and aesthetic), the plastic (creative, organic), and the expressive (representing the parts of the whole). Like Coleridge he recognized the insufficiency of the understanding and common sense in man's effort to penetrate the mysteries outside of himself as well as within himself.

He noted further that Coleridge taught the English *to recognize in the imagination an important factor not only in the happiness but in the destiny of man*. Here Lowell pointed to an important insight, however much he failed to develop the idea. This emphasis on the tragic aspect of the imagination, such as is later found in the novels of Thomas Hardy, is an element without which no great literature or art can come into being.

Thus Lowell transcended the aesthetics of the established norm to examine the profundity of the creative imagination. As a teacher, moreover, he communicated a sense of the importance of literature in both its substantive and formal aspects. In his incidental characterization of Petrarch, for example, he anticipated symbolism with his reference to "that rhetorical art by which the music of words supplants their meaning, and the verse moulds the thought instead of being plastic to it. . . ."[62]

A close view of the authors treated in this chapter points to a common aesthetic that reveals, in varying degrees of intensity, a struggle between instinctual drives and the ways of cold reflection. Implicit in all of them was a quest for the means of transcending that conflict. Thus Hawthorne strove to free the imagination from the shackles of social vulgarity and insensitivity to beauty. Melville made an heroic effort to assimilate the elemental (the oceanic) in nature and in man. Whitman's unanimism was a lyrical embrace of the one and the many and an invitation to the nation to meet its poets at least half way. In Lowell there was an ironic note that is symptomatic of an awareness of the conflict between traditionally established norms and the dynamics of the creative imagination. Ultimately, Lowell's aesthetic took its cue from Coleridge.

6

CONCERTED EFFORTS AT AN AESTHETIC STRUCTURE (1860-90)

THE PEDAGOGIC MOTIVE

John Bascom (1827–1911)

As late as 1862 the preface to Bascom's *Aesthetics* showed a hesitancy in using the term: "[At] the risk of some offence, we have ventured to style our work Aesthetics." The alleged object of the book, which consisted of twenty lectures, was "to aid the ordinary students of the beauties of the external and ideal worlds."[1] Here "aesthetics" indicated the way in which beauty enters the mind, that is, through the senses.

For Bascom, beauty depended on the changes in the relations of parts in a whole. Objects are its occasions, but expression is its primary condition. Aesthetics and the science of beauty are interchangeable terms.[2] He suggested, rather obliquely, that the pleasure man finds in such phenomena as earthquakes, storms, and scenes of desolation may be traceable to primordial psychic states: the presence within him of the dark, the wild, and the sad. Man finds these states

in nature through a process of projection,[3] suggesting an amplifica-
tion of Ruskin's pathetic fallacy. In general, Bascom's work presented
a genetic approach to the aesthetics of pleasure in the unpleasant.

Influenced by Lessing's *Laocoön*, Bascom maintained that, in
sensory terms, a poem is abstract, analytic, and suggestive. Its emotional force is derived from the interest of the action and the facility
with which the reader follows it. If, for example, the poet is to deal
with the shield of Achilles, he does not merely describe its many
devices; he shows how the varied images rose with truly volcanic
fury from Vulcan's forge. Similarly, the poet, as Bascom suggested,
is most forceful when he can show how objects are related in time,
rather than merely describing their positions in space.[4]

George Fisk Comfort (1833–1910)

More concerned than Bascom with the place of aesthetics in pedagogy, Comfort, in his "Esthetics in Collegiate Education," wrote at
a time of rising interest in the structure of higher education in
America. Comfort maintained that in most American colleges no
provision had been made to open the student's thoughts to beauty
within or without him.

In an ideal educational system, he suggested, equal prominence
should be given to the moral, the scientific, and the aesthetic.[5]
Noting that American travelers, while eagerly admiring cathedrals
and other works of art in Europe, did little to promote the art of
their country,[6] he urged that all college students should receive a
high aesthetic culture. Such a development, by broadening the range
of intellectual activity, would also have benefited American technology and science.[7]

Comfort suggested that if instruction in aesthetics and the fine arts
is to be effective, it should deal systematically with three principal
areas of inquiry: the theoretical, the practical, and the historical.
The theoretical will include the general science of aesthetics, or the
philosophy of the beautiful, and its place in a system of philosophy,
as well as the classification and mutual relations of the fine arts and

the means by which the applied arts may receive life, grace, and beauty from them. The practical will be devoted to such subjects as carpet ornamentation, furniture, wallpaper, dress, machinery, and the application of mathematics to drawing. Finally, the historical aspects of the fine arts will be necessary for an understanding of the rise and fall of cultures and of history in general.[8] Only when aesthetics and the fine arts are thus placed on a level with philosophy, science, theology, and morals, Comfort maintained, could America have a well-balanced culture and civilization.[9]

Henry Noble Day (1808–1890)

Like Bascom and Comfort, Day was moved partly by pedagogic purposes when he wrote *The Science of Aesthetics: The Nature or Kinds, Laws and Uses of Beauty*, "in closest practical connection with the study and teaching of rhetoric."[10] Citing Wolfgang Menzel and Robert Zimmerman for their contrasting views of beauty, he noted Menzel's declaration: "The science of aesthetics itself is nothing but the theory of objective beauty." Zimmerman, on the other hand, maintained that "the exposition of the beautiful from its subjective origin, not from its objective laws, is the fundamental principle of all aesthetics after Kant, with the exception of Herbart."[11] Day also approved Sir William Hamilton's observations that form as object and imagination as subject are correlative, and that the active and passive phases of imagination are conjoined.[12]

By 1872, when Day's book was published, many American scholars were already familiar with virtually all aesthetic ideas that had developed in Germany from Alexander Baumgarten through Winckelmann, Lessing, Kant, Schiller, Herder, Schelling, Karl Wilhelm Solger, Friedrich Schleiermacher, Johann Friedrich Herbart, Hegel, and Christian Weisse.[13] In his assessment of Baumgarten, who first used the term "aesthetics," Day noted the imperfect and partial nature of that scholar's work. Baumgarten's principles, largely derived from the passive side of the imagination, suggested a theory of the beautiful based primarily on purely sensory considerations. Day admitted, however, the influential role of the term "aesthetics" in the development of the science of the beautiful.[14]

In its subject matter and in its logical systematic development, aesthetics is a true science. Indeed, it may be described as the very portal of all knowledge, because man perceives truth only through the aesthetic sensibility that makes him aware of form. Thus, according to many German aestheticians, form and idea, or the perception of form, constituted an indissoluble unity. For Day, such an approach expressed a confusion typical of an age more concerned with metaphysical idealism than with a sensory perception of reality.[15]

In his insistence on the separation of form and idea, however, Day failed to recognize the inner relationships of the two in aesthetic theory. Théodore Jouffroy, for example, maintained that every aesthetic object represents an interplay of the visible and the invisible, the sign and the thing signified, or idea: "Of these two elements that which acts upon us aesthetically is the invisible."[16]

Closely allied to this interplay of the visible and the invisible is the fruitful idea, which Day culled from Ruskin, that "every light is a shadow compared to higher lights, till we reach the brightness of the sun; and every shadow is a light compared to other shadows till we reach the darkness of night."[17] This remark suggests a Rembrandtian exposition of the dramatic struggle of light and dark, of the chiaroscuro in the aesthetic experience itself.

Brother Azarias (Patrick Francis Mullany) (1847–1893)

Although Brother Azarias was not an innovator in aesthetic theory, his *Essay Contributing to a Philosophy of Literature* (1874)[18] is an important compendium of philosophical thought, comprising remarks on Plato, Vico, Schlegel's *Lectures on Dramatic Poetry*, Schiller, Madame de Staël's *Germany*, Victor Cousin, Hegel, Schelling, Johann Gottlieb Fichte, and Taine.[19] Azarias described three forms of beauty: intellectual, moral, and physical. He especially admired Schelling, Fichte, and Hegel for their conceptions of the identity of subject and object and the manifestation of the idea in all of nature.[20]

In discussing pleasure, pain, and the general malaise of the nineteenth century, he referred to Schopenhauer, Chateaubriand, Byron, Heine, Nikolaus Lenau, Leopardi, Henri Frédéric Amiel, Edouard von Hartmann, and William H. Mallock. He quoted from Lenau's "Die Zweifler":

> *Es braust in meines Herzens wildem Takt,*
> *Vergänglichkeit, dein lauter Katarakt!*
>
> (Transitoriness, your loud cataract
> Rages in my heart's wild beat!)

Leopardi's "The Broom," with its expression of infelicity, was also mentioned. The notion of pain as a positive state and pleasure as negative received further documentation in Amiel's *Intimate Journal*, von Hartmann's *Philosophy of the Unconscious*, Charles Richet's "La Douleur: Etude de psychologie physiologique" (in the *Revue philosophique* for November, 1877), Mallock's *Is Life Worth Living?*, and in the Book of Job. Schiller, Azarias noted, suggested that art can bring tranquility to life.[21]

William Greenough Thayer Shedd (1820–1894)

As a minister and professor of systematic theology at the Union Theological Seminary, Shedd approached aesthetics from the point of view of religious education. Accordingly, in "The True Nature of the Beautiful and Its Relation to Culture"[22] he expressed his concern that American culture "will go the way [of] Grecian and Roman culture, and from the same cause: an undue cultivation of the aesthetic nature, to the neglect of the intellectual and the moral."[23]

Shedd argued that if the beautiful is only the glittering garment of the universe, then the aesthetic sense is a luxury rather than a necessity of the soul. Furthermore, if art is merely and purely an expression of truth, why would not every subject be a fit one for the artist?[24] In his argument Shedd may have failed to understand that, for many artists, the whole universe may be taken as a frame for the expression of beauty, and so with every part in it.

The problem of art, in every instance, is to attain an exact correspondence between matter and form. Its vocation is to sensualize, to bring down the idea of the human mind (a purely intellectual entity) into the sphere of sense, and there materialize it into colors and lines and outlines and proportions for the sense. For Shedd, the unmixed, unbalanced effect of the beautiful is mental enervation. Shedd pointed, for example, to Benvenuto Cellini.[25] Art, he believed, should be subservient to morality. Comparatively speaking, puritan nature owed little to aesthetic culture. Milton's art, for example, essentially puritan, is beautiful only as it is severe and grand. His beauty is superinduced on the true and the holy.[26]

Approaching the problem of the relation of art to science, Shedd delivered the tiresome shibboleth that all art and all literature is the antithesis of science, and that the poetic vision and the scientific vision are contraries. The sole end of one is beauty; of the other, truth. In accordance with the idea that science is the death of poetry, he suggested that the study of Kant injured Schiller's poetry and that Coleridge suffered equally from his study of philosophy.

These poets, said Shedd, might have written more had not their imagination been subjected to the severe processes of the intellect. In his confusion, he added that their art is all the higher for the restraint imposed on their poetic nature. Thus the connection between science and poetry seems close, after all, because the former has a heuristic and disciplinary effect on the latter.[27]

THE ANALYTICAL AND HISTORICAL APPROACH

G. Stanley Hall (1844?–1924)

A year after receiving his doctorate at Harvard (1878) and while engaged in further studies in Germany, Hall published the article

"Is Aesthetics a Science?"[28] Without answering his own question, Hall presented the various aspects of a critical and analytical approach to the art process and its concrete products, refuting any metaphysical approach to the problem.

Artists, said Hall, care nothing about philosophical discussions of art and consider them irrelevant to their métier. For many, art, like taste, is a purely individual matter. Some are satisfied with Hegel's formula: Art is the absolute idea immediately presented to sense. Others find illumination in Schopenhauer's declaration that in a work of art we not only find relief from pain but are absorbed in the Platonic ideal or the purest objective form of will that it illustrates.

Hall made references to Adolf Zeising and to Gustav Theodor Fechner's experimental work with the so-called golden section and to psychophysical analysis of the sensations of sound. Hall mentioned Castel's visual harpsichord, which combined color and sound in a close association on mathematical principles and led to an interest in synaesthesia among the symbolist poets. Should poets and painters, however, study the graphs and calculations of scientists in their analysis of sound and color? Certainly science has not yet disclosed the foundations for a radically new synthesis of any art, Hall admitted. He nevertheless preferred scientific discussion of art to "the inane speculations about the nature of the Beautiful and Sublime which fill so many pages of textbooks on aesthetics." He could not believe that fashion would ever be set or children's playthings chosen by a quadrennial congress of professors of aesthetics.

Hall suggested, however, that the artist of the future should be more fully instructed in the scientific aspects of his art and less fearful of impairing his creativity by the cultivation of critical acumen. He indicated, too, that the understanding has a sort of satisfaction peculiar to itself, which may justly be called aesthetic.

John Steinfort Kedney (1819–1911)

Kedney's two major works were both analytical and historical. *The Beautiful and the Sublime*, subtitled *An Analysis of These Emotions and a Determination of the Objectivity of Beauty,* was published in New York in 1880. *Hegel's Aesthetics, a Critical Exposition* appeared in Chicago in 1885.[29]

In *The Beautiful and the Sublime*, Kedney traced the emotion of the beautiful to man's discovery of a wondrous adjustment and harmony in nature and in the human form. Kedney based this insight on the Pythagorean assertion of the law of numbers underlying the structure of the universe.[30] Dissatisfied with explanations of the sublime, which is one form of beauty, he noted that sublimity involves both a dignified seriousness and a profound exultation, as in the works of Beethoven, Shakespeare, Michelangelo, or Aristotle. The natural elements themselves provide a setting for the sublime.[31] Moral sublimity is that form of all aesthetic emotion which has the largest element of pain. It is less attractive than moral beauty. Kedney believed that moral sublimity is abnormal and springs out of that which should not exist.[32]

In a critical supplement, Kedney gave a rather hurried sketch of various theories of beauty and sublimity. In his opinion, subjective theories failed to realize that beauty is inherent in the constitution of the universe. Objective theories established this principle, but failed to analyze completely the subjective element in the emotion. After dismissing Cousin, Burke, Archibald Alison, Henry Home (Lord Kames), and Johannes Christian Oersted as having said interesting things about beauty but having failed to convince him either in their discussions or in their definitions of beauty, he cited Washington Allston's introduction to his *Lectures on Art*. Kedney credited Allston with following the true method in examining first the emotion of beauty, so as to find its conditions and describe it. Allston, however, failed to follow objective beauty to its last definition. Nor did he define the conceptions intermediate between beauty and sublimity, such as elegance, grandeur, and majesty.[33] For Kedney, "elegance" is an impure form of the beautiful dependent on conventional tastes. "Grandeur," equally vague and conventional, is an impure form of the sublime.

Later in his appendix, Kedney examined Kant, Schiller, and Hegel. According to Kant, the proper place for the aesthetic judgment was between the speculative and the practical reason: "The reflective judgment, when aesthetic and not teleological, has to do with subjective or formal adaptation, and not with objective or material." Kedney noted that this principle was not precisely identical with Schiller's endeavor to find a place for aesthetic freedom or the "play impulse" between the passive condition of perception and the active one of reflection and volition.

Kant's thought expressed the reflective judgment of the philosopher; Schiller's, the empirical judgment of the poet. For Kant, the beautiful was that which, through the harmony of its form with the human faculty of knowledge, aroused a disinterested universal and necessary satisfaction. The beautiful is a symbol of the moral good. Schiller, reproducing Kant with his own end in view, asserted that the play impulse was both passive and active; that we advanced into the realm of idea without leaving the sensuous world; that beauty was both object and a condition of the subject.

In the main, Schiller added nothing new to Kant's exposition. He amplified the notion that the disappointed cognition, after the failure of imagination, caused us to fall back on the consciousness of freedom as an indemnity and a safe refuge from all difficulties and disorders in the intellectual and moral world.[34] This important insight suggested the therapeutic value of art.

For Kant, the idea itself could arouse emotion only in conjunction with the symbol. The physical world is a symbol. To penetrate the symbol we need the activity of the imagination, which imparts its own life to the symbol. The foundation for both the sublime and the beautiful is as much within us as without us.[35]

Hegel always spoke of the sublime as "separating idea and form." Kedney, disagreeing with this, argued that the genesis of the emotion is an endeavor to combine and not to separate, to find the idea in the form—to annul the separation.[36] In his critical exposition of Hegel's *Aesthetics*,[37] Kedney objected strongly to Hegel's dictum that no criterion exists by which to determine the degree of beauty in the objects of nature, and that no vindication can be made of higher and purer taste.

The tendency in Hegel's philosophy was to exalt thought and

underrate feeling. Treating imagination synthetically rather than analytically, he applied the term to a congeries of qualities and modes of activity. Hegel, however, seems to have been the first to accomplish an objective classification of the arts and to have marked by appropriate epithets the overlapping periods through which art has moved in the evolution of the human mind: the symbolic, classic, and romantic. Although these terms, according to Kedney, are very useful, they must not be taken to indicate an absolutely determined consecutive movement. A reversal of this order may occur, as in Hebraic art, which had no classic period.[38]

The symbolic period can be understood in terms of the evolution of the human mind discovering itself enveloped in, and as a part of, nature. At the same time man, as a body, finds himself in the midst of vast and overwhelming forces and in the face of a riddle he cannot penetrate. The instinct to unify, derived from his own unity as a self, prompts him to seek a cohering thread and a center in all phenomena in order to make them intelligible. Experimenting in thought, he locates this center now here, now there: in sky, sun, fire, water, or something else. With a constant shifting of references, the mind, in its fertility, makes a new synthesis and thus imparts something of itself to the natural object or aggregates of objects.

In each attempt, however, the idea itself is vague and fluctuating, and can only fix and clarify itself by finding some outward expression. The vague idea must be expressed through a symbol. Because the symbol cannot transcend the idea, however, it must exhibit its own inadequacy, and thus start the mind on a new enterprise after a new solution.[39] Baudelaire aptly summarized this condition:

> La Nature est un temple où de vivants piliers
> Laissent parfois, sortir de confuses paroles;
> L'homme y passe a travers *des forêts de symboles*
> Qui l'observent avec des regards familiers.

> (Nature is a temple where living columns
> Emit, at times, jumbled words.
> Man passes there through forests of symbols,
> Which observe him with knowing looks.)[40]

Man, seeking meaning in nature, passes through "forests of symbols." Because the symbolic tendency cannot be entirely transcended as long as enigmas persist, an abundance of symbolism occurs in modern poetry and music. Even the classic period was not devoid of the symbolic process.[41]

Romantic art can have at least three distinct objectives: (1) to express the vision of the ultimate perfection in symbol, (2) to deal with nature and human life as material to be worked up according to subjective caprice, and (3) to exhibit the characteristics of the transitory. Nature and human life may be dealt with realistically or idealistically, reviving the classical ideal or clarifying the romantic, or combining the two. The characteristics of the transitory—contradiction and conflict—constitute the reign of the pathetic and the sublime, at which point the interest in romantic art culminates. Indeed, the pathetic may become the sublime.[42]

In Chapter 4 of *Aesthetics*, "The Romantic Arts," Hegel stated that painting, music, and poetry illustrate, as architecture and sculpture do not, the idea of romantic art. Because poetry alone can develop the totality of thought, it is *the universal art*. Its sweep is arrested only when the mind, in its loftiest conception, having only an obscure knowledge of its own thought, can no longer represent it under the symbolic forms of external nature. (For Hegel the ideal to be reached in all the arts was the absolute itself, which is *spirit*.)[43]

In lyricism, painting yields to poetry and music. In poetry, sound is a means to an end; in music, it is the end itself. Here Kedney's gloss stated that music consists of liberty in law, that is, the coalescence of freedom and necessity. Like music, poetry contains the immediate perception by the soul of itself.[44] Thus the expression of the inner power and meaning of the human soul was given for the first time in romantic art. In it, intuition was discovered as struggling to unravel its own nature through full and clear expression.[45]

On the relationship between speculative and poetic thinking, Kedney remarked that both coordinate and demand unity. However, speculative thinking deals with ideas and relations, while poetic thinking is concerned with their concrete manifestations and *feels*, as the other does not, the correspondence of *all* the elements of absolute being. It thus makes a complete synthesis, which appeals not to the cool reason only but to the entire sum of the soul's activities. Poetry (poetic thinking) is the first form under which the mind seizes the *true* before the *general*, to be afterward connected by the process of reasoning. *Poetry makes dull thought living.*[46]

Hegel concluded that philosophy finds its worthiest occupation in the effort to coordinate the idea of the beautiful and all the forms of art. The study of art is neither merely amusing nor instrumental; *it is rather the attempted deliverance of the mind from the trammels of finite existence.* It is the best recompense for the rude travail to which man is condemned in the order of science and knowledge. In Kedney's view, Hegel showed how the eternal idea of the beautiful has haunted the human race. Man perpetually seeks solace in the imaginative representation of the ideal.[47]

Henry Webster Parker (1822–1903):
A Scientist's View of Aesthetics

Parker was a naturalist who, influenced by Darwin, approached the nature of beauty and aesthetic speculation genetically. His investigation led him to an examination of the animal mind. He quoted Victor Hugo as having said: "Animals are nothing but the forms of our virtues and vices, wandering before our eyes, the visible phantoms of our souls."[48] The animal appetites and passions are embodied in man. But man is the only intelligent creature to appreciate the beautiful, which "bathes, shapes, and colors the whole universe," and to realize that "the aesthetic in nature has intelligent cause."[49]

Man and nature are each other's mirror. Any other view involves an unexplained and unexplainable correlation between the world and man's high intellectual, aesthetic, and moral needs. Ernst Haeckel asserted that "Spirit exists everywhere in Nature," and Goethe declared that "matter can never exist and act without spirit."[50] Parker credited Kedney with having brought out the subjective element of the aesthetic—the spontaneous going forth of the human spirit into all forms of beauty. Man is propelled by the need for a symbolic realization of the craving and prophecy of his own intellectual and spiritual being.[51]

The yearning for beauty was expressed by the romantic poets. "I live not in myself," said Byron, "but I am become portion of that around me; and to me high mountains are a feeling." H. T. Finck, who quoted these words in his *Romantic Love and Personal Beauty*, added: "[It] is a poetic anticipation of Schopenhauer's doctrine, that for true aesthetic enjoyment, it is necessary that the percipient subject be completely merged in the perceived object."

In spite of the repeated use by philosophers of the words "enjoyment," "pleasure," and "admiration," Parker objected that they are equally applicable to a sight of roast turkey or a Belgian giant. Contrary to physiological aesthetics,[52] Parker held that it is not the germ, the lowest experience, but the full flower and glory of experience that reveal the nature of the beautiful.[53] He quoted Shelley:

> Spirit of Beauty, that dost consecrate
>   With thine own hues all thou dost shine upon . . .
> Thy light alone, like mists o'er mountains driven . . .
> Gives grace and truth to life's unquiet dream.

One of the most interesting essays in Parker's *The Spirit of Beauty: Essays Scientific and Aesthetic* is "Lessons in Crystals." After pointing out that everything in nature, like the face of a jewel, may reflect light and "give some gleam of spiritual beauty," he remarked that light gives beauty to the enduring flowers of the mineral world, and that "there are many coincidences between aspects of the human mind and the geometrical forms of crystals." Just as a perfectly symmetrical crystal is comparatively rare, so is a perfectly symmetrical mind:

> Human crystallography—the formation of mind, of character, and of society—is the most suggestive branch of the subject. The conditions necessary to the production of large and perfect crystals are freedom and time—freedom among the molecules

to arrange themselves, and time to do so with regularity and prolonged consecutiveness. This also holds for the normal growth of institutions in society.[54]

The mind, like the crystal, must beware of foreign substances that mar the luster. To be sure, all men are shaped by outside influences, including historic tradition, but they must guard against having their vision overcast "by transient forms of fashionable error."[55]

Parker's specific treatment of literary aesthetics was limited. Besides his references to some of the romantic poets (Coleridge among them), he adverted to Spencer's essay on style. Here, all effect in literary style was resolved into economy of attention and of feeling demanded in apprehension, or of ease in production.

Parker charged Spencer with ignoring that all art taxes the creator as well as the consumer of art with utmost labor and effort and with "just such a struggle as the theory of spiritual longing and movement towards perfection admits." This charge, I believe, is not exactly just. Implicit in Spencer's essay on style was the belief expressed explicitly in his essay on personal beauty: "the aspects which please us most are the outward correlatives of inward perfections."[56] Spencer was as well aware as Parker that perfections are never attained without exertion and labor.

According to Parker, the imagination creates the ideal, which is the perfect idea embodied in form. The beautiful is realized through the imaginative projection of man's inmost being into the ideal.[57] He concludes with an apostrophic (if not sermonizing) note, calling for the union of the spiritual and the material through an inspired vision of beauty created by art.

George Trumbull Ladd (1842–1921): The Psychologist's Interest in Aesthetics

A year before the appearance of his later widely known text, *The Elements of Physiological Psychology* (1887), Ladd published his *Outlines of Aesthetics*, consisting of dictated portions of Hermann

Lotze's lectures, which were delivered in the summer semester of 1856.[58] Ladd's translation was part of a growing interest among American philosophers in the work of Lotze, as shown in the writings of Josiah Royce and Borden P. Bowne, who had studied with Lotze, and in Francis Bowen, Bascom, and Hall.

William James's library revealed the extent of his concern with Lotze. Not only did it contain Lotze's work on medical psychology (*Medizinische Psychologie oder Physiologie der Seele* [1852]); it also contained such works as *History of Aesthetics in Germany* (1868) and the *Dictate*, comprising the lectures on aesthetics that Ladd was to translate, as well as *A Critical Account of the Philosophy of Lotze* (1895), by Henry Jones.[59] In 1889, George Santayana, a pupil of Josiah Royce and William James, presented his doctoral thesis, *Lotze's System of Philosophy*. Chapter 5 of this work discussed Lotze's aesthetics.[60]

Outlines of Aesthetics did not provide a concise definition of beauty or show how "things" can be objectively beautiful. Lotze stated that more general agreement exists on the *agreeable* than on the beautiful. Because the agreeable is more closely related to the individual than to the universal, no uniform standard for "beauty" can be established.[61]

Even though things may enjoy their own beauty, no tangible equivalent exists for the pleasure of the subjective impression that beauty provides. Beauty can be apprehended only in the form of an idea. Lotze approached a definition in this statement: *"Beauty is the appearance to immediate intuition of a unity among those three powers which our cognition is unable completely to unite"* (italics added).

Reality has three interrelated realms or *powers*: (1) the realm of universal laws; (2) the realm of real substances and forces, which are active according to the universal laws; and (3) the definite and specific plan according to which these elements of reality are brought together in order to realize a definite action according to universal laws. Cognition fruitlessly seeks for a connection among these three powers. Somewhere between the realm of the true and the good, feeling intervenes in the impression of beauty. It actualizes and manifests itself in (1) the universal forms of space, time, and motion on which all reality is built; (2) the definite typical species of individual and actual beings; and (3) the world of events into which the latter are interwoven.[62]

In order to effect an impression of beauty, art must: please the senses (physiological); satisfy all the general laws of ideation, feeling, and volition (psychological); and correspond to the spirit. The work of art fulfills these conditions if it is mindful of: a circle of general laws valid beyond its own peculiar limits, thus showing itself to be part of a picture of reality; its obligation to bring before us a definite and concrete form of life which, though following the aforesaid laws does not follow from them alone; and its ability to cause this form of life to appear to us as part of a capacious plan of the world and a contribution to it.[63]

On the arts of music and poetry, Lotze made a number of specific points. Tones are the natural symbol for all activity that fills up time: becoming, beginning, and ceasing to be. Proceeding from resounding bodies, they reveal the motion of their interior parts and are in all respects adapted to the expression of the interior life of the spirit. Tones therefore immediately show the essential interior condition of things. Through gradations of intensity, they can imitate, in the most manifold forms of crescendo and diminuendo, all those formal predicates of consistency and firmness, of yielding and transition, of gradual movements of will and sudden bound, of elasticity and sleepiness, that exist in every spiritual life as possible forms of its course and that are of the greatest significance.[64]

Because mathematical relations are not experienced in music, Lotze considered them of no aesthetic interest. An ascending series of the number of vibrations is experienced not as a series of numbers but as increasing pitch of the tone. In this so-called quality of pitch lies the expression, so infinitely significant aesthetically, of one power surpassing another, as in "lower tone."

The second aesthetically significant feature in the series of tones is the existence of harmonies. "Coloring" depends on the nature of the instrument, producing a noteworthy individuality. Melody depends on the relations in the harmony of the chord. The essential element of melody consists in the special form of the movement with which it weaves itself about the firmly fixed tones of its chord.

Transition into another key, with a final recurrence to a previous one, is a condition necessary to aesthetic satisfaction. Threats of disturbing the equilibrium add to the aesthetic experience, in the suggestion of deviation and return. Thus, although music cannot translate feeling directly, it can remind the listener of a particular feeling.[65]

In his discussion of poetic art, Ladd (basing himself on Lotze) made the following pancalistic statement:*

> All universal sciences—ethics, philosophy of nature, history—
> if they pursue their subject-matter into the minute details in
> which its full significance becomes apparent for the first time,
> issue at last in poetry. That is, they can only exhibit what is
> of most worth when they cease to proceed in accordance with
> universal categories, and furnish a portrayal of the innumer-
> able tender and individual relations on which what is par-
> ticular depends.[66]

Tragedy and comedy have the same fundamental end: to show how every finite nature fails when it seeks to dominate the infinite. In tragedy powerful characters are overthrown by vast forces; in comedy insignificant figures, by ordinary accidents.[67]

Such fundamental ideas, derived from Lotze, were characteristic of Ladd's contribution to the development of literary aesthetics in America.

Charles Carroll Everett (1829–1900)

A professor of theology at Harvard, Everett nonetheless derived his theories of the imagination in part from such scientific works as John Tyndall's "The Scientific Use of the Imagination." According to this essay, all great discoveries were made when science left the region of the seen and the known and followed the imagination into

---

* For a definition of pancalism, see Chapter 11, passim.

new paths. Tyndall showed how by the aid of the imagination science reaches a point that by its very nature can never be discerned by the senses. Everett used the term "imagination" to express that insight which anticipates the result of conscious analysis and induction.[68]

In this interpretation, man's first scientific discoveries came as poetry, that is, as products of the imagination.[69] Indeed, the fullness in nature, which escapes the understanding, can only be perceived through an imaginative perception of the ideal.[70] Everett, like H. W. Parker, recognized an intimate relation between the religious and the aesthetic sense,[71] as did such modern theologians as Paul Tillich and Mircea Eliade.

Not satisfied with a definition of poetry as merely the language of passion and meter, Everett extolled the beauty of spirit above that of sound, color, and form. He valued thought above passion. But thought in itself is not beautiful, because it is the result of abstraction from all the lower forms of existence. To be beautiful, ideas must be transformed into ideals. They must become sensuous, in Milton's sense. The illusory quality of beauty (and of poetry that expresses it) was expressed thus by Emerson (whom Everett quoted) in his apostrophe:

> Thee gliding through the sea of form
> Like the lightning through the storm,
> Somewhat not to be possessed,
> Somewhat not to be caressed . . .
> Thou eternal fugitive
> Hovering over all that live.[72]

If Everett grasped the illusionism of Emerson at all, he failed to appreciate fully its importance for an aesthetic of fluidity. Instead, he saw in it a text for the support of a pietistic *touch-me-not* of beauty. Yet he did appreciate the scene of Don Quixote at the puppet show, where the Knight of the Sad Countenance forgets that the scene before him is an illusion, and strikes with his sword to defend the innocent.

The aesthetic attitude enables men, within a play or a poem, to make playmates of the wild beasts pain and fear and thus to tame them. Remembering the illusory nature of the performance, men play with grief as actors do upon the stage.[73] Milton and Shelley placed at the head of their utterances of grief not the names of the friends for whom they sorrowed but strange names like Lycidas and Adonais, as if to say: It is not our sorrow that we utter; it is the world's sorrow.[74]

Everett saw the poet "idealist" as the "realist" in the truest sense. Thus Whitman's poetry is not composed merely of lists but of pictures as well. Some may be repulsive and terrible, some beautiful. Everett likened Whitman's poems to faces that peer at us for a moment in a dream. He was happy to add that now and then Whitman manifested his strength without the extravagances into which false theories of art had led him.[75]

Some of the materials that the moralist would exclude from art on moral grounds Everett would exclude on artistic grounds. Poetry may remove the spirit from grossness. To bolster this contention, he quoted from Tennyson's "Palace of Art," which portrayed the tragedy of a soul . . .

> That did love Beauty only . . . seeing not
> That Beauty, Good and Knowledge are three sisters
> That never can be sundered without tears.[76]

In a section entitled "The Poetic Aspect of Nature," Everett compared Mill's essay "Nature" with Emerson's on the same subject. "If we consider," he said, "that the stability of the universe depends upon the steadfastness of the laws of nature, the criticism of Mill will seem trivial."[77] Everett was apparently offended by Mill's remark that nearly all the crimes for which men are hanged or imprisoned constitute nature's everyday performances of suffering and death. Actually, how "steadfast" is an earthquake, a storm, a flood, an epidemic, or a stroke of lightning?

As Mill recognized, the projections of the mind onto a universe that knows nothing of these laws matter nothing to it in its explosive phases. The soul of the poet, however, inspired by inscrutability and the ineffable itself, creates lyricism, beauty, the sublime which, together, constitute man's greatest weapon against nothingness.

When Everett came to Emerson, he did admit that, in spite of the contrast between these two essays, both contain much truth: the forces of nature certainly have no respect for persons. But again Everett deplored science, which, at first exalting nature by its revelations, in the end makes the universe appear prosaic.[78] He failed to understand that, far from diminishing the grandeur of nature, science is the one poem that continues to reveal it.

Everett pointed to Mill's discovery of the soothing power of nature as expressed in the poetry of Wordsworth (one thinks also of A. N. Whitehead's affinity for Wordsworth and Shelley). Emerson found in the wilderness "something more dear and connate than in the streets and villages. . . . In the tranquil landscape and especially in the distant line of the horizon, man beholds something as beautiful as his own nature." Everett was aware, finally, that a fundamental paradox exists in nature: its indifference and its beneficence.[79]

Man's response to nature is in many respects like that of other animals. He builds houses as birds build nests, and his political institutions are as natural as those of the bees and the ants. Still, men do not feel the same in a city street as they do in the forest.[80] Nature is indeed the mother of man and was so recognized by the Greeks and the Romans. In Homer there is awareness of natural beauty. Lotze sought a view of nature that might supply to us the loss of this elder consciousness. At the same time men have a keener delight in nature than ever before.[81]

With Christianity, a cleavage was introduced between the spirit and earthly life, a chasm between the spiritual and the natural. Later, men attempted a return to nature as to a companion. The chasm between man and nature was bridged by music in an amalgam that united man with the cosmos.[82]

Everett followed Hegel to a considerable extent. The universal must, by its very nature, take shape in that which is partial, and the partial is always antagonistic. The universal makes progress only through the dialectic of division and contention.[83] Tragedy reflects this dialectic, in which struggle demands repose and collision some sort of solution. Because the repose in sight is at best temporary, a deeper form of it is found in death. Indeed, the word "tragedy" has come to involve death.[84] In its presence the will is dwarfed and all caprice seems impertinent. Death is the symbol of the real solution of the tragic conflict and thus of the highest repose. Lear's scepter is meaningless after all his sorrows and losses. Love is triumphant in Cordelia's death.[85]

Turning to comedy, Everett remarked in an anticipation of Freud that the sense of the ludicrous must be placed among those great elements of human nature that have shown themselves to be rooted in the deep unconscious life of man, as when people laugh without being able to tell why.

Two principles have been variously recognized as forming the essence of the comic: (1) a certain incongruousness in objects or relations and (2) the sudden recognition of some lack or inferiority in others that leads to self-satisfaction in one's own superiority. Laughter may also occur as a discharge of energy in the presence of an object or an event that threatens to identify us with the object of laughter. We fear that *we* might be the highly dressed up gentleman who is now bespattered with the custard pie or is lying full length on the sidewalk because of a banana peel. We laugh at what we fear; laughter is a discharge of that fear. The defect one discovers in another is simply a form of incongruity upon which one can look down with some contempt.[86]

Alexander Bain did not agree that the comic consists of the incongruous. He argued that a decrepit man under a heavy burden, a fly in the ointment, or an instrument out of tune will not produce laughter.[87] Much, of course, depends on the particular situation. If I meet a friend both of whose arms are full and I ask him for a match, the response will certainly be laughter. Incongruity without pain equals the comic; with pain, it equals the tragic.

A great deal of the comic has its tragic side. Falstaff and Don Quixote may be taken as outstanding examples. Socrates insisted on the kinship of comedy and tragedy. He said: "He who is by art a tragic poet is also a comic one." Everett pointed out that the relation of Socrates to the Athenian state formed the tragedy of Greece; but the fate of Socrates was the legitimate outcome of the comedy of Aristophanes.[88]

In Everett's opinion, Schopenhauer was the only writer who laid a real foundation for the philosophy of the comic. When we expect one meaning but find this strikingly out of place, we may have the sense of the ludicrous. A joke, in its way, is like a piece of music or a statue. Thus, *beauty is a matter not of reasoning, but of recognition*. Everyone finds something ludicrous in Don Quixote.[89]

By transferring the comic from the objective to the subjective world, Schopenhauer made a very important advance. The outer world, however, as it exists for us, is practically the result of our own process of thought. Our most real objects are embodied categories or classes. Thus the comic, though subjective, is no more so than many of the solid facts with which we contrast it. The causes for the comic belong to the realm of science, and to it nothing is ludicrous. Neither is anything comic to the heart. Thus the comic may be regarded as the froth and foam of life.[90] Wit separates form from reality. Humor feels a deep sympathy with the reality. Kant's view of the comic was very narrow; he seems to have found it only in the jest, as Schopenhauer found it only in the blunder.[91] In the course of evolution, laughter was apparently helpful and therefore endured.[92]

Daniel Cady Eaton (1834–1895)

American awareness of aesthetic ideas abroad continued throughout the nineteenth century, notably in the periodical *New Englander*, which published Eaton's articles "Bits of Commonplace Aesthetics" and "Modern French Aesthetics."[93]

College graduates wishing to pursue advanced studies were advised (even as Henry Adams was by James Russell Lowell in 1858) to go to Berlin. By comparison with the Germans, the French were still considered "shallow pated heathen, scatter-brained immoralists, or at best but plausible hypocrites."[94] As if to counteract this prejudice, François Guizot advanced "the pompous boast" (in his *History of Civilization*) that no idea became universal until France had accepted it and then passed it on to the rest of mankind.

Speaking for himself, Eaton confessed that, after reading German "metaphysikers" and "aesthetikers" for years, and after giving the whole thing up in despair, he finally found rest, comfort, and delightful refreshment in French authors and in French translations of German authors. Finding that Hegel in the original was beyond him, he resorted to Charles Bénard's French translation.[95] After throwing some darts at the *Gelehrte* for their interminable sentences and mystifying words, he added:

> Aesthetics has not only a pedantic sound, but conveys the idea of an assumption of superior refinement and of the possession of more delicate organs for the detection and enjoyment of the beautiful. It is bad enough for a man to display superior knowledge, but to have him in addition claim to be a creature of finer and more ethereal fibre is intolerable. Aesthetics has this prejudice against it.[96]

This complaint against the exclusivistic and snobbish attitude of aesthetics was raised before, as I have pointed out, by Channing and Day.

Eaton's "Modern French Aesthetics" provided the readers of his day with a compact summary of the history of aesthetics, although his real theme was French aesthetics in particular. Beginning with the etymology of the word "aesthetics"—from the Greek word meaning "to perceive, to apprehend or notice by the senses"—he continued from the Greeks through Saint Augustine, Baumgarten, Kant, Schelling, Hegel, Friedrich Theodor Vischer, Karl Julius Ferdinand Schnaase, and Johannes Adolf Overbeck.[97]

In his "Bits of Commonplace Aesthetics" Eaton pointed out that Christian Wolff, Baumgarten's master, declared that the object of metaphysics was the perfecting of knowledge; that knowledge was either the product of thought or the result of observation; and that because logic could occupy itself only with the higher knowledge, that is, thought, another and inferior science was needed to occupy itself exclusively with the knowledge derived immediately from perception, that is, with sensations. Baumgarten therefore devoted himself to developing such a science.[98]

Little did he dream of the questions and controversies that would subsequently arise. Is beauty a mere sensation produced in some part of ourselves, entirely subjective, without foundation or stability? Or has it independent existence apart from individual taste, fancy, or the dictates of fashion? Generally impatient with Baumgarten, Eaton did admit his importance in turning thought onto the study of aesthetics through his *Aesthetica* (1750), a work not named by Eaton.[99]

For Eaton, Kant was the greatest of all German aestheticians. Obtaining a French translation of the *Critique of Judgment*, including the aesthetical writings, he was assisted by the translator's critical explanation. He was also impressed by Hegel's observations on the fine arts.[100]

Finally, Eaton recalled that his theme was, after all, modern French aesthetics. The French, he said, are orderly and believe in standards, as in the competition proposed by the French Academy in 1858: "Inquire which are the principles of the science of the Beautiful; verify them by applying them to the most obvious beauties of nature, poetry, and the arts, as well as by a critical examination of the most celebrated systems to which the science of the Beautiful has given birth: both in antiquity and more especially modern times."

The prize was awarded to Charles Lévêque, a member of the French Institute and a professor at the Collège de France, who had distinguished himself as a philosophical writer. His essay was the most psychological of those submitted. Eaton thought that his tendency to rhapsodize was somewhat reminiscent of Schelling.

The work of his competitor, Paul Voituron, affirmed that beauty is not an individual expression but a judgment that imposes itself upon the reason of all: "[There] must be an abstract notion of the Beautiful . . . that [belongs] to all . . . just as all possess abstract notions of truth and justice." Although Voituron devoted a chapter to the metaphysics of the beautiful, he did not provide a definitive definition of beauty.[101]

Eaton urged that every child's education include some phase of art. If beauty is an element of divinity, it should be studied and practiced on a level with goodness, mercy, justice, and love. Everyday life has a claim on aesthetics. The sense of beauty is universal, as is its manifestation.[102] Beauty is an entity, a real thing, not a mere subjective sensation. The soul instinctively hungers for it. The longing for beauty is therefore the same as the longing for truth and goodness: "So the mission of art is sacred, and aesthetics is the catechism of art."[103]

In the four decades covered in this chapter, there was a growing effort to incorporate the subject of aesthetics into general education in America; the pioneers in this objective were men like Bascom, Comfort, Day, and Eaton. The period was also marked by a concerted attempt to present aesthetic matters both analytically and historically. In this effort, foreign sources such as Kant, Hegel, Lotze, and Schopenhauer served as background. While Shedd and Everett saw a relationship between aesthetics and theology, Parker pointed to its connection with science, and Ladd presented a connection with psychology.

THE SCIENTIFIC BACKGROUND
OF MODERN AESTHETICS

Fred Newton Scott (1860–1931)

Despite the work of the numerous scholars already discussed, aesthetics did not begin to receive recognition as an independent scholastic discipline until about 1890. In that year Fred Newton Scott, an assistant professor of rhetoric at the University of Michigan, produced his pamphlet *Aesthetics: Its Problems and Literature*.[1] Describing the fundamental issues of aesthetic theory, this work also provided a critical bibliography notable for its many references to Scott's *A Guide to the Literature of Aesthetics*, compiled with assistance of Charles Mills Gayley (1858–1932).[2]

In Scott's view, both aesthetics and philosophy pose a basic question: What is it about things that makes them aesthetic objects? In answer, Scott proposed the term "aesthetic value" for the more ambiguous "beauty." He also cited the work of such scholars as Bascom, Day, Everett, Kedney, and Eaton. Kedney was particularly commended for his detailed exposition of the whole *Aesthetics* of Hegel, although Scott added somewhat unjustly: "Unhappily the author has followed the plan of substituting his own theories for those of Hegel at every point wherein he differs from the latter."[3]

The position of aesthetics in Scott's time is suggested generally by an entry in the eighth edition of the Encyclopaedia Britannica:

> *Aesthetics.* A term . . . employed by the followers of German metaphysicians to designate philosophical investigations into the theory of the Beautiful or Philosophy of the Fine Arts, which they are disposed to regard as a distinct science. . . . Aesthetic speculations do not appear to have contributed anything to the improvement of the fine arts, or to our real knowledge of mental phenomena.

Certainly, this English source did not greatly clarify the subject, and Scott noted the characteristic weaknesses of English aesthetics in general.[4] As a corrective, he cited Bernard Bosanquet's masterly paper "The Part Played by Aesthetics in the Development of Modern Philosophy."[5] The student was also directed to Bosanquet's "The Aesthetic Theory of Ugliness" as the ablest single article on the subject"[6] and to James Sully's article on aesthetics in the ninth edition of the Encyclopaedia Britannica. Sully's *Sensation and Intuition: Studies in Psychology and Aesthetics* (1874), well known to American students, included the section "The Possibility of a Science of Aesthetics."

Scott further described the contemporary condition of aesthetics in his *An Introduction to the Methods and Materials of Literary Criticism: The Bases in Aesthetics and Poetics* (1901):

> What the inquirer wants is guidance, not dogmatic formulation of principles, but systematic presentation of the problems that must be solved and of the information available for the process. The present consciousness of literary criticism is dynamic, transitional. It has outgrown unquestioning acquiescence in tradition, authority, personal bias or prejudice. But it is not yet fully alive to its possibilities.

In any study of aesthetics, Scott believed, scholars must recognize the connections among literature, art, criticism, and many other disciplines. Indeed, for him, criticism was actually a comparison of alternatives,[7] as in a study of the relationship between literature and science.[8] On this point, Scott cited *Studies in the Evolution of English Criticism* (1894), a doctoral dissertation by Laura Johnson Wylie, who was apparently influenced by Brunetière's *Evolution of Criticism*.[9] Brunetière maintained that there was an evolution in literary "genres" analogous to evolution in living organisms.

Bosanquet is again commended by Scott, particularly for his *A History of Aesthetics* (1892), the only adequate historicocritical survey of the subject then extant outside of Germany. John Dewey, in his *Psychology* (1887), had already discussed aesthetic feeling, imagination, and intuition,[10] as had Charles Carroll Everett in *The Science of Thought* (1882).[11]

Part of William Knight's *The Philosophy of the Beautiful* was recommended as a good historical guide on the subject, but Scott had reservations about Part II, which was devoted to theory.[12] On the special subject of the relationships between the arts, Scott cited Ellen Frothingham's translation of Lessing's *Laocoön* (1890) and Edward Lorraine Walter's study *The Boundaries of Poetry and Painting*.[13]

The relationship between poetry and philosophy was discussed in another work listed by Scott, George Sylvester Morris's *British Thought and Thinkers* (1880). Basing his work on a study of Shakespeare, Morris found that while philosophy is the theory of life, poetry is the exposition of life. Although the philosopher and the poet share many insights, the poet, said Morris, is universal because he reports the intrinsically real. He creates only the form of that which he tells. He has the substance of the philosopher, but his work is uplifted by his message, not held down by its weight.[14]

Among other writers who contributed the aesthetic theory of Scott's time, one of the most notable was the great British philosopher John Stuart Mill, whose *Dissertations and Discussions* was published in the United States in 1865. In the section "Thoughts on Poetry and Its Varieties," Mill described poetry as

> feeling confessing itself to itself in moments of solitude, and embodying . . . itself in symbols which are the nearest possible representations of the feeling in the exact shape in which it

> exists in the poet's mind. . . . In poetry emotions are the links
> of associations by which ideas are connected. . . . What is
> poetry but the thought and words in which emotion spon-
> taneously embodies itself?[15]

The role of melancholy in poetry, which was not alluded to by Mill,
was discussed by Edmund C. Stedman in *The Nature and Elements
of Poetry* (1892).

Emil DuBois-Reymond (*1818–1896*)

Scott's emphasis on the interrelationships of aesthetics and other
disciplines was reflected in such philological studies as Francis Barton
Gummere's "On the Origins of Poetry"[16] and, in Europe, Hiram M.
Stanley's *Studies in the Evolutionary Psychology of Feeling* (1895).[17]
A particularly notable contribution was made by the physiologist
Emil DuBois-Reymond in his address "On the Relation of Natural
Science to Art" (1891).[18] Declaring that science and art are essentially separate, he maintained nonetheless that human intellect shines
brightest where glory in art is coupled with glory in science,[19] recalling Henry Thomas Buckle's thesis in his *History of Civilization in
England*.[20] DuBois-Reymond contended further that aesthetic speculation is most dominant during periods of diminished creative power,
and he cited Lotze's *History of Aesthetics in Germany* (1868) as a
wearying account of abstract definitions of the essence of beauty.

The labels that philosophers apply to beauty—unity in multiplicity,
fitness without a purpose, unconscious rationality, the transcendent
realized, the enjoyment of the harmony of the absolute—no more
describe the sensation of beauty, said DuBois-Reymond, than light
and sound waves describe the qualities of human perception.[21] Why
not admit that in the presence of beauty man senses something
inexpressible, though nonetheless distinctly felt—something without
which life would be dull and cheerless?[22]

Mechanical beauty (that is, automatic, unstudied beauty) yields
readily to analysis. It answers, more or less, to the definition of

"unconscious rationality" (Frost would call it a "wildness of logic"), an unconscious perception of the right means having been used, with the greatest possible profit in the transmission of force and the smallest waste of material (corresponding to Maupertuis's law of minimum action). Beauty is thus symbolized in the economy of movement with which a spreading oak proudly distends its vigorous branches toward air and sunlight.[23]

In painting and sculpture, science contributed greatly in such matters as linear perspective, the geometrical construction of shadows, rules of equilibrium, aerial perspective, the chemistry and physiology of color, and, in music, the nature of harmony. DuBois-Reymond was therefore shocked that Ruskin, "who enjoys in England the reputation and veneration of a Lessing," forbade his pupils the study of anatomy in his lectures "The Relation of Natural Science to Art." DuBois-Reymond was less surprised when Ruskin prohibited the study of the nude, and felt that this "preposterous doctrine" hardly deserved a refutation.[24]

On science and art in general, DuBois-Reymond regarded the artistic conception of natural problems as defective when it is confined to theoretical abstractions instead of penetrating the causal connection of events to the limits of human understanding. He went on to remark, however, that "it cannot be denied that artistic feeling may be useful to scientific men." DuBois-Reymond thus admitted a connection between the aesthetic aspect of experience and mechanical beauty, postulating an aesthetic in which thought and feeling are inextricably related.[25]

Arthur Lincoln Frothingham (1859–1923)

In attempting a positive definition of art, Frothingham first criticized some of the imperfect aesthetic definitions that were still accepted in the 1890s:

1. *Art is a representation, in sensible form, of ideas of sublimity and beauty and the picturesque.* This was not adequate (Frothingham said) because the greater part of art is an embodiment of the

principles of the horrible, of deformity, of the grotesque, and of subjective reality.

2. Art is *"the union of the objective and subjective in the human spirit . . . something inward, a content, and something outer which has that content as its significance."* This was too broad, for it did not distinguish art from every fact of existence. Every actuality has an internal and external, a subjective and an objective element.

3. *Art is that which gives pleasure.* Not all art has pleasure as its object. The aim of a great body of works of art is to cause pain through the representation of destructive force, misfortune, and death, as in tragedy.

4. *Art is subjective only.* By making art subjective only, one removes its civilizing function and misrepresents its very nature. Art is the embodiment by the human mind of the objective reality of things both above and below itself, by means of its own subjective reality.

5. *Art is idealism and symbolism (versus naturalism) and is identifiable with imitation.* This did not constitute a definition of art, because, in addition to the art of symbolism, much art is founded on naturalism and on romanticism, as well as on imitation and material realism. Imitation is only the lowest function of the depraved type of art.

6. *No work of art can be great but as it deceives (Edmund Burke).* This was most untrue, because a work of art formed on this principle represents the most superficial form even of realism.

7. *Art consists of form supplied by technique; the subject is irrelevant, as is the ideal content (Schiller).* The ideal content is the very substance of art, giving the created object reality and universal significance.

8. *Art is the significant, the characteristic, the expressive.* This favorite definition of Frothingham's contemporaries (and ours) was both vague and insufficient for two reasons: (1) these terms are usually used to express only the individual element in art; and (2) no distinct artistic principles are presented as the ground of reality (whether objective or subjective).

To be sure, expression, characteristic delineation, ideal significance must all be recognized in art; but even then a definition of art has not been presented. Such a definition must be derived from ontologic principles that constitute the objective reality of art and from psychic principles that constitute the subjective reality of the human mind.[26]

Frothingham attempted to provide such a definition: *Art is the universal organon for the representation (in intellectual form, or in thought) of the total ideality of existence, both actual and potential.*[27] For Frothingham, art presents the total ideal capacity of man in the various spheres of human activity. It is an ideal objective world in communion with the subjective ideal world in the mind of man; it has reality both outside the mind, as object and, within the mind, as subjective experience.[28]

Art, then, has three missions: historic, interpretive, creative. In its historic mission, it incarnates in sensible form the changes of actual life, so that future humanity may not be confined, for the sources of its knowledge, to present experience. The interpretive mission is to make clear to thought the ideal significance of human realization and to point to a higher plane of consciousness. The creative mission is to conceive and to incorporate in adequate sensible form the un-actualized possibilities of human nature.

According to Frothingham, these three kinds of ideality require three different kinds of artistic mental power: (1) the man of talent and fancy, (2) the man of genius and imagination, and (3) the man of inspiration and reason. The first creates fanciful, ephemeral forms by comparing things that are, internally, either in discord or without real relationship. The second, with intuitive insight into generic and specific law and relation, creates those things he has seen lying dormant in the natural man and in nature. The third, endowed with prophetic vision of eternal truths, sees the universal principles of being, non-being, and becoming. He incorporates in the intellectual symbolism of the imagination the supernatural intuitions and conceptions of the reason and the sentiment.

Frothingham's aesthetic brings to mind William Blake's ideas on the poet and his vision. For Blake, the highest category in the creative mission of art is to symbolize in the natural world the spiritual existence that cannot be realized on earth.

The logical intellect bruises its beauty, said Frothingham, with critical energy, pulls it to pieces to find out its mechanism, and contemplates its lifeless members with contempt, blind to the light and beauty it has destroyed. Frothingham nonetheless regarded all creative activity as a process marked by historic necessity and the invariable laws of the natural world.[29]

Frothingham, who opted for an aesthetic responsive to Christian theism, felt that only a false idealism could lead some theorists to a principle that would unite such opposites as the beautiful, the deformed, the terrible, and the ludicrous under the name of beauty. He admitted that great art exists in the tragedies of Aeschylus and Shakespeare and in Dante's *Inferno,* all of which made use of the incongruous, the chaotic, the discordant, the horrible, and the licentious. But he wondered whether these works were representations of beauty. They depress and paralyze the mind and soul with terror and contract them to their lowest possibilities.[30] Frothingham did not recognize Victor Hugo's theory of the grotesque as suggesting a new view of the attractive through contrast and opposition to the merely pleasant—of the beautiful as a complexity of these contrarieties.[31]

George Lansing Raymond (1839–1929)

In the same year that Frothingham's article appeared, George Lansing Raymond published his *Art in Theory: An Introduction to the Study of Comparative Aesthetics.*[32] In his preface, he asserted that nowhere can the prevailing method of historic criticism do more harm than in aesthetics. He denied that art is the expression of the spirit of the age and that all art is thus of interest to the artist. Great artists like Raphael, Michelangelo, Titian, Shakespeare, Goethe, and Beethoven are moved, he said, as much from within as from without. Emphasizing the psychological method, Raymond saw art not only as form but as a continuing manifestation of subjective states.[33]

Art is distinctively a product of the imagination, the faculty that perceives the image of one thing in the form of another. Although science may find a single form or fact interesting in itself, art, at its best, never does. It looks for another form with which the first may be compared, demanding a parallel fact of fancy, of which the first furnishes a suggestion.[34] The very beginning of the mental tendency that culminates in art is a suggestion to the imagination of a relationship existing, primarily, between forms, and secondarily (because both are necessarily connected) between the methods or laws that these forms illustrate.[35]

Only in art is the mind drawn to a necessity of recognizing the law of correspondence or analogy, which may go beyond a justifiable scientific continuation of the impression received from nature. (Raymond was apparently not aware that scientific models are themselves analogies.) Thus such successful inventors as Fulton, Morse, and Bell initially studied some form of art, and indeed perhaps no great discovery is possible to one whose mind cannot go beyond the customary limits of science.

The human mind is incapable of taking in any form without being informed of something by it. Raymond felt that art may therefore constitute a bridge between religion and science and that aesthetic studies are needed to complete and unite the separated intellectual influences of the two. Like Dr. Johnson, he believed that art must hold the mirror up to nature and make of all nature a mirror[36]—a dictum reminiscent of Emerson's "The laws of moral nature answer to those of matter as face to face in a glass."[37]

Anticipating Freud, Raymond suggested that behind all conscious intelligence an unconscious intelligence of some kind is in operation. He added a remark of Schelling that the function of the work of art is to "rend the veil" behind which reason is hidden in nature; he also cited Hegel's statement that "beauty is the revelation of mind or the idea through sensuous appearances." Raymond also singled out the view of Morris Carrière's *Das Wesen und die Formen der Poesie* that beauty is the unity of the idea underlying various and different individual and concrete forms of sense.[38]

Raymond objected to both Kant and Hegel when they seemed to grant to art a monopoly of the beautiful; only reluctantly did they allow a place to beauty in nature.[39] He agreed with William Wetmore Story:

Nature is not an aggregation of facts—it is an idea in the mind derived from a long series of varying impressions and experiences. When we say a work of art is natural, it is because it answers to this ideal, not because it is true to some particular fact.[40]

Finally, for Raymond aesthetic pleasures blend the results of what is most important in both the physical and the mental areas of activity, widening one's outlook and sympathies especially in the direction—and this is distinctive in them—of enabling the imagination to perceive subtle correspondences between things material and spiritual that otherwise might not reveal their essential unity.[41]

Henry Rutgers Marshall (1852–1927)

Marshall was particularly influenced by the work of the British philosopher Grant Allen, whose *Physiological Aesthetics* was published in London in 1877. Allen in turn based much of his thought on the writing of Spencer, Alexander Bain, Hermann Ludwig von Helmholtz, and Darwin. Asserting that aesthetic predilections are the necessary result of natural selection, he believed that they must be understood in terms of "the general relation of pleasure and pain to our organism and its circumstances."[42]

Allen wished to exhibit the aesthetic feelings as constant subjective counterparts of certain definite nervous states. The following statement by him may still meet with the applause of some American aestheticians:

The subject of aesthetics has so long been given over to transcendental rhetoric and vague poetical declamation, that the name alone upon a cover is sufficient to deter most scientific readers. I have therefore qualified it by an epithet which at once exhibits the positive point of view from which the volume was written. . . . I am not myself an excessive devotee of fine art in any form. . . . I count this as [a] gain in attempting the psychological analysis of aesthetics: because as Helm-

> holtz well observes, the worshipper of art is liable to bring with
> him into the consideration of its simplest elements those en-
> thusiastic feelings which are aroused in him by its highest
> developments.[43]

Allen concluded that the object of his work is 'to elucidate physiologically the nature of our aesthetic Feelings."[44]

For Allen the aesthetic feelings belong to the emotional rather
than the intellectual part of our being. He began his inquiry with
the physical aspect of pleasure and pain. Pain is to be understood in
terms of oxidation effects, and pleasure in terms of an increase in
vital function. Pain is associated with a decrease in vital function.
When a waste of tissue ceases to be pleasurable and begins to be
painful, it has exceeded the ordinary powers of repair. Thus, said
Allen, the human organism may be said to possess a reserve fund
or working capital; it is, in fact, a self-regulatory machine. He
accounted for the innumerable variations of opinion by regarding
them as expressions of the personal equation* of aesthetics.[45] Allen
believed, moreover, that touch is as important as sight and hearing
in the fine arts and poetry, and he urged aesthetic consideration of
tactile phenomena.[46]

Citing Spencer's declaration that every cognition is a recognition,[47]
Allen discussed the intervention of the intellect in the aesthetic experience. Intellectual pleasure results from the sudden solution of
a difficult problem; intellectual pain is the product of fatigue and
wasted effort.[48]

Allen was convinced that "every aesthetic Feeling, though it may
incidentally contain intellectual and complex emotional factors, has
necessarily for its ultimate and principal component, pleasure of sense,
ideal or actual, either as tastes, smells, touches, sounds, forms." In
any event, intellectual exercise is aesthetic only when it is used on
aesthetic objects for an aesthetic purpose. Allen gave as examples
the intellectual pleasure provided by symmetry and the awareness

---

* The *personal equation* in science is the variation in computation resulting
from personal errors, and the compensating correction. In aesthetics, this expression refers to the variation in taste and response arising from individual
differences.

of the exquisite architecture of a snowflake.[49] (Allen did not define "aesthetic object" or "aesthetic purpose.")

Allen divided literature into the scientific and the aesthetic. The first includes works of natural science, philosophy, and history. The second comprises poetry, romance, and belles lettres in general. Poetry, said Allen, owes most of its effectiveness to its ideal factors.[50] The words that it uses are seldom either pleasant or painful in themselves. As poetic symbols, they call up into consciousness a faint form of certain previously experienced sensations or emotions, singly or in groups. Thus poetic genius may be defined as the power to combine and arrange such evocative elements in a harmonious whole.[51]

Allen's aesthetic ideas were recalled in Henry Rutgers Marshall's influential *Pain, Pleasure and Aesthetics* (1894). Unlike William James, who, in his *The Principles of Psychology* (1890), omitted all discussion of the pleasure-pain theory in aesthetics, Marshall devoted much thought to this idea.

On the relationship of science and art, he cited the importance of the imagination in both areas. Imagination is the life force of art, but it also provides science with "those hypotheses without which there were no scientific advance." Marshall described Darwin as a victim of overspecialization, with his alleged failure to appreciate poetry, and urged that science learn the lesson of humility in the presence of aesthetic genius. Art, on the other hand, should acknowledge more fully its indebtedness to science and seek to learn from scientific advances.[52]

Having rejected the vague word "feeling,"[53] Marshall applied his term "algedonics" to the science of pain and pleasure, and "hedonics" to the science of pleasure.[54] For him, pleasure-pain is not sensation, although closely bound up with it; it is not emotion, although closely related to it.[55] Pleasure and pain are not determined by percepts, as emotions are; they partake of the elements that make up these percepts, as well as of the simpler states called sensations. Objects that produce pleasure may also produce pain. Emotions are complexes of pleasure and pain.[56]

Like Hall, William James, and Santayana, Marshall approached his work with a great deal of skepticism. In Chapter 3, "The Field of Aesthetics," he remarked:

> A great deal of attention has been given by thinkers in the
> past to the subject of Aesthetics, but for all that we find our-
> selves today without any Science of Aesthetics, and without
> any Philosophy of Art which is comprehensive and widely
> acknowledged as valid.

He could find no special movement of thought with which one could
identify the aesthetic state of mind.

Considering pleasure evanescent, Marshall adopted the following
hypothesis:

> That object is to be considered beautiful which produces
> a psychosis that is permanently pleasurable in revival. Each
> pleasure may form an element of impression in an aesthetic
> complex; but only those pleasures are judged to be aesthetic
> which, relatively speaking, are permanently pleasurable in
> memory.

From a psychological point of view, said Marshall, nonhedonistic
aesthetic theories resulted in failure.[57] Earlier introspective thought
emphasized sensualism, and indeed the very term "aesthetics," in its
derivation, had a sensory connotation. Baumgarten first used it
because he considered the beautiful to be the perfection of *sensuous
knowledge,* and Kant's "Transcendental Aesthetic" treats of the
a priori principles of sense.[58]

At this point, Marshall referred to Allen, whom he credited with
perhaps the most thoroughgoing statement of the strictly sensualistic
position, in his *Physiologic Aesthetics.* Like Allen, Marshall adverted
to the role of the "personal equation." He objected, however, to
Allen's, as well as to Helmholtz's, overemphasis on the sensational.
For Marshall, Allen's physiological theory of aesthetics was less
important than the purely psychological.[59]

In reviewing past theories, Marshall differed from Schiller and
Kant in the theory that the "art impulse" is especially connected with
the "play impulse." This notion of Schiller's (derived from Kant)
represented a revival of Stoic thought. Both the poet and the philosopher felt the play impulse to be wider than the art impulse and

were therefore inclined to derive the latter from the former, because both arise without definite ends in view. By "play" was meant spontaneous activity, with no objective except the expenditure of accumulated energy, or, as Spencer noted: "The activities we call play are united with the aesthetic activities by the traits that neither subserve in any direct way the processes conductive to life."[60]

Marshall noted that both Edmund Burke and Jean Marie Guyau gave prominence to the "love" element in art. Implied in Guyau's thought was the idea that intense and unextended pleasures are, in their very nature, unaesthetic. Actually, Marshall added, all notable aesthetic psychoses are summational hedonic complexes—in current terms, cumulative libidinous drives. Aesthetic impression is very different from aesthetic judgment.[61]

Marshall's preoccupation with the aesthetics of music in relation to the algedonic principle led him to study Edmund Gurney's *The Power of Sound* (1880).[62] According to Gurney, the force of musical expression is often generated by indefiniteness, which in turn induces "dreaminess." Particulars are forgotten in the general effect, which is an aesthetic complex.[63] Precisely such a complex is of paramount importance in the development of symbolism and the symbolist movement in literature and art.

The "dreaminess" is closely related to desire (a "pent-up stream of action"), which is the persistent image of the realization of an unrealized objective idea. This dreaminess is also metaphorical. "To wake up," said James Sully, "to a resemblance between two things hitherto kept apart in the mind is always an agreeable experience."[64]

In the musical or the poetic experience a plurality of effects is fused in a unity of experience. To some extent, this situation also exists in the thought process. Ideas haunt each other and induce pain at the point of greatest intensity; the pain gives way to pleasure when they are resolved in unity.[65]

Marshall's *Aesthetic Principles* (1895) offered two ways of looking at aesthetic problems: from the standpoint of the observer and from that of the artist. The artist must alternate between the attitude of the producer and that of the observer, and he must be his own sternest critic. The more of a scientist and critic the artist can become without doing violence to his art instinct, the greater will he be as an artist. Leonardo and Goethe were cited as examples. Such great artists were fully aware that technique is only a tool for the production of beauty.[66] In this work, too, Marshall described the subjective quality of pleasure, noting further that not all pleasures are aesthetic.[67]

The art instinct, said Marshall, works to attract others to ourselves, unconsciously but certainly. It tends to overthrow isolation and to promote sociability and sympathy. For this reason, Marshall, like Guyau and Ernst Grosse, strongly opted for the social view as nobler than the individualistic or the art-for-art's sake view.[68]

Elaborating this social view, Marshall related the question of standards to aesthetic pedagogy. Society, he believed, should work to develop within the young and ignorant those capacities and mental activities that would lead them spontaneously to search out art work of high value. As for the standards themselves, Marshall adopted a relativistic and tolerant attitude. By studying other people's standards, our own may be improved.[69]

Marshall's awareness of the struggle between artist and critic, in which creativity seems inimical to critical formalism,[70] served as a prologue to the subsequent struggle between historians of literature and the so-called New Critics. The genuine critic, Marshall believed, must not only be a deep student of the philosophy of art: he must be conversant as well with the artist's technical methods and his personal aims. Both the critic and the artist, who must consider first the delights of immediate impression, must never ignore the more durable pleasures. Thus Marshall called for responsibility in the critical attitude, which must work in the direction of positive aesthetic good.[71] The science of aesthetics, confronting the facts of pain and ugliness, however, would produce its most valuable effects by surmounting them.[72]

On the role of reason as a normative factor in aesthetics, Marshall referred to *Amiel's Journal* for May 23, 1863:

> All that is diffused and indistinct, without form or sex or accent, is antagonistic to beauty, for the mind's first need is

light. Light means order, and order means, in the first place,
the distinction of the parts; in the second, their regular action.
Beauty is based on reason.

Although Marshall himself pointed out that exclusively rationalistic views of aesthetics are not tenable, he did agree that an object
that presents no strong interests, but merely a conglomerate of mod-
erate pleasures, soon cloys. The great artist follows *the principle of
the satisfaction of expectancies,* as in the masterpieces of Wagner
and Shakespeare.[73] Such artists base their aesthetic on the body and
its sensations of pain and pleasure, uniting them with a yearning
for the mysterious essence beyond mortality.

Thus the study of aesthetics in America made important strides
in the 1890s. It was promoted by Scott through his critical bibliography and his exploration of the connections between aesthetics
and other disciplines. DuBois-Reymond, whose lecture on the relationship between the arts and the sciences was discussed here, suggested that a plenitude of the intellect is achieved through a coupling
of the two disciplines. A definition of art as a universal organon for
the representation of the total ideality of existence was offered by
Frothingham. Imagination was defined by Raymond as the faculty
that perceives the image of one thing in the form of another. He
anticipated Freud in referring to an unconscious intelligence. He also
echoed Emerson and Baudelaire in maintaining that there were subtle
correspondences between the spiritual and the material. Marshall,
dissatisfied with the vague term "feeling," contributed the theory of
an *algedonic* aesthetic, which took into account the roles of pleasure
and pain in aesthetic experiences. He believed that great art would
obey the principle of the satisfaction of expectancies.

AN ORGANIC APPROACH:
GEORGE SANTAYANA
(1863-1952)

THE SENSE OF BEAUTY

Santayana's aesthetic philosophy ranged from nineteenth-century idealism to twentieth-century organicism. His approach to aesthetics was perceptual and valuational, and took susceptibility into account. Monroe C. Beardsley was therefore justified in describing Santayana's *The Sense of Beauty* (1896) as primarily a psychological study.[1]

Unlike several recent aestheticians,[2] Santayana "studied sincerity rather than novelty." As a philosopher, he certainly displayed "sanity of judgment" and as a poet, "distinction of taste."[3] For all his skepticism as to the value of "aesthetics" as an independent study, he maintained an interest in the subject from the time of his introduction to the work of Lotze, first by William James and Josiah Royce at Harvard, and then by Friedrich Paulsen in Berlin. His doctoral dissertation, *Lotze's System of Philosophy* (1889), was devoted in part to a discussion of aesthetics.[4]

Basic Principles

The principal ideas in *The Sense of Beauty* concerned the nature of aesthetics and art, the theory of perception in relation to sensibility and imagination, the connection between beauty and pleasure, the definition of beauty, and the classes of beauty.

For Santayana, "aesthetics is the theory of perception or susceptibility," and "art is a rehearsal of rational living—a model as well as a constituent of the life of reason." He noted further that the comprehension of the passion of love is necessary to the aesthetic appreciation of the arts. Among the senses, sight is perception par excellence. In fact, "aesthetics is the theory of perception par excellence, since we become most easily aware of objects through visual agency and in visual terms."[5] In order to imagine *things*, "the idea of these *things* had to be constructed out of the materials already present to the mind."[6]

Santayana's view of beauty as "pleasure regarded as the quality of a thing" (pleasure objectified) underwent a change during the three decades following the publication of *The Sense of Beauty*. In his article "The Mutability of Aesthetic Categories" (1925) he remarked that he would not now use the phrase "objective pleasure," because he saw that "a term does not become subjective merely because an intuition of it occurs." Pleasure, like colors, is neither objective nor subjective but neutral.[7] He did not provide, however, a precise description of "neutral" pleasure.

Clearly, the problem of the experience of beauty, whether objective or subjective, concerned Santayana as much as it had previous philosophers. At the conclusion of *The Sense of Beauty*, he suggested a resolution of the problem: "Beauty is a pledge of the possible conformity between the soul and nature."[8] Beauty is, in other words, a conformity between subject and object.

Santayana divided beauty into three classes: (1) material (colors, sounds), (2) form (symmetry, proportion), and (3) expression. In expression, he distinguished two terms: (a) the object actually presented (the word, the image, the expressive thing) and (b) the object suggested (the further thought, emotion, or image evoked—the thing expressed).[9]

Although Santayana did not investigate the physical basis of pleasure, he did discuss the effects of color and sound. One passage recalls the concern of the symbolist poets with synesthesia, the mingling of sensory impressions: "There are certain effects of colour which give all men pleasure, and others which jar, almost like a musical discord." Santayana suggested that "A more general development of this sensibility would make possible a new abstract art, an art that should deal with colours as music does with sound."[10]

Santayana's treatment of the physiology of form recalls Grant Allen. He indicated that an awareness of physical proportion acts physiologically to produce pleasure, as in the perception of bilateral symmetry, which results in a sense of stability.[11] He therefore regarded form as "the unity of a manifold" and symmetry as "a kind of unity in variety, where a whole is determined by the rhythmic repetition of similars."[12]

On the effect of stimuli in general he noted: "Nothing is objectively impressive; things are impressive only when they succeed in touching the sensibility of the observer, by finding the avenues to his brain and his heart." For this reason, as he remarked in his introduction, "the sense of beauty has a more important place in life than aesthetic theory has ever taken in philosophy."[13]

For Santayana, aesthetic principles are not confined only to art or beauty in nature, but apply beyond them to "every idea which is formed in the human mind, every activity or emotion," because all have "some relation, direct or indirect, to pain and pleasure." Here he recalls Marshall's algedonic theory. Thus, in the idea of democracy (the leading moral idea of our time) "there is a strongly aesthetic ingredient, and the power of the idea . . . over the imagination is an illustration of the effect of multiplicity in uniformity."[14]

Santayana spoke of an "ascending series of aesthetic satisfactions" that saves man from a stultifying uniformity or monotony of judgment.[15] Without specifying the steps in that series, Santayana insists that it implied degrees of beauty and a subjective bias that may lead us to prefer, for example, a rose to an oyster or a lion to a monkey.

But among these steps there is a continuity, so that "we recognize in the greatest connoisseur only the refinement of the judgments of the rudest peasant." He granted that gropings after beauty have value as signs of aesthetic vitality; but in themselves, he believed, they are abortive and indicate the impotence of the imagination:

> Sentimentalism in the observer and romanticism in the artist are examples of this aesthetic incapacity. Whenever beauty is really seen and lived, it has a definite embodiment; the eye has precision, the work has style, and the object has perfection.[16]

Santayana's use of the term "romanticism" was ambivalent. On the one hand, romanticism characterizes "the beginning of all aesthetic life"; on the other, it is pejorative and reductive, suggesting "indulgence," "confused suggestion," "turgid force"—all of which must be corrected through education and "attentive labor." On this point, however, Santayana offered a warning: .

> The breadth of our inspiration need not be lost in the process of clarification, for there is no limit to the number and variety of forms which the world may be made to wear; only, if it is to be appreciated as beautiful and not merely felt as unutterable, it must be seen as a kingdom of forms. Thus the works of Shakespeare give us a great variety, with a frequent marvelous precision of characterisation, and the forms of his art are definite although its scope is great.[17]

Clearly, Santayana found the label "romanticism" unavoidably useful, but one suspects that one of the reasons for his aversion to romanticism was that he associated it with sentimentalism.

There was at least a touch of Walter Pater in Santayana's union of the contemplative spirit with the aesthetic:

> To learn to see nature and to enshrine in the arts the typical forms of things; to study and recognize their variations; to domesticate the imagination in the world, so that everywhere beauty can be seen, and a hint found for artistic creation—that

is the goal of contemplation. Progress lies in the direction of discrimination and precision, not in that of formless emotion and reverie.[18]

Here, again, as in the case of "romanticism," Santayana seems to have apologized for the term "contemplation" by counterposing "discrimination" and "precision." Suggested here is a passage from his novel *The Last Puritan* (1936):

> The trouble with you philosophers is that you misunderstand your vocation. You ought to be poets, but you insist on laying down the law for the universe, physical and moral, and are vexed with one another because your inspirations are not identical.

In *The Sense of Beauty* perception, understanding, and enjoyment are shown to be elements of a single process. The perceptibility of a thing is

> a certain prophecy of its beauty; if it were not on the road to beauty, if it had no approach to fitness to our faculties of perception, the object would remain eternally unperceived. . . . The sense . . . that the whole world is made to be food for the soul . . . is *the poetical reverberation of a psychological fact— of the fact that our mind is an organism tending to unity* (italics added).

This organicism was further stressed by Santayana's statement: "The mind that perceives nature is the same that understands and enjoys her." Thus, although the idea that nature can be governed by an aspiration toward beauty might be rejected as a confusion, "this confusion is founded on a consciousness of the subjective relation between the perceptibility, rationality, and beauty of things."[19]

Reminiscent of Greenough's emphasis on function was the following statement of Santayana on the relationship of form to function:

> The beauty is in nature a result of the functional adaptation of our senses and imagination to the mechanical products of our environment. . . . [Beauty] is the result of the intentional

adaptation of mechanical forms to the functions which our
senses and imagination already have acquired. This watchful
subservience to our aesthetic demands is the essence of fine art.
Nature is the basis, but man is the goal (italics added).

Although, in Santayana's view, the beautiful is constituted by the
imagination in ignorance and even in contempt of the practical, it
is not independent of the necessary, because "the necessary must also
be the basis of the type, and of all its imaginative variations."[20]

Literary Aesthetics

In Santayana's discussions of literary aesthetics, he spoke not only
as a philosopher but as a poet. Language, he said, preserves the fruit
of experience, which is "distilled and concentrated into a symbol."
Primarily a sort of music, it tends to give form to experience. Grammar, philosophically studied, was, for Santayana, akin to the deepest
metaphysics because "in revealing the constitution of speech, it reveals
the constitution of thought. . . ."[21]

The creator of superb sonnets, he remarked that in that form

we have, by dint of assonance, a real unity forced upon the
thought; for a sonnet in which the thought is not distributed
appropriately to the structure of the verse, has no excuse for
being a sonnet. By virtue of this inter-relation of parts, the
sonnet, the *non plus ultra* of rhyme, is the most classic of
modern poetical forms; much more classic in spirit than blank
verse, which lacks almost entirely the power of synthesizing
the phrase, and making the unexpected seem the inevitable.[22]

The most exacting of the forms of composition, in Santayana's
opinion, is the drama. While the poet-musician (lyricist) gains his
effects "by the marshalling of sounds and images, by the fugue of
passion and the snap of wit," the dramatist (psychologist) gains his
effects not so much through the intrinsic mastery of language as
"by the closer adaptation of it to things."[23] Plot is the formal element
of the drama as such (in keeping with Aristotle), but the ethos and

sentiments are the expression, while the versification, music, and stage settings are the materials. Such dramatists as Shakespeare, Molière, and Calderón excelled in ethos rather than in plot. Modern dramatists have excelled in expression rather than in form.[24]

The ideal character in drama—Hamlet, Achilles—is not a collection of salient traits common to a class of man. He is an individual whose actions and words emanate from his inner nature. The fiction, said Santayana, becomes the standard of naturalness,[25] and the poet-dramatist, endowed with pliability and definiteness of imagination, expresses the inward tendencies that have remained hidden in the majority of men.[26]

Santayana maintained that the conventions of the tragic stage are more favorable to psychological truth than the conventions of real life. He illustrated this by quoting Othello's speech:

> Speak of me as I am . . .
> Of one that lov'd, not wisely, but too well. . . .
> And say besides, that in Aleppo once
> When a malignant and a turban'd Turk
> Beat a Venetian and traduc'd the state,
> I took by the throat the circumcised dog,
> And smote him, thus.

Santayana commented: "The height of passion is naturally complex and rhetorical. *Love makes us poets, and the approach of death should make us philosophers*" (italics added).[27] An awareness of the hero's liberation purges the spectator of his own pity and fear and awakens him to a sense of the sublime, which, in Santayana's view, is essentially mystical: "It is the transcending of distinct perception in favor of a feeling of unity and volume."[28]

This feeling of unity originates in the organism, which, by definition, functions as a harmony of parts, and therefore carries within it a sense of unity or monism. This sense is prelogical and presents itself as a feeling, as an emotion of pleasure in harmonious cofunction and of pain at disharmony. A philosophy of monism is therefore a poem in praise of harmony and equipoise, such as that provided by the catharsis of the drama.

Santayana approached this organismal view when he stated that the life of the imagination consists of the disintegration of mental forms as well as of their reintegration: "It is a spiritual process of birth and death, nutrition and generation. . . . All the qualities of discourse, wit, eloquence, cogency, absurdity, are feelings incidental to this process, and involved in the juxtapositions, tensions, and resolutions of our ideas."[29]

Santayana introduced the subject of the comic by asserting that "Fun is a good thing, but only when it spoils nothing better. . . . In fact, there is a kind of congruity and method even in fooling. . . . Nonsense is good only because common sense is so limited." Wit, whose process consists in quick association by similarity, "belittles one thing and dignifies another." It makes use of both flattery and irony.[30] The author pointed out that "the only way in which the ridiculous can be kept within the sphere of the aesthetically good is [by] abstracting it from its relations, and treating it as an independent and curious stimulus. . . . "

In aligning humor with tragedy, Santayana showed that the former combines amusing weakness with amicable humanity, while in the latter "the depth of the woe we sympathise with seems to add to our satisfaction." In both, the painful suggestions must be balanced by agreeable elements. The reaction is both aesthetic and sympathetic —or, we should say, aesthetic *because* sympathetic.

As might be expected, Santayana cited the figure of Don Quixote here, with his mixture of madness, wit, honor, idealism, absurdity, simplicity, and goodness. Discussing such a mixture, Santayana remarked: "As humour becomes deep and really different from satire, it changes into pathos, and passes out of the sphere of the comic altogether." A similar conclusion was reached by the great Spanish philosopher Miguel de Unamuno, author of *The Tragic Sense of Life* (1913), in his study of *Don Quixote*:

> Do not adhere to the miserable juridical criterion of judging a human act and the temporal hurt inflicted on the victim. Try to grasp the intimate meaning and to understand how much depth of feeling, of thought, and of desire is involved in the

truth that there is greater value in a hurt inflicted because of
a holy intention than in a beneficent act rendered with a per-
verse intention.[31]

Santayana, deriving his literary aesthetic from a recognition of the
organic relationship between sorrow and joy, humor and tragedy,
showed how one may suggest the other: "Good wit is novel truth,
as the good grotesque is novel beauty."[32] This organic sense was also
expressed in a number of other remarks in *The Sense of Beauty*:

> Beauty, as we feel it, is something indescribable; what it is
> or what it means can never be said.

> Beauty is a pledge of the possible conformity between the
> soul and nature, and consequently a ground of faith in the
> supremacy of the good.

> The aesthetic value of vital functions differs according to
> their physiological concomitants; those that are favorable to
> ideation are of course more apt to extend something of their
> intimate warmth to the pleasures of contemplation, and thus
> to intensify the sense of beauty and the interest of thought.
> The sense of beauty is its realization.[33]

Is a thing of beauty a joy forever? Replying in the affirmative,
Santayana nonetheless noted the necessary limitations of organic existence: "Mind is a fluid; the lights and shadows that flicker through
it have no real boundaries, and no possibility of permanence.[34]

THE LIFE OF REASON

Nine years after *The Sense of Beauty*, Santayana published his
Reason in Art (1905) as part of the series *The Life of Reason*. Elaborating on ideas expressed in his earlier work, he maintained that all
art "has an instinctive source and a material embodiment." If it has
anything to do with modifying the environment, it "may be expected
to subserve all parts of the human ideal, to increase man's comfort,

knowledge and delight."[35] In social terms, art contributes to the
life of a nation, which may be deemed truly successful only when
"a minimum of its labor is servile and a maximum of its play is
beneficial."[36] Santayana noted, however, that in the United States
the liberal arts had not yet achieved full spiritual expression either
in terms of the natural environment or on the basis of modern technology.[37] He therefore emphasized the importance of cultivating
music, language, and the other arts as a means of achieving full
spiritual development.

Music and Language

In music, said Santayana, man gains a sense of freedom from the
restrictions of daily life. Sound, sweeping through the body, engenders both joy and melancholy.[38] Language, to the extent that it
is governed by the principles of euphony and phonetics, is actually
a form of music and denotation, making imaginative use of euphony,
meter, and rhyme as musical elements in the communication of
meaning.[39]

Man's intellectual progress has two phases: the poetic, in which
he imagines the world; and the scientific, in which he sifts and tests
the products of his imagination.[40] These phases, of course, do not
occur in an absolutely linear sequence. Indeed, scientific procedure
is inherently imaginative, while imagination is largely based on the
sensory experience that is also important in science. Both are essential
elements of the life process.

In its oscillation between mere euphony and strict denotation,
language is both significant and wasteful. Its musical aspect involves
a certain equivocation, even though music is essential to its aesthetic
nature. Its very indefiniteness allows language to suggest new horizons
of thought, so that it becomes capable of dramatizing virtually the
whole range of human experience. Thus language, as Santayana
observed, epitomizes man's struggle to understand his world—his
attempts at persuading the sphinx to propose a riddle more intelligible
than that which presently confronts him.[41]

The great significance of language, Santayana declared, lies in its power to stir emotion, as in the sublime works of primitive poetry. Such poetry, representing both the essence and the outer form of experience, derives its force from rhythm, sound, and suggestion rather than from analytical discourse. This primitive force largely disappears when a poetic idea loses its connotations, when it is confined to a particular meaning. In such a process, feeling gives way to information, and the poetic idea becomes a mere instrument of communication and thus ceases to function as an emotive force.[42]

This process, of course, as many philosophic semanticists have noted, is never complete. Virtually every element of language retains a certain emotional quality, and an aura of emotion hovers around almost any supposedly prosaic statement. For this reason Santayana asserted that the necessity of distinguishing fact from fancy does so much violence to the inner man that not only poets but theologians and philosophers protest against it. Language thus represents a continuing struggle between the practicality of prose, with its demonstrable object, and the incorrigibility of the transcendental flight of poetry.[43]

After ascribing poetic indulgence to youthful aspirations and prosaic habits to the mature, Santayana suggested that an art of speech, if it is to add any ultimate charm to life, must go beyond the set of signals found in simple denotative prose. Thus prose, if it is to have any aesthetic significance, must convey its matter with a certain amount of art. Constituting a poetry that is faithful to rational function, it must delight while it instructs. Poetry, properly used, may make palatable the most rigorous discourse, as in the works of Lucretius and Racine. Racine, conceiving his plays prosaically with the calculated skill of a physiologist, is memorable because of the music of his medium. He "clothed his intelligible characters in magical and tragic robes."[44]

Santayana believed that poetry stands in the same relation to cognition that myth does to science. Indeed, in his essay on Lucretius he remarked: "The mind was a born mythologist, and projected its feelings into their causes." Thus every poet represents a mixture of fidelity to nature and some false fancy. The degree in which his imagination dominates reality is the exact measure of the poet's importance and dignity.[45]

Santayana discussed both rational and irrational poetry, as well as a mixture of the two: "Poetry is an attenuation, a rehandling, an echo of crude experience; it is itself a theoretic vision of things at arm's length."[46] Noting that a poetic element in thought precedes its prosaic development, Santayana related taste to moments when the aesthetic emotion is massive and distinct, and to youth, because (as he put it) half our standards come from our first masters, and the other half from our first loves.[47]

The Psychology of Aesthetics

In the article "What is Aesthetics?" Santayana discussed the source of the aesthetic principle. Holding that there is "no single agency in nature, no specific organ in sense, and no separable task in spirit, to which the aesthetic quality can be attributed" and that "like life itself it opens out for reflection into divergent vistas," he admitted that psychology may occasionally deal with aesthetic questions. The latter, however, are also a concern of moral philosophy. Aesthetic elements represent animal and sensuous values that are absorbed in a rational life: "for reason will immediately feel itself called upon to synthesize those imaginative activities with whatever else is valuable.[48] Thus aesthetics cannot be studied in terms of any one science alone, but must be examined in the context of the totality of human knowledge.[49]

Here Santayana clearly showed the influence of Croce's *Aesthetics as Science of Expression and General Linguistic* (1902), which he reviewed in 1903. Noting Croce's tendency toward digressive criticism of other aesthetic theories, Santayana discussed the Italian philosopher's belief that nothing is aesthetic except the art of intuition or imagination, and that nothing is a work of art except the inner momentary product of fancy. This polemic, said Santayana, merely showed "the barrenness of any strictly transcendental philosophy." When a critic maintains that all art or beauty "must fall within a 'transcendental unity of apperception,'" he simply banishes most critical problems without solving or clarifying them.[50]

On the other hand, Santayana found Croce's history of aesthetics a remarkable and comprehensive survey of the subject, especially in its treatment of Giambattista Vico and Friedrich Schleiermacher. The former, often regarded as the true founder of aesthetic science, is especially notable for his dictum: "Men at first feel without being aware; next they become aware with a perturbed and agitated soul; finally they reflect with an undisturbed mind.[51] This view generally accords with Croce's own outlook, as does Schleiermacher's statement: "The inner image is the virtual work of art."[52]

Of the three levels on which human life moves—sensation, apperception or intuition, and thought—the second alone, said Santayana (following Croce), is aesthetic and consists entirely in intuition or expression, that is, art. The true work of art is expression itself. Art has no existence apart from active imagination. All men are artists.

Linguistics and aesthetics are identical. Technique, subject, associations, purposes, moral affinities are all irrelevant to the spiritual and poetic essence of beauty. Croce did not deny that sensuous and rational considerations may have legitimate weight in determining an attitude toward works of art. He did suggest, however, that a thing painful to sense and morally repulsive may yet be entirely beautiful.[53]

In general, Santayana found Croce's system superficial. If intuition has nothing to do with sense or reason, so much the worse for intuition. An art that is merely an irresponsible and private exercise of fancy is a visionary indulgence. Santayana especially cited Croce's view of language: a word being an expression, a synthesis reached by creative genius is not a sign. Santayana supposed that Croce might admit that such a synthesis could ultimately become a sign. Precisely this characteristic renders language different from music.[54]

If speech never became symbolic, it would not have become an instrument for practical or rational discourse. Thus the communication of ideas is a function that even "aesthetic" language occasionally performs. Discourse without concepts and objects without charm may be momentarily sufficient, said Santayana sardonically, for that

contemptible entity, the abstract poet, whose mind is a barren kalei-
doscope for the endless intuition of everything. But they are nevertheless singularly tedious to the sensitive, political, and thinking
animal called man.[55] Again, this conception of the wholeness of man
reflected Santayana's organic approach to art.

Santayana's reference to the "thinking animal called man" was
related to his concept of "animal faith," fully developed in his
Scepticism and Animal Faith (1923). Rousseau's declaration that
"the man who thinks is a depraved animal" implied a warning that
it is unwholesome for man to cut himself off from the chain of the
animal kingdom of which he is a link. A faith in that fact could
help him to relate the external world to essences. It could also help
him to confront the dialectic of matter and spirit without having to
embrace either a facile idealism divorced from matter and generative
process or a specious materialism based on mere appearance. Accordingly, Santayana's concept of "animal faith" is a recognition of matter
as a matrix for the aesthetic of the spirit.

PHILOSOPHICAL AND PSYCHOLOGICAL APPROACHES TO AESTHETICS

Alexander Thomas Ormond (*1847–1915*)

A former pupil of James McCosh at Princeton, Ormond dedicated his *Foundations of Knowledge* (1900) to his teacher. In it, Ormond posited an experiential philosophy whose two modes of knowledge were the spiritual and the mechanical. He insisted that, in their articulation of reality and in their reach for the unity of the true and the good, the spiritual categories were entitled to an equal hearing with the mechanical. Ormond believed further that the world was, in the last analysis, spiritual, and that mechanism itself would ultimately concur in this. He also stated his conviction that in their quest for world unity the aesthetic and the scientific modes were united, although the one sought it under the category of beauty and the other under the categories of mathematics and dynamics.[1]

Ormond adopted a general philosophical approach to aesthetics. The aesthetic, he said, is one of the three strata of conscious activity; the others are the mathematical and the dynamic. Each is a source of epistemological categories that mediate the evolution of man's intuition of the world. Aesthetic consciousness demands a congruity between its own nature and that to which it will react with pleasure rather than with pain. Thus, for Ormond, congruity is the fundamental aesthetic principle.[2] Reflective aesthetic consciousness represents a persistent drive for a self-regulated unitary system. This unity, although subjective in origin, is as completely objective as the categories of cause and substance.[3]

In accordance with his unitary conception, Ormond declared that the categories of scientific and aesthetic truth have been kept apart too long. Men must recognize the aesthetic texture of all modes of conceiving. Both the artist and the scientist seek representations of a unified world view, the former (as was said above) in the category of beauty, the latter in terms of mathematical or dynamic principles. The category of unity is itself a distinctive product of the aesthetic consciousness.[4]

The essential element of all representation, Ormond declared, is symbolism. A symbol is any form or object that is used to represent a certain content indirectly through its direct representation of other content, as in the use of the word "lion" for strength. In time, the indirect may give way to a more direct mode of representation:

> In truth, we might define symbolism as an analogical mode of representing meaning. The symbol may be simply a halfway station on the way to the concept. . . . But *it is a fact of the vitalest import that the symbol stands at the end as well as at the beginning of knowledge* (italics added).[5]

The definition of symbolism was important for such later works as Susanne Langer's *Philosophy in a New Key* (1942). Indeed, Ormond was perhaps the first American thinker to emphasize the role of symbolism in aesthetic matters.

Lewis Edward Gates (1860–1924)

Although Gates was not a professional aesthetician himself, his *Studies and Appreciations* (1900) made an impression on several American aestheticians. He responded early to such French critics as Sainte-Beuve, Taine, Jules Lemaître, Ernest Renan, and Émile Hennequin, and to the German philosophers and aestheticians Winckelmann, Herder, Lessing, and Wilhelm Dilthey. He was fully aware of the idea of literature as an organic growth and of the spreading of this concept from Montesquieu, Winckelmann, and Herder to Goethe, Coleridge, and Emerson.[6]

Gates particularly appreciated Taine's recognition of the relationship between history and aesthetics, and his understanding of the force of the aesthetic response:

> A man does not produce all he is capable of unless, having conceived some artistic form or some general idea, he finds it so beautiful that he prefers it to anything else (especially to himself) and adores it like a goddess whom he is too happy to serve.[7]

Francis Barton Gummere (1855–1919)

American students are indebted to Gummere's *The Beginnings of Poetry* (1901), which discusses a number of problems in poetics and literary aesthetics. His earlier dissertation, *The Anglo-Saxon Metaphor* (1881), is also valuable for its discussion of metaphor, which Gummere described as antecedent to simile.[8] He also cited Baumgarten's definition of poetry: *oratio sensitiva perfecta*, speech that brings to mind a distinct and perfect picture, and speech so charged with energy that it demands metrical expression.[9]

Fred Newton Scott (1860–1931)

Scott, who was discussed in Chapter 7 for his survey of aesthetic literature, may be considered here in his approach to the philosophy of language. His article "The Most Fundamental Differentia of Poetry and Prose"[10] described several means of distinguishing the two modes of literary expression according to their respective degrees of imagination, emotive force, artistic quality, and form.

Judgment on the basis of imaginative content generally represents a false distinction because a confrontation of, for example, Burke's prose with Pope's poetry reveals the former to be far more imaginative than the latter. As for emotion, Ruskin's *Modern Painters* shows more passion than all of Landor's verse. The degree of artistic quality may be a test of the relative values of different specimens of art, but it cannot serve to differentiate poetry from prose, because the latter is not simply an undeveloped form of the former.

With regard to form, Scott cited Gummere, who showed that the essential fact of poetry is rhythm: "Poetry is rhythmic utterance . . . With mainly emotional origin." Gummere, however, did not offer meter as a fundamental basis of difference but merely as a sign of distinction.

Scott went beyond this outward sign, which did not touch the essence of poetry.[11] Considering the genetic aspect of the problem, he found that the primary need for self-expression in primitive life is most keenly felt on festal occasions. There, the sense of communication is absorbed in the lust of expression. Scott described such a feeling as communication for the sake of expression, which he contrasted with expression for the sake of communication. He used the metaphor of a bowman shooting an arrow. The "twang" of the arrow is communication for the sake of expression; expression for the sake of communication is the "chug" of the arrow as it buries itself in the target.[12]

Scott concluded that the difference between poetry and prose derives from the difference between two recurring social situations: one in which an individual is moved to verbal utterance primarily by the desire to communicate something—expression being present but subordinate; and another, in which an individual (or a group in concert) seeks to express feelings or ideas that must have a motor outlet. In each case, the character of the situation colors the quality of the utterance and determines the form of the expression.

Applying his formula to poetry and prose, Scott found that the former is communication in language for the sake of expression; the latter, expression in language for the sake of communication. As he acknowledged, his ideas were derived from Mill's "Thoughts

on Poetry and Its Varieties," with its two fundamental principles:
(1) the distinction between poetry and prose is common to all the
arts; and (2) "eloquence is heard; poetry is overheard."[13]

Ethel Dench Puffer (1872–1942)

For Puffer, the "literary" treatment of art, like the "emotional" treatment of literature, necessarily involved a detailed aesthetic analysis.
The lack of such analysis, she found, was responsible for such phrases
as Gates's: "the splendid and victorious womanhood of Titian's
Madonnas." In art, said Puffer, the essential element is the visible
beauty, not the moral conception.[14] She found even Pater lacking
in sound analytical ability,[15] and cited the importance of a scientific
approach to aesthetics.[16]

Admitting the complexity of the aesthetic experience, she did not
agree with Santayana that philosophical aesthetics must confuse the
import of an experience with the explanation of its cause. She was
not satisfied with his idea that "beauty [is] objectified pleasure."
She defined the aesthetic experience as a combination of a favorable
stimulation and repose. This state involves "a distinctive feeling tone
and a characteristic trend of activity aroused by a certain situation"
and can be no other than an emotion.[17]

Puffer found Guyau nearest to her point of view. For him:

> The beautiful is a perception or an action which stimulates
> life within us under its three forms simultaneously [sensibility,
> intelligence, and will] and produces pleasure by the swift con-
> sciousness of this general stimulation.[18]

She considered Guyau's analysis successful because it took into
account both diffused stimulation and the mutual checking of antagonistic impulses producing an equilibrium. This, in effect, is the
aesthetic experience: the experience of the perfect moment of the
union of stimulation and repose that constitutes the unique aesthetic
emotion.[19]

Puffer's psychology of creativity (in both the arts and the sciences) included an account of the mysticism in which the self is merged or absorbed in the subject. For Bernard of Clairvaux, "the individual disappears in the eternal essence as the drop of water in a cask of wine." For Schopenhauer, the contemplation of the beautiful caused the will of the individual to be merged in "the pure subject, the clear mirror of the object." One could add here that Baudelaire spoke of "the vaporization of the self," and, indeed Puffer referred to the temporary evaporation of the consciousness of one's own personality.

In the contemplation of the beautiful, as in the mystical experience, the observer is lost in the object. Indeed, he draws the object into himself or becomes one with it, as when he contemplates a tall pine tree by gazing up and down its length and out to the ends of the branches.[20] Such contemplation produces the musical moment, Schiller's musical mood, in which beauty appears in the guise of a unified object and from which poems emerge. In this atmosphere, all things become magically suggestive, translating dreaming expectation into works of art.[21]

In her discussion of literary aesthetics, Puffer found language, meaning, and experience closely interlocked. Thus the material of literature is life itself. On the question of style, she brought together the dicta of Spencer, Pater, and Raleigh, all of whom cited the importance of economy, unity in the association of ideas, and the cumulative effect of past meaning in words. Puffer's statement that words do not *have* meanings but are meanings anticipated MacLeish's famous dictum: "A poem should not mean/But be."[22]

The emotional experience in the drama is not, for Puffer, as simple as Aristotle would make it. Pity and fear do not in themselves produce pleasure, relief, and repose.[23] She concluded that the mysterious catharsis, the emotion of the tragedy, is a unique aesthetic emotion. It is involved in the singular characteristic of drama, the face-to-face confrontation of forces, as in the confrontation of Lear and his daughters.[24]

In tragedy, said Puffer, such conflicting forces are irreconcilable and destructive; in comedy, a reconciliation occurs. Both forms, however, are closely related, as Puffer indicated in a quotation from Everett:

> The tragic is, like the cosmic, simply the incongruous. The
> great Tragedy of Nature—the Struggle for Existence—results
> simply from a greater or lesser incongruousness between any
> form of life and its surroundings. The comic is found in an
> incongruous relation considered merely as to its *form,* while
> the tragic is found in an incongruous relation taken as to
> its reality.[25]

Puffer also cited Meredith's essay on the comic spirit, in which
he noted that the element of conflict is common to both comedy and
tragedy.[26]

In "The Beauty of Ideas", Puffer reverted to Santayana's attempt
to establish an organic relation between form and idea. Analyzing his
definition of beauty as the objectification of pleasure, she questioned
his designation of form as "beauty in the first term" and expression
as "beauty in the second term." Although Santayana stated that only
the first can exist alone, Puffer wondered whether the second cannot
be felt in objects without the intrinsic worth of form. She suggested
that Santayana's explication of "beauty in the second term" as the
power to suggest feeling through the medium of associated ideas
did not necessarily imply aesthetic character. Even the greatest ideas
—such as those found in the works of Aristotle, Spinoza, and Kant—
do not constitute great art in themselves,[27] although Unamuno speaks
of Spinoza, for example, as a lonely poet in the world of thought.

Puffer thus confronted the dualistic view that great creations of
art are the expression of great truths under the laws of poetic form.
She asked: *Is the aesthetic expression indeed the recognition of truth
plus the feeling of beauty of form, or is it a fusion of these into a
third undivided pulse of aesthetic emotion?* She thus proposed a
unitary theory of the beautiful, noting that a true aesthetic principle
recognizes the close union of form and idea, as in the use of *le mot
juste* in literature.

Discussing this unity, Puffer described a feeling of "rightness" in
music when the awaited note slips into place, or in narrative when
the inevitable consequences of a plot unfold in proper order.[28] On
this point Edmund Gurney said that when the listener thinks that
he is yearning after the unutterable, he is really yearning after the

next note; when he seems to find pleasure in the yearning he is actually rejoicing in a triumphal acceptance of the melodic rightness of that note.

Puffer maintained that the much-discussed catharsis, or emotion of tragedy, is not the experience of emotion or pleasure in the experience represented but rather pleasure in the experience of ideas tinged with emotion, which belong to each other with precisely a musical rightness. She therefore described catharsis as the triumphant acquiescence in the rightness of relations. Thus the tragic emotions of pity or fear are not in themselves aesthetic; they become so only if they appear in tragedy as part of a unified and reciprocally harmonious group of experiences.[29]

For Puffer then, aesthetic experience is based on the principle of unity in harmonious functioning, in which the law of internal relation and of fitness for imitative response applies to all embodiments of beauty.

The psychophysical state of aesthetic pleasure thus consists of three primary elements: (1) a kind of physiological equilibrium, a "co-existence of opposing impulses which heighten the sense of being while it presents action," as in the impulse to movement corresponding to geometric symmetry; (2) a psychological equilibrium in which the flow of ideas and impulses is a circle rounding on itself, all associations, emotions, expectations indissolubly linked with the central thought and leading back only to it, and proceeding in an irrevocable order, which is yet adopted to the possibilities of human experience; and (3) a quietude of the will in the acceptance of the given moral attitude for the whole scheme of life.

These three orders of mental life—the physiological, the psychological, and the will in a state of equilibrium—constitute the perfect unity and self-completeness of Puffer's aesthetic ideal.

Hartley Burr Alexander (1873–1939)

Alexander's general approach to aesthetic problems was eclectic. He made use of the insights of evolution, sociology, and psychology. In his discussion of the evolution of poetic spirit, Alexander referred to Gummere's *The Beginnings of Poetry* as "the most satisfactory exposition of the Social origins of poetry."[30] The lyric cry is, for Alexander, a judgment as well as a desire and a demand for a clearer revelation of the worth of life. Like so many before him, in discussing the individual and universal aspects of art and poetry, he referred to Guyau's "keen little volume," *L'Art au point de vue sociologique* (1899).

For Guyau, the individual is already a society, an epitome of that greater whole in which he moves and has his being: "We say *I*, and we could as well say *We*." From this point of view, the agreeable becomes beautiful in the measure of its solidarity, the sociability that exists among all elements of human existence.

Alexander argued, however, that the *We* is still an *I*, that its sociality is only the expression of the organic complexity of its unity.[31] Citing two works by Théodule Ribot,[32] he maintained that the work of the imagination is, first, the enlargement of man's world through the widening vitality of comprehension; second, it is an awakening and a revelation of the nature hidden beneath the surface of communal thinking. Such an imaginative creation, unlike the visions and syntheses of Copernicus or Newton, requires only the ratification of those to whom it appeals. The standard of judgment is here wholly subjective and the sole test is appreciation.[33]

In the imaginative process, Alexander said, memory plays an important part. The artist, however, remembers only the material he needs. Imaginative creation involves selection and synthesis, which are signs of the so-called picturesque memory, or "painter's memory."[34] Alexander therefore characterized imaginative imagery "as spontaneous mental embodiments of sensuous elements so synthesized as to possess an organic unity not to be distinguished from the unities of real things."[35]

He posited three main reasons for the failure thus far of any attempt to analyze the emotional elements of the imagination: (1) the unsatisfactory state of the psychology of emotion; (2) the discord of common notions of the value and function of emotional life; and (3) the constant intrusion of bias by traditional interpretations in aesthetics. As an example of this failure, he cited the absurdity of traditional hedonism, which seems to have forced its bias even on the psychology of aesthetics, as in Santayana's anomalous conception of beauty as "objectified pleasure." Alexander indicated that this definition did not differentiate the pleasure of beauty from other pleasures.[36]

The true nature of aesthetic satisfaction, Alexander suggested, can be made clear only by reference to its analogue in rational thinking. Just as the feeling of certitude makes for logical assent, so the feeling of fitness and completeness makes for the recognition of beauty. Neither satisfaction, however, is to be identified with pleasure, which is commonly an accompaniment of activity; judgment, of the logical or aesthetic sense, marks the termination of a mental action.[37]

Alexander's thought here was rather vague. Emotion is an action in response to pleasure or pain. If by *pleasure* Alexander meant *sexual* pleasure, he failed to say so. If a poem, a painting, a play, or a sensation does not bring us pleasure, what does it bring? If aesthetic discrimination is not in the direction of that which rouses our emotions in conjunction with the recognition of beauty, then what is the function of aesthetics?

In fact, Alexander did link aesthetics (albeit obliquely) to emotions in their various manifestations. He recognized that they may respond to an imaginative occasion and that all are related to an artistic representation of life.[38] He also recognized the importance of imaginative reconstruction and transmutation, as in his quotation of Elizabeth Barrett Browning's sonnet "Motive and Inspiration":[39]

> This song of soul I struggle to outbear
> Through portals of the sense, sublime and whole,
> And utter all myself into the air.[40]

As this quotation suggests, Alexander believed that beauty is "quite as truly a subjectification of reality beyond the self as it is objectification of the self's ideal life." Ultimately, "an interpretation of an ideal felt by only one or two will not be esteemed apart from the personal equation." We judge as character and aptitude force us to judge.[41] Alexander remained vague on the role of personality in aesthetic experience. He concluded that beauty is as much in the aspiration as in the ideal image. All realization leads to renewed aspiration.[42]

Elizabeth Kemper Adams (1872–1948)

Approaching the aesthetic experience from the point of view of functional psychology, Adams concluded that much confusion resulted from treatment of that experience in isolation from everyday life.[43] For her, the term "aesthetic" characterized a certain type of concrete conscious experience, involving a sense of immediate and specialized value inhering in a more or less definite object, and possessing a strong, pleasantly colored "feeling tone." It referred to a specific type of consciousness, not to subsequent reflection on it, and to the aesthetic object only as the core of the consciousness, not as studied independently. In this usage, "aesthetic" is both wider and narrower than the term "artistic," being inapplicable to the study of the object apart from its immediate apprehension in the experience.[44]

The aesthetic experience always involves a cluster of activities— an "equilibrium of tensions." Here Adams is reminiscent of Puffer's idea of aesthetic repose as representing an "equilibrium or balance of forces." She cited Santayana directly: "Only when the aesthetic ingredient becomes predominant [in our life] do we exclaim 'How beautiful!' "[45]

Elaborating this point, Adams maintained that "aesthetic sympathy" is always at the heart of a social determination of reality. In that sympathy, the opposition between individual and society breaks down,[46] as she suggested in a quotation from Tolstoi's *What Is Art?*:

> A real work of art destroys in the consciousness of the receiver the separation between himself and the artist. . . . In this freeing of our personality from its separation and isolation, in this uniting it with others, lies the chief characteristic of the great attractive force of art.[47]

Although the primary source of art is an individual impulse, the secondary effect of the exteriorization of a feeling state is the awakening of similar feelings in others.[48]

For Adams, every aesthetic experience has a particular emotional reverberation. Its "feel" results from a particular combination of elements, although two experiences made up largely of different elements may have approximately the same "feel," as in the previously mentioned phenomena of synesthesia. Thus Berenson called Michelangelo the Milton, and Titian the Shakespeare, of Italian painting, while to Adams, Beethoven suggested both Michelangelo and Milton, Chopin suggested Shelley, and Wagner, Browning.[49]

In both comedy and tragedy, the unfolding of the aesthetic experience is complex and concentrated. An elaborate balance of parts maintains a moving equilibrium. In *Macbeth*, for example, the swift succession of events in the first part, the tense excitement and horror caused by the murder of Duncan, are balanced by the slower succession of lesser and somewhat confused events, with the frequent shifting of scene in the second part.[50]

Adams noted that comedy may be described according to at least three theories: (1) "degradation," (2) "baffled expectation," and (3) "incongruity." The first presupposes an identification of the spectator with the comic protagonist who is brought low from a supposedly high position. The laughter evoked diverts the spectator from himself to the spectacle. *Example:* A person who is highly esteemed is delivering a solemn speech. Suddenly, because of an untoward movement of his hand while he is intoning a special point, he turns over the pitcher of water in front of him and splashes his face and his shirt front.

The theory of "baffled expectation" presumes the spectator under necessity of having to make a sudden shift from an image that he has been entertaining ardently for some time to an object that confronts him in actuality. The laughter which ensues acts as a palliative for the disappointment. *Example:* A lover has arranged with his sweetheart a secret rendezvous in his apartment. When he finally responds to the much-expected knock, the person in the doorway is the sweetheart's mother.

The theory of "incongruity" takes into account the disparity between an image in relation to social congruence and an object that departs radically from that relation. *Example:* A wedding guest appears at the ceremony dressed in a dinner jacket and dungarees.

In all instances cited, there is the element of surprise. Unlike tragedy, however, comedy presents only a partial view of existence.[51]

On the sublime, Adams differed from Burke and Kant. Kant maintained that whereas beauty brings with it a feeling of the furtherance of life, the sublime is associated with a checking of it; it therefore causes a stronger outflow of the vital powers. Beauty may thus be described as a promise of happiness (as Stendhal believed), sublimity as a denial of it.[52] Adams considered the experience of the sublime as a comparison of the condition of the self in two experiences, or of the self and the object embodying grandeur or power. The comparison contributes to an enlarged view of one's personal experience.

She could not agree with Santayana that "unity by inclusion gives us the beautiful" and that "unity by exclusion, opposition, and isolation gives us the sublime." For her, the sense of the sublime arises just because the felt unity includes so much. She agreed, however, that the awareness is of the unity rather than of its various elements, and she accepted Santayana's further description:

> Both [that is, beauty and sublimity] are pleasures; but the pleasure of the one is warm, passive, and pervasive; that of the other cold, imperious, and keen. The one identifies us with the world, the other raises us above it.

Citing this passage, Adams noted that beauty brings out all the implications and possibilities of ordinary life; the sublime lifts men above the ordinary to the strange and the occult.[53]

She regarded "ugly" as a limiting term that marks one sort of initiation into the aesthetic. Like the grotesque, the ugly becomes a contributory factor in a total aesthetic experience.[54]

On the nature of the so-called lyric cry with its all-enveloping sense of melancholy and sadness, Adams discussed the balance of stimulation and recuperation in the aesthetic experience. The poignancy of beauty, she said, belongs to the moment when emotional satisfaction suffuses the entire organism, and the immediate and unified perception of the experience begins to disintegrate,[55] as suggested by Keats:

> She dwells with Beauty—Beauty that must die;
> And joy, whose hand is ever at his lips
> Bidding adieu.

Like Ormond, Adams concluded that every process of judgment has an aesthetic aspect resulting from the sense of unity attained at the conclusion of the process—Adams's "pause of satisfaction."[56] She thus anticipated the work of two other American aestheticians, Kate Gordon and James Baldwin.[57]

Kate Gordon (1878–1944?)

Kate Gordon's ideas on aesthetics were expressed in her essay "Pragmatism in Aesthetics" (1908) and in her textbook *Esthetics* (1909). Her basic argument was that aesthetic experience illustrates and confirms the teaching of pragmatism: that the ultimate meaning of beauty is to be found in concrete acts and that the function of art is to produce new experience. As a pragmatist, Gordon sought final explanations in terms of purpose. She found reality in experienced satisfaction.[58]

For Gordon, an artist was anyone who seriously attempted to express his emotions through one of the recognized media of artistic production. She would have agreed with Hirn that every normal person is at some time in his life an artist. The successful master has expressed not only his own feelings but also those of others.

The motives for the production of art are varied: money, love, emulation, fear. All are present among primitive people. The artistic impulse is derived from the tendency to imitate, to attract by pleasing, and to expend surplus energy, as well as from the impulses toward self-exhibition and self-expression to relieve emotion and to objectify feeling. It is also allied to instinct, play, and sociability.[59]

The work of art mediates between the producer and the admirer. It may stimulate unexpected interest and reactions, producing an element of adventure. The instinct for excitement and a longing for novelty, which are present in every human being, encourage the artist to develop new emotions and new means for expressing them, thus initially alluring the observer.[60]

The pragmatic attitude evaluates the aesthetic moment according to its purpose.[61] The meaning of art, however, can never be precisely defined. Thus aesthetic appreciation and logical judgment are notably different. The function of art is to preserve and present meanings at their emotional stage, before they have become explicit, definite, or solved. Art lives on the factors that resist it.[62] From a pragmatic point of view, man creates his own life, thus producing, as Oscar Wilde noted, an imitation of art. If art, however, is the "image of life," it is more a prophetic than an historic image. After seeing a Turner, Gordon pointed out, one sees more form and color in a sky. Life and nature are experienced, essentially, as products of art.[63]

In her *Esthetics*, Gordon regarded aesthetic speculation as a branch of advanced psychology. For her, the essentially creative moment in thinking is that in which the mind sees likenesses, when it perceives a similarity or partial identity that did not appear before. Galileo discovered a likeness between the cathedral lamp and the earth; Newton, between the falling apple and the planet. Watt found that the steaming of a teakettle might be imitated in a new device—the locomotive. Similar discoveries occur in artistic composition through the use of analogues and the observation of similarities, as in the development of metaphors and similes.[64]

Gordon cited the factor that she called "repeat" as one of the important characteristics of poetry. This conception covers rhyme, assonance, refrain, and recurrence of phrases; it also takes into account emotion, which is expressed in repeating, rhythmical language. The poetic imagination is rendered sensuous by rhythm, rhyme, assonance, and thought imagery, as in Keats's "The Eve of St. Agnes."[65]

Figures of speech or tropes are not merely ornamental; they are essential parts of literary thought. When the mode of conceiving a subject is capable of definite elaboration and exact proof, a scientific statement results; but when the comparison, or mode of conceiving, is new (and not destined for further definition or proof) a literary statement is necessary. Gordon believed that literary comparisons are suggestive and scientific ones definitive—that poetic thought often initiates a comparison that, when taken up by scientific thought, is reduced to a critical restatement.

Critical thought, said Gordon, is the reduction of tropes to facts. She quoted Gertrude Buck's statement that "figures represent a necessary intermediate stage in every completed process of thought." As Goldsmith noted, "Passion itself is very figurative."[66]

Gordon was not quite successful in her analysis of the pleasure produced by melancholy and sadness. She called for further research on the psychology of art as a means of accounting for the influence of these elements on poetry.[67]

In prose, Gordon found, the principal sources of pleasure are rhythm and assonance, as in the works of Browne, Pater, and Ruskin. Browne's rhythms are stately and orchestral; Pater's are incantatory (reminiscent of Browne) and graceful; while Ruskin's are marked by a cumulative intensity.[68] Such elements may be present even in the essay, and the development of thought itself—through induction, complication, exposition, elaboration, climax, and conclusion—may be presented in highly artistic fashion,[69] as in the writings of William James and Bergson. Again, Gordon noted that the artist transmutes and transfigures the objects with which he deals. His reality is creation, not imitation.[70]

William Davis Furry (1873–1940)

Furry's thought represented an attempt to deal with the continuing philosophical problem of dualism—the conflict between content and form, existence and thought.[71] In his principal work he asserted that the aesthetic experience represents a mode of conscious determination in which the two aspects of thought (content and control) are recognized and reconciled by the rise of a new mode of immediate experience. The essential character of this type of experience is the "*semblant*"[72] treatment of meanings already present for the sake of obtaining further meaning.

Furry claimed that the aesthetic experience had passed through a series of stages of development at each of which it reflected the principal epistemological problem then present. Because the aesthetic experience is neither theoretical nor practical, it can reconcile these two areas of human activity, bringing about a unity in man's mind.[73] Thus the aesthetic experience produces a form of life richer and more complete than that provided by thought or will or both together, because in it the "genetic dynamogenies as well as the static dualisms are mediated."[74]

Furry cited A. E. Taylor's definition of consciousness as, in its first appearance, immediate and a-dualistic. As William James noted, "The child does not see light, but is light." Francis H. Bradley stated: "There was a time when the separation of the outer world as a thing apart from our feelings had not even begun." In James Mark Baldwin's *Thought and Things* James was also quoted: "Pure experience is the name which I give to the original flux of life before reflection has categorized it. . . . Pure experience . . . is but another name for feeling or sensation."[75]

Furry, following these views, sought a unity of consciousness in the aesthetic experience. He agreed with Baldwin that new dualisms would arise, but these would be of fact, not of meaning.[76]

As we have seen in this chapter, a number of American aestheticians have brought fruitful insights to their subject. Ormond called attention to the use of symbolism and analogy long before Susanne Langer (who leaned, in this respect, on Ernst Cassirer). Gates helped to promulgate the idea of literature as organic growth. The genetic approach to poetry and the emphasis on the central role of metaphor in it was Gummere's contribution. Scott, who had furnished important guides for the study of literary aesthetics, presented a cogent view of the differentia of poetry and prose. Puffer made the interesting suggestion of aesthetic repose representing an equilibrium or balance of forces. Like Ormond, she proposed a unitary theory of the beautiful, recognizing the close union of form and idea. Whereas Santayana regarded beauty as objectified pleasure, Alexander insisted that it is to be found as much in aspiration as in the ideal image. Reminiscent of Puffer, Adams, in discussing the nature of the so-called lyrical cry, spoke of a balance of stimulation and recuperation in the aesthetic experience. She referred to the sense of unity attained at the conclusion of the process as the "pause of satisfaction." As a pragmatist, Gordon regarded the function of art to be the production of new experience. For her, the artist's reality is a creation, not an imitation. And Furry, coming to grips with the dualism of content and form, posited the *"semblant"* as a new mode of experience, by which the two (content and form) are reconciled. In this way, meanings already present yield further meanings.

CRITICISM AND

AESTHETICS

Kate Gordon remarked that "criticism may be called the aesthetics of particular cases."[1] This chapter will examine the aesthetic doctrines of a number of prominent American literary critics.

Joel Elias Spingarn (*1875–1939*)

In 1910 Spingarn, a famous professor of comparative literature at Columbia University, opened his lecture "The New Criticism" with a sentence borrowed from one of Flaubert's letters: "What dull creatures those college professors are whenever they talk about art."[2] Clearly, the professor used the shock method to alert his audience of future professors to the necessity of *thinking anew* about matters critical and aesthetic.

In this lecture he declared that the first need in American criticism was for education in aesthetic thinking; this had to be followed by the scholarly discipline that would provide both a deep national insight and a wide international outlook. Such humane scholarship, as opposed to pedantry, would substitute the quest for a larger self for the worship of monuments and ancestors.

Even more urgently required, according to Spingarn, was a deepened sensibility that would counteract the prevailing deadness of artistic feeling. To this end he called for the development of taste, by which he meant not the so-called good taste of the dilettante and amateur collector but the quality of the creative moment shared by both the artist and the observer.[3]

In undertaking the difficult task of providing a definition of taste, Spingarn attempted to avoid mistaking virtuous platitudes for art. He accepted no facile generalizations about the place of poetry, for example, among the humanities. The true critic, he believed, would see the essential unity of art, philosophy, religion, and morals in the life of the spirit. Such a critic, in his search for beauty, would be satisfied with nothing less than truth.[4]

Throughout history, Spingarn suggested, impressionism (or enjoyment) and dogmatism (or judgment) represented opposite approaches to criticism, although the idea of expression is implicit in both.[5] The German aestheticians first conceived criticism as the study of expression, but the fundamental expressive nature of literature was often obscured, as Croce had shown.[6]

Spingarn noted that Croce's aesthetic called for an inversion of the statement *art is expression* to the declaration that *expression is art*. This revolutionary approach dispensed with such elements as "rules," "conventions," and "genres." It rejected the idea of technique as separate from art, discarded the concept of literary "evolution," and condemned the old division between genius and taste.[7] "Genius is to aesthetics what the ego is to philosophy, the only supreme and absolute reality," said Schelling. Spingarn, following this view, suggested that while criticism could examine certain aspects of the nature of art, it could not discover the source of its power.[8]

Some years later, however, Spingarn modified these views. In 1922 he wrote that at the time of his earlier work "the pedants and the professors were in the ascendant" and that the critical writer was obliged to assist the creative artist. By the 1920s the pendulum had swung from the "professors" to the journalists who treated an imaginative work as if they were describing fireworks or a bullfight.

The critic therefore had to insist on discipline, knowledge, and thought, as in Spingarn's "Essay on the Divergence of Criticism and Creation."[9]

Although he asserted that America had neither inherited nor created a tradition of aesthetic thought, he proudly cited those elements of American aesthetics that anticipated modern critical concepts. In particular he praised Jefferson's literary consciousness, as shown, for example, in a letter to William Wirt (1816) in which he expressed contempt for artificial canons of criticism and asked only whether a work is animating and interesting. (For full quotation of this letter, see Chapter 1).[10]

Spingarn turned next to Poe's conception of poetry as "the rhythmical creation of beauty" and to Emerson's kindred idea that beauty, like truth, is "an ultimate end. . . . Beauty is its own excuse for being." Spingarn recalled Poe's remark: "The only proper method of testing the merits of a poem is by measuring its capabilities of exciting the Poetic Sentiments in others." Such views, said Spingarn, should warn the critic against overemphasizing the didactic elements of art. He regretted, however, that the views of these American thinkers had not been fully incorporated into the body of American criticism.[11]

Once again, therefore, Spingarn insisted on the importance of truly aesthetic principles in criticism. The latter, as an expression of taste, or that faculty of imaginative sympathy by which the reader relives the vision created by the artist, must be firmly grounded in principle. Even dilettante criticism, however, is preferable to the dogmatic or aridly intellectual criticism of the professors, because the dilettante at least shares some of the artist's enthusiasm, while the intellectualist or moralist is precluded by his temperament and theories from ever understanding the primal thrill and purpose of the creative act.

Logic is not the arbiter of art. Reason and judgment must be accompanied by generous forms of feeling.[12] Any philosophy of art must be founded on a philosophy of life; without this, all aesthetic formulas will seem empty. The true artist, moreover, can transcend the external and moralistic aspects of art. This element of transcendence is, for Spingarn, the test of all art. It is inherent in the very nature of the creative imagination.[13]

Albert Mordell (*1885–*   )

In *The Shifting of Literary Values* (1912) Mordell asserted that past literature was "a large mausoleum in which lie the effigies of the old movements, dead beyond resurrection."[14] Conceptions of beauty change. The modern image of woman, for example, is not that of the age of chivalry. She is no longer the pale, immaculate creature of the knights or the vile object of the monks, and books that present her in this light are false.[15]

Mordell called for the development of aesthetic principles without regard to the theories of the distant past. He considered Nietzsche, Taine, and Pater greater moralists and stylists than Marcus Aurelius, Bunyan, and Thomas a Kempis. In his view, Goethe, Ibsen, Balzac, and Byron were greater than Milton, Aeschylus, Spenser, and Tasso.[16] Mordell took issue with Victor Hugo, who declared (in his *Shakespeare*) that in Homer and Dante literature reached a climax and that no one can surpass these poets because art is not progressive.[17]

Mordell found no essential conflict between intellect and feeling, or between poetry and science. The characters of Balzac, he said, are more intensely engrossed in their passions than the characters of Homer, in spite of Balzac's judgment and intellect. Thought neither stifles the emotions nor corrupts the imagination. Critical acuity does not damage literary performance, as shown in the works of Poe, Coleridge, Heine, and Goethe. Combinations of the critical and imaginative faculties also occur in French literature, in the works of such writers as Voltaire, Diderot, Stendhal, Théophile Gautier, the Goncourts, and Baudelaire. Mordell agreed, then, with others who have held that the literary man discovers new ideas just as the scientist discovers new facts.[18]

For Mordell, ideas were more important than form. He referred to Pater, "one of the greatest stylists we have had," who maintained that substance decided greatness in art. *The Red and the Black* and *Crime and Punishment* are not remarkable for style, but they are among the greatest literary productions of mankind. Rabelais and Cervantes live solely because of their ideas. Historical criticism, said

Mordell, has one great fatality; it attempts to reduce our minds to the level of those whom we have outgrown and finally dulls our judgments.[19]

Literary criticism is subjective; it can never become a fixed science. The changing literary reputations of Blake and Stendhal represent a travesty on human judgment. Mordell, recognizing this transitory nature of human judgment, felt that the excessive domination of the classics had led to an atrophied intellectual development and a restriction of artistic growth.[20] His attitude recalls that of the Scotch poet John Davidson, who declared that literature would be able to start afresh only when the influence of Shakespeare was dissipated.

Edward Howard Griggs (*1868–1951*)

Griggs's aesthetic was founded not on a restatement of criticism and philosophy but on the extensive study of works of art in each of the areas mentioned in the title of his book: *The Philosophy of Art: The Meaning and Relation of Sculpture, Painting, Poetry and Music* (1913).[21] Using the comparative method, he examined the effect of selected masterpieces on the senses, emotions, imagination, and intellect.

For him, all art was expression, but not all expression was art. He offered this definition: Art is the adequate and harmonious expression of some aspect of man's life or relation to nature, through the medium of personality, in definitely limited form.[22]

Art is at once real and ideal. It never merely echoes nature, but transmutes it through the medium of the artist's personality. Resorting to a figure of speech, Griggs said that a work of art is like a wondrous shell thrown up on the shore of time by the ocean of humanity. We hold it to our ear and hear the music of the artist's life and character.[23] In so doing, one might add, we also hear the music of our own being.

Griggs's discussion of the meaning and function of music and its relation to the spirit is relevant to an understanding of poetry. Music can reveal the infinite, as when Browning's Abt Vogler speaks of this miracle: "That out of three sounds he frame not a fourth sound, but a star." Griggs frequently cited Lessing on the relationship of poetry to sculpture and painting. The relationship of poetry to music is even closer than to the spatial arts.

In relation to the human spirit, poetry is the widest and most universal of the fine arts. Prose, however, can sometimes suggest the union of the arts, in the organlike tones of De Quincey, the North Sea storm in Carlyle, the tableaux of Victor Hugo, and the subtly tender melody in the exquisite prose of Pierre Loti.[24]

Although each art has its specific function, all must express the unity of the human spirit, which all the arts serve in a common aesthetic cause. The intellect must strive for abstract conceptions, in the effort to discover the unifying type behind the individuals given in nature; but the abstract concept is barren until it is given creative expression in some concrete form.

Wagner held that in music drama, poetry and dramatic action constitute the center, with music as an associated art. His disciples held that music was the center, and that the other arts were subordinate to it. Griggs considered the music drama an interesting illustration of the law of evolution from a homogeneous basis, through differentiation, to unity on a higher plane.[25]

The danger, in art, that the sensuous may pass over into the sensual was symbolized for Griggs in the Witches' Kitchen scene in *Faust*. Faust can see the vision of the ideal body and face only as he stands reverently away from the mirror; when he steps forward in an attempt to grasp the form, the vision fades. The same truth is expressed in a saying often heard in Parisian studios: "If you want to be an artist, you must hang up your passions with your hat and coat before you enter the Studio."[26] Oscar Wilde also expressed this struggle of the artist:

> To drift with every passion till my soul
> Is a stringed lute on which all winds can play.
> Is it for this that I have given away
> Mine ancient wisdom, and austere control?[27]

Like others before him, Griggs realized the elusive quality of
beauty, which escapes definition. It contains something deeper than
the principle of the harmony of the parts in a whole. On this point
Griggs quoted Emerson's "Each and All":

> I thought of the Sparrow's note from heaven
> Singing at dawn on the alder bough;
> I brought him home, in his nest, at even;
> He sings the song, but it cheers not now.
> For I did not bring home the river and sky;—
> He sang to my ear,—they sang to my eye.

Griggs echoed Emerson's organicism and Greenough's function-
alism when the latter spoke of the harmony of an organism to its
function, or a thing made to its purpose—the harmony of content
and form: "All appreciation of beauty in nature is a coming to consciousness of a rhythm already existing between our senses and the
nature of the world."[28] Despite the difficulty of defining beauty, art
helps man to appreciate the world as it is and life as it ought to be.
It also helps men to benefit from the healing and exalting influence
of beauty.

Like Havelock Ellis, Griggs cited one supreme art to which all
are called—*the art of living*. The service of art, he said, is not limited
to the few, but is universal.[29] A similar view was expressed in Ellis's
The Dance of Life: "It has always been difficult for Man to realize
that his life is all an art." Ellis borrowed a further observation from
Jules de Gaultier: "Morality is a fact of sensibility; it has no need
to have recourse to reason for its affirmations."[30]

George Edward Woodberry (1855–1930)

Woodberry's ideas were expounded in his address "Two Phases of
Criticism: Historical and Esthetic" (1913).[31] Adverting, like Griggs,
to Taine, Woodberry regarded works of art as terms in a temporal
series, giving rise to a history of art. Taine's method emphasized the
objective element in the genesis of art. Whereas to the psychologists

the individual was all, Taine attempted to escape from personality. The former idealized idiosyncrasy as the bound and substance of genius, causing criticism to lose itself in biography and medicine. Thus Woodberry suggested Freud and Max Nordau when he remarked that defective, delinquent, degenerate genius seemed hunted to his lair in the subconscious self.

In addition to the sociologists and the psychologists, Woodberry cited a third group (really a hybrid of the other two), namely, the comparatists. These men have been preoccupied with such key figures as Petrarch, Rousseau, and Goethe, and with the intricate problems of influences between nations and epochs. The tendency among such scholars to dissect literary works has often turned criticism into a mere anatomy of texts.

In all these divagations, criticism became ever more removed from the work of art. It left the matter of life, which art is, for the matter of knowledge. If the purpose of criticism is to obtain an understanding of the state of mind of a man at a past moment, the historical criticism becomes an indispensable preliminary.[32] While citing the importance of such an approach,[33] however, Woodberry remarked that especially in the world of art, which is the most intense realm of life, one is often inclined to ask: "Is there no rescue from the reign of death which is history, and how shall it be accomplished?"[34]

He asked further whether critics are mistaken when they relegate art to the dead past and translate it into history? Does the personality of art, like the human personality, change in time? He declared that the revolt against the historical treatment of art arises from a belief that in such a treatment art loses its own nature and is degraded into mere knowledge.[35]

Through expression, the artist externalizes his mind. His work of art becomes part of the external world. An observer's re-creation of a work of art depends on his own nature. Every man has the artist's soul; he is not merely a spectator, but a participant. A new poem suggests new powers of feeling, evoking a fresh passion for life, a transforming and exalting power. Thus, whereas the end of science is to know, the end of art is to be.[36]

I might add, however, that art does provide the feeling that something new has been revealed, suggesting a deeper knowledge of life. The *I think* is added to the *I feel* in a combination that constitutes true being. The artist's discovery of life therefore depends, I believe, on both knowledge and feeling. This combination makes art a growth of freedom and gives it, as Woodberry said, a prophetic quality.[37]

William Crary Brownell (1851–1928)

In Brownell's view, the historical method, for all its services, has two erroneous tendencies. Imposing its historical theory on literary and aesthetic facts, it discerns their historical rather than their essential character. It accepts its "documents" as final rather than as the subjects of its concern.[38] History, moreover, cannot be divorced from psychology, any more than aesthetics can be separated from philosophy. The so-called document is itself a semantic sign and as such is functionally and intimately related to the aesthetic experience.

Brownell noted that history itself (sometimes referred to as philosophy teaching by example) often suffered from the submergence of its examples by its philosophy.[39] He followed Sainte-Beuve's observation that the business of criticism is to occupy itself with examples and ideas associated with them, not with theories and the systems they threaten. Thus, for Brownell, the crown of critical achievement is the solution of the mystery of human personality.[40]

In his view, critical practice, fortified by general culture, seeks to establish initially some central conception of the subject, follows with an analysis of detail confirming or modifying this conception, and concludes with a balanced synthesis. This process is based on a standard of reason that rules out individual whim or formulated prescriptions. As exemplars of this rational approach Brownell cited Saint-Beuve, Edmond Scherer, Arnold, and "such straightforward apostles of pure good sense" as Francisque Sarcey and Émile Faguet.[41] Such writers, he believed, represent the optimum union of the aesthetic and the historical in criticism.

In his book *Standards* (1917) Brownell asserted that criteria belong to sense rather than to reason. They are felt as ideal exemplars for measurement by comparison, not deduced as criteria of absolute authority. He noted an instinctive hostility to standards, arising from the tension that conformity imposes both on the artist and on the appreciator of art. Standards also seem to conflict with spontaneity and the vital outflow of energy.

He alluded to two types of spontaneity, however: that of an *elevated order* and that of an *elementary order*.[42] On this categorization, he quoted Édouard Manet: "People desire to popularize art, without perceiving that art always loses in height what it gains in breadth." Further, in his discussion of the "elevated order," Brownell cited Gide's observation that "the admirable French tradition" of good taste was maintained by the cultured men who mediated between the rigid formalism of the court of Louis XIV and the free naturalism of the general public (the pit).[43]

At one time, said Brownell, the art-loving public consisted of cultivated people: their standards were narrow, but they had standards. In the modern public the elements least sensitive to art and letters are disproportionately large. Brownell blamed this condition on the prevalance of vocational training and specialization, which usurped the place of the liberal arts in the educational system. As a result, contemporary society has no real community of educated people with common intellectual interests and standards.

The present public demands sensation, novelty, "something different." Brownell discussed the emotional nature of this recoil from disciplined thought and noted the widespread feeling that intellectual standards are undemocratic.[44] He deplored the disappearance of the sense of awe from the inner life of modern man. Few of his contemporaries, he remarked, shared Kant's rapture over the starry heavens and the moral law.[45]

Brownell admitted, however, that to deny the need of new standards would be to expose oneself as smug and Victorian. The only solution was to increase the "remnant" in art and letters and to spread the standards; otherwise art would be reduced to a standardless caprice. The artist who functions for himself alone has obtained his catharsis, but has not provided one for his fellow man, as Aristotle urged. Because mankind as a whole is wider than any one man, its cooperation in arts and letters is quite as important as that of their professional representatives.

As an example of a true community, Brownell cited France, where an entire people is animated by the perpetual renewal of a national art.[46] This renewal results from a constant shift of standards beyond the comfort and smugness of the individual. Such a shift can be achieved only by the individual, however, as Max Eastman suggested when he urged Americans to make their own poetry. Following this view, Brownell observed that it is best to do one's thinking in solitude—in solitude but not in isolation from the concerns of mankind.[47]

Van Wyck Brooks (1886–1963)

Like Brownell, Van Wyck Brooks was disturbed by the state of American culture, which he described in his essay "The Critics and Young America" (1917).[48] Anticipating many writers of the 1960s, he wondered whether the older generation ever suspects the existence of an inherent weakness in a culture that has so lost control of a really well-disposed younger generation as to leave in its wake a society so little civilized.

How does it happen, Brooks asked, that we who are gradually becoming receptive to so many influences of the past feel the chill of the grave (or, as Alfred Stieglitz once put it to me, "the smell of the morgue") as we look back over the spiritual history of our own race?[49] Our field of action has been preempted by our acquisitive instincts, and we have never developed a national fabric of spiritual experience. As a result, we are unable to think and feel in international terms. We share only vicariously in the heritage of civilization.

We have flocked around Carlyle, Browning, Meredith, Ibsen, and Nietzsche for entertainment; but they have said nothing real to us because we have nothing in our lives to make their message real.[50] One thinks of Frost's remark that America failed to produce a Dostoyevski because of nothing less than too much comfort. Literature with us is either an amusement or a soporific. Our slogan is: Let's have cheerfulness and forgetfulness. American writers live in a world of externalities. Could one ask, said Brooks, for a more essential declaration of artistic bankruptcy?[51]

Our industrial process has produced a poor quality of human nature. In Europe, on the other hand, the human spirit has been kept alive by a long line of rebels, such as Nietzsche, Ernest Renan, William Morris, Rodin, Marx, and Mill, who have reacted violently to the desiccating influences of the industrial system. Rebelling against the oppressive conditions of their environment, they have been able to keep alive the tradition of a great society by assimilating for human uses the positive by-products of industrialism itself—science and democracy.

By pointing to the degradation of society and the poverty of their lives, they built a bridge between the greatness of the few in the past and the greatness of the many, perhaps in the future. Thus the democracies of Europe rose above their dead selves. In America the only son of Abraham Lincoln, who liberated the slaves politically, became the president of the Pullman Company and was the first to exploit the freed men industrially. Throughout his essay Brooks charged that our environment has given us personally no sense of the significance of life.[52] (But, when one is mindful of a Europe that produced Hitler, Mussolini, and Stalin, then Brooks's remarks are in need of revision.)

Now that the acquisitive life had lost the sanction of pioneering necessity, Brooks felt that his age (1917) called for intensive cultivation of the creative life. But for that, Brooks lamented, how ill-equipped we are! The young found themselves born into a race that had drained away all its spiritual resources in a struggle to survive, and so continued to struggle in the midst of plenty because life itself no longer possessed any other meaning.[53]

In this essay, as we can now see, Brooks clearly forecast many of the dominant concerns of the 1970s. These concerns were adumbrated in most of his writings, including *The Flowering of New England* and *New England Indian Summer*. He pointed out that the gospel of self-expression, makeshift though it be, has revealed a promise in America that has been taken too much for granted.

America's task is to build a program for the conservation of our spiritual resources.[54]

Irving Babbitt (1865–1933)

The question of self-expression and spontaneity in art, as well as the restraining role of discipline—all of which arise in the reflections of Spingarn, Brownell, and Brooks—became especially important in Babbitt's writings, notably in his essay "Genius and Taste."[55] Here he made Spingarn and his master Croce the special butts of his argument, attacking their exaltation of spontaneity and free expression, and describing them as primitivists. He quoted Diderot: "Genius calls for something enormous, *primitive* and barbaric."[56]

According to the primitivist, the genius must let himself go both imaginatively and emotionally, and the whole business of the critic is to receive so keen an impression from the resulting expression that, when passed through his temperament, it issues forth as a fresh expression. By participating in the creative thrill of genius, the critic becomes creative in turn, and insofar as this situation occurs, genius and taste are one, as they were for Spingarn. Babbitt noted, however, that Schlegel's similar view antedated that of Croce and Spingarn by at least a century, especially in his declaration that genius and taste are "indivisibly one." Babbitt found, moreover, that Spingarn's aesthetic closely paralleled Oscar Wilde's in *The Critic as Artist*, which concluded that "Criticism is the only civilized form of autobiography."[57]

Babbitt maintained that the basis of the whole movement from the original genius of the eighteenth century to Wilde and Spingarn was the craving for an indeterminate vagabondage of imagination and emotion—an emotional emancipation of the imagination from any allegiance to standards or central control. Thus Spingarn's ideas on genius and taste encourage conceit or megalomania, which Babbitt found to be extremely dangerous, especially when a whole nation comes to feel its intoxication as an ecstatic "idealism."[58]

The whole conception of genius and taste had about it, for Babbitt, the flavor of a decadent aestheticism. Using Arnold's phrase, he attacked the term "creative critic" as "the grand name without the grand thing." In an age marked by the disintegration of traditional values, the critic must be creative in an important sense; he must create standards with the aid of the ethical imagination. Critic and creator are truly united in their common allegiance to critical standards.[59]

Spingarn declared that the opening night of the International Exhibition of 1913 was one of the most "exciting adventures" he had ever experienced. For Babbitt, such an attitude represented a late stage of a movement that from its rise in the eighteenth century was unable to distinguish between the original and the aboriginal. Nothing, he suggested, is more tiresome than a stale eccentricity. Is this country, he asked, always to be the dumping ground of Europe? Can we not create our own standards, without such primitivistic affirmations as Spingarn's statement that the "art of a child is art quite as much as that of Michelangelo"?[60]

Clearly, Babbitt placed Spingarn among the corrupters of the literary conscience, among those who made the imagination the irresponsible accomplice of the unchained emotions.[61] Many will agree that when Babbitt spoke of art as creating "the illusion of a higher reality," he meant by "higher reality" that sanctioned by Calvinism; whereas Spingarn, who also believed in the creative illusionism of art, meant illusion sanctioned by the human spirit free of all parochialism.

Thomas Stearns Eliot (1888–1965)

Eliot, a pupil of Babbitt and Santayana at Harvard, headed his essay "The Perfect Critic" with a quotation from Rémy de Gourmont's *Letters to the Amazon*: "To build into laws personal impressions is the great effort of a man if he is sincere."[62] Thus, for Eliot, the artist is to be depended on as a critic; his criticism will be objective evaluation, not merely the satisfaction of a suppressed desire. Eliot supported this view with a further quote from Gourmont: "The writer whose style is abstract is almost always a sentimentalist, at least a sensitive soul. The writer who is an artist is practically never a sentimentalist, and very rarely a sensitive soul."[63]

Much of Eliot's thought was derived from Coleridge, whom he regarded as perhaps the greatest of English critics. Eliot felt, however, that Coleridge's metaphysical interest was tinged with emotions. He declared that a literary critic should have no emotions except those immediately provoked by a work of art. Everything that Aristotle said, for example, illuminated the literature that is the occasion for saying it. Such a statement is only occasionally true of Coleridge.

For Eliot, Aristotle was the prototype of the scientific, or as Eliot would have said, the intelligent mind. Only Gourmont among modern critics could approach him, with his remarkable combination of sensitiveness, erudition, sense of fact and sense of history, and generalizing power—all factors, apparently, that in Eliot's opinion combined to make the great critic.

The critic, said Eliot, should have a superior sensibility to impressions.[64] He observed further that the two directions of sensibility —criticism and creativity—are complementary. Sensibility, however, is rare, unpopular, and desirable; the critic and the creative artist are therefore frequently the same person. Eliot obviously had himself in mind as that representative individual when he remarked that the poetic critic criticizes poetry in order to create poetry. He believed, moreover, "historical" and "philosophical" critics had better be called historians and philosophers quite simply.[65]

Emphasizing the importance of literary tradition, Eliot maintained that the best parts in a poet may be those in which his ancestors (the dead poets) asserted their immortality most vigorously. Thus a poet cannot be evaluated apart from his relation to a tradition. "I mean this," said Eliot, "as a principle of aesthetic, not merely historical criticism." He noted in addition that the past is altered by the present as much as the present is directed by the past,[66] and he expressed his sense of the aesthetic of history: the historic imagination transposes, transmutes, and rearranges past events. An awareness of such a metamorphosis, Eliot suggested, is essential for the poet.

Eliot attempted to eliminate personal emotion from the enjoyment of poetry, citing Arnold's description of the highest purpose of art: to see the object as it really is, "to see life clearly and see it whole." Bad criticism is, for Eliot, only an expression of emotion.[67] The progress of an artist is a continual self-sacrifice, a continual extinction of personality, as in the remark by Keats that the poet has no "personality." In this depersonalization, art approaches the condition of science.

Here Eliot used the analogy of the catalyst, which causes chemical compounds to combine, forming a new compound. The combination takes place only if the catalyst is present, but the newly formed compound contains no trace of the catalyst, which is apparently unaffected by the combination.

The mind of the poet, Eliot believed, is such a catalyst. It may operate partly or exclusively on the experience of the man himself, but the more accomplished the artist, the more completely separate in him will be the man who suffers and the mind which creates—the more perfectly will the mind digest and transmute the passions that are its material.[68] The poet is only a medium (not a personality) in which impressions and experiences combine in peculiar and unexpected ways.[69]

Thus, Eliot asserted, the business of the poet is not to find new emotions, but to use the ordinary ones and, in working them up into poetry, to express feelings that are not in actual emotion at all. The obscurity of this conception of emotion, together with Eliot's indication that only a rare individual can recognize an expression of significant emotion,[70] suggests that he credited very few people with the ability to respond to a poetry and even fewer with an understanding of the philosophy or aesthetic of that art.

Henry Louis Mencken (*1880–1956*)

Mencken, an aggressive, epigrammatic journalist, was also an admirer of the lyrical and even the sentimental in literature and music. Secretly respecting the philological scholarship that he outwardly derided, he was dominated by Nietzsche and by his love for music. For him, the ideal critic, like the artist, was capable of expressing his inner compulsions articulately and with a positive sense of the importance of the self.[71]

Because the feelings of the critic are largely derived from those of other men, as expressed in art, he must, said Mencken, possess the intellectual agility and enterprise that will allow him to move from the work of art to the vast and mysterious complex of phenomena behind it. Lacking this capacity, he remains "no more than a fugleman or policeman to his betters." If the critic, however, possesses something of the genuine artist in himself, he will inevitably move from the work of art to life itself. His own expression will therefore acquire a dignity that it would not otherwise attain. The critic, then, is an artist whose self-expression comprises both art and life. Through him one work of art begets another, and in this sense the object before the true critic is always less interesting than the feelings within him.[72]

In Mencken's view, such a critic does not force a work of art to conform with any transient theory of aesthetics. Rather, he attempts to relieve his own tensions, transforming them into "plausible" and ingratiating expressions, therefore gaining the attention and respect of his equals. The works of such critics as Carlyle and Macaulay are notable for their charm—a quality that Mencken found much more important than truth. Indeed, he believed that criticism should be less concerned with discovering truth than with exposing error,[73] because, in aesthetics, nothing is permanently true.

Mencken attributed the vitality of such diverse works as *Hamlet*, the Mona Lisa, *Faust*, "Dixie," *Parsifal*, Mother Goose, "Annabel Lee," and *Huckleberry Finn* not to correct demeanor but to the quality of creative passion that emanates from them. In recognition of this quality, the critic should produce writings based on sound structure and marked by the charm of an uncommon and independent personality. Mencken noted again that he could not imagine any aesthetic idea that is palpably and incontrovertibly sound, and he declared that no artist has ever improved his work as a result of so-called constructive criticism.[74]

Although Mencken thus seems to have derogated the idea of a "science" of aesthetics, he nevertheless welcomed a renaissance of the doctrine that aesthetic matters are important, and that a man might do well to take them seriously. He cited the importance of conflict in aesthetic issues, as during the period when, he said, literature was kept alive by the dispute between Poe and those he criticized. In a later period, when Howells, mild-mannered and beneficent, was the typical critic, literature survived upon the tomb of the Puritan culture.

Mencken conjectured that if Poe had been surrounded by admiring professors, he would probably have written poetry as hollow as Woodberry's. It took the unfair and sometimes dishonorable opposition of Rufus Wilmot Griswold to stimulate Poe to his highest efforts. And Mencken hailed the critical strife of his own day (the 1920s), which no longer allowed the Paul Elmer Mores and Hamilton Wright Mabies to "purr in peace."[75]

In the article "Criticism of Criticism of Criticism,"[76] Mencken pointed to the divergent views of the critics on their own art, which are as varied as their views of the other arts. One group tries to police the fine arts according to moral principles. Another demands that they be concerned with beauty only. Still another declares that a literary work is a psychological document and should help man to know himself. A fourth group reduces criticism to an exact science.[77]

Refuting the moralistic critics, Mencken quoted Spingarn's *Creative Criticism*: "To say that poetry is moral or immoral is as meaningless as to say that an equilateral triangle is moral and an isosceles triangle is immoral." Mencken parodied the moralistic view in his remark: "This cauliflower would be good if it had only been prepared in accordance with international law." He particularly attacked "Prof. Dr. W. C. Brownell, the Amherst Aristotle, with his eloquent plea for standards as iron-clad as the Westminster Confession."[78] Mencken classed Brownell with such writers as William Lyon Phelps, Percy H. Boynton, Stuart Pratt Sherman, and Paul Elmer More, for whom, he said, criticism was little more than a branch of homiletics.[79]

Despite some reservations, Mencken generally admired Spingarn, for whom "aesthetic judgment and artistic creation are instinct with the same vital life." Spingarn, of course, erred in his failure to recognize fully the social and even the moral implications of art. The finale of Beethoven's C-Minor Symphony, for example, is not only colossal as music; it is also colossal as revolt. It says something against something. Still, as Mencken admitted, Spingarn did dissipate many false views and came closer to the truth than his colleagues.[80]

The critic most admired by Mencken was James Huneker. In him, as in Poe, Mencken found a sensitive and intelligent artist who could re-create the work of other artists. For Mencken, however, Huneker's use of the word "creative" seemed somewhat flamboyant. He would have substituted "catalytic," because for him, as in some respects for Eliot, the critic acts as a catalytic agent to initiate a reaction between two elements—the work of art and the spectator. Thus the critical process should produce the very factors that the artist has attempted to convey: understanding, appreciation, and intelligent enjoyment.[81] In general, Mencken's strident criticism of American culture helped to create an awareness of its weaknesses as well as of its possibilities for aesthetic improvement.

This chapter has presented a wide spectrum of critical opinion. Spingarn, a disciple of Croce, maintained that the philosophy of art must be based on a philosophy of life, while Mordell regarded the worship of the past as an incubus on the free development of ideas. For him there was no conflict between poetry and science. In line with Mordell, Woodberry held that the historical treatment of art obscured its nature by degrading it to mere knowledge. The prophetic quality of art was the result of the combination of knowledge and feeling. Brownell envisioned human personality in the heart of critical achievement. What mattered was art rather than any system of viewing it. He was equally opposed to rigidity of standards and to standardless caprice.

Brooks was chiefly concerned with the oppressive effect of industrialism on the creative process. Accordingly, he warned against the easy dismissal of self-expression in the arts. In the "creative criticism" sponsored by Spingarn, Babbitt could only see a vagabondage of emotion and imagination. The illusion of a "higher reality" in art needed, in Babbitt's view, an "inner check" (that of Calvinism), whereas for Spingarn it needed freedom from all parochialism.

T. S. Eliot maintained that the true mark of the critic and the creative artist (essentially the same person) was the possession of a higher sensibility. Eliot was obscure in his assertion that the poet's business was to express feelings that were not at all in actual emotion. Mencken saw the critic as one who was able to move from the work apart to the complex phenomena behind it. His aesthetic ideal, a combination of good sense, urbanity, and lyricism, aimed especially to counteract the crass materialism of the "booboisie."

AESTHETICS AS A
UNIFYING VISION

James Mark Baldwin (1861–1934)

Baldwin's philosophy was directed "to all those who find Art the Noblest Instrument of the Spiritual Life."[1] His aesthetic theory, which he called "pancalism" (from the Greek meaning "all beautiful") was based on a reasoned approach to art. He particularly admired the theory of affective logic (a logic that takes emotion into account), which, he noted, is distinctly French, just as *Einfühlung* (empathy) is distinctly German. The aestheticians Théodule Ribot and Theodor Lipps were respectively connected with these influential movements in psychological and aesthetic theory.[2]

Baldwin believed that only the aesthetic experience can reunite "self-reality" (or inner control) and "thing-reality" (or external control), which are divided in the process of intellectual analysis. The aesthetic imagination rejects the incomplete knowledge offered by narrow cognition. Indeed, as studies in affective logic have shown, the aesthetic element in man has generally been the unifying force in the dualisms created by the partial motives of cognitive and practical interest.[3]

The sense of reality is based on interest and satisfaction. The mind comprehends actuality through the imagination—the vehicle of the prospecting, postulating, schematizing, and desiring functions.

Through these functions, man's perceptions of actualities are enlarged, defined, and enriched. Thus the scientific imagination not only discovers the true but also postulates the ideal of truth.

Reality is progressive, unfinished, and dynamic. It has an ideal meaning, which is never actually achieved either through mere knowledge, which is excessively confining, or through mere freedom of thought, which excludes profound insights. A true sense of reality is neither impersonal nor capricious.[4]

Although Baldwin generally aligned himself with the instrumentalism and pragmatism of John Dewey and William James, he called attention to their limitations. He declared that philosophy should not disparage certain functions to dignify others. Men, he said, should be informed by knowledge and moved by feeling, not divided between the two. In this approach Baldwin recalls Lotze, who also rejected partial solutions to the problem of human existence.[5]

Baldwin's *Genetic Theory of Reality* (1915) showed that by their very nature the categories of thought ignore and disparage the most direct experiences of life, resulting in a stifling of cognition. In the rivalry between rationalism (based on the intuition of "pure reason") and voluntarism (based on "practical reason"), imagination again constitutes a unifying force between cognition and mechanism. It merges the ideals of thought in the intense perception of aesthetic contemplation, forming a reality of reconciliation and completeness. Men comprehend the real through their enjoyment of the beautiful.[6]

Aesthetic contemplation is concerned solely with immediate perception. Reflective knowledge, unable to solve its own contradictions, reconstructs its objects in the form of ideas and systems. According to Baldwin, however, certain "secondary presuppositions" always "haunt the house of every ontological theory of reality." The aesthetic experience knows no "other" than its own object; the relation of subject to object is part of its content, but it is not itself subject to this distinction. Its higher immediacy and completeness deny the relativities of inner and outer, earlier and later, actual and ideal, true and false, affirmative and negative, good and bad. The world, said Baldwin, cannot remain incoherent, disorganized, and radically pluralistic, if it becomes artistic and beautiful.[7]

Baldwin's affectivism denied the competence of either reason or

will to serve as an exclusive organ of reality. He asserted that an
immediate synthesis of function is found in aesthetic contemplation,
a state that may be described as one of feeling. This feeling had too
often been left at the level of impulse or regarded as an empty form
of transcendental reason, instead of being considered in its true role
as an instrument of epistemology.

Baldwin therefore called for a theory of imagination that would
express the ideals of the will in a union of cognition and feeling.
Through such a theory, the two great currents of affectivism—the
mystical and the rational—would be joined.[8] Baldwin cited Wilbur
M. Urban's prospect of a "Beautiful Vision" ensuing from "a form
of contemplation which transcends will and thought alike" and which
must be the goal of all metaphysics. Pancalism, then, was yet another
organic approach to aesthetics, through which man could express the
whole of his nature in the awareness brought by his sense of beauty.[9]

DeWitt Henry Parker (1885–1949)

A pupil of William James, Royce, Santayana, and Ralph Barton
Perry at Harvard, Parker moved slowly toward a theory of beauty,
publishing his *Principles of Aesthetics* in 1920. In that year I took
Parker's course in which this work was used as a text. I can still
recall the quiet flame that seemed to burn as Parker spoke. He communicated aesthetic ideas without the narrowly logical obfuscation
that sometimes pervades more recent discussions of the subject. Matters of great moment were stated simply and explicitly. The subject
was always man's abiding fascination for beauty.

For Parker, as for Baldwin, feeling was of paramount importance.
Apparently influenced by Coleridge's idea of the "willing suspen-
sion of disbelief," he indicated that aesthetic belief implies an aban-
don sufficient to allow the suggestibility of a work of art to work on
our feelings. He attached the same meaning to the terms "experience
of art," "aesthetic experience," and "beauty."[10] For him, art involved
value judgment based on selection and comparison.

Although he stated at one point that a work of art is a logical system, he also noted that its purpose is sympathetic vision, not scientific truth or edification: "The tyranny of the scientific and the moral is the death of art." He was quick to add, however: "I do not mean, of course, that art may not express the mystery and the wonder of science." In the first statement he nonetheless brings to mind the famous remark that Descartes, as the personification of science, cut the throat of poetry.[11]

In his concrete application of aesthetic theory to the arts, Parker began with music, believing that all arts contain a musical element. He suggested that a succession of tones comes to express the changing process of the inner life. Here Parker followed the general as well as the detailed ideas of Schopenhauer, Lotze, Wilhelm Wundt, and Lipps in holding that "music expresses the abstract aspects of action in all its divagations" and that the "content of music becomes not a mere form of life, but life itself."[12]

Music and poetry are akin in that both are arts of sound with rhythm as the principle of their order. They are twin-born in song. The incursion of definite meaning in poetry differentiates it from music. We may argue, however, that the powerful impact of poetry very often results in suggestions that are not at all clearly defined— that poetry is, in fact, like music, "the spontaneous overflow of powerful feelings."[13]

Parker described the four basic functions of words: (1) the expression of sound and movement (heard and uttered), (2) the embodiment of meaning (concrete or abstract), (3) the communication of total experience (the self as well as the object), and (4) the suggestion of transcendental meaning in concrete images. This definition of words as articulations of sound and meaning, expressive of feeling and evocative of images, led Parker to a study of sound, meaning, feeling, and imagery in a synthetic view of the nature and function of poetry.[14]

The best poems, Parker believed, are at once musical, imaginative, and thoughtful. The various elements are often in conflict, however: the music may obscure the thought; the meaning may become vague because of an overelaboration of imagery; and both imagery and euphony may be shut out by subtlety of thought. Swinburne, for example, covered philosophical thought with sensuousness and musicality, while in Browning subtlety of thought precluded musicality.

Emotional thought represents a union of music and imagery.[15] Thus lyric poetry shows nature as merely a reflection of moods. Its subject matter is identifiable with its musical expressiveness. Even dramatic poetry contains an important lyrical element. In both forms, life seems to move in the actual present, whereas in the epic the time of the storyteller (the present) and that of the events he relates (the past) constitute a duality.[16]

Prose rhythm is fundamentally "a rhythmical movement of ideas." In this it resembles poetry, but without its regularization. Parker seems to have suggested a developmental charm in which the progressive links are words (language), ideas (thought), and images, as in poetry. Parker used a telling metaphor to describe the beauty of prose in relation to its content: "The transparent medium of prose shares the beauty of its content, just as a perfect glass partakes of the color of the light which it transmits." Because prose literature lacks, for the most part, the musical element, Parker regarded it as "incompletely beautiful." That very lack, however, enables it to represent life fully and in detail: "The unmusical character of prose style is not determined by weakness, but by adaptation to function."[17]

Prose fiction, which represents a psychological need for self-revelation, is basically related to history, although imaginative inventiveness makes it less than completely factual. In Parker's estimation, fiction is a compensation for loneliness and boredom; yet it is not unrelated to the world of reality. We might say with Valéry that fiction (really poetry) is a musicalization of experience. By delineating life, the art of fiction clearly becomes a criticism of life.[18]

Herbert Sidney Langfeld (1879–1958)

In *The Aesthetic Attitude* (1920) Langfeld declared that the aesthetic experience is enriched through a knowledge of the nature of appreciation. Attempting to show that "the perception of beauty is one of the most useful of man's experiences," he suggested that the nature of an individual's artistic response depends to some extent on his previous development.[19]

Following Croce, however, Langfeld asserted:

> The Romanticists are correct in their belief that appreciation as well as production [of works of art] should be intuitive. . . . Artistic response is a direct perception . . . whatever may have been the preceding intellectual preparation.[20]

At the same time he agreed with the intellectualists that an observer should have a rational background for response, and he indicated that the two positions can be reconciled. He followed John Livingston Lowes, who observed that the artist "must hold an imperial sway over his impressions, selecting, clarifying, ordering, moulding, filing and refiling them."[21]

Langfeld recognized that psychological analysis did not furnish all the data necessary for aesthetic appreciation. Thus he felt that Allen's *Physiological Aesthetics* ignored most of the problems of aesthetic enjoyment, including the nature of beauty. Among those who had made progress toward a theory (or at least a description) of beauty, Langfeld singled out Hugo Münsterberg, Puffer, and Edward Bullough.

He admitted the cogency of the theory of repose advanced by Münsterberg and his pupil Puffer—the repose found in the aesthetic object through its detachment and isolation from its surroundings. He argued, however, that one is hardly in an isolated attitude in the case of the drama, with its rising tension.

Bullough's theory of "psychical distance" (not unrelated to the theory of repose) was, for Langfeld, one of the most valuable descriptions of the conditions underlying beauty. The term "distance" was used metaphorically, not in a spatial or temporal sense. "Psychical distance" is a condition for aesthetic experience or enjoyment, as when a person on a ship threatened by a storm enjoys the color of the water and the shapes of the waves. At the moment that the waves threaten to strike, however, the "psychical distance" is lost and the aesthetic attitude gives way to an attitude of bodily resistance. (The waves themselves are, of course, both spatial and temporal.) Another example is that of a man watching *Othello* and imagining his wife in the place of Desdemona and identifying himself with Othello. The man has lost the aesthetic attitude and has ceased to "repose" in the object.

Bullough's rule of "the antinomy of distance" called for our having as little distance as possible without losing it entirely. Langfeld criticized Bullough's use of the word "distance" because it covered two distinct facts: the amount of appeal, which is one of the factors underlying the attitude; and the aesthetic attitude itself. Langfeld's argument was that we can have varying strength of appeal to our wishes in terms of distance, but we cannot have degrees of aesthetic attitude. The less distance, the greater the likelihood of loss of aesthetic attitude.[22]

On the fundamental aesthetic problem of unity, Langfeld noted that when an observer is confronted with a multiplicity of objects, he becomes restless. Accordingly, he seeks some principle for relating the objects to one another. Thus the quest for monism originates in the psychological need for repose and balance. From this point of view, desire plays itself out in accordance with the aesthetic principle of unity so often discussed by philosophers.[23]

Langfeld categorized unity in art according to three separate expressions: (1) unity of form, (2) unity of content, and (3) unity of form and content. Only when the three are brought to perfection is complete aesthetic enjoyment possible. In literature this pleasure is secured only through the genuine unity of mood and a dominant point of view.[24] Balance and symmetry are equally important, as in drama, where the strain of conflicting forces should be presented in every scene, so that the major crisis appears as a natural summation of the minor crises depicted throughout the play.[25]

Beauty, for Langfeld, is primarily a matter of successful unified adjustment to a situation, with an accompanying feeling of aesthetic pleasure. The absence of such an adjustment produces ugliness and aesthetic pain. Beauty is neither in the object nor in the organism;

it is a specific relation of the two. Because men differ, different kinds and degrees of beauty will exist. The great function of art is to provide an expressive outlet for the varying responses of individuals to their inner drives and impulses.[26]

Laurence Ladd Buermeyer (1889–1969)

Buermeyer's *The Aesthetic Experience* (1924) indicated that art must be relevant to daily life, in the sense of Ellis's statement that all arts are a part of life.[27] Art thus vivifies an "impoverished and denuded world."

For Buermeyer, aesthetic quality is an aspect of all intelligent or reasonable perception, not a mere embellishment of it. Art is the intelligent transformation of instinct. Man contributes to creation by a sympathetic and imaginative entry into a heterogeneous mass of perception, stabilizing his feelings in the repose that is the condition of art.

Like Dewey and Warner Fite, Buermeyer maintained that all experience furnishes occasions for aesthetic appreciation.[28] In the midst of the chaos in which men live, they find an area of order that Buermeyer likened to the ring of light about a lamp, which shades off into darkness on every side. Art counterbalances the evasions of life. Through the imaginative grasp and conquest of desire, art compensates men for their tenuous grip on reality; it offers "the peace that passeth understanding."[29]

By defining art as *expression in a medium of sense*, Buermeyer linked it to desire, and matter to form. He suggested that art is conduct and feeling enlightened by "fundamental brain-work." In this connection he pointed out that romantic love (as differentiated from sexual attraction) is the product of those who have given aesthetic expression to fundamental emotions.[30] As examples he quoted Marlowe's description of Helen's "face that launched a thousand ships," and Pater, for whom the Mona Lisa suggested "what in the ways of a thousand years men had come to desire."[31]

Following Dewey's declaration that experience is art, Buermeyer

declared that art is life: if it is to flourish it must be cultivated by
all men. Science and philosophy may also contribute to a vision of
unity in the human experience. Indeed philosophers and artists may
often express a similar aesthetic intent, as in the cases of Schopenhauer and Thomas Hardy.[32] No art of life can exist for slaves, however. Those who see an opposition between democracy and art are
still subject to the view of art as something apart from life.[33]

Thomas Munro (1897–   )

Probably no one in America did more to promote study and research
in aesthetics than Thomas Munro, the able and energetic editor of
the *Journal of Aesthetics and Art Criticism*, founded in 1941. His
influential *Scientific Method in Aesthetics* (1928) discussed the
experimental approach to a variety of aesthetic problems, providing
a research program that has subsequently been carried out by a
number of scholars.[34]

In his preface Munro expressed his indebtedness to Dewey's conception of experimental method, of valuation, and of aesthetic experience and to Santayana's conception of the place of art in the
life of reason and of aesthetics in a naturalistic philosophy. In criticism, he cited the works of Albert Coombs Barnes on plastic form,
as well as his analysis and historical studies of form in painting.

Fully aware of the difference between the "plumbing" of science
and its philosophy, Munro, like Einstein, did not discount the at-
tractiveness and function of mystery in human experience and
imagination. "If science must mechanize and deaden what it penetrates," he said, "let us be in no hurry to extend it to the arts and
to the spontaneous enjoyments of life."

For him, scientific method is not absolutely identical with quantitative measurement. In 1876, Gustav Theodor Fechner proceeded
to formulate, in his *Introduction to Aesthetics*, an aesthetic based on
inductive principles and experimental findings, as a result of which
he arrived at a series of aesthetic laws, such as unity in variety and
the correct mean. Munro believed that Fechner's quantitative procedure had failed to touch the central problem of artistic value.

Further, he held that Fechner's approach and that of metaphysics are remote from the aesthetic experience itself.

Art criticism is, he believed, much closer to concrete issues. Even if its "observations" of works of art are mixed with personal feelings, the latter are themselves important to aesthetics. In such criticism, the very lack of systematic method and the clash of standards are facts that a theory of aesthetics can observe and attempt to interpret. This activity was precisely the material of Munro's journal, which was devoted to "a study of recurrences and variations in human behavior toward works of art."[35]

Although much art criticism prior to Munro had displayed no steady aim or consistent method, he discerned two tendencies in his generation: one toward psychology and the other toward the analysis of form. The first involved genetic explanation, studying the work of art in terms of the artist's or critic's personality and "the psychic and environmental mechanisms which determined his product or judgment."[36] The second tendency represented a reaction against the psychological approach and a denial of a link between psychology and aesthetics. Some critics did agree, however, to "a sensible use of psychology" in the analysis of form.

In general, Munro urged that past theories be utilized as suggestions for further investigation. Thus critics should consider Plato's theory of the effects of certain kinds of music on the will and Aristotle's theory of tragedy as catharsis—the one outside of its philosophical context, and the other in relation to present psychoanalytical thought.[37]

In Munro's view, form is not a detachable framework but the distinctive "mode of handling" (Pater's phrase) the subject and materials. Perception can be sharpened through the comparison of forms and media, leading to a systematic classification of aesthetic experiences. Munro cautioned, however, against an emotional attachment to definitions, systems, or philosophies that tend to oversimplify developments in the history of art or criticism. The concentrated study of particular works of art should supplement theories of the "romantic," the "sublime," or the "decadent."[38]

Munro recognized the general aesthetic significance of psychoanalysis even before it became widely accepted:

Its technique of exploring the depths of imaginative life, its
bold attempt to adapt scientific method to study of phenomena
apparently beyond the reach of science, are worthy of respectful
consideration by the aesthetic psychologist.

Munro suggested further that for the understanding of complex
affective responses, general psychology could profit greatly from
literature, which, as Freud well knew, is a vast repository of as yet
uninterpreted data.[39]

Finally, on the question of valuation in art and aesthetics, Munro
would largely replace general standards with intelligent analysis. He
described certain common factors in the experiences of individuals
but noted that "general standards of value are, and always must be,
used by every one, as a means of bringing to bear the past experience
of himself and others."[40]

Certainly, aesthetics cannot develop reliable standards of value by
coercion. Recognizing this, Munro advocated a systematic comparison
of responses to identical forms, thus substituting an experiential
approach for abstract theory.[41] Such a system of applied aesthetics
would not seek to direct the intuitive impulse but would allow it to
find its own patterns of adventure and growth, by dissolving the
routines of mechanical habit.[42]

Curt John Ducasse (1881–1969)

For Ducasse, art was not a quality of things but an activity of man.
Oddly enough, he held that art does not necessarily seek the creation
of beauty, because many works of art are ugly. The creator of an
ugly work of art will insist that he was not concerned with the creation of beauty but with giving objective expression to his feelings.
Beauty itself is variable: some beautiful things are not works of art,
and some works of art are not beautiful.[43]

On the nature of art in relation to language, expression, and feeling, Ducasse examined the work of Eugène Véron, Tolstoi, Jespersen, Grace De Laguna, Max Meyer, Lascelles Abercrombie, and
Croce. According to Véron, he noted, art is essentially language that

originates in cry and gesture. Originally imitative expressions become essentially arbitrary abstract thought and symbols that do not attempt to resemble the objects they represent.

Language is then divided into prose and poetry. The former involves the expression of facts and ideas by means of symbols in which the imitative character is attenuated or lost. In the latter, the goal is the expression of the concrete signs abandoned by prose.

Véron defined art, as "the emotional expression of human personality." Artistic genius is the capacity to find expressive forms for emotions through a kind of immediate intuition "in which reflection and desire intervene only as later additions." Art is therefore much wider in scope than beauty. The beautiful does not contain art; art contains the beautiful, just as it contains the terrible, the sad, the ugly, and the joyous.[44] Véron's aesthetic views, including his understanding of the sincerity of the artist, all reappeared in Tolstoi's *What Is Art?*[45]

Ducasse believed Tolstoi may have been influenced by Véron in much larger measure than the few merely critical references in the book would suggest. Through Tolstoi, however, the doctrines of art as the language of feeling and of art as independent of beauty have exerted their greatest influence. Like Véron, Tolstoi declared that art is essentially the language of feeling. Whereas a man transmits his thoughts by words, he transmits his feeling by means of art.[46] Words, of course, transmit feeling as well as thought.

In his study of language, Ducasse (like Dewey, with whom he often differed) was influenced by Jespersen's *Language, Its Nature, Development and Origin* (1922). According to this work, language did not originate in the endeavor to transmit thought or feeling. It was first used exclamatively as in the baby's cry, not communicatively, forming an utterance from an inner craving of the individual, without thought of any fellow creature.[47]

Dewey denied the name "language" to such utterances; they become language, he said, only in the context of mutual assistance, when communication occurs.[48] For Ducasse, language is an intentional, external expression of an inner psychic state. Art, like the language of feeling, is essentially expression.[49] Here, Ducasse cited

Abercrombie's remark that "the essence of [artistic] activity is communication" and juxtaposed the following quotation in rebuttal: "That transportation of certain acids can be effected only in stoneware carboys is a fact; that stoneware is very convenient for this purpose is possible; but it is nonetheless true that stoneware is not thus defined."[50]

Ducasse found that both Véron and Tolstoi used the term "expression" ambiguously. Tolstoi believed that true art is infectious; counterfeit art fails in this respect. Ducasse said that Véron and Tolstoi were right, however, in conceiving art to be the language of feeling; but he thought Tolstoi wrong in the idea that feeling can actually be transmitted from mind to mind. Véron was right in taking language to consist essentially in expression; but he failed to qualify "expression" so as to exclude expressions of feeling that are not art.[51]

Ducasse urged a cautious reading of Croce, who regarded art as essentially *expression*. When Croce spoke of "expression," he meant the "spiritual aesthetic synthesis." Ducasse felt that the Italian philosopher used the word "expression" irresponsibly in his studies of aesthetics. Thus, for Croce, beauty is the "hedonistic accompaniment" of expression. Aesthetic expression is necessarily expression in images. The physical work of art is nothing but a subsequent mechanical *copy* of the image that the artist has created and glimpsed in imagination.

For Ducasse, Croce's doctrine of the theoretical relation of "expression" to "intuition" was obscure. Why, he asked, use two words when they are really one? Croce is also in error, Ducasse insisted, in his views on the nature of the physical work of art. Illumination comes not in the act of creative expression but only in the subsequent contemplation of its product.[52]

Helen Huss Parkhurst (1887–1959)

Without contradicting other theories on the objectification of inner states in outward expression, Parkhurst suggested that "art is the natural and necessary precipitate of the wild sea of conflicting yet intricately related elements of which [man's] consciousness is composed." Her descriptions of man's inner divisiveness and its resolution in art expressed the unifying vision of her aesthetic:

> If man were not thus divided against himself he could experience not half so deeply the urge to artistic expression. . . . [Such] art as he fashions is the natural and necessary precipitate of the wild sea of conflicting yet intricately related elements of which his consciousness is composed.[53]

Parkhurst thus found a relationship between creativity and the emotional conflicts of human existence. She suggested that "the artist's work proceeds not from a finished imaginative experience to which the work of art corresponds, but from passionate excitement about the subject-matter"—that is, from emotion. Noting that the emotions instigate creativity, she recalled Santayana's view that emotion "is primarily about nothing and much of it remains about nothing to the end . . . objectless emotion chokes the heart with its dull importunity; now it impedes right action, now it feeds and fattens illusion."[54] Because emotion seeks a unifying objective, it may in some cases create its own illusory goals, as in many romantic and mystical works.[55] In other cases it may create great art.

To illustrate her unifying approach, Parkhurst mentioned Guyau's memorable defense of the high emotional values of the combined experience of temperature and taste as shown by a man drinking a glass of milk on a mountain top after a hot and difficult climb. She added:

> This case might seem to be an ambiguous one. For presently he was at the same time feeling upon his skin the cold winds of those upper spaces; feasting his eyes upon a wide and beautiful panorama of country below him; and possibly receiving a rich complex of sensations: sound and lights and sweetness replete with poetic associations. . . . Sensations seldom if ever come singly, and perhaps the capacity of a sensory quality to attract to itself the meaning of a number of scattered perceptions, thus producing an effect of emotional unity, is just the needed proof of its aesthetic significance.[56]

This concept of the aesthetic significance of unity was the foundation of Parkhurst's aesthetic theory.

On the separability of substance and form, Parkhurst wondered whether the meaning of a work of art is not really resident in the human spirit itself rather than in the objective elements of the work. She quoted Santayana:

> [Beauty] cannot be preserved mummified in any external object. . . . The only Venus which is inalienably beautiful is the divine essence revealed to the lover as he gazes, perhaps never to be revealed to another man, nor revealed to himself again.[57]

For Parkhurst, aesthetic form in poetry is a matter of surprise in the midst of regularity, a departure that constitutes a form of irregularity. The poignancy of poetry is secured by the contrasts and oppositions.[58] She accounted for the difference in ideal length between a symphony and a poem by suggesting that "the unity of effect in a poem is strictly dependent upon the maintenance of a single mood, while unity in music is compatible with a crowded procession of moods."[59]

Poetry and prose, said Parkhurst, differ only in degree, especially in blank verse.[60] She concluded that the difference between prose and poetry is the difference between the speaking voice and the singing—qualitatively distinct, yet incapable of exact description. She went on to say:

> There are passages . . . for which the inner silent voice of the reader is undeniably lifted—changed from the soberer quality of plain speech into the voice of singing—with the keen wail of pain, the quickened breathing of terror, the throaty utterance of passion, the moan of desolation, or the breathless cry of sheer ecstasy.[61]

Parkhurst suggested, however, that the rhythms of prose are far more numerous and varied than those of verse, and she observed: "In poetry and prose alike, the purely formal aspect of audible rhythm with its blend of the expected and the unexpected constitutes their common participation in the quality of music."[62] Prose, she noted further, is not entirely free of an appeal to emotion, as in Lincoln's speeches and Schopenhauer's essays. Thus, as Fred Newton Scott has suggested, no content is the exclusive property of poets.[63] Indeed, in the unity that is literature, the varied arts of poetry and prose have much in common.

Discussing the unifying effect of metaphor, Parkhurst noted that through it we may witness

> the impinging of the spatiality of colours upon the space-lessness of odours; the assimilation of the corporeality of solid shape to the incorporeality of sound; the merging of the non-sensuous into the sensuous richness of the palpable and the visible; the transition from the warm immediacy and concreteness of the world of sense to the clear cold air of pure intellection.[64]

Another unifying element in literature is the combination of love and death as a recurring theme:

> The exceeding beauty that we discover in the vanishing qualities of the world is, beyond question, intensified by our perception of its omen of our own brief futility. . . . It is quite impossible to tell how seriously impaired might be our appreciation of what now seems to us an infinitely haunting melody, an ecstatic lyric, or a solemn building or carving, if the conflict between craving for permanence and unceasing subjection to the unenduring were removed altogether from our experience.[65]

Turning from thematic to technical unity in the play and the novel, Parkhurst pointed out that Ibsen was scrupulous in observing the Aristotelian unities of time, place, and action, which, however, restricted his choice of plots. She noted that, in art, extraneous detail must always be avoided. The goal of the artist is cohesiveness in the absorption of the arhythmic with the rhythmic, of detail in a totality of organization.[66]

Thus, for Parkhurst, all art partakes of the unifying quality of metaphor: "The conceiving of a character, or the development of a plot, thus reduces to the contriving of effects describable in no better terms than those of metaphor—that strange alchemy by which the essence of one order is blended with the essence of another."[67] For Parkhurst, as for the other writers discussed in this chapter, aesthetics is indeed a unifying vision.

ART AND EXPERIENCE: JOHN DEWEY (1859-1952)

Dewey set the tone of his experiential approach to aesthetics in his early article "The New Psychology" (1884). Here he criticized the old psychologists, who pruned experience "till it presented a trimmed tameness which would shock none of their laws" and "preyed upon its vitality till it would go into the coffin of their abstractions." The new psychology believed "that truth, that reality, not necessary beliefs about reality, is given in the living experience of the soul's development."[1]

THE AESTHETIC EXPERIENCE

The essence of the aesthetic experience was described in the section "Aesthetic Feeling" in Dewey's first book, *Psychology* (1887). The most general property of beauty, he wrote, is harmony, or variety in unity. It is "the feeling of the agreement of some experience with the ideal nature of the self." Related to harmony are the ideas of adaptation and economy, which occur when the means in an aesthetic experience are accurately fitted to the end.[2]

Feeling and Art

For Dewey, feeling was something more than passive enjoyment of beauty; it was the impetus, or spring, to creative activity in the form of the fine arts: "As the intellectual feelings, as springs to action, take the form of wonder, so the aesthetic feelings take the form of *admiration*. Admiration is love of beauty, as wonder is love of knowledge."[3] The fine arts, then, which include poetry in its various forms, are attempts to satisfy the fundamental emotional impulses of mankind.

In the development of these art forms, therefore, mere formulas should not, said Dewey, replace the living reality of experience based on feeling:

> Every attempt to set up the ideal as *ultimate* has two evil effects . . . it stifles the efforts of the individual, and substitutes for . . . spontaneous freedom of action which is the essence of aesthetic production a rigid obedience to externally imposed rules. . . . It fossilizes the ideal into cut-and-dried formulae . . . [and] becomes a burdensome command to produce nothing new.[4]

In *Experience and Nature* (1926) Dewey elaborated this view. For him, "intellectual piety toward experience" was a precondition for freedom. Consciousness itself, when not dull and torpid, is a product of the imagination:

> Cosmogonies are mythological, not because savages indulge in defective scientific explanations, but because objects of imagination are consummatory in the degree in which they exuberantly escape from the pressure of natural surroundings. . . . The congenial is the first form of the consistent.[5]

Delight in free experience results from "the esthetic character of logical coherence rather than its tested coherence with fact."[6]

Thus, for Dewey, every genuine work of art transforms man's

vision of himself and of his relationship to the world, constituting, in Arnold's phrase, a criticism of life in the highest sense: "For art fixes those standards of enjoyment and appreciation with which other things are compared; it selects the objects of future desires; it stimulates effort."

In a community, art, more than anything else, determines the direction of ideas and supplies the meanings in terms of which life is esteemed and criticized.[7] Through art man overcomes the apparent hostility of nature, which Josiah Royce described when he observed: "The spirit is dissatisfied with the mathematical order and feels unfriendliness among the eternities."[8] As opposed to these external threats, the inner experience of beauty becomes a constant adventure in readjustment that renews and refreshes the vision.

The Inner Life

The escape into one's inner life as a road to freedom was not original with modern man. Savages, the oppressed, and children took that path, said Dewey, "long before it was formulated in philosophical romanticism." The conscious awareness of this need, however, added a new dimension to modern experience, producing new forms of art as well as new theories of aesthetics, as Dewey showed in his discussion of Santayana:

> Mr. Santayana is a thinker whose intent and basis are at one with classical thought. But if we note the importance assumed in his thinking by the "inward landscape," there is before us a measure of the pervasive influence of the kind of experience that was seized upon by Romanticism as the exclusive truth of experience."[9]

In this passage, Dewey warned against an excessively individualistic approach to experience:

> Romanticism has made the best and the worst of the discovery of the private and uncommunicable. . . . [It] has created

a vast and somnambulic egotism out of the fact of subjectivity. For every existence in addition to its qualitative and intrinsic boundaries has affinities and active outreachings for connection and intimate union. It is an energy of attraction, expansion and supplementation. . . . Sociability, communication are just as immediate traits of the concrete individual as the privacy of the closet of consciousness.

A dualism ensues from the ambiguous nature of the self: man is both an individual and a social being.[10] Both elements of man's nature motivate his creation of art through "the tang of overt conflict and the impact of harsh conditions." In the process of creation, the self overcomes "external necessities by incorporating them in an individual vision and expression."[11]

The duality inherent in the creation of art leads inevitably, said Dewey, to the strife between classic and romantic. Classicism represents embodied objective order; romanticism, the freshness and spontaneity that arise from individuality. Romantic art is marked by desire for the strange and the unusual, the exotic; it attempts to incorporate the strange into the ordinary, as Carlyle suggested: "[In art] the infinite is made to blend with the finite; to stand visible and as it were attainable there."[12]

Even the "classic," when it was first produced, bore the marks of adventure and experiment:

> This fact is ignored by classicists in their protest against romantics who undertake the development of new values, often without possessing means for their creation. That which is now classic is so because of completion of adventure, not because of its absence. The one who perceives and enjoys esthetically always has the sense of adventure in reading any classic that Keats had in reading Chapman's "Homer."[13]

Dewey, moreover, found a similarity between the venturesomeness of the poet's imagination and the experimental quest of the scientist or philosopher. Poets and scientists alike are "full of many wonders of the spheres." Thus, Dewey concluded, inclusiveness is the mark of the true aesthetic experience:

Not absence of desire and thought but their thorough incorporation into perceptual experience characterizes esthetic
experience, in its distinction from experiences that are especially "intellectual" and "practical."

He points to the experience of reading Keats's "The Eve of Saint
Agnes," in which thought is active but not apart from other elements.
The experience is marked "by a greater inclusiveness of all psychological factors than occurs in ordinary experiences. . . . How can
experience that is rich as well as unified be reached by a process
of exclusion?"[14]

The Unity of Art

For Dewey, contemplation was "a name for the perception of significant characters, plus an emphatic allusion to an accompanying
esthetic emotion."[15] What part did this emotion play in the development of knowledge? Modern psychology certainly recognized the
emotional aura that accompanies all knowing, although the mere
enjoyment of an idea does not in itself validate the idea as verifiable
knowledge.

If, with the Greeks, we regard knowledge as contemplation rather
than as a productive art, then art will be secondary to the aesthetic,
"creation" will be secondary to "taste," and the scientist will assume
a lower rank than the dilettante. "But," said Dewey,

. . . if modern tendencies are justified in putting art and
creation first . . . [it] would then be seen that science is an art,
that art is practice, and that the only distinction worth drawing
is not between practice and theory, but between those modes
of practice that are not intelligent, not inherently and immediately enjoyable, and those which are full of enjoyed meanings.

Once this is seen, there "would disappear the separations that
trouble present thinking: division of everything into nature *and*
experience, of experience into practice *and* theory, art *and* science,—
useful [art] *and* fine, menial *and* free." Here again aesthetics appears

as a unifying vision, eliminating, among other dualities, the age-old imagined conflict between art and science.[16]

Art, as an active productive process, was defined by Dewey as a combination of two perceptions, the aesthetic and the operative: "In complete art, appreciation follows the object and moves with it to its completion. . . . Art, free from subjection to any 'ism,' has movement, creation, as well as order, finality."[17] Those who would make art wholly esoteric are therefore confronted by Dewey with two alternatives: either art is a continuation of natural tendencies, or it is a peculiar addition to the nature of something springing exclusively from within man. If it is a continuation of natural tendencies, "aesthetic appreciation is of the same nature as enjoyment of any object that is consummatory [that is, completed with an end in view]. It is the outcome of a skilled and intelligent art of dealing with natural things for the sake of intensifying, purifying, prolonging and deepening the satisfactions which they spontaneously afford." If art is a peculiar addition, it has an occult, esoteric character; and those critics who adhere to this isolation of art hold that it is the expression of the emotions and that "subject-matter is of no significance except as material through which emotion is expressed." For them, true art is the "reduction of subject-matter to a mere medium of emotion."[18]

Dewey argued, however, that emotion is a response to an objective situation and indicates a more or less excited participation in some scene of nature or life. The art process is a spontaneous emotional response to a situation occurring without any reference to art, "and without 'esthetic' quality save in the sense in which all immediate enjoyment and suffering is esthetic."[19]

Dewey maintained that the term "significant form" denoted a selection for the sake of emphasis, purity, and subtlety. An artist may select forms discriminatingly or by "a kind of sympathetic vibration." Some contemporary art, Dewey believed, was at its worst, "scientific" rather than artistic and represented "technical exercises, sterile and of a new kind of pedantry." At its best, it assisted "in ushering in new modes of art by education of the organ of perception in new modes of consummatory objects; they enlarge and enrich the world of human vision."[20]

THE CONTINUITY OF EXPERIENCE

In *Art as Experience* (1934), Dewey insisted that it is the task of the philosopher of the fine arts "to restore continuity between the refined and intensified forms of experience that are works of art and the everyday events, doings, and sufferings that are universally recognized to constitute experience."[21] He defined experience as "the result, the sign, and the reward of that interaction of organism and environment which, when it is carried to the full, is a transformation of interaction into participation and communication." Any oppositions of mind and body in this participation are "marks of contraction and withdrawal." Thus, "art is . . . prefigured in the very processes of living."

Intellectual experience cannot be sharply marked off from the aesthetic. Intellectual experience, if it is to be complete, must include aesthetic elements. Thus the intellectual experience itself "has a satisfying emotional quality because it possesses internal integration and fulfillment reached through ordered and organized movement."[22] Dewey asserted, moreover, that the thought of the artist is as profound as that of the scientific inquirer:

> To think effectively in terms of relations of qualities is as severe a demand upon thought as to think in terms of symbols, verbal and mathematical. Indeed, since words are easily manipulated in mechanical ways, the production of a work of genuine art probably demands more intelligence than does most of the so-called thinking that goes on among those who pride themselves on being intellectuals.

Clearly, then, "the esthetic is no intruder in experience from without, whether by way of idle luxury or transcendental ideality—it is the clarified and intensified development of traits that belong to every normally complete experience."[23]

On Creativity

The process of creativity involves expression, which arises from inner agitation and impulsion. In this process, said Dewey, the poet and the novelist have an immense advantage over an expert psychologist in dealing with emotions. Instead of describing the sensation in intellectual and symbolic terms, "the artist 'does the deed that breeds' the emotion. . . . In the development of an expressive act, the emotion operates like a magnet drawing to itself appropriate material."

This turmoil, if it is to produce more than mere exclamation, must be shaped and embodied in an artistic form. Even lyrical expression, which appears to be unpremeditated, is controlled material. Thus spontaneity, Dewey said, is actually the result of long periods of activity, or else it is so empty as not to be an act of expression at all.[24]

Here Dewey was clearly influenced by William James's observations in *The Varieties of Religious Experience*:

> A man's conscious wit and will are aiming at something only dimly and inaccurately imagined. Yet all the while the forces of mere organic ripening within him are going on to their own prefigured result, and his conscious strainings are letting loose subconscious allies behind the scenes which in their way work toward rearrangement, and the rearrangement toward which all these deeper forces tend is pretty surely definite, and definitely different from what he consciously conceives and determines.[25]

This, Dewey commented, is true not only of artists but of scientists who "do not operate by conscious wit and will to anything like the extent popularly supposed." Both scientists and artists engage in "emotionalized thinking." Artists

> . . . have for their subject-matter the qualities of things of direct experience; "intellectual" inquirers deal with these qualities at one remove, through the medium of symbols that stand for qualities but are not significant to their immediate presence. The ultimate difference is enormous as far as the technique of

thought and emotion are concerned. But there is no difference as far as dependence on emotionalized ideas and subconscious maturing are concerned.[26]

Artistic Form

Having emphasized the importance of formal elements as controlling factors in creativity, Dewey rejected the concept of the separation of substance and form. Such a dichotomy, he said, serves only to divide "the live creature" from its environment. Indeed, he notes that form in one context is substance in another or even in the same work of art.[27]

Rhythm, an aspect of form in art, derives from the very relationship of man to nature:

> [The] participation of man in nature's rhythms, a partnership much more intimate than is any observation of them for purposes of knowledge, induced him to impose rhythm in changes where they did not appear. The apportioned reed, the stretched string and taut skin rendered the measures of action conscious through song and dance. . . . The formative arts that shaped things of use were wedded to the rhythms of voice and the self-contained movements of the body, and out of the union technical arts gained the quality of fine art. Then the apprehended rhythms of nature were employed to introduce evident order into some phase of the confused observations and images of mankind. Man no longer conformed his activities of necessity to the rhythmic changes of nature's cycles, but used those which necessity forced upon him to celebrate his relations to nature as if she had conferred upon him the freedom of her realm.[28]

Rhythm, a universal element of existence, underlies all the arts. It arises from a resistance to the immediate expression of emotion, creating a tension that in turn produces periodic accumulation and release:

> Esthetic recurrence . . . is vital, physiological, functional. . . . [Each] recurrence is novel as well as a reminder. In satisfying

an aroused expectancy, it also institutes a new longing, incites
a fresh curiosity, establishes a changed suspense.

This process of recurrence is the mainspring of artistic and scientific creativity. It is the source of energy that leads to discovery and
testing, proof and exploration, closure and awakening.[29] As a unifying force, emotional energy "evokes, assembles, accepts, and rejects
memories, images, observations, and works them into a whole toned
throughout by the same emotional feeling. Thereby is presented an
object that is unified and distinguished throughout."

In this connection, Dewey supported his own ideas by quoting
Santayana:

> Perceptions do not remain in the mind, as would be sug-
> gested by the trite simile of the seal and the wax, passive and
> changeless, until time wears off their rough edges and makes
> them fade. No, perceptions fall into the brain rather as seeds
> into a furrowed field or even as sparks into a keg of gunpowder.
> Each image breeds a hundred more, sometimes slowly and sub-
> terraneously, sometimes (as when a passionate train is started)
> with a sudden burst of fancy.[30]

In a further elaboration of the relationship between rhythm and
creativity, Dewey cited Schiller's description of the peculiar musical
mood, or *Stimmung*, that precedes the creation of a poem. This mood
is marked by a "penetrating quality," which unifies discrete perceptions into an organic whole, leaving, however, an aura of mystery,
which Poe described as "a suggestive indefiniteness of vague and
therefore spiritual effect."[31]

In verse, said Dewey, meter acts as a rhythmic expression of
emotional energy to produce a unified sensation or mood. Again, the
immediate expression of emotion encounters resistance, resulting in
the development of rhythmic form. On this point, Dewey cited
Coleridge, who traced the origin of meter "to the balance in the mind
effected by that spontaneous effort which strives to hold in check
the workings of passion." Dewey added Coleridge's remark that every

work of art must have about it something not understood to obtain its full effect.[32]

The Nature of Criticism

Dewey's ideas on creativity and form provided the basis of his approach to criticism. Like Spingarn, he believed that the critic must share the experience of the artist:

> We lay hold of the full import of a work of art only as we go through in our own vital processes the processes the artist went through in producing the work. It is the critic's privilege to share in the promotion of this active process. His condemnation is that he so often arrests it.[33]

Thus equipped, the critic will be able to carry on his most important function—expanding the experience of the observer of art.

The absence of such an approach to criticism led, Dewey believed, to the oversimplification that often reduced the whole work of art to one isolated element, as in much psychoanalytic criticism. Another fallacy was the failure to recognize that art has its own ideas—that the artist does not simply use preexisting "acceptable" material, which he renders palatable by emotional or imaginative coloration.[34] Both failures resulted from a critical failure of empathy in regard to the unique experience of the artist.

Dewey's holistic approach to experience, which emphasized the complexity of the *whole* over the mere sum of the parts, led him to side with Wordsworth on the relationship of science and art:

> If the labours of men of science should ever create any material revolution, direct or indirect, in our condition and in the impressions which we habitually receive, the Poet will sleep then no more than at present . . . he will be at their side, carrying sensation into the midst of the objects of science itself.

Dewey added: "But poetry will not on that account be a popularization of science, nor will its characteristic values be those of science."[35]

Although Dewey's remark indicated a certain continuing belief in the duality of science and art, he asserted that both depend on the imagination for their creativity and that both may contribute to an expansion of human experience:

> The arts of science [note the phrase], of politics, of history, and of painting and poetry all have finally the same *material*: that which is constituted by the interaction of the live creature with his surroundings. They differ in the media by which they convey and express this material, not in the material itself.

He observed, therefore, that science and art are intimately related: "Science uses the medium that is adapted to the purpose of control and prediction, of increase of power; it is an art. Under particular conditions, its matter may also be esthetic."[36]

THE QUALITY OF LIFE

Dewey's approach to literary criticism was based on the belief that art could enhance life through its particular relation to experience: "Art is the quality that permeates an experience; it is not, save by a figure of speech, the experience itself." In the process of reorganizing past experience in the light of present knowledge, the artist attempts to effect an imaginative union of past and present,[37] seeking thereby to heighten the quality of experience. In this process, "the sense of relation between nature and man in some form has always been the actuating spirit of art."[38]

Art thus becomes a re-creative force derived from works of the imagination through conflict and resistance: "Friction is as necessary to generate esthetic energy as it is to supply the energy that drives machinery." The widening of experience through imaginative re-creation would lead, Dewey suggested, to increasingly meaningful leisure time and to the enrichment of the quality of life in society as a whole.[39]

Dewey and the Romantics

With his expansive philosophy of art, Dewey recalls the Romantic poets, whose ideas on the expansion of experience were propounded in Shelley's "Defence of Poetry":

> Poetry . . . is at once the center and circumference of all knowledge; it is that which comprehends all science and to which all science must be referred. . . . Poetry awakens and enlarges the mind by rendering it the receptacle of a thousand unapprehended combinations of thought.

Following this view, Dewey observed that in both the production and enjoyment of works of art, knowledge is transformed: "it becomes something more than knowledge because it is merged with intellectual elements from an experience worth while as an experience."[40] He also noted with approval Shelley's remark on the imagination as "the great instrument of moral good," which makes possible the expansion of experience and "the identification of ourselves with the beautiful which exists in thought, action, or person, not our own."[41]

Similarly suggestive views in the works of Keats particularly impressed Dewey, as when Keats observed that the artist may look " 'pon the Sun, the Moon, the Stars, and the Earth and its contents as material to form greater things, that is ethereal things—greater things than the Creator himself made." Dewey used the phrase "ethereal things" as the title of a chapter in *Art and Experience* "to designate the meanings and values that many philosophers and some critics suppose are inaccessible to sense, because of their spiritual, eternal, and universal characters—thus exemplifying the common dualism of nature and spirit."

Keats's identification of the artist's attitude with the live creature was especially important for Dewey. Both man and the hawk, said Keats, engage in movements toward a goal: "There may be reasonings, but when they take an instinctive form, like that of animal forms and movements, they are poetry, they are fine; they have grace."[42] According to Dewey, "reasonings" have an origin like that of the movements of a wild creature toward its goal: "they may become spontaneous, 'instinctive,' and when they become instinctive are sensuous and immediate, poetic."

Dewey noted further that no "reasoning" as reasoning, that is,

> . . . as excluding imagination and sense, can reach truth. Even "the greatest philosopher" exercises an animal-like preference to guide his thinking to its conclusions. He selects and puts aside as his imaginative sentiments move. "Reason" at its height cannot attain complete grasp and a self-contained assurance. It must fall back upon imagination—upon the embodiment of ideas in emotionally charged sense.[43]

Here Keats and Dewey were clearly aligned in their views on the impact of experience.

Dewey did not, of course, overlook the famous lines, "Beauty is truth; truth beauty—that is all/Ye know on earth, and all ye need to know" and, in conjunction with this, Keats's prose statement, "What the imagination seizes as beauty must be truth." Dewey suggested that "truth" as used by Keats denoted the wisdom by which men live; it was independent of positive statement. The critical words were "on earth," where men's "irritable reaching after fact and reason" confuses and distorts existence instead of illuminating it. In Dewey's view, the philosophy of Keats, like that of Shakespeare, entails an acceptance of life and experience in all its uncertainty, mystery and doubt, a wandering "in faery lands forlorn."[44]

The enrichment of experience made possible by such a philosophy was further suggested for Dewey by Keats's observations on the nature of the poetic imagination:

> As to the poetical character itself . . . it is not itself. It is everything and nothing—it enjoys light and shade: it lives in gusto, be it fair or foul, high or low, rich or poor, mean or elevated. . . . It does not harm from its relish for the dark side of things, any more than from its taste for the bright one.

. . . A poet is the most unpoetical of anything in existence, because he has no identity—he is continually in and for, and filling some other body.[45]

The ethical, and indeed the sociological implications of the free play of this imaginative faculty were clearly understood by Keats:

> By every germ of spirit sucking the sap from mold etherial, every human being might become great, and Humanity instead of being a wide heath of furze and briars with here and there a remote Pine or Oak, would become a grand democracy of Forest Trees![46]

From Wordsworth Dewey derived support for his idea that poetic art does not merely lead to but actually constitutes an experience, as in the poet's vivid poetic expression of Tintern Abbey. After discussing the integration of form and matter in the poet's work, Dewey pointed to Wordsworth's own record of his "poetic history" and his "consciousness of the infinite variety of natural appearance" —his development from the conventional (and its language) to a more complete perceptiveness, to an experience that, as Dewey said, corresponded more subtly and sensitively to the rhythm of natural change (and its language) and to an ever-deepening enrichment of experience.[47]

Also relevant to Dewey's philosophy was Coleridge's term "esemplastic," which Coleridge used to characterize the process of imagination in art. Dewey interpreted this process as a "welding together of all elements, no matter how diverse in ordinary experience, into a new and completely unified experience." Coleridge's further distinction between imagination and fancy had little attraction for Dewey, who favored the poet's definition of imagination in its synthesizing rather than in its analytic aspects.[48]

Shelley's influence on Browning paralleled his influence on Dewey, as shown in Browning's essay on Shelley. Browning noted that when the average person ("the general eye") has absorbed all he can through his senses, the poet, with his loftier vision, will lift his fellows, "with their half-apprehensions, to his own sphere."[49] Those who follow, however, will merely subsist on "food swallowed long ago by a supply of fresh and living swaths." The world must then await the appearance of a new poet, who will get

> . . . at new substance by breaking up the assumed wholes into parts of independent and unclassed value, careless of the unknown laws for recombining them (it will be the business of yet another poet to suggest these hereafter), prodigal of objects for men's outer and not inner sight, shaping for their uses a new and different creation from the last, which it displaces by the right of life over death.

Thus, as Dewey observed, "Art has been the means of keeping alive the sense of purposes that outrun evidence and of meanings that transcend indurated habit."[50]

Santayana's influence on Dewey's ethical views was suggested by Dewey's citation of the statement, "Value lies in meaning, not in substance: *in the ideal which things approach*, not in the energy which they embody" (Dewey's emphasis).[51] Dewey, however, refuted Santayana's complaint that Shakespeare lacked a philosophical system, replying:

> An artist may be instinctively repelled by the constraint imposed by acceptance of any system. If the important thing is [as Santayana said] "not this or that system but some system," why not accept, with Shakespeare, the free and varied system of nature itself?[52]

Shakespeare's art was faithful to the many potentialities of nature rather than to any fixed philosophy. It thus constituted a clear model for Dewey's philosophy of experience.

Qualitative Thought

Further evidence of Dewey's concern with the quality of life may be found in his essay "Qualitative Thought."[53] Noting that "the world in which we immediately live . . . is pre-eminently a qualitative world," he observed that science is concerned with relations, not with qualities. A persistent logical problem involves the relation between two types of propositions, one referring to objects of physical science and the other to qualitative objects.

The terms "feeling" and "felt" are the names for a *relation* of quality. Feeling is the first stage in the development of explicit distinctions. Reflection and rational elaboration spring from and make explicit a prior intuition. Dewey thus favored Bergson's contention that intuition precedes and penetrates more deeply than conception. Thought is the transformation of an intuition, which "signifies the realization of a pervasive quality such that it regulates the determination of relevant distinctions."

Such ejaculatory judgments as "Good," "Oh," "Yes," "No" supply perhaps the simplest example of qualitative thought in its purity: "Language fails not because thought fails, but because no verbal symbols can do justice to the fullness and richness of thought." The logic of the artist is the logic of qualitative thinking:

> Without an independent qualitative apprehension, the characteristics of a work of art can be translated into explicit harmonies . . . only in a way which substitutes mechanical formulae for esthetic quality. The value of any such translation in esthetic criticism is measured, moreover, by the extent to which the propositional statements return to effect a heightening and deepening of a qualitative apprehension. Otherwise, esthetic appreciation is replaced by judgment of isolated technique. . . . *Construction that is artistic is as much a case of genuine thought as that expressed in scientific and philosophical matters*, and so is all genuine esthetic appreciation of art, since the latter must in some way, to be vital, retrace the course of the creative process.[54]

AESTHETIC ANALYSIS AND THE PHILOSOPHIC DIMENSION OF CRITICISM

David W. Prall (1886–1940)

Prall's major work, *Aesthetic Analysis* (1936), was clearly indebted to Dewey, especially in its emphasis on the qualitative presentation of the world. For Prall, consciousness was awareness of felt qualitative content. The movement from mere qualitative surface to active participation in discrimination of quality and the realization of the character of things constitutes the aesthetic aspect of experience. No experience is totally aesthetic or, for that matter, totally anaesthetic.

Like Dewey, Prall believed that men are all self-preserving nodes in the intrinsic and infinite matrix of natural flux. They experience the aesthetic the moment they are not totally anaesthetized.[1] Prall also shared Dewey's belief that the aesthetic is differentiated by the same elements that mark off a particular experience from experience in general.

The concrete object of aesthetic perception, said Prall, is the determinate and emotionally intuited content. In an aesthetic experience, the observer finds the world presented immediately through his senses, which function only as instrumentalities of the integrated organism in a response involving emotional tone. Thus, for Prall, aesthetics is neither physics, nor psychology, nor physiology. It is not process at all: it is color and sound, not physical wave motions; it is attracting, exciting quality; deep rich color, moving, emotional sound, not nerve currents or accelerated breathing or pulse.[2] If qualities have relations, then qualitative wholes may be amenable to scientific treatment, which deals with relations and abstract structures.[3]

The concrete apprehension of an aesthetic object is in its very nature *feeling*. This feeling, however, is aesthetic only if it is directed exclusively to the object, not to some irrelevance suggested by some incidental aspect of it. Contemplation that does not attend and discriminate is either not aesthetic contemplation at all, or it is the aesthetic contemplation of something else—bodily states instead of the presented object.[4]

Aesthetic analysis is not itself aesthetic appreciation. Aesthetics is a branch of knowledge; it is knowledge of qualities in their immediacy and their immediately grasped relations, directly apprehended in sensuous structures. Although aesthetics will not teach men how to write poetry (or, I might add, how to make bread), it may teach them something about the nature of their enjoyment of it.[5] The aesthetic is the element that is present in the medium apprehended. It depends, of course, on immediate experience, not simply on vague awareness.[6]

All works of art are concretely experienced presentations of sensory-imaginal content. In poetry, for instance, language expresses feeling or emotion as the qualitative character of imagined content. Feeling simply is concrete direct experience. The sensuous presentations of art directly embody feeling. Qualitative terms are simply the names for the way things feel. Feelings thus consist of sensuously qualified content.[7]

An aesthetic object that is at all absorbing presents complexity that must yet be sufficiently simple to be apprehended as a qualitative unity. Technical aesthetic perception helps to apprehend qualitative character and to discriminate the technical and aesthetic constituents of the effect. Following Dewey, Prall said that, with the aim of art being expression, art is necessarily the nearest approach possible to anything like adequate communication.[8]

Analysis accomplishes its purpose in aesthetics only when all that it describes as elements and patterns are seen to be integrated in the affective quality or feeling that is the unitary aesthetic character of the given work of art analyzed. The adequate critic, Prall believed, needs full acquaintance with the traditional technical material as well as with all the historically developed aesthetic forms and instrumentalities. He also needs flexibility to enable him to go beyond the object immediately before him.[9]

Prall considered the qualitative element in both art and science. In art, the qualitative has taken a marked intrinsic significance for human beings. According to him, it is also the starting point in science; logic itself begins in qualitative distinctions. The final goal of natural science, however, is not acquaintance with qualities and their directly felt relations and structures, but with the conditions of their occurrence, their dynamic relations, and the control of the processes that involve them.

In aesthetics, on the other hand, one seeks a direct acquaintance with content and structure as actually presented through sense. Such a general acquaintance makes possible a full grasp of the character of particular works of art as well as of the aesthetic aspects of nature.[10]

Aesthetics itself is theory, not appreciative aesthetic experience. Aesthetics has not reached the point where a fully adequate analysis of a whole concrete experience can be made out, partly because it has not been seriously cultivated and also partly because such an analysis would involve all the findings of all the sciences—a complete knowledge of the organic conditions of the response and a complete knowledge of all that may be the subject of a response, whether inside or outside the organism. Given these limits of aesthetic analysis, it is completely valid as scientific knowledge.[11]

Aesthetics is primarily a theory of the nature of the arts, the total subject matter of which is the qualitative nature of things directly presented through sensory-affective organic functioning. Men demand structure composed of discriminable constituents in apprehended relations. The qualitative sensory-affective surface of the world generates interest and this, in one way or another, amounts to the demand for novelty. Art is expressive, not merely representative. Even strictly aesthetic analysis cannot avoid the technical aspects of the arts.[12]

Prall said relatively little about literary aesthetics. He mentioned pitch variation in both music and verse, and showed that rhythm is not divorced from sense. The meaning of words, he said, is to be found only in concrete, nonverbal content. Thus an indirect symbolic medium like language may function aesthetically in two ways:

(1) Words may be not heard but heard *through*, presenting not themselves but their meanings. When language provides content by such transparent functioning, this content is not verbal at all, but fully imaginal and emotional, as suggested by Sapir's remark: "Gentlemen, words are only words."

(2) Words may be so placed and so integrated in specific contexts that a reader finds them in rhythm and skillful connotation—which again is not verbal but imaginal. Words thus used suggest feelings that do not arise from the meanings of separate words, phrases, and sentences, but from presented feeling—a content actually received by way of the sounds of words, the total meaning determined both by perceived sounds and by presented imaginal content.[13]

Stephen Coburn Pepper (1891–   )

Pepper, in his *Aesthetic Quality: A Contextualistic Theory of Beauty* (1937),[14] expressed his indebtedness to William James, Prall, and Dewey, among others.[15] He maintained that "the full justification of an aesthetic theory extends far beyond the bounds of the aesthetic field. . . . It depends . . . on a philosophy." Citing the work of I. A. Richards as a good example of the eclectic method, Pepper remarked that, like a book of proverbs, it was full of wisdom, but also of half-truths, and consequently of half-falsehoods, and of implicit and even explicit contradictions. It lacked, in an eminent degree, objectivity.

Pepper charged that all the mechanistic features arbitrarily selected by Richards can be found implicitly, if not explicitly, in Santayana's

The Sense of Beauty. The idealistic features in Bernard Bosanquet's *Three Lectures in Aesthetics* and the work of Santayana and Dewey (*Art as Experience*) carry one along by a sort of momentum into the universe of facts with which they deal. This, said Pepper, cannot be said of Richards's book.[16]

Although Pepper was committed to a contextualistic interpretation, he did not believe that it represented "the only justifiable or profitable point of view." He stated outright: "I have no desire to make the contextualistic theory appear to conquer all others . . . for a submergence of the other good theories would be very unhealthy both in theory and in criticism." Furthermore, two theories equally good may compensate for each other's possible omissions or distortions.[17]

The objectivity of science, said Pepper, is disintegration; that of fine art, integration. Science seeks to control its results by a maximum elimination of outlying effects, while fine art seeks to control its results by a maximum encompassing of outlying effects:

> *Fine art conscripts elements to function in the mutual determination of one another*, having no faith in the self-determination of an element. For there is nothing in art so variable as an isolated element such as a single visual line, a single color, a single word. *But place any of these in a skillfully framed context and its character becomes as specific as anything in the world* [italics added].[18]

Here, then, is the central idea of contextualism.

For Pepper, the aesthetic encompasses the quality of events. The quality can be understood only through intuition, so that aesthetics depends on intuited qualities. Intuition is centripetal. The aesthetic experience, arising from the vivid sense of the quality of an event, is no mere emotional superfluity or cosmic luxury. On the contrary, Pepper insisted, it is the most illuminating of activities. It gives a direct insight into the nature of the world and the substance of reality—it realizes events: "*To feel the quality of an event is to feel the actual working part of the world process* [italics added]. . . . It is to stop swimming and rest upon a wave, and feel the cosmic currents, and the movement of the world swell." This metaphor recalls Bergson's use of analogies to water.

Pepper continued:

> Art is thus fully as cognitive, fully as knowing as science,
> so that contextualists are fond of calling the intuition of quality
> a *realization*. If scientific, analytical knowledge has scope, it
> nevertheless lacks intimacy and realization. The artist like the
> scientist is a man whose function it is to lead to a better knowl-
> edge of nature—not, however, by showing us how to control
> her, but how to realize her.[19]

Pepper was reminiscent of Bergson when he said that a given
event is a section of continuous duration or temporal flow, even
though the very act of naming it seems to stop it and freeze it.
Quality is continually changing. A line is a process, as is an area
of color, or a combination of a line and color.

Pepper called processes *strands* and described a set of interrelated
strands as a *texture*. A strand is a single discriminated process; a
texture is a connected pattern of strands. But a strand may reveal
itself to be a texture in its own right composed of still finer strands.
Similarly, a texture may assume the function of a strand in a still
larger texture. The analysis of a texture is, accordingly, the singling
out and the following out of its strands, while the intuition of a
texture is the realization of its fused quality.[20]

Thus, for Pepper, analysis and intuition were interrelated. No
texture exists in isolation; it has connections through its strands in all
directions. Some of these connections are essential to a full understanding of its analytical nature. These connections, said Pepper, are
mainly inferential and not discoverable by direct discrimination of
the details of a given event.[21]

Pepper asserted that the perceived character of a work of art is
just as much a revelation of oneself as it is of the work. In this sense,
all qualities are relative, as is all aesthetic experience. The qualities
represent a cooperative result of an interaction between a personal
and an impersonal continuous texture. An individual work of art
is a progressive coupling of many single perceptions.[22]

Pepper described a *relationship quality* that accounts for the fusion
of various perceptions in one *aesthetic quality* or experience. He cited
two important types of relationship quality: one discloses similarity;

the other, individuality. Similarity consists in two or more textures having strands that converge, or that tend to converge, on another texture or on a strand of another texture, which is said to be common to the first two textures. Similarity spreads a thin quality wide; if belabored, it tends rather quickly to reduce the qualitativeness of events. Its use is consequently mainly analytical, and it enters the aesthetic field only in a somewhat subsidiary way.[23]

The relationship quality of individuality represents the central principle of massive aesthetic experience. It involves the sense that cables of strands carry over from one event into another and even when spread apart can be reassembled and spun again. This carry-over is made possible by the continuity and flow of events.

The underlying ground for relationship quality is clearly the continuous physical textures of the body.[24] The event quality of each successive perception becomes gradually enriched in a process called *funding*. A great work of art has no limits to this enrichment.[25] Thus *quality is the immediate intuited aspect of an event. The aesthetic field is that of intuited quality. Beauty is enhanced quality.*[26] Analysis, however, seems to drain events of quality: "A moment's thought is passion's passing bell."[27]

Believing that in essence Croce's theory calls for the elimination of conflict, analysis, and regularity, Pepper reacted against it because he held that the greatest enhancement of quality is not obtained this way. Paradoxically, it is obtained through the incorporation in art of activities hostile to quality.[28] In aesthetic practice, the three deadening activities—analysis, conflict, regularity—reduce to two—conflict and organization—because regularity is by and large the method of organization, and analysis consists of simply rendering explicit the elements of the method.

Both conflict and organization, if properly controlled, contribute directly to the increase of quality, the one by vivifying the quality of occurrence, the other by extending it. These two ways of increasing beauty are, moreover, somewhat antithetical, because intensity of quality tends to reduce extent, and extension tends to reduce intensity. The artist must find that nice adjustment between these opposing tendencies which produces the maximum of quality with the available materials.[29]

Two factors lead to the intensification of quality: novelty and conflict. Novelty is the tearing off of habit.[30] Men who have grown old
and stiff in habits have to fabricate materials that children find
everywhere with no effort. Pepper believed that everyone could con-
firm in his own memory Wordsworth's recollections:

> There was a time when meadow, grove and stream,
>   The earth and every common sight to me did seem
> Apparell'd in celestial light,
>   The glory and the freshness of a dream. . . .
>   But yet I know, where'er I go,
> That there hath passed away the glory from the earth.[31]

Pepper also quoted a passage from Romain Rolland's *Jean Christophe* in which Jean is fascinated by the variety and menacing quality
of clouds. In another long passage the child steals up to the piano
and is lost in the mystery of the sounds emitted from the keys.
When Melchior teaches Jean Christophe how to play, analysis begins
to steal away the spirits, making them familiar and indifferent.[32]

A word is a very paradigm of habit. The principle of intrusive
novelty is particularly evident in words. Such novelty acts as a scin-
tillating light that plays over the surface of life and art. Although
it produces no deep beauty, it gently reminds men of the qualities
of things. It is the best substitute for the fresh experiences of childhood.[33]

Conflict, said Pepper, is an extreme case of intrusive novelty. In
conflict, the artist is quick to perceive an agent of great aesthetic
value. Like fire, it must be confined and induced to warm its maker,
not left free to consume him. The greatest art, with few exceptions,
is composed of this inflammable and flaming material. The more
violent and extensive the conflict, provided it can be controlled, the
greater the potentiality of quality.[34]

The inflammable potentialities of a purpose, the extent and intensity of quality that it can produce, depend partly on the tenacity
of its drive, partly on the strength of the obstacles placed in its path,
partly on the capacity of the organism to master its faculties for the
problem. Hunger, love, jealousy, fear, hate, and ambition are powerful drives. The ideal aesthetic material seems to be a rich, resourceful,

and strong personality stirred by a powerful drive to some end and confronted by formidable obstacles to its attainment.[35] Every art is susceptible to emotion, which is the very spirit of dramatic conflict. Such emotion is most easily exhibited in the novel and the drama. In architecture (which Goethe called "frozen music"), the drama occurs among lines, surfaces, and volumes. The architect extends his conflicts through space instead of through time.[36]

Emotion, Pepper admitted, is the most intimately felt and the least satisfactorily understood of all objects of experience. It baffles analysis and yet influences our lives. The paradox disappears when one considers that emotion is the very essence of quality. It is a relative term; its correlate is analysis.

A surge of passion such as inspired Shelley's "Swiftly walk o'er the western wave,/Spirit of Night" would be an emotion. A concentration of quality, with no great massiveness of intensity, constitutes a sensuous feeling, as in an observer's absorption in the violet of a night sky. The spell of a soft evening—saturating thought, movement, and utterance—would be a mood.

Feeling and mood may become emotion when an accumulation of intensity and extensity occurs. All these elements differ only in degree. Thus Pepper accepted James's theory of the emotions, enlarging it to include not only bodily sensations but all feelings, and insisting explicitly on the fusion of all sensations.[37]

Emotion, arising from conflict, may be presented in art in three often intermingled ways: direct stimulation, representation, and expression. Given this variety, the wise artist will not disparage emotion as a false element or as mere sentimentality. Indeed, the normal aesthetic experience represents a balance between emotional fusion and analytic discrimination.[38] The very concept of good taste forms a middle ground between the layman's sentimentality and the arid intellectuality of the critic.[39] On this point Pepper again agreed with James, that if one lacks the capacity for "seizure" and ecstasy in a work of art, then one has also lost the power for full realization.[40]

Pepper stated further that quality is the life of art and organization its body. Conflict and analysis can depict an event of quality, and both can be used to intensify and increase quality, by giving it spread and depth. Conflict and analysis, however, are intrinsically antagonistic.

Pepper's aesthetic therefore presented three paradoxes: (1) conflict as a source of frustration and even destruction of quality and, at the same time, as a source of the intensification of quality; (2) analysis—which forms the internal structure of organization—with its ability to drain an event of quality, but also with the capability to increase quality, not by enhancing its vividness but by giving it spread and depth; (3) the antagonism of conflict and analysis and their common antagonism to quality. In practice, analysis dissolves conflict, and organization is nearly synonymous with harmony. Yet the organization wanted in art is one that produces harmony without dissolving conflict. Thus quality, not analysis, is the essence of beauty.[41]

The bulk of aesthetic criticism, Pepper suggested, is directly or indirectly concerned with types. In general, he pointed out, a type is a system of strands that fully (or almost fully) appears in an individual object and is repeatable in other individual objects. This characteristic of full appearance in an individual object constitutes the intrinsic character of a type. The concept of a system implies that the references of the strands constituting the type mutually involve each other and do not vary widely.

A sense of system arises from a mutuality of reference among the strands of a texture, as in the Petrarchan sonnet. Such a sonnet must be strictly followed in its principal features or the reader is jarred into intellectual analysis and a consequent diminution of quality. A properly constituted type, therefore, is not merely an organizing tool; it has a character and a quality of its own. Discriminating analysis reveals the quality, and the quality in turn is the revelation of the analysis.[42]

"Pattern" is an intrinsic mode of organization, as Pepper showed in his analysis of the Shakespearean line "Shall I compare thee to a summer's day?" In this line the regular pattern is felt, but not said or heard. The rhythm of the verse is thus a simultaneous combination of two patterns: the skeletal and the axial.[43] He said that no division exists between symmetry and balance, and he described the use of repetitive rhythms. In a poem, the reader first notices words and syllable sounds, gradually understanding the overall pattern of lines and stanzas—stanzas in verse that are unrestricted in their repetitions.[44]

A theme is any pattern composed of any sort of elements that is capable of recognizable repetition or variation. It must be strictly a pattern so that it can be grasped as a whole. Recognizability becomes the prime factor in the principle of theme and variation, which extends the limits of interest further than any other single principle of design; it holds monotony longest at bay. The limit of a man's ability to learn without fatigue is all that prevents theme and variation from representing virtually unlimited fruitfulness in design. A theme, however, cannot be greater than a rather simple organization of elements.[45]

Because Pepper defined beauty as enhanced quality of texture, any texture of vivid quality was, for him, an object of beauty. The primary aesthetic judgment for Pepper's theory was expressed in the statement, "This is a texture vivid in quality." Without vividness of quality, the texture is not aesthetic. Thus Pepper's hypothesis suggested that no ugliness exists but that degrees of beauty occur —degrees of intensity of enhancement and degrees of extensity of texture.

Throughout his work Pepper was guided by two standards of aesthetic excellence—*vividness of quality* and *spread of quality*. To these he added a third standard—*depth*. Individual textures acquire a depth and a solidity of character when they participate in social interests. The highest beauty, then, is an individual texture: (1) *vivid* in quality, (2) of great *spread* and (3) of *depth*. This threefold discrimination constituted Pepper's basic aesthetic judgment. The texture of appreciation changes, however, with such factors as fatigue, irritability, or a change in the object. One must also consider such personal conditions as a receptive mood and adequate experience (good taste). By the receptive mood Pepper meant a general readiness of the system of personal strands to splice themselves into the system of impersonal strands and generate the total organized texture to the full capacity of the spectator or the participant in a work of art.[46]

The personal strands should be relevant to the impersonal strands and relevant to each other. Coleridge's "imagination" is nothing other than the prolongation of the impersonal strands into the personal system and the enrichment produced by the personal strands in the generation of the total aesthetic work of art. *Imagination, in short, is the personal contribution to the aesthetic work of art.* Without the imagination, all that is left is the physical work of art, which is describable only in the analytical relational term of physics.[47]

Pepper described the operation of the imagination as follows: The physical work of art presents certain relations to be filled out by personal strands. First an act of *perception* occurs. The observer brings into the texture of his perception the relevant qualities of the schemes in which the physical relations participate. These factors constitute "funded interest." The perception is enriched and deepened by these interests into an *apperception*, and the apperception spreads into image and idea.

Meanwhile, during all this imaginative construction, intrusive novelties, dramatic conflicts, and emotions arise and saturate the texture with vitality. In this way, an aesthetic work of art is created out of a physical work of art. The physical continuity exists, however, only as a fragile system of schematic relations, the primary objective being the imaginatively constructed work.[48]

Because every experience is qualitatively unique, the aesthetic experiences of two spectators are necessarily different; everyone has different modes of imagery. The images of a poem will differ greatly for different people according to their image habits, and yet poems rely greatly on images.

In spite of such differences, no diminution of objectivity need occur in the specific realization of such a line as Keats's "And gathering swallows twitter in the Skies." The visual image occurs in the reference to the spatial location "in the skies"; the auditory image exists in "twitter," and the line of flight through "gathering"—all relevant images. A blind man, of course, cannot perceive visual relations. A color-blind man misses the hues. A man without a rhythmic sense misses balance and the swing of line and the subtleties of repetition. The normality supposed here is that of the average man —raised to the fullness of his capacities.[49]

The assumption of normality lifts aesthetic works of art out of the category of dreams and converts them into social objects, endowing them with an authority as extensive as the society in which this normality endures. When a man is said to have good taste, he is presumed to possess the full capacity of imaginative construction relevant to the work of art or type of art under consideration. One thing is certain: a work of art that is totally lacking in vitality is worthless.[50]

Pepper concluded that quality is the very essence of life and nature. A man ignorant of depth of quality does not know the substance of life or nature even if he is erudite or efficient. He will not know the inner meaning of his erudition or efficiency. His effectiveness will depend on the insights of other men who did once know. In the end, nothing is valuable but the quality of something.[51]

Theodore Meyer Greene (1897–1969)

Greene's *The Arts and the Art of Criticism* (1940) is less valuable to us now as an original contribution to aesthetics than as an example of a work prestigious in its day. Greene himself admitted that his volume dealt with broad issues discussed for centuries by critics and philosophers, and he was aware that in the estimate of some critics his book did not give the reader a sense of the excitement of artistic creation or of critical appraisal.[52]

In his discussion of literature, Greene analyzed words, verbal meaning, and metaphor. A word, he said, is a sound or visible mark with an ideational meaning and is therefore essentially symbolic in character. Verbal language is a system of auditory symbols with visual equivalents. Three types of verbal meaning occur: (1) conceptual, (2) imagistic, and (3) emotive-conative.

The conceptual core, the associated images, and the emotive-conative suggestions of individual words can all acquire greater precision in a meaningful context, and, by skillful manipulation, words can be made to convey new concepts, fresh images, and novel emotive-conative states devoid of ambiguity. Words uttered have timbre, pitch, intensity, and duration, and in conjunction with intervening pauses form the basis of metrical and nonmetrical rhythm, or verbal tonality ("musical quality").[53]

In every metaphor two ideas are related in such a way as to illuminate and vitalize one another. The metaphorical relation is essentially one of revealing analogical comparison. Citing Buchanan's *Poetry and Mathematics* (1929), Greene remarked that analogy is of prime importance in every universe of discourse, in mathematics and science, philosophy and history, as well as in literature. Metaphor represents a juxtaposition of ideas one of which is more general, the other more particular. Thus in the metaphors "glaring error" and "marble brow," *error* is more general and *glaring* more particular, *marble* is more abstract, *brow* more particular.

Metaphors may be expanded into similes, similes into parables or fables and finally into allegories in which abstract ideas of great complexity are set in analogical relation to images of comparable complexity, as in *The Pilgrim's Progress, The Divine Comedy*, and *The Faerie Queene*. Metaphorical relation can be studied in such lines as Shelley's "Life, like a dome of many-coloured glass,/Sta·ns the white radiance of Eternity" and Coleridge's "A sunny pleas· re-dome with caves of ice!"[54]

Time is itself the occasion for metaphoric expression, as when Greene spoke of the *moving* "present" of the narrative in portions of *Tristram Shandy*, in which there is an overlapping of three distinguishable "present" moments. Similarly, William James described the specious present as the "saddleback" of time, and Rossetti defined the sonnet in terms of time, as "a moment's monument."[55]

Literary composition involves a "translation" of written or printed symbols into their auditory equivalents, and then into their ideational meanings. The central meaning of each word is its conceptual reference to a universal, as in Wordsworth's

> A motion and a spirit, that impels
> All thinking things, all objects of all thought
> And rolls through all things.[56]

The literary artist must take into account a factor ignored by the scientist—the immediate expressiveness of sound. In Spinoza the words catch fire from the subject matter; in Wordsworth, the words are themselves on fire. Literary composition thus arises from an interplay of the conceptual, the imagistic, and the emotive-conative meanings.[57]

In the section devoted to principles of criticism, Greene discussed the roles of historical inquiry, sensitive re-creation, and judicial appraisal. He lists five levels of critical appraisal: (1) formal excellence, (2) artistic quality, (3) artistic integrity, (4) artistic truth, and (5) artistic greatness.

In discussing artistic greatness, Greene quoted T. S. Eliot: "The 'greatness' of literature cannot be determined solely by literary standards; though . . . whether it is literature or not can be determined only by literary standards." He also quoted Shelley: "Poetry enlarges the circumference of the imagination by replenishing it with thoughts of ever new delight, [with] the power of attracting and assimilating to their own nature all other thought."[58]

Like many earlier aestheticians, Greene discussed the relationship between science and art:

> Not only does the artist's generic attitude differ from that of the scientist, he seeks to attain and express a different kind of insight from that which the scientist strives to attain and formulate. Art and science focus upon different aspects of reality and human experience, and the farther they advance, the more pronounced the difference between them becomes. But they resemble one another in being, each in its own way, extensions of man's normal every-day experience. Both the scientist and the artist not only start with the apprehensions of the common man, they are at pains not to lose contact with the world of ordinary sense-perception.[59]

The artist, said Greene, addresses himself to the particular, but if his work of art is rich in meaning, it transcends the particular, so that the artist becomes as much concerned as the scientist with the apprehension and the interpretation of the universal. The aesthetic factor of elegance is present in art, science, and crafts.[60] In art, as in science, clarity of thought and clarity of expression are complementary aspects of a single process.[61]

Greene considered artistic perfection as the resolution of three polar tensions: (1) simplicity versus complexity, whose resolution is the mean of organic unity; (2) order versus novelty, whose mean is expressive originality; and (3) the denial versus the idolatry of the medium, whose resolution is the expressive exploration of the medium.[62] Artistic vitality is always a product of a synthetic resolution of conflicting tendencies, any one of which would, if uncontrolled, destroy all artistic merit.[63]

In this chapter I have dealt with the analytical approach to aesthetics as presented in the work of Prall, Pepper, and Greene. Prall's aesthetics was concerned with the knowledge of qualities directly apprehended in sensuous experience. Language, a symbolic medium, may function aesthetically through rhythms and connotations that carry imaginal and emotional meaning. Pepper's "contextualism" maintained that any experience is a strand whose specific nature becomes clear within the frame of a wider content or texture, which is itself a set of interrelated strands.

For Pepper, the aesthetic field is that of intuited quality, which is intensified by novelty and conflict. Intrusive novelty, of which conflict is an extreme case, is particularly evident in words. Emotion, the very essence of quality, lends vitality to imaginative construction, which transmutes a physical work of art into an aesthetic one. The realization of depth of quality depends largely on intuition and very little on erudition.

Greene's contribution was mainly pedagogic. He presented various schematizations: one of verbal meaning (the conceptual, imagistic, and emotive-conative), another of the levels of critical appraisal (form, quality, integrity, truth, and greatness), and another of artistic perfection as the resolution of three polar tensions: simplicity versus complexity, order versus novelty, the denial versus the idolatry of the medium.

SYMBOLISM AND OTHER
AESTHETIC TONALITIES

Susanne Langer (1895–   ): Symbolism

Langer's *Philosophy in a New Key: A Study in the Symbolism of Reason, Rite and Art* (1942) was concerned with many of the major issues of literary aesthetics, including problems of language, metaphor, the science-poetry polarity, and symbolism in general.[1] In her approach to language, Langer differed with such philosophers as Bertrand Russell, Ludwig Wittgenstein, and Rudolf Carnap, for whom language had no meaning except possibly as an expression of feeling and desire, though not of thought. Langer believed that human thought itself is only "a tiny, grammar-bound island, in the midst of a sea of feeling" and that "Nature speaks to us, first of all through our senses."[2]

On the relationship of reason to feeling, Langer cited Creighton's suggestion that feeling itself must participate in knowledge: "The character of the feeling in any experience may be taken as an index of the mind's grasp of its object."[3] Following this view, Langer sought to define the articulate forms of feeling. Language, she argued, is generally unable to convey fully "the interplay of feelings with thoughts and impressions"; music is therefore "the kind of symbolism peculiarly adapted to the explication of the 'unspeakable.'"[4]

In her speculations on the nature of language and metaphor, Langer discussed Otto Jespersen's idea that speech and song may have had a common source, as suggested by J. Donovan in "The Festal Origin of Human Speech."[5] Langer also cited Philip Wegener, who recognized two general principles of linguistic development: emendation, which begets the syntactical form of speech; and metaphor, the source of generality.

All discourse involves two elements: the context (verbal or practical) and the novelty. To designate the novelty, the speaker will have recourse to *logical analogy*; the context will make it clear that the speaker "cannot mean the thing literally denoted, and must mean something else symbolically." The context indicates, for instance, that the statement, "The king's anger flares up," contains no reference to a physical flame; it is to be taken metaphorically.[6]

According to Wegener, our literal language is a repository of "faded metaphors." Examples given by Langer include: "The brook *runs* swiftly"; "A rumor *runs* through the town"; "A fence *runs* round the barnyard." Although the reader does not think here of actual running done by legs, the primitive imagery (the unconscious analogy with functions of the body) of *running* underlies the expression.

Wegener said that "the process of fading . . . represents the bridge from the first [one word] . . . phase of language to the developed phase of a discursive exposition." Langer added that metaphor is the force that makes language "essentially *relational*, intellectual, forever showing up new, abstractable forms in reality. . . ."[7]

Image making, symbols, metaphor, and myth are all closely connected in a line leading from primitivism to modern sophistication and philosophic formulation. This continuing development is marked by new discovery. It arises from a contemplation that touches the whole cycle of human emotions. Myth is the primitive phase of metaphysical thought, and metaphor facilitates the discovery of new ideas.[8]

In her discussion of poetry, Langer noted Urban's statement that the poet does well to keep to symbolic form rather than to literal expression. She also took into account Urban's suggestion that "poetry is covert metaphysics" and that it is "only when its implications,

critically interpreted and adequately expressed, become part of philosophy that an adequate view of the world can be achieved."

What is this critical and adequate expression, Langer asked, if
not literal interpretation?[9] But later she asserted that artistic symbols
were untranslatable. Thus poetry is not concerned with the literal
assertion but with the way in which the assertion is made: the sound,
the tempo, the aura of associations. Poetry is "a form compounded
of sound and suggestion, statement and reticence, and no translation
can reincarnate that."[10]

In *Feeling and Form*[11] Langer discussed Schiller's concept of
Schein, or "semblance," as a liberating force for perception; it frees
the mind from practical tasks and enables it to dwell on the sheer
appearances of things. Langer, influenced by this idea, declared that
the function of artistic illusion is not "make-believe" but disengage-
ment from belief: "The knowledge that what is before us has no
practical significance in the world is what enables us to give attention to its appearance as such." On the inseparable nature of image
and sight, she cited Rémy de Gourmont's statement that only the
visual-minded can "write." Similarly, William H. Prescott regarded
the line, "The quality of mercy is not strained," as unpoetic because
it suggests nothing visible.[12]

For modern pragmatists, the two essential functions of language
are the conveyance of information and the stimulation of feelings
and attitudes in the listener or reader. From this point of view,
Langer said, the criticism of poetry must be concerned with such
questions as "What is the poet trying to say?" "What is the poet
trying to make us feel?" For her, however, the fundamental question
was: "What has the poet made and how did he make it?"

Words are only the materials from which the poet derives his
poetic elements. He then creates the semblance of events—"a piece
of virtual life."[13] A poem, therefore, is not factual statement versified;
it is the creation of a "symbol of a feeling." As such, it does not recall
"objects which would elicit the feeling itself," but weaves "a pattern
of words—words charged with meaning, and colored by literary
associations."[14]

Langer frequently cited Barfield's *Poetic Diction, A Study in Mean-*

ings (1924), which revealed, she said, "the same relationships between language and conception, conception and imagination, imagination and myth, myth and poetry, that Cassirer discovered as a result
of his reflection on the logic of science."[15] Langer considered Ernst
Cassirer's laws as exactly similar to Freud's scattered canons of symbolization. Both depended on the concept of "mythic consciousness,"
which Durkheim found in the evolution of totemism, and which
Owen Barfield noted in "poetic meaning" or "true metaphor." Freud's
principle of ambivalence comes into play, she said, because emotional
opposites, like joy and grief, desire and fear, "are often very similar
in their dynamic structure and reminiscent of each other."[16]

The problem of "pure poetry" elicited from Langer numerous references to Henri Bremond's *La Poésie pure* (1920), in which "essence"
was equated with "magic." Langer believed that the so-called quality
of "poetic magic" depends on sound, imagery, meaning, and emotion
—and on nothing else. She noted that Bremond, like Poe, Shelley,
Coleridge, and Swinburne, sought poetic essence to the exclusion of
didacticism and discursiveness.[17]

On the larger question of the meaning of poetry, Langer quoted
Prescott's declaration that poetry is certainly not printed words on
paper; its essential element is "dream-like" and "cannot be steadily
or attentively contemplated, but may be seen only in glimpses"; true
poetic beauty is inexplicable.[18] Ultimately, Langer regarded Prescott's
theory as muddled, because "none of its 'principles' really works,
freely and without exception, in all instances."

Langer delivered herself of a number of rather dubious, if not
downright queer, assertions:

> Ideas and emotions are *dangerous* subjects for poetry, the
> former because a weak poet may be led into discourse on his
> topic, the latter because he may be tempted to direct utterance,
> exclamation and catharsis of his own feelings.

If ideas and emotions are dangerous, what then is left for the poet
to use?

Langer suggested that the *good* poet uses every bit of the subject matter for artistic effect. She did not, however, define her concept of the "good poet," offering only a rather hackneyed observation: "Everything actual must be transformed by imagination into something purely experiential; that is the principle of poesis."[19]

In her analysis of "dramatic" illusion, Langer quoted Charles Morgan's statement: "Illusion . . . is form in suspense." Form, latent in the drama, finally moves toward fulfillment.[20] As Langer observed, "Drama is neither ritual nor show business, though it may occur in the frame of either one; it is poetry, which is neither a kind of circus nor a kind of church."[21] If drama is poetry, why not say then that it is poetry in the form of dialogue, which, through its verisimilitude, induces in the spectator an illusion of reality? On this point, Langer quoted Eric Bentley's observation that "all 'theatre arts' are means to one end; the correct presentation of a poem."[22]

Langer largely refuted Unamuno on the nature of tragedy. Unamuno's central idea (essentially Pascalian) was that man's greatness and dignity can be found in his "tragic sense of life." Because Unamuno's poetic metaphysics could not be argued with in terms to which Langer was accustomed, she declared that "he cannot be taken seriously," although she conceded that "he cannot . . . be worsted in argument."[23] Langer's work, however, suffers from a lack of precisely that poetic spirit which informed Unamuno's thought, as in Ferguson's description of "Purpose, Passion (or Suffering) and Perception."

Unamuno's "We created God to save the universe from Nothingness"[24] might be matched by the reflection that we create beauty in the form of tragedy to save our lives from meaninglessness. This idea recalls Ashley Thorndike's observation that tragedy "brings home to us the images of our own sorrows, and chastens the spirit through the outpouring of our sympathies, even our horror and despair, for the misfortune of our fellows." Thorndike's assertion, "It is the function of Literature to unite the world of experience and the world of vision,"[25] may be matched by Unamuno's declaration that the basic problem in philosophy is to conciliate self and cosmos. Such views were often inadequately appreciated in Langer's work.

On the role of intuition, Langer considered Bergson and Croce.

Croce's intuition, as she saw it, was not Bergson's blind "taking possession" or emotional experience of "reality." For Croce, it was an act of perception whereby content is turned into form. Langer charged Croce with looseness of language and with some logically inadmissible steps that led to his metaphysics of "the Spirit." The result for aesthetics is, she believed, a confusion resulting from the identification of intuition and expression. A work of art is essentially in the artist's mind and is only duplicated in its material form.[26]

Langer attempted to impose "logic" on Croce: ". . . for by expression he means what I have called 'logical expression,' no matter how much he might protest the word 'logical.'" In her view, Croce's "science" of nonintellectual knowledge needed a recognition of nondiscursive symbolization: "All cognition of form is intuitive; all relatedness—distinctness, congruence, correspondence of forms, contrast, and synthesis in a total *gestalt*—can be known only by direct insight which is intuition." Although Langer relied here on the authority of Ernst Cassirer,[27] her views at this point closely resembled those of Croce.

Unlike Croce and R. G. Collingwood, however, Langer did not define "technique" as tantamount to "manufacture." Noting that the crafts provide opportunities for the creation of works of art, she insisted that the artist must know beforehand what he is about to create and what form he is to give it. Mere feeling on the part of the artist might lead to "aestheticism." She declared further that the products of the artist's creation outgrow the compass of his personal life.[28] Her assertions here were reminiscent of Keats's notion of the "impersonality" of the artist, and her observations on the work of art and its public closely resembled those of Jean-Marie Guyau and Dewey.

In *Mind: An Essay on Human Feeling* (1967), Langer remarked that Santayana's process of objectification resembled her own idea of "projection." His concept, however, implied not symbolic projection but the supposed process of "projecting" sensations actually occurring in our own bodies onto an outside world as qualities of "matter." Langer, however, found Santayana's ideas dated largely as a result of a shift from the psychology of sensation and association to a concept tentatively built on principles of symbol and meaning. In general, she dismissed the resemblances between Santayana's theory and her own.[29] She noted further that Santayana's term "projection" was more explicitly defined by Bernard Bosanquet as "symbolic projection."[30]

In her examination of the nature of poetry, Langer turned to Eliot's "objective correlative," through which emotion is referred to a set of events that become the formula for a given emotion. She noted that this principle failed to provide a means by which the artist could transform his feelings into objective expression. Her views here are reminiscent of George Eliot's observation: "To be a poet is to have a soul . . . in which knowledge passes instantaneously into feeling and feeling flashes back as a new organ of knowledge."[31]

Langer herself summarized the significance of her work as follows:

> The theory itself [that of the Art Symbol], which I have here set forth, is not really one person's work. It is a step—and I think, an important one—in a philosophy of art on which many aestheticians have already labored, the theory of expressive form. . . . It was Cassirer—though he never regarded himself as an aesthetician—who hewed the keystone of the structure, in his broad and disinterested study of symbolic forms; and I, for my part, would put the stone in place, to join and sustain what so far we have built.[32]

Philip Wheelwright (1901–1969): Poetry, Logic, and Myth

Wheelwright's background for the study of literary aesthetics was enviably rich in both range and depth. He combined the probing discrimination of the philosopher and the sensitivity of the poet. He wrote on general philosophy, Aristotle, Heraclitus, metaphor, literary criticism, and the nature of poetry.

In "Toward a Metaphysic of Literary Criticism" Wheelwright proposed a threefold task for literary criticism: (1) to define, analyze, and, by implication, evaluate "the sphere of reality to which a given work refers"; (2) to estimate "the adequacy of the work to the sphere of reality thus defined"; and (3), on the basis of (1) and (2), to determine the value of the work.

Although the critic should recognize the distinction between his subject and those of the scientist and the philosopher, he should also "accept a metaphysic that attributes a genuine reality to his field as to theirs." Wheelwright used the test of the function of metaphor in philosophy and in literature. Whereas in the former, metaphor tends to be merely illustrative, in the latter it is a necessary form, without which "the reality to which the work refers would not be the same."[33] He seems to have agreed with Ramón Fernandez, whom he quoted, that "the fundamental problem of aesthetics is no other than the metaphysical problem of being, but transposed to the plane of imagination"—that, in general, "aesthetics must be an imaginative ontology."[34]

In his "Poetry and Logic," Wheelwright expressed his indebtedness to Louis Grudin's *A Primer of Aesthetics* (1930). This work, which is concerned with verbal logic, tried to establish aesthetics as an area of authentic and verifiable knowledge. Grudin discussed energy as a symbol of change in physics and quoted A. N. Whitehead to the effect that "energy is merely the name for the qualitative aspect of a structure of happenings." He did not *explicitly* indicate, however, that the poetic process involves a transformation from physical energy to psychic energy (that of will).

Grudin saw the poet and his poem bound together as contextual symbol. For him, a poem has a signatory role: "A poem may mean different things to different readers, yet remain fixed as a verbal context in each case."[35] Beauty was identifiable with "ultimately significant" symbolization: "[The] strictly contextual relation called *beauty* is distinct from the relation called the symbol's truth respecting the object. The relation of *truth* is meant aside from the relation of beauty." For Grudin, prose begins and ends with a signatory order. Prose remains such, even when there is a lapse from truth, "while a lapse from beauty produces banal poetry rather than prose."[36]

Following Grudin, Wheelwright mentioned the distinction between the poetically intelligible and the logically intelligible. Philosophic language, he felt, falls short of "the verbal chemistries that poetry effects"; the abstractions of philosophy cannot give birth to a *King Lear.*[37]

In a much later essay, "Poetry, Myth and Reality," Wheelwright asserted that lack of poetic response may be a very serious matter, for it may indicate "the general sickness of our contemporary society." He pointed out the utter disaster that is to be faced in three prestigious doctrines: behaviorism, instrumentalism, and semantic positivism. They have in common a positivistic materialism for which the only truth is experimental truth. For them, poetic truth is a fiction that supplies a certain "emotional heightening."[38]

Our modern dilemma, as Wheelwright saw it, goes back to Descartes. The Ego-Phenomena (EP) axis cuts across the Myth-Community axis. Today, he maintained, the philosophy of the EP axis has reached its most intractable expression in behaviorism, instrumentalism, and semantic positivism—all of them reducing the human mind to what can be proven experimentally. Impersonal experimentalism and voluminous literalism have led us into a blind alley.[39] The way out, Wheelwright suggested, is through a proper understanding of myth as the expression of a profound sense of togetherness, not merely on the plane of intellect but on that of feeling and the wholeness of living. In Wheelwright's opinion, poetry today is inhibited by a dearth of shared consciousness of myth, which has a history.

To his remark that what matters is the myth consciousness of the next generation,[40] I might add that a new Edenic myth (compounded of freedom, love, and "one's own thing") is now growing apace among the young. It is too early yet for the process to have evolved a clear-cut aesthetic. Many signs, however, already indicate that it may be more closely related to the chthonic and the unconscious than to any sophisticated semantic.

No investigation of the nature of poetry is possible without an examination of the nature of language. Wheelwright addressed himself to this question in *The Burning Fountain: A Study in the Language of Symbolism.*[41] He noted that "this book is about expressive language . . . which is to be described as poetic." In general, he called

the language of poetry *expressive language*; the language of plain
sense "as it becomes logical" he called *steno-language*. One is not
cut off from the benefits of the other.

The poem, as an instrument of sensitivity, implies a rich coalescence of knowledge and feeling in the creator and a stimulus for the
re-creation of that amalgam in the reader. Poetry

> . . . quickens and guides man's associative faculty, keeps it
> in athletic trim and thus actually generates new meanings—
> meanings that would lose their identity outside the context of
> the individual poem, but which are authentically real within
> the poem.[42]

Metaphor, central in the poetic structure, was for Wheelwright
not a stratagem of grammar but of semantic import. As he saw it,
the difference between metaphor and simile is merely one of rhetorical strategy. He found no semantic difference between the statement "He dances like a clumsy elephant" (simile) and "That clumsy
elephant gets in everyone's way."

Wheelwright noted that Aristotle called simile "a metaphor with
a preface." For Wheelwright, a real metaphor is characterized by
the factor that Martin Foss called "energy tension." Indeed, living
language as such is marked by tension, especially in poetry.[43] Any
discussion of metaphor involves "the mind's primary activity of
integration"—what Coleridge called "the primary imagination."
Wheelwright concluded *The Burning Fountain* with several telling
metaphors:

> The end of the turning wheel is the still axis which is the
> *arché* of its turning. The end of the cosmic dance is the
> quietude of love beyond desire. The end of dying is the ever-
> renewed threshold experience of potential rebirth.[44]

In *Metaphor and Reality* Wheelwright, like Langer, credited
Cassirer's *The Philosophy of Symbolic Forms* with having entered
deeply into "the interrelations of sense-awareness, mental judgment,
use of language, myth, and art."[45]

The tensive character of language is especially felt in poetry, which is essentially "dramatic" and has overtones of universality. By reason of its openness, poetic language tends toward semantic plenitude and toward the "polysemous" (Michel Bréal's term). Wheelwright cited the use of the word "key" in T. S. Eliot's lines: "I have heard the key/Turn in the door once and turn once only." The word in question carries other meanings besides itself, implying metaphoric use.[46]

Wheelwright also referred to Wallace Stevens and to Sister Bernetta, both of whom identified metaphor with symbolic metamorphosis. Such an approach involved the molding and remolding of essences and forms into new configurations by metamorphic insight.[47] For Stevens and Frost, poetry was essentially a matter of metaphor. For Wheelwright, the most interesting metaphors were those in which *epiphor* and *diaphor* are combined.[48]

Wheelwright offered a broad definition of the term "symbol":

> A Symbol, in general, is a relatively stable and repeatable element of perceptual experience, standing for some larger meaning or set of meanings which can not be given, or not fully given, in perceptual experience itself.

Steno-symbols (indispensable to science) must have a public exactitude. Tensive symbolism is never perfectly exact. The tensive symbol draws life from a multiplicity of associations, for the most part subconscious. Wheelwright showed that Carlyle was speaking about tensive symbols when he wrote: "[In] a symbol there is concealment and yet revelation . . . silence and speech acting together."[49] Archetypal symbols, like "light," for example, carry the same or very similar meanings for most of mankind. This symbol seems to be particularly well fitted to represent mind with its discriminatory power.[50]

Myth, as Wheelwright saw it, involves an interplay of human thought, feeling, imagination, and language. Because imaginative language is basically metaphoric, a natural collision occurs between metaphor and myth in man's attempts to discover and utter "the inner meaning of the universe and of human life."[51] Both epiphoric and diaphoric activities occur in early developments of symbol and myth.

Epiphor appears wherever man sees through the immediate to some lurking, "higher" reality. A diaphoric mythoid (an incipient myth) involves a synthesis of two or more forms charged with immediacy. To exemplify a mythoid in which the diaphoric element is observable and strong, Wheelwright pointed to the triple symbolism of Woman (A), Cow (B), and Crescent Moon (C). This pattern is repeated in various cultures. Each of the three images is likened to each of the others by a particular characteristic. A and B both give milk; A and C have monthly periods; B and C wear horns —and to that extent their relations are epiphoric. The total triadic grouping, however, when viewed in a single apperception by early man, is diaphoric.[52]

Wheelwright came close to dealing with a universal mathesis in which poetry and science are conjointly involved in the quest of reality. Thus, he did speak of a poetically significant I—the *I* that enters into the making and reception of a poem—which consists of visual, auditory, motor, and structural images. Such images, he said, point and hint at something beyond.

For Wheelwright, reality was perspectival; he believed that any treatment of reality will show forth its own ontological limits. Something always exists "beyond." Wheelwright's thought implied a poetic power that can break through all rigid and therefore arrested forms of thought and feeling. This approach is of extreme importance for an aesthetics of literature.

Bernard C. Heyl (1905–   ): The Multiple Meanings of Art, Beauty, and Artistic Truth

In a work published prior to Wheelwright's *The Burning Fountain*, Heyl treated the crucial aspects of artistic analysis—the multiple meanings of "art," "beauty," "artistic truth," "objectivism," "subjectivism," and "relativism"—against the background of semantics.[53] He cited Carnap, Langer, Wheelwright, I. A. Richards, A. J. Ayer, and

Samuel I. Hayakawa, among others. Curiously enough, Heyl's quotation from Sir Charles Sherrington's *Man on His Nature* (1941)
seems to have given the lie to the semantic positivists, who too often
gave the impression that *finitude* or *finality* in meaning was possible:

> Kant seems to assume the human mind to be a finished thing,
> a completed item of existence. But the human mind is part of
> a tide of change which, in its instance, has been latterly and,
> we may think, still is, running like a mill-race. Many living
> things are all the time busy becoming something other than
> what they are. And this, our mind, with the rest. It is being
> made along with our planet's making. We do not know that
> it ever will be finished.[54]

What is true of mind is true for the means of expressing it, namely,
language. Meanings change with contexts. Because the transaction
between mind and its environment is necessarily fluid, so is the
expression of that transaction. We should not wonder, then, at the
diversity of interpretations of the terms "art" and "beauty" and the
inadequacy of contemporary art criticism and aesthetics, to which
Heyl pointed. Accordingly, he felt that "it is both unnecessary and
undesirable to use the epithet 'artistic truth' in esthetics and in art
criticism."[55]

Value judgment is equally devious and quixotic, even among
famous critics. Heyl's six criteria for determining the so-called "expert"
resolved themselves to educational and technical equipment. He
agreed with Dewey that "the idea that unless standards and rules are
eternal and immutable they are not rules and criteria at all is
childish."[56] If pressed for the meaning of such terms as "beauty,"
"artistic quality," and "esthetic quality," the so-called objectivist
critic will be forced to consider them unanalyzable. Thus Theodore
Meyer Greene was cited as saying: "Like color and sound, beauty
is an irreducible, unique, and ineffable quality."[57] Heyl maintained
that the objectivist is engaged in a metaphysical chase for a non-
existent entity and that his very goal may be aesthetically and
psychologically dangerous.[58]

The alternative to objectivism is subjectivism, which is repudiated by those who seek a basis for reasoned estimation and discrimination. Again Dewey was quoted:

> The conception that mere liking is adequate to constitute a value situation makes no provision for the education and cultivation of taste and renders criticism, whether esthetic, moral, or logical, arbitrary and absurd.

Intervening between the subjectivists and the objectivists, the art historian Kurt Koffka stressed the interdependence of the ego and its objects.[59] Heyl advocated "some tenable theory" that would avoid the extremes of objectivism (the single-scale idea) and of subjectivism (the supposition no common scale exists). He favored a "wholesome elasticity and variety" in criticism.[60]

Bertram Morris (1908–   ): *The Satisfied Imagination*

In the same year that Heyl's book appeared (1943), Bertram Morris's *The Aesthetic Process* was published. Impressed by the works of Samuel Alexander, Dewey, Whitehead, and Bergson, Morris intended "to construct a positive aesthetic theory, which we may call the theory of the satisfied imagination."[61] He recognized in *empathy* one of the most significant psychological concepts in aesthetics. As Theodor Lipps remarked, "The object is myself and by the very same token this self of mine is the object."[62]

The concrete, aesthetic object is to be found in feeling, which is consonant with activity: "In art, gay colors leap, distressing sounds groan, dolorous tones cry." In the aesthetic experience the object is the embodiment of feeling.[63] The theory of the satisfied imagination was implicit in Morris's definition of beauty—"the expression of a purpose in a sensuous medium."[64]

Like many other aestheticians, Morris ran into the problem of the polarity between science and art. With the end of developing the thesis that "expression of purpose is the unfolding of meaning," he compared some of the salient features of scientific inquiry with the art process. Science, he said, refuses to accept purposive relations; in art, purposiveness engenders the contemplative. Although purpose in science is intellectual and confirmable, in art it is sensuous and emotional.[65] Morris felt that Dewey oversimplified the identification of scientific operational procedure with the aesthetic. Morris went so far as to say that "The externality of the relations in the one [science] as compared with the internality in the other [art] makes the identification a travesty."[66]

Morris's insight into aesthetic activity as being more closely related to a drama of imagery than to trains of imagery is worth stressing.[67] One might paraphrase this by saying that the aesthetic activity is dialectic rather than merely linear. In this dialectic, feeling is, as Morris said, the productive factor, and images bring feeling to dramatic expression. Mere intellectualism will not produce art. Poets mean more than they intend.[68]

For Morris, aesthetic analysis was far removed from mathematical analysis: "If beauty could be proved, art would not admit of new interpretations." Propositions cannot mediate the aesthetic object, and technique is not a guarantee of art: "The virtue of metaphorical judgment consists in its expressiveness . . . in its feeling-tone. . . ."[69]

Morris's reflections on symbolism led him to certain remarks on sentimentalism. He stated that where the symbolic dominates art, sentimentalism necessarily results, as when, for example, the sight of the handkerchief recalls the beloved."[70] I have had occasion earlier to note the rather *facile*, pejorative references to *sentimentality*, without taking into account the full nature of so-called sentimentalism. If the literary symbol is meant to be a mere objet d'art (a thing of words . . . just words), why not say so? If, on the other hand, words in poetry (literature) are meant to signify something beyond themselves, then what argument can be raised against the wistfulness and the sense of painful regret generated by an object once associated with someone now gone?

If by sentimentalism is meant specious or false feeling, then let us address ourselves, in our aesthetic reflections, to this problem. Who is to determine the probity of feelings roused by a poem or any work of art? Morris quoted Eliot: "The sentimental person, in whom a work of art arouses all sorts of emotions which have nothing to do with art whatever, but are accidents of personal associations, is an incomplete artist." One hears here the stentorian voice of the Mogul Critic who blares out from his mountaintop: "Thou shalt not commit non-T.S. Eliot feelings in responding to poems or you will be damned as a philistine and a sentimentalist who knows absolutely nothing about ART." The "complete adequacy of the external to the emotion," which for Eliot constituted "artistic inevitability,"[71] is something that everyone feels intuitively or not at all. Intuitions are not to be instructed by constantly brandishing before them the heresy of the sentimental.

The principles of criticism are closely related to the theory of the satisfied imagination. Within them, Morris felt, aesthetic theory will find validation to the extent that they relate concretely to our actual appreciation.[72] Aristotle, Dewey, and Whitehead, among others, insisted that the real meaning of art is experience itself. It is a way of coming to grips with the world.[73]

Morris offered the following categorization of criticism: (1) genetic criticism, (2) aesthetic criticism, and (3) higher criticism. The first, most fully used by art historians, is, in Morris's opinion, incompletely aesthetic. The second rests on the principles of the metaphorical judgment. Whitehead said that great art "transforms the soul into the permanent realization of values extending beyond its former self." The so-called higher criticism stems from "those rare critics who are able to bring to life again the dormant virtues of neglected art."[74] For Morris, aesthetic criticism comes closest to serving the objectives of the satisfied imagination. Eventually, all these forms of criticism tend to converge in their common cultural interest. It is worth repeating Morris's statement that "art is a liberating activity which gives direction to human power."[75]

Morris Weitz (1916–): Toward a New Analysis

In his *Philosophy of the Arts* (1950), Weitz cited Clive Bell's opinion that literature can never be pure art because it is concerned primarily with facts and ideas and, as such, is primarily intellectual. To this,

Weitz added that poetry becomes pure only when it is resolved into music.

Weitz pointed out that unlike Bell, who distinguished between the aesthetics of painting and literature, R. E. Fry attempted to explain all the arts by means of the principle of significant form. For him, the essence of literature was to be found in the relation of inevitability—"the vivid sense of the inevitability of the unfolding of events."[76]

Weitz found in this idea two serious internal difficulties: (1) It is incomplete because it deals only with tragedy. (2) In making inevitability the essence of literature, literature is reduced to the instinctual level of experience, "from which it follows that there can be no aesthetic emotion so far as our response to literature is concerned."[77]

Weitz maintained that "to say that art is significant form is to say that it is also significant content." In this he found himself sustained by DeWitt H. Parker, A. C. Barnes, and A. C. Bradley, in spite of their superficial distinction between form and content. In any concrete work of art an organic relation exists between the two.[78]

For the best statement of this principle as it applies to poetry, Weitz singled out that of Cleanth Brooks and Robert Penn Warren in their *Understanding Poetry*. A poem, they said, does not consist of "a group of mechanically combined elements—meter, rime, figurative language, idea, etc., put together to make a poem as bricks are put together to make a wall." They suggested that a poem is comparable to a plant. The organic theory repudiates the distinction between the *what* and the *how* (content and form).[79]

For Weitz, then, a poem is an organic complex of expressive elements: words, images, allusions, metrics, subjects, themes. It is always "much richer than its *printed* meanings." The cult of unintelligibility, he seems to have suggested, can be overcome by grasping the symbols within a poem. He took "The Love Song of J. Alfred Prufrock" as an example. Here we have the symbols of the etherized patient, the coffee spoons, Prufrock himself, and the act of drowning. Weitz followed Cleanth Brooks in seeing in this poem "the unfolding of a tremendous double metaphor"—life and death on the meaningless plane of conventionality and life and death as directed toward salvation, with Prufrock himself as "the epitome of the conflict between the two ways of life and death."[80]

Recent theory, especially that of I. A. Richards,[81] has raised the important question of whether art is only emotive or whether it is referential as well. Thus, T. M. Greene maintained (at length) that art can lay claims to "propositional truth," while Heyl and John Hospers succeeded, Weitz believed, in exposing the inadequacies of Greene's position.

As a way out of this controversy, Parker posited the concept of "depth meaning." When, for example, Frost says, "Nothing gold can stay," "gold" has both its surface meaning and its depth meaning, the more universal idea that nothing valuable can abide. Weitz pointed out, however, that other instances contain truth claims as surface sentences (Longfellow's "A Psalm of Life" or Shakespeare's "Let me not to the marriage of true minds") and not necessarily as depth meanings. Weitz concluded that "the emotive theory is simply false in its assertion that no art contains referential meanings."[82]

Recognizing the noble efforts of Brooks and Richards, Weitz felt, nevertheless, that a new analysis was needed. He began with the fundamental contribution of the New Criticism, namely, that

> . . . a poem is an organic complex of constituents, including the theme. Toward these, but especially the theme, when it functions as a truth claim, there are at least four cognitive attitudes that one can assume: indifference or unconcern, make-believe, acceptance of belief, and rejection or disbelief.

Richards, Weitz claimed, was not at all clear whether poetry cannot be referential and embody truth claims or ought not to be so. What ought to be challenged is Richards's underlying idea—that truth claims fall within the province of science, not of poetry. This, said Weitz, is false. No psychologist has equalled a Proust or a Dostoyevski in the assessment of human motivation.

The wisdom of literature is lacking in science. Accordingly, Richards's indifference to truth claims in art will not do. The recommendation that we treat poetic claims of truth as if they were true is cognitively false. The assumption is that they are really false.

The make-believe theory has no explanations for the attitude of the readers who do find that much of poetry does embody truth or truth claims.[83] Reading well, which Brooks underlined as important for the understanding of poetry, was, for Weitz, reading with an eye for rich human possibilities and "the liberating effects they offer us." For him, it was "the liberating function of the aesthetic experience."[84]

Under "Voluntarism," Weitz considered Freud's as well as Parker's theories of art. Parker agreed with Freud that artistic activity is akin to the dream and that the dream itself is dominated by desire. The imagination, dominated by desire, exists, in fact, for the purpose of satisfying desires. The imaginative satisfaction of desire that takes place wholly within the person is as genuine as that which comes from the appropriation of some object from the environment.

Weitz sided with Parker in this view, as against Curt Ducasse, who was Parker's most severe critic. Finding Freud's psychology limiting, Parker claimed that artistic activity is the satisfaction of desires—but not merely of frustrated desires. For Weitz, the aesthetic experience was not a form of sublimation: "It is as real and direct a form of satisfaction of desire as our satisfying our sexual desire in the experience of sexual intercourse."[85]

Weitz further examined the contemplation theory held by Ducasse, Bell, Edward Bullough, and Roger Fry. Ducasse interpreted contemplation as a mild form of emotional indulgence or infection. To this Weitz was strongly opposed because of its reductive quality and its tone of prohibitiveness for a full artistic expression. Bullough's theory of contemplation, which Weitz considered more adequate, involved a bipolarity of action and detachment that Bullough called "psychical distance," which I have discussed earlier.

With Bell and Fry, Weitz regarded the contemplative attitude toward art as a way of securing a unique experience, one that is not "caused by an indulgence in the emotion of the art object but by the contemplative experience itself. It is in this sense that appreciation is a legitimate emotional experience."[86]

On the question of criticism, and the expression of taste that goes with it, Weitz admitted that he knew of no refutation against Ducasse's claim that any ultimate criterion in evaluation is an emotive preference and not something referential and objective. Still he felt that this is tantamount to nihilism, which, while irrefutable, is (at least for him) totally unacceptable.[87] Weitz, too, asked, "What about the sentimental and the saccharine in art?" Is a work like *The Sorrows of Werther* as good, aesthetically, as Hamlet?

Weitz admitted that here an axiology is involved that may meet with skepticism on the part of some.[88] I have already indicated my own reflections on this problem. Here I wish to add that open-faced confrontation of the facts of the human condition in the vast context of the cosmic swirl reduces the human comedy to a sentimental blink. It is precisely this blink, however, that affords us our sentimental education, which turns on such matters as beauty, drama, the grotesque, and musical moments in an aesthetic response that is constantly changing.

THE NEW CRITICISM

The New Criticism defies definition, except by contrast with the older criticism. Whereas older criticism related itself to history, biography, philosophy, and even to some branches of science, the New Criticism regarded all such relationships as irrelevant for a true understanding of literature. Its poetic ontology recognized only structural tensions and their resolutions within the literary work itself. The elements to be dealt with were diction, rhythm, metaphor, symbol, semantic pointers, and texture. Life was, at best, a tangential consideration. Tradition was a desideratum only insofar as it revealed tonalities of literary pattern.

Douglas Day (1932–   )

In "The Background of the New Criticism," Douglas Day stated that the so-called New Criticism began in the first decade of the twentieth century. Although the work of the New Critics differed from Joel Spingarn's brand of "creative" criticism, they welcomed his emphasis on the sensibility of the poet and the inseparability of form and content. Further, despite their rejection of Irving Babbitt's moralism, the New Critics agreed with his emphasis on the importance of form and the critic's need for an erudite sense of the past.[1] They also responded to the influential theories of Rémy de Gourmont and Thomas Ernest Hulme.

For Gourmont, poetry presented a three-stage process: sensation, image words, and sentiment words (words expressing feeling). Stage one (the sensuous apprehension of concrete experience) vitalizes the other two stages.[2] Gourmont's linkage of sensibility with the poetic description of concrete, physical experience is definitely echoed, Day felt, in T. S. Eliot's objective correlative.[3]

Hulme, according to Sir Herbert Read, derived much from Gourmont, but Gourmont's concept of the poem as dependent largely on the sensibility of the poet, showed him, as Day perceived, to be closer to romantic impressionism than would be acceptable to Hulme. Hulme asserted that the romantic is a *sentimentalist* (that ghost again!) who is much concerned with his "damp" feelings. By contrast, the classical poet will be dry, emotionless, and concrete. He will deal with the finite instead of flirting with the infinite.[4] The classical poet is characterized by his concentrated state of mind and by his self-control in the expression of his perceptions.[5]

The complexity of a poem arises from the use of metaphorical analogies. Each "part of a poem is modified by the other's presence, and each is, to a certain extent, the whole."[6] As a disciple of Bergson, Hulme held that the organic form of a poem is a function of intuition. The artist must be able to transcend appearance to perceive a reality beyond it.[7] As was the case with Gourmont, in Day's view, Hulme did not actually break away from the romantic expressionism he opposed.[8]

Although Hulme is still remembered as the founder of the imagist movement, the movement was actually under Ezra Pound's control from his introduction of *Les Imagistes* in his *Ripostes* in 1912 until, as Day put it, Amy Lowell usurped his throne in 1914.[9] T. S. Eliot was greatly influenced by Pound, whom he described as the better craftsman (*"Il miglior fabbro"*). From Pound he supposedly learned the necessity for a return to a poetry of impersonality and unemotionality, which would convey the reality of everyday experience through concrete imagery.[10]

Eliot was also deeply obligated to Poe for his views on the independence of poetry from morals, politics, and biography. He was further influenced by Poe's idea that the emotions provoked by a poem are different from those arising in the mind of the poet. His thoughts on the poet's "impersonality" were anticipated by Keats, while his idea of the poem as an independent organism is actually derived from Coleridge. On the role of sensibility, he was instructed by his master, Rémy de Gourmont.[11]

Eliot's notion of the objective correlative, which emphasized the work itself as a structure, was to become, Day pointed out, the touchstone of the New Criticism. According to that notion, the poem is an objectification of the emotions that arise within the poet; it should therefore constitute the critic's principal concern.[12] In consonance with such critics as Murray Krieger and Eliseo Vivas, Day contended that Eliot's thought is a complex blend of classicism and the extreme form of romanticism that he and his contemporaries had presumably opposed.[13]

The work of Eliot served to transmit the crucial ideas found in Gourmont, Hulme, and Pound. It thus provided a general attitude for the New Critics. Their critical method, however, was actually provided by I. A. Richards's *Principles of Literary Criticism* (1924). Here Richards described two ways in which impulse may be organized: inclusion and exclusion, or synthesis and elimination.

Richards indicated that the poetry of inclusion is the worthier of the two, in that its aim is the presentation of a maximum number of conflicting impulses. This sort of poetry lends itself to critical analysis. The poetry of exclusion, seeking the presentation of a minimum number of conflicting impulses, is little more than a direct statement of a single attitude, and is therefore not particularly rewarding as a subject for extensive critical analysis. Inclusive poetry makes use of a factor that Richards calls *irony*:

> Irony . . . consists in bringing in the opposite, the complementary impulses; that is why poetry which is opposed to it is not of the highest order, and why irony itself is so constantly a characteristic of poetry which is.[14]

The critic's task is to unravel the complex network of meanings provided by the poet's skillful use of irony, paradox, and ambiguity.

Some critics welcome obscurity because it provides an opportunity for the exercise of their ingenuity. At any rate, Day saw Richards as one who contributed to modern criticism a method of textual interpretation that could do away with subjective generalities.[15]

Day concluded that the New Critics were classical in only two respects: their requirement that the poet limit his imaginative faculty to the treatment of the world perceived by the senses, and their demand that poets and critics alike pay closer attention to form and structure. Although Eliot and Richards made significant contributions in these respects, Day argued that their theories must finally be classified as broadly romantic, because they stress the abnormal sensibility of the poet and the organic autonomy of the poem. This inherent divisiveness in the New Critics prevented them from reaching any common ground on which to found a unified critical theory.[16]

John Crowe Ransom (1888–   )

Perhaps the most prestigious critical summary of the New Criticism was offered by Ransom. This approach, he said, had been damaged by its use of a psychological affective vocabulary. He noted that Richards subordinated the cognitive element in experience to the emotive, and the emotive to the conative. In the interest of objectivity, Ransom preferred the terms "cause," "character," and "consequence," respectively, to "cognition," "emotion," and "conation."

In opposition to the romantic and psychological view of the arts as vehicles for raising and communicating passion, Ransom maintained that whereas art starts with feelings and passions, it "proposes to find and explore the appropriate objects and in that sense to objectify and lose them."[17] Ransom persisted in associating Richards's view of poetry with romantic escapism and morbid self-indulgence. But Ransom's cavilling skirted the ridiculous when he pretended not to understand Richards's characterization of Eliot's technique as "a music of ideas." Surely, Ransom knew that this phrase suggests the sense of harmony and tunefulness invoked by certain ideas in poetry and even in philosophy. His casuistry became high-handed when he asserted: "Emotions themselves are fictions, and critical theory could not with a straight face have recourse to them."[18]

As might be expected, Ransom balked at the inclusion of "feelings" in Richards's description of the four separate meanings of a poem: sense (thought or meaning), feelings, tone, and intention. The critic, Ransom argued, need attend only to the objective situations: "The feelings will be their strict correlatives, and the pursuit of feelings will be gratuitous."

Richards described sentimentality as an overly facile or excessively copious affective response by the reader. For Ransom and Eliot, sentimental responses are stock responses to poems that do not warrant them. Thus most poets appear to stand condemned of indulging in affective activities that are not grounded in precise cognition. Only they—Ransom, Eliot, and company—are capable of precise cognition. Even Richards is excluded from this elect hierarchy.[19] On the question of beauty in a poem, Ransom concluded that, lacking any satisfactory accounts of beauty, anyone may make his own definition.[20]

Ransom recognized that in the analysis of metaphor Richards had furnished two extremely important terms: "tenor" and "vehicle." The first is the original context, the given discourse; the second is the importation of foreign context. Thus, in lines quoted by Richards from "Cooper Hill," Sir John Denham addressed the Thames:

> O could I flow like thee, and make thy stream
> My great exemplar as it is my theme!
> Though deep, yet clear; though gentle, yet not dull,
> Strong without rage; without o'erflowing full.

Here, Richards commented, the poet's mind is the tenor and the river the vehicle. And he pointed out that the last two lines contain a repeated alternation of the relative positions of tenor and vehicle and of the direction of the shift between them.[21] Ransom believed that the stream should be taken as the tenor, because Denham begins with it and calls it his "theme," while, for Ransom, the speaker's mind is actually the vehicle. Metaphor, Ransom remarked, is usually more spontaneous than this.[22]

According to Ransom, the study of Coleridge caused Richards to modify his earlier views. Particularly influential was Coleridge's concept of the poetic imagination as an "esemplastic" faculty that unifies opposites. It furnishes a kind of "interanimation" between the opposed parts of the metaphor (the tenor and the vehicle in Richards's terms).

Ransom believed that the metaphor is "a sort of second poem attached to the given poem, like the epicycles by which the Ptolemaic theory complicated the pure orbits of the heavenly bodies." He conceded (rather condescendingly) the existence of an "obvious intelligence" in Richards's declaration that metaphor is the "omnipresent principle of language" (a fact, incidentally, recognized by philologists before Richards).

In an illustrative anecdote Ransom remarked that a scientist of "correct" habits told him that he had been fighting with his colleagues over the technical advisability of introducing any analogies whatever into scientific argument, because of the difficulties of holding the mind to the exact "point of analogy."[23] Such scientists as J. Bronowski and Gaston Bachelard, however, offered other views on the role of analogy and metaphor in the play of the imagination in both art and science.

Bronowski, a scientist of a high order and also an author of one of the best books on Blake, wrote:

> He [the active scientist] knows that science is not something which insects or machines can do. What makes it different is a creative process. . . .
> The world which the human mind knows and explores does not survive if it is emptied of thought. And thought does not survive without symbolic concepts. The symbol and the metaphor are as necessary to science as to poetry.[24]

The gaucherie and limitation in Ransom's thought can be seen in his adherence to a sort of Chinese Wall between science and poetry. He failed to recognize a truth observed by many first-rate scientists and poets, namely, that man is the cosmos thinking, or, as Emerson put it, "The universe is the externization of the soul."[25]

Ransom felt that Richards had varying success in his analysis of the problems of tragedy, irony, and associated forms of wit. For Ransom, Richards's account of the conflict between pity and terror is more rhetorical than realistic. Tragedy, in Ransom's view, belongs to a biological-logical category.[26]

After Richards, Ransom discussed Eliot, whose *The Waste Land* he called "the most famous poem of our age." In Eliot, Ransom saw the clash of a Dr. Jekyll (the critic) and a Mr. Hyde (the poet). In *For Launcelot Andrews* (1928)—where Eliot declared himself a classicist in literature, a royalist in politics, and an Anglo-Catholic in religion—he described poetry as autelic—that is as having itself as an end, independent of anything else.

Because Eliot used historical studies for the sake of literary understanding, Ransom felt that Eliot might be called an historical critic, a critical scholar in the tradition of Dryden or Dr. Johnson. If Eliot, said Ransom, was one of the most important sources of a new criticism, it was because here (in the new criticism) was in part the recovery of old criticism. No poet can be valued apart from a tradition to which he belongs.[27]

Ransom followed Eliot's ideas on the relative roles of emotions and feelings in the creative act: "Probably the most important thing in Eliot's statement is his recognition of *big* emotions as set off against *little* feelings. . . . [The] emotion attaches to the main *structure* [of the poem], the feelings attach to the local *texture*." He went on to say that Richards would hardly have talked, as did Eliot, about a fusion of "feelings, phrases, images into one compound."[28]

Surprisingly, Ransom complained that Eliot's pronouncement had something painful to the humble reader "when he suggests that there is something esoteric in the vocation of criticism and that while Eliot is initiated the humble reader is not."[29] Ransom came close to recognizing his own superciliousness in another critic.

For Eliot, sensibility was the organ that produced feelings. Ransom, however, seems to have opposed a psychological magic that valued feeling above thought. He favored something

> . . . much tamer and more credible: the procedure of suspend-
> ing the course of the main thought while we explore the private

character of the detail items. We stop following the main thought, and take off in a different direction, as we follow the private history of an item; then we come back to the main thought.[30]

Ransom also analyzed Yvor Winters's *Primitivism and Decadence* (1937), in which Winters cited Mallarmé's idea that words have an obvious (that is, a rational) meaning, and an essential fringe of feeling. Following this, Winters maintained that the element peculiar to the poem and wanting to the prose is precisely the "fringe of feeling" that constitutes everywhere in the poem a vivid texture, and that this is clearly essential.

Many postromantic poets, however, seem to have ignored the idea that a poem is more than its rational content. Winters believed that the feeling in certain poems is inseparable from what we call poetic form—form being the shaping of a given experience. The poem consists in the relationship between the rational content and the feeling.[31] Ransom wished that Winters's evaluation of Baudelaire had dispensed with "the business of the 'moral evaluation' and the 'spiritual control'"; Baudelaire was "beyond good and evil at the stage when he is writing poetry; he is not practically moved by them."[32]

In the course of his rather cluttered discussion of Winters's two essays "The Experimental School in American Poetry" and "The Influence of Meter in Poetic Composition," Ransom struck an Emersonian note when he stated that

> . . . nature is almost inevitably the symbol for aesthetic experience. Nature is nearly all texture, with such multitude of forms as to be practically formless. Probably the hardest problem of the artist handling it is to find the dominating structures to attach the textures to.[33]

Ransom found suggestions for an ontological account of poetry in the semantic system of Charles W. Morris, who recognized three irreducible forms of discourse: science, art, and technology. Discussing the credibility of aesthetic discourse, Morris declared that, like scientific discourse, it is objective and knowledge-giving. Ransom noted, however, that whereas scientific signs have no character other than that of referring to one another, aesthetic signs are "icons" or images. Thus, "man" is the scientific sign, whereas "this particular man" is the iconic sign. The icon of Hamlet, for example, is never twice the same. Such principles, Ransom reflected, are ontological. Art, concerned with the qualitative value of the actual world, defies the restrictiveness of science.[34]

In accord with the ontological analysis of poetry, Ransom believed that the development of metrical content parallels that of meaning, as indicated by the endless revisions of poets. The veteran poet senses the aesthetic value of the interplay, in the total structure of the poem, of indeterminate sound and indeterminate meaning: "Ontologically, it is a case of bringing into experience both a denser and a more contingent world, and commanding a discourse in more dimensions."[35]

Throughout his discussion, Ransom showed interest not in the poetry of Robinson, Frost, Robert Bridges, Yeats, or even Hopkins, but in that of Pound, Eliot, Tate, Stevens—the so-called modernists. In discussing the "indeterminateness" of such writers, he often became vague, speaking, for example, of *"indeterminateness* of the *positive* sort."

Further, he referred to modernist poetry as being "an ontological density which proves itself by logical obscurity."[36] One is lost in a broken-mirror room of paradoxes. Ransom's pontificating tone and language, however, were part of the story of the New Criticism and its correlative quixotic aesthetic.

Stanley Edgar Hyman (1919–1970)

Hyman's approach to criticism was indicated in his preface to *The Armed Vision* (1947), where he cited a particularly relevant passage from Sir Walter Scott:

> As to the herd of critics, it is impossible for me to pay much attention to them, for as they do not understand what I call

poetry, we talk in a foreign language to each other. Indeed, many of these gentlemen appear to me to be a sort of tinkers, who, unable to make pots and pans, set up for menders of them, and, God knows, often make two holes in patching one.[37]

Hyman defined art as the manipulation of human experience into meaningful and pleasurable patterns. Criticism, he said, is an autelic art. As a kind of poetry, it gives pleasure. This definition of criticism clearly differed from that of Eliot, who declared: "No exponent of criticism . . . has, I presume, ever made the preposterous assumption that criticism is an autelic art."[38]

In a further examination of critical principles, Hyman analyzed Richards's declaration that aesthetic experiences are "not in the least a new and different kind of thing" and that they can be studied in the same fashion as other experiences. This view, as Hyman pointed out, was anticipated by Conrad Aiken and even before him by John Dewey.[39]

With the penchant for contention characteristic of so many critics, Hyman listed Max Eastman, V. F. Calverton, and Henri Peyre among the bad and infuriating contemporary critics. Peyre, however, should certainly be credited with his recognition of the excitement inherent in creatively used erudition. Precisely because of his mastery in this respect he could see, as Hyman admitted, that

> Modern criticism is still groping for its method and enthu-
> siastically experimenting with several techniques. It has not yet
> outgrown the primitive stage in which physics similarly fumbled
> before Bacon and Descartes, chemistry before Lavoisier, soci-
> ology before Auguste Comte, and physiology before Claude
> Bernard.

Hyman charged that, having made the above statement, Peyre went on to make his sharpest attack on precisely those who represented the attempt of criticism to outgrow the primitive stage he described: Richards, William Empson, Kenneth Burke, and R. P. Blackmur.[40]

In his section on Eliot, Hyman pointed out that, contrary to Ransom's assessment of that poet-critic as "the historical critic [who]

uses his historical studies for the sake of literary understanding,"
Edmund Wilson saw Eliot as the very type of the unhistorical critic
—one who treated literature as though it existed in a temporal
vacuum.[41] Quite astutely, Hyman realized that Eliot absorbed his
influences so smoothly that he gave the impression of being a primary
source. Actually, his work was highly derivative. One need only
refer to Pound (to whom *The Waste Land* is dedicated), Hulme,
and Richards (whose influence Eliot frequently acknowledged), not
to speak of foreign influences, especially Gourmont.[42]

Here Hyman raises the question of consistency in a creative artist,
such as Eliot, who combined within himself the poet and the critic.
As F. O. Matthiessen argued, Eliot's essay "The Music of Poetry"
refuted "the fallacy that there is no harmony between his 'revolutionary' creative work and his 'traditionalist' criticism." Hyman
thought that the *Quartets* won many over to Matthiessen's view.
Others, however, would agree with William York Tindall, who maintained that Eliot's criticism was, "whatever its ostensible subject, a
criticism of his own practice"[43]—we might say, a defense of his own
practice.

Much of Hyman's criticism was concerned with the application
of various forms of psychology to criticism and literary aesthetics.
Like many others, he cited Maud Bodkin's *Archetypal Patterns in
Poetry: Psychological Studies of Imagination* (1934). This work is
based on Jung's theory of archetypes or unconscious primordial
images. These "psychic residua of numberless experiences of the
same type" were shared by modern man's primitive ancestors and
have been inherited in the structure of the brain.

For literary expression, the basic concepts are the collective unconscious and its archetypal patterns. Here Hyman noted E. E. Stoll's
attack on the application of the psychological method to the analysis
of literature and the defense it elicited from Bodkin. She argued
cogently that we must not dismiss one of our most valuable modern
insights—psychological awareness—as "an enriched apprehension."
(On Bodkin's use of Lowes's *The Road to Xanadu*, Hyman maintained that she was as oblivious as Lowes to the obvious sex symbolism of the caverns and mountains in *Kubla Khan*.)[44]

Although the application of psychoanalysis to the study of literature may perhaps go back to Freud's *The Interpretation of Dreams* (1900), it was not until Freud's visit to the United States in 1909 that his ideas, with the help of A. A. Brill, gained currency here. In Hyman's estimation, another important beginning was made in 1912 when Frederick Clarke Prescott applied Freud's *The Interpretation of Dreams* (not yet translated then) systematically to the interpretation of poetry in the article "Poetry and Dreams" (1919).

Prescott declared that poetry, like dreams, is the disguised fulfillment of repressed wishes. Freudian mechanisms found in "dream work" are also to be found in "poetic work." Hyman felt that in Prescott's *The Poetic Mind* (1922), Freudian psychoanalysis was watered down "to fit a new romantic mysticism and Shelley worship." It did anticipate Empson's "ambiguity" by insisting on plural meaning.[45]

Hyman's thoughts on Conrad Aiken should be examined in reference to Houston Peterson's study of Aiken, notably in the remark, "And our minds grow more complex as we contemplate theories of their complexity." Aiken, like so many of his contemporaries, has been subject to what Peterson called a "mania psychologica." Quite correctly, Peterson saw in Aiken a romantic who took modern psychology seriously. He attempted "to convert poetry into a kind of absolute music."

In *The House of Dust*, Aiken wrote: "Let us return, hear music and forget." In this poem his psychological burrowing can be seen in such lines as

> Our own brute minds—in which we hurry, trembling,
> Through streets as yet unlighted. . . .
> We are all searchers in a house of darkness,
> A house of dust; we creep with little lanterns. . . .

But what, one may ask, does this mean aesthetically?

> Why should we bring this need to seek for beauty,
> To lift our minds, if there were only dust?

The answer is in the sudden opening of a door and hearing "a sudden music."

The aesthetic quest is precisely for the musical moments in life or time and the nature of one's identity that seems to beckon, and to escape, from one expression of it to another.

So often Aiken set Freud to music—a music in which the repetitive theme is Festus's (that is, Aiken's) question:

> But am I then . . . in a cavern
> From which I dare not grow—
> Into the universe which is myself?

Through such psychological insights (those gained from Freud and Jung) Aiken came to understand that a poet-critic's pronouncements on the work of others really constitute a defense, as Peterson put it, of his own brand of poetry. They represent "a slow distillation of his temperament through his reason."[46]

Hyman showed that Aiken derived his basic attitude of contemporary criticism from Freud. Aiken even anticipated Richards's statement that poetry is a human product satisfying human needs and that its origins and functions may be open to analysis. Hyman believed, however, that the most penetrating use of psychoanalysis for criticism was made by Kenneth Burke in his "Freud and the Analysis of Poetry." Burke also drew heavily on gestalt psychology in order to achieve an integrated, "phenomenological" approach. He praised Caroline Spurgeon's *Shakespeare's Imagery and What It Tells Us* (1935) as one of the three most fertile works in literature since Eliot's *The Sacred Wood*, the other two being the volumes of Richards and Empson.[47]

According to Hyman, Burke's notion of literature as symbolic action may be traced to Plato's *Republic*. Socrates spoke of man's natural desire to find relief from misfortune in weeping and lamentation. He referred to the poets who delighted in presenting this feeling through controlled expression. For Hyman, however, Aristotle was the true father of symbolic action. In the *Poetics* Aristotle said that "happiness and misery are not states of being, but forms of activity." Pity and terror are not audience states but audience symbolic actions. Here Hyman aptly cited D. H. Lawrence's Freudian remark: "One sheds one's sickness in books."[48]

Burke's "dramatism," in Hyman's estimation, was derived from Aristotle and perhaps also from Scott Buchanan's *Poetry and Mathematics* (1929). Burke equated Aristotle's four causes—formal, material, efficient, and final—with act, scene, agent, and purpose. ("Act," "scene," and "agent" are the three terms central to the philosophy of drama embodied in Henry James's prefaces).

Burke also equated his categories with Aristotle's six elements of tragedy: plot as act, character as agent, thought as purpose, melody and diction as agency, and spectacle as scene.[49] Burke's analysis of Freud caused some critics to charge him with the use of "jargon" and has tempted Hyman to indulge himself in a sardonic bon mot. Hyman reflected that Burke received so little of the world's "increment" that he was forced to devote himself to its "excrement."[50]

Finally, Hyman made noteworthy reference to the divided modern mind, with its many levels of meaning and its concomitant many-leveled criticism. Thus Charles Baudouin (*Psychoanalysis and Aesthetics*, 1924) spoke of a "multiple parallelism," comparable to a polyglot Bible; Richards, of a "multiple definition" or "multiple interpretation"; Burke, of a "multiple causation"; Erich Fromm, of a "palimpsest" reading of Kafka in psychoanalytic, social, and religious terms; Prescott, of "multiple significance"; Philip Wheelwright, of "plurisignation"; and Austin Warren, of "concurrent multivalence."[51]

Richard Foster (1928–)

By 1962, Richard Foster felt that "a reappraisal of the New Criticism" was in order. He offered such a reappraisal in *The New Romantics*, with the quoted words serving as a subtitle. Here Foster argued that on close examination of the New Critic's aesthetics, epistemology, and metaphysics, he emerges as a romantic rather than as a classicist. He is to be identified by his sensibility rather than by his use of reason.[52]

Foster paid tribute to Murray Krieger's *The New Apologists for*

Poetry (1956), which provided Foster with his own point of departure. He considered his own discussion complementary to Krieger's.
They both viewed the sensibility and criticism of the New Critics
as "romantic." The claim of the New Critics that poetry provided
knowledge beyond reason and science was, in Foster's opinion, tantamount to a metaphysics of revelation.[53]

For Foster the New Critics

> . . . are twentieth-century romantics whose sensibilities as
> *romantics* overbalance whatever traditionalist viewpoints they
> may explicitly subscribe to . . . they have tended to oppose
> poetry to science . . . and . . . like the Romantics, in order to
> raise that opposition above the level of a merely desperate
> emotional reaction, they have developed and promoted a sup-
> porting theoretical doctrine that poetry is a high form of
> knowledge.[54]

Richards himself, in Foster's interpretation of *Coleridge on Imagination* (1935), shifted from mechanism to vitalism and in doing so
exhibited a romantic frame of mind. Those who followed Coleridge
would find themselves centered, not in the object but in their awareness of it. We might ask: What then would become of the hallowed
"objective correlative"? This question did not occur to Foster. Coleridge's notion of the "coincidence of an object with its subject"[55]
may be only a partial answer to that question.

William Elton (1921–   )

In "A Guide to the New Criticism" (1949),[56] Elton stated that
while the New Criticism has achieved a singular triumph in being
adopted in the college teaching of poetry, "its theories remain im-
penetrable and misunderstood" and that for this "its terminology
is largely to blame." He therefore attempted to provide a glossary.[57]

Elton saw the New Criticism as one of a series of critical replies
to the chaos of standards between two world wars: the neohumanism
of Paul Elmer More and Irving Babbitt; the economic determinism

of Granville Hicks; and the aesthetic or New Criticism of John Crowe Ransom.

In his glossary, Elton did not pretend to give final definitions of critical terms. He simply attempted to clarify the terms current in the New Criticism. In the process he ventured some critical remarks of his own. The student will find in his little guide thumbnail information on such items as Empson's seven types of ambiguity, and Philip Wheelwright's remark on Empson's confusion; form, irony, and poetry as knowledge; metaphor, ontology or the reality of being within a poem; and sensibility, structure, texture, symbol, tension, and wit.

Particularly pertinent here are Elton's definitions of "structure" and "texture." He culled his definition of structure from Ransom, Cleanth Brooks and Robert Penn Warren. Brooks took *The Rape of the Lock* as an illustration:

> The structure is not the heroic complex as such, or the canto arrangement . . . [or] that of the mock-epic convention. . . . [It] is a structure of meanings, evaluations, and interpretations; and the principle of unity which informs it seems to be one of balancing and harmonizing connotations, attitudes, and meanings. . . . It unites the like and the unlike.

The unity is not one of reduction and simplification. It is an achieved harmony. In such a structure we have "the frequent occurrence . . . of such terms as 'ambiguity,' 'paradox,' 'complex of attitudes' and . . . 'irony.' "[58]

On the question of "texture," Elton pointed out that Ransom directed attention from the semantic to the psychological—"the poem as a work on the order of a Freudian dream, having not only a *manifest* and possible content but a *latent* and suspected content." Ransom related the manifest content to the so-called public argument of structure, and the latent content to the free detail of texture. It is not at all clear, however, how in Ransom's system the thought work becomes the ego's while the play on substance becomes the id's. Because Ransom omitted the superego, the third member of the Freudian group, Elton suggested that it operates in the social relations of the poem, in the human functioning of structure and texture. Later Ransom abandoned Freudian probing.[59]

The Chicago School and Other Critics

Ronald Salmon Crane, a leading member of the so-called Chicago school of critics found two errors (ultimately, really one) in the New Criticism: (1) It approaches a variety of poems in the same way; it looks in all of them for one and the same structure (paradox, irony, complex meaning). (2) It is preoccupied with intellectual content; it seeks for structure exclusively in terms of thought rather than in anything that may be the distinctive unifier of a given poem. Thus, the New Critic's reading—as is the case, for instance, in Cleanth Brooks's analysis of Gray's *Elegy*—gives us not a poem but a subtle piece of dialectic.[60]

Another member of the Chicago Group,[61] Elder Olson, offered the following explanation of the emotive basis of art:

> We feel some emotion, some form of pleasure or pain, because our desires are frustrated or satisfied; we feel the desires because we are friendly or hostile to, or favour or do not favour the characters set before us . . . and we are friendly or hostile to the characters because of their ethical traits; in brief, *we side with the good against the bad* or . . . with the oppressed against the oppressor.

To speak this way, John Holloway commented, is to speak of those who boo the stage villain or cheer the hero.[62]

In his article "The Aesthetics of Textual Criticism" James Thorpe raised the interesting question of whether printers' errors are unwitting improvements on an author's version of his work and whether editorial emendations are real improvements on the original text. Paul Valéry declared that "once published, a text is like an apparatus that anyone may use as he will." Besides, if an author "knows well what he meant to do, this knowledge always disturbs his perception of what he has done." Thorpe commented: "We may be suspicious of anything that can be called authorial intention, for fear of committing the 'intentional fallacy.' "[63]

One of the main points made by Thorpe was that "the intentions of the person we call the author . . . become entangled with the intentions of all the others [printers, editors, commentators] who have a stake in the outcome, which is the work of art."[64] Because of this entanglement, the work of art is "always tending toward a collaborative status." No ultimate authority for the textual critic was claimed by Thorpe. He simply made a plea for a consistent set of aesthetic assumptions in terms of which the textual critic could recover and preserve the integrity of the text.[65]

The problem of "intention" engaged the attention of T. M. Gang, who accepted William R. Wimsatt's and Monroe C. Beardsley's position that criticism should concern itself with the poem "objectively" rather than with the mental processes that engendered it, or those that it produces.[66] For all that, Gang was not willing to ignore all information about the author or the historical context of the poem.

For Gang, "to mean" has two senses (often simultaneous): that of *intending* and that of *signifying*. When we ask what the poet meant, we are asking what he intended to signify. It is probably better, Gang said, to talk about the meaning of *King Lear* than about Shakespeare's intention in writing the play. Where external data (notebooks, prefaces, letters) contribute to our construction, the author's literary intention will be worth invoking.[67]

The concept of "subconscious intention" should be considered, Gang felt, because the unconscious is invoked not merely in conjunction with the neurotic but with the *discoverable* source of all behavior and of all art. Images and patterns are present in the unconscious quite apart from the artist's awareness. The "unconscious meaning" of a symbol, said Gang, is like the dictionary meaning of a word: we can look up our book of archetypal patterns to find out what it is. Gang's final conclusion is that we need not be afraid of the word "intention" and that even while using it we can treat the poem as something objectively existing.[68]

Along with the intentional fallacy, the New Critics, in their struggle to establish the autonomy of the individual work of art, combated the so-called biographical fallacy. René Wellek declared categorically in 1949, as Carlos Baker pointed out, that "No biographical evidence can change or influence critical evaluation." The following year, however, Leslie Fiedler counterattacked this as "a central dogma of much recent criticism."

With good humor, Baker related that in the 1940s "all a man needed to set himself up as Pontifex Maximus Scriblerus was wit, sensibility, imagination, a gift of gab, his bare hands—and a poem or a story to analyze the hell out of." In the late 1960s critics were no longer as cocksure as they had been in the 1940s about the irrelevance of history and biography in the effort to plumb or assess the products of the creative act. Had not an outstanding poet like Wallace Stevens declared before this—and Baker quoted these words:

> It is often said of a man that his work is autobiographical in spite of every subterfuge. It cannot be otherwise. . . . The truth is . . . that a man's sense of the world dictates his subjects to him and his sense is derived from his . . . temperament . . . over which he has little control. . . .

Baker himself reported that as a result of reading the letters of Stevens and Lawrance Thompson's biography of Frost, his understanding of these poets was deepened. His concluding remark, then, was that sensible critics will find relevance in biographical and historical material for a full understanding of poetry and literary products.[69]

Twelve years earlier, in writing a report for English readers on the state of criticism in America, Wimsatt struck a pessimistic note: "as usual, and perhaps necessarily, criticism is in a state of confusion and mess." Because of underlying difficulties, his prognostication was that criticism was "likely now and in the future to renew and sustain the confusion."[70]

One student of art and its history, Patricia Gebhard, has found the aesthetic of the New Criticism able to provide the means for examining the syntax and structure of the various arts. In defining a poem as the organization of man's experiences into an autonomous whole, the New Criticism presented the possibility of evaluating the other arts in terms of the same type of organic whole. When used thus, the New Criticism becomes an aesthetic theory that can aid in the understanding and enjoyment of all the arts.[71]

Although the aesthetic of the New Criticism has never been definitively defined, certain principles do emerge. Historically, it goes back to Plato and Aristotle and forward to Kant and Coleridge. In England, the chief proponent of what was to be named the New Criticism by Ransom was Richards, who was heavily indebted to Coleridge. The more immediate sources of New Criticism as it developed in America were Rémy de Gourmont and Hulme. Its central idea was that a work of art (especially a poem) is an organic, autonomous whole.

THE MODALITIES AND
DIALECTICS OF POESIS

In the periodic shifting of values, literary aesthetics has undertaken a constant reexamination of the nature of the creative process in terms of the structure of language and the relationship of poetry to cognition. This chapter deals with two sophisticated observers of literary-aesthetic ideas, particularly during the second two decades of our century—John Livingston Lowes (1867–1945) and Max Eastman (1883–1969)—and two poets who reacted critically to their craft—Robert Frost (1874–1963) and Wallace Stevens (1879–1955).

CONVENTION AND REVOLT:
LOWES AND EASTMAN

The theme of Lowes's *Convention and Revolt in Poetry* (1919) was *permanence in flux*. For him, convention entailed concurrence with certain accepted methods of communication as well as the acceptance of illusion (depth in a painting, time in a play). In both Wordsworth and Henri Amiel he found support for the idea that the poet's truth depends not on actuality but on illusion: "[The] very essence of poetic truth is accepted illusion and illusion to which we consent is the very tap root of conventions of poetry."[1]

In the conventions the poet finds the tools of his craft. Through a balance between recurrence and variation, convention often comes to life again. Thus, as Lowes indicated, a revival of the *ubi sunt* formula ("Where, oh where are?") occurred in Edgar Lee Masters's *Spoon River Anthology*:

> Where are Elmer, Herman, Bert . . . ?
> Where are Uncle Isaac and Aunt Emily . . . ?
> All, all, are sleeping on the hill.[2]

Admitting that the old could not be transformed forever, Lowes pointed to the irony that the new stays so only for a fleeting moment, as it were, and that the striving for newness often results in the display of devious tricks. He believed, further, that at its height the finest art would not only transcend but transmute the public taste.[3]

The relative roles of *denotation* and *connotation* were brought into the argument concerning the differentia of poetry and prose. Suggestions and connotations of words, Lowes maintained, are the very elements of poetry; a contrary situation prevails in scientific prose:

> *For words stir our feelings, not through a precise delimitation of their sense, but through their enveloping atmosphere of associations* [italics added]. . . . Not one word in a poem produces its effect through what a dictionary can afford.

As an example, he cited a passage from Robert Louis Stevenson's "Requiem":

> Home is the sailor, home from the sea,
> And the hunter home from the hill. . . .[4]

In this passage practically each word, although common enough, is, in the poetic context, richly freighted with an association of ideas. Because of this association, which Lowes did not express, the words have the power to waken within the reader that wistfulness, that metaphysical shiver, which evokes a darkly lyrical atmosphere. The shift of values becomes evident in comparison with the romantic belief that words had intrinsic poetic values, which, according to

Lowes, "conferred plenary absolution from the pains of thought upon poet and reader alike."

Such a doctrine later provoked a reaction in the form of the so-called New Poetry, especially among the imagists. Even earlier, however, Goethe had urged that the true master be revealed through *Beschränkung* (restraint), and Théophile Gautier challenged poets to look down "on facile measure":

> *Sculpte, lime, cisèle;*
> *Que ton rêve flottant*
> * se scelle*
> *Dans le bloc résistant!*

These lines were translated by Santayana:

> Chisel and carve and file,
> Till thy vague dream imprint
>   Its smile
> On the unyielding flint.[5]

Lowes, however, in his discussion of the "plenary absolution" of the romanticists from difficult workmanship, must have known better than most that Shelley and Keats, to mention only two romantic poets, often slaved over their poems, as their manuscripts reveal.

On the relative uses of thought and feeling in poetry, Lowes regarded poetry that embodied thought alone as prose disguised as verse: "But however feeling may render plastic the stuff of poetry, the poem, if it be worthy of the name, is forged in the brain." Looking at "the ruck of recent verse" in the monthly periodicals of his day, he found creative imagination utterly absent.[6]

In *The Literary Mind* (1931) Max Eastman found Lowes's *Convention and Revolt in Poetry* fundamentally unsound in its disregard of psychology and the logic of science. Rejecting Lowes's dictum that the very essence of poetic truth is accepted illusion, Eastman did not believe with Shelley and Wordsworth that poetry is the breath and finer spirit of science, although he did think that it can breathe a fine spirit into knowledge or science. In his remark that poetry cannot be the criticism of life but can be the life of criticism, he did not clearly indicate whether he meant that poetry can make criticism lively or that criticism can itself be a form of poetry. Like many earlier critics, he understood that in such writers as Goethe, Taine, and William James, poetry and science approached each other, if they did not indeed merge. James, wrote Eastman, was in fact "a great psychologist with poetry in his pen."[7]

IN PURSUIT OF POETIC IMAGINATION

The response to Lowes's *The Road to Xanadu: A Study in the Ways of the Imagination* was quite different. Stanley Edgar Hyman, for example, described it as "a major study in the operations of the poetic imagination," praising it further as a work in which "even the pursuit of sources becomes a critical activity."[8]

In such a study Lowes of course dealt with Coleridge's distinction between fancy and imagination—a distinction recently supported by Kenneth Burke. Lowes arrived at the conviction that these factors are not two powers but one: "The valid distinction which exists between them lies, not in the materials with which they operate, but in the degree of intensity of the operant power itself." In this opinion he was sustained years later by Lascelles Abercrombie, who declared outright that fancy was nothing but a degree of imagination and that "the degree of it concerns, not the quality of the imagery, but the quality and force of the emotion symbolized by the imagery."[9]

With great ingenuity and unflinching effort, Lowes traced Coleridge's imaginative process from a small manuscript notebook found at the British Museum to the emergence and completion of "The Rime of the Ancient Mariner" and "Kubla Khan." Indeed, an examination of this notebook prompted Lowes to follow Coleridge through his numerous primary and secondary sources.[10] In this search he may have been aided by Coleridge's revelation, in *Anima Poetae*, of the secret sources of both "Kubla Khan" and "The Rime of the Ancient Mariner": ". . . the imagination—the true inward creatrix, instantly out of the chaos of elements or shattered fragments of memory, puts together some form to fit it.[11]

Lowes hesitated to use the term "unconscious," resorting to Coleridge's suggestion of the twilight realms of consciousness.[12] To support Coleridge's views on the origins and operations of poetic creativity, Lowes cited a modern instance bearing the authority of a scientist, Henri Poincaré's *Science and Method*. In this work Poincaré maintained that the unconscious work of the imagination actually involves laborious preparation, and that the sudden illumination of the mind, after prolonged periods of unconscious work, remains mysterious, unless the conscious preparation is considered.

> [Let] us represent the future elements of our combinations as something resembling Epicurus's *hooked atoms* [*atomes crochus*]. When the mind is in complete repose these atoms are immovable. . . . Thus complete repose may continue indefinitely without the atoms meeting . . . without the possibility of the formation of any combination. . . . On the other hand, during a period of apparent repose, but of unconscious work, some of them are detached from the wall . . . and set in motion. . . . Their mutual collisions may then produce new combinations. . . . [We then have] unexpected coupling.[13]

Lowes also cited Dryden's description of fancy: "in its first Work [initial stage], moving the sleeping Images of things towards the Light, there to be distinguished, and then either chosen or rejected by the Judgment."[14] Finally, Lowes offered Coleridge's own concise definition: "the streaming nature of association which thinking curbs and rudders."[15]

Lowes understood that poetic creativity will always involve "something inscrutable which no analysis can reach." His primary concern was with Coleridge's association of ideas—his combination of *atomes crochus*.[16] On the role of psychoanalysis in such a study, Lowes stated categorically that he was dealing only with the material content of the dream, not at all with the latent.[17]

His dubious description of the dreamer as merely a detached and unsolicitous spectator was subsequently corrected:

> The sole factor that determined the form and sequence [of] the dissolving phantasmagoria [in "Kubla Khan"] was the subtle potency of the associative links. There was this time no intervention of a waking intelligence intent upon a plan . . . and it is largely that absence of deliberate manipulation which has made it possible to disengage, to a degree unattainable in our study of "The Ancient Mariner," the bewildering hooks and eyes of the memory which were the irresponsible artificers of the dream.[18]

In Coleridge's previously quoted description of the imagination, Lowes found the ultimate statement of the poet's views on form and dream.[19]

One of the pervasive questions in literary aesthetics involves the role of fact in the creative process. The fact may itself be the *romance of the mind*, a phrase used by Henry Osborn Taylor as the title of his book (devoted to his humanistic approach to science). In the measurement of civilization various types of facts have to be taken into account: the material, the intellectual, the moral, the political, and the aesthetic. Although the idea of number (measurement) has been applied in varying degrees to all of them, the first is the most susceptible to measurements, while the last can be measured only with difficulty, if at all.[20]

To what extent does *fact* of the material kind play a role in the creative imagination? Lowes stated forthrightly that the notion that the creative imagination has little or nothing to do with the facts "is one of the *pseudodoxia epidemica* which die hard. . . . For the imagination never operates in a vacuum. Its stuff is always fact of some order, somehow experienced; its product is that fact transmuted."[21] The artist, of course, must prevent facts from overwhelming imagination—a danger also confronted by the scientist, for whom a theory is a scientific poem, and science itself, as Gaston Bachelard noted, the aesthetic of intellect. With Coleridge, certainly, the mind was not merely "a lazy looker-on on an external world,"[22] but a force actively concerned with the unity of mind and the object of its contemplation. The maintenance of such a view of the mind is *the* essential problem of aesthetics.

IMAGISM

In 1931, when Glenn Hughes published his *Imagism and Imagists,* the movement was still alive, although it had ceased to be the center of critical controversy. Hughes discussed six "official" representatives of the period: Richard Aldington, H. D. (Hilda Doolittle), John Gould Fletcher, F. S. Flint, D. H. Lawrence, and Amy Lowell. He added the name of Ezra Pound "because of his importance to the movement as an organizer."[23]

Pound invented the term imagism[24] and described the four basic principles of the movement: (1) direct treatment of matters subjective or objective, (2) economy in the use of words, (3) composition "in sequence of the musical phrase, not the sequence of a metronome," and (4) conformity to the doctrine of the image. Pound defined the image as "that which presents an intellectual and emotional complex in an instant of time." He added that "it is better to present one Image in a lifetime than to produce a voluminous work."[25]

The principles of imagism were further defined by Aldington and Lowell[26] as essentially those of all great literature: the use of the common, exact, rather than the decorative word; the creation of new cadences that carry new ideas; freedom in choice of subject; the presentation of exact images that avoid the vague and the "cosmic"; and a general adherence to modern life, with, however, a rejection of certain of its uninspiring elements.[27]

Lowell was particularly concerned with the problems of *vers libre,* which she called "cadenced verse":

> It is the sense of perfect balance of flow and rhythm. . . . The unit of *vers libre* is not the foot, the number of syllables, the quantity, or the line. The unit is the strophe, which may be the whole poem, or may be only a part. Each strophe is a complete circle. . . . [The] circle need not always be the same size, nor need the times allowed to negotiate it always be the same. . . . Also circles can be added to circles, movement upon

movement to the poem, provided each movement completes itself, and ramifies naturally into the next.[28]

She used "H.D." 's "Oread" as an example:

> Whirl up, sea—
> Whirl your pointed pines,
> Splash your great pines
> On our rocks,
> Hurl your green over us,
> Cover us with your pools of fir.

In this poem each line is a cadence composed of time units in which the number of syllables is immaterial and which are to be read at varying tempi.[29]

Reactions to Imagism

Conrad Aiken, one of the most vocal adversaries of imagism, charged that its adherents constituted a mutual admiration society, that they lacked emotional force and were therefore unable to stir the reader, and that, except for Fletcher, they were all "music deaf."[30]

Another adversary, William Ellery Leonard, declared that the imagists could not see straight, feel straight, think straight, or talk straight.[31] As an example, he quoted Amy Lowell's "Bullion":

> My thoughts
> Chink against my ribs
> And roll about like silver hailstones
> I should like to spill them out.

Leonard's comment to this was: "Dear lady, I wish you might; you would feel easier."[32] He continued: "Their words don't spring to life, as wisdom from power. . . . [They] are sought for, hunted out, not prayed for, waited for. . . ." His final estimate was that the imagists were guilty of quackery.[33]

Yet another critical response to imagism, and again particularly to the poems of Amy Lowell, came from John Livingston Lowes himself. He restated in crystallized form the imagist credo: "Hard, clear images embodied in unrimed cadence; precision of delineation linked with flexibility of rhythm." Then, stimulated by Witter Bynner's remark that "George Meredith has thousands of imagist poems incidental to each of his novels," Lowes printed as prose three passages from Lowell's *vers libre* poems, concluding that "Miss Lowell's free verse may be written as very beautiful prose; George Meredith's prose may be written as very beautiful free verse. Which is which?"

Lowell's own answer was, "There is no difference." She added that typography is irrelevant and that a comparison of Meredith's lyrical passages from his prose with his own metrical poetry would reveal the advantages his imagination enjoyed in using freer forms.[34]

And so the battle continued. In 1917, T. S. Eliot declared emphatically that *vers libre* did not exist, that it was simply "a battle-cry of freedom in art," that "the ghost of some simple meter should lurk behind the arras in even the 'freest verse,' " and that "freedom is only truly freedom when it appears against the background of an artificial limitation."[35]

The idea, said Hughes, that cadence should be substituted for meter, and that the result could be distinguished from prose, was at the very heart of the imagist credo.[36] John Gould Fletcher argued that the basis of English poetry was "rhythm, or, as some would call it, cadence." Using geometric metaphors to represent the difference between prose and poetry, he envisiond thought and emotion as expressed in prose, developing in a straight line, from the point of view of a flat surface. Breadth is secured by the grouping of sentences in a paragraph; the sensation of depth is obtained by the arrangement of blocks of thought "in a rising climacteric progression, or in parallel lines, or in a sort of zigzag figure." In poetry, on the other hand,

> . . . we have a succession of curves. The direction of thought is not in straight lines, but wavy and spiral. It rises and falls on gusts of strong emotion. Most often it creates strongly marked loops and circles. The structure of the stanza or strophe

always tends to be spherical. Depth is obtained by making one sphere contain a number of concentric or overlapping spheres.

Fletcher concluded that the difference between poetry and prose is "a difference between a general roundness and a general square-ness of outline."[37] Fletcher's geometrical analogies also suggest a difference between the maleness of prose and the femaleness of poetry and a bisexuality in cases where poetry has an admixture of prose and where prose contains poetry.

These discussions of free verse were illustrated by Eastman's in-genious juxtaposition of two passages:

> (A) Any space is not quiet it is so likely to be shining. Dark-ness very dark darkness is sectional. There is a way to see in onion and surely very surely rhubarb and a tomato, surely very surely there is that seeding.
> (B) I was looking at you, the sweet boy that does not want sweet soap. Neatness of feet do not win feet, but feet win the neatness of men. Run does not run west but west runs east. I like the strawberries best.

Eastman took one of these passages from Kraepelin's *Clinical Psy-chiatry* and the other from a work by Gertrude Stein. Now which is which? Passage A is by Stein, whom Edith Sitwell credited with revivifying the language through her very anarchy.[38] Thus the cult of unintelligibility seems to attempt everything from the annihilation of syntax to typographical peculiarities. To what end? The work of Robert Frost may suggest an answer.

TWO POETS AND THE CREATIVE PROCESS

Robert Frost (1874–1963)

Ezra Pound, who met Frost in London in 1912, found that New Englander to be a birch that could not be bent "down to stay" ("Birches"). No, Pound could not make an imagist disciple of him.

Everything Frost took—or took to—he made conform to his own style. Many of the forces that affected Frost's early development are explained in Lawrance Thompson's three-volume biography,[39] which describes Frost's early exposure to Swedenborgian symbolism and correspondences; to Wordsworth, Bryant, and particularly to Emerson. From his mother he learned to appreciate Poe. He read Cooper, Francis Parkman, William Hickling Prescott, Thomas Gray, and Sir Walter Scott. He was impressed by the death poems of Edward Rowland Sill and was even more fascinated by the somber wit and terse statements in Emily Dickinson's poems. With Elinor (his future wife) he read Shelley, and while working in the Arlington Mill, he read Shakespeare and Thomas Hardy, who taught him "the good use of a few words." Frost also read Keats, Tennyson, and Browning and he was moved by Francis Thompson's "The Hound of Heaven." In his reading of Virgil, as Lawrance Thompson noted, Frost became aware of the entire range of pastoral poetry, while the Iliad and the Odyssey made him familiar with the scope of epic art.[40]

At Harvard, Frost felt the influence of William James (then on leave).[41] Half a century later, when I asked Frost whether he "had" George Santayana, he replied (not without the dawn of an ironic smile), "Yes, he had me."

Frost's early humanistic interest in astronomy was deepened by his reading of Richard Proctor's *Our Place among Infinities* (1876), while his interest in earth science was aroused by Nathaniel Southgate Shaler's course in historical geology. Thompson suggested that historical geology interacted with Frost's interest in astronomy, furnishing many metaphors and images that were subsequently incorporated in his poems.[42]

Writing about Nathaniel S. Shaler, William James remarked, "Of all the minds I have known, his leaves the largest impression," and he described Shaler's *From Old Fields* as "a great epic wind of sadness blowing through it all."[43] Whether or not young Frost read that volume of poems on the Civil War, its "touch of Thomas Hardy's feeling for fate" must have emerged in Shaler's lectures, particularly impressing the young Frost. Certainly, this "touch" is evident in Frost's "A Question":

A voice said, Look in the Stars
And tell me truly, men of earth,
If all the soul-and-body scars
Were not too much to pay for birth.[44]

Here the influence of Schopenhauer has joined that of Proctor, Shaler, and Hardy.

Frost appreciated *Walden* as being "near the height of poetry." And Emerson's essays and poems expressed for him "the rapture of idealism." As a teacher at Pinkerton, he read with his classes Longfellow's "Evangeline" and "The Courtship of Miles Standish," Hawthorne's *The House of the Seven Gables* and Maeterlinck's *Blue Bird*.[45] The influence of Hawthorne was particularly strong, and Frost must have been moved by such passages as the following:

> The northwest wind has swept the sky clear. The window is distinctly seen. Through its panes, moreover, we dimly catch the sweep of the dark, clustering foliage, outside, fluttering with a constant irregularity of movement, and letting in a peep of starlight. . . . These glimpses illuminate the Judge's face. . . . The moonbeams fall aslant into the room. They play over the Judge's figure and show that he has not stirred throughout the hours of darkness. . . . They gleam upon his watch. His grasp conceals the dial-plate; but we know that the faithful hands have met; for one of the city clocks tells midnight.[46]

This poetic amalgam of the elements of nature, of the dramatic dialectic of light and darkness, of man's loneliness, and of death reappeared throughout Frost's poetry. In "I Will Sing You One-O," for example, the wind and the cold suggest a fear that they "Had checked the pace/Of the tower clock," recalling Hawthorne's "one of the city clocks [telling] midnight." Here and elsewhere Frost and Hawthorne showed a common companionship with the night and with the dramatization of "finalities."

French literature also had its impact on Frost, although not to the same extent as on Stevens. At the State Normal School in Plymouth, New Hampshire, Frost had his students read Rousseau's *Émile*. In

1911 he read the newly published American translation of Bergson's *Creative Evolution*, in which he found many metaphors on the contending forces of mind and matter.[47] Thompson did not notice that Bergson quoted some words from a work by Frost's professor of geology:

> A geologist whom we have already had occasion to cite, N. S. Shaler, says excellently: "When we come to man, it seems that we find abolished the ancient subjection of mind (spirit) to body, and that the intellectual aspects develop with extraordinary speed, while the structure of the body remains identical in all essentials."[48]

In 1939, the French reciprocated Frost's compliment with a long article on Frost in the influential *Nouvelle Revue française*.[49]

After receiving full recognition as a poet with the publication of *A Boy's Will* in England in April, 1913, Frost was encouraged to philosophize about his craft. He may have been moved to do so by the prevalance of the technical "palaver" of the literati among whom he then moved. Thus he wrote to a friend that contrary to the notion of some successful poets that "the music of words was a matter of harmonised vowels and consonants," he "alone of English writers" had consciously set himself "to make music out of what he might call the sound of sense."[50]

Frost subsequently expressed the following principles:

> A sentence is a sound in itself on which other sounds called words may be strung.
> [The] sentence sound often says more than the words. . . .
> [There] is always danger of overloading [the sentence with words].
> I like to drag and break the intonation across the meter as waves first comb and then break stumbling on the shingle.[51]

In the years after his return to America in 1915, Frost described many other principles of the poetic art. Considering poetry as education, he maintained that crude enthusiasm could be educated into taste by metaphor. He would go so far as to make metaphor "the whole of thinking," noting that "unless you are at home in the meta-phor, unless you have had your proper poetical education in the metaphor, you are not safe anywhere. . . . "[52] Here Frost was remi-niscent of Bachelard's statement, "A poetic spirit is purely and simply a syntax of metaphors,"[53] and in the following remark he reminds one of Emerson:

> Greatest of all attempts to say one thing in terms of another
> is to say matter in terms of spirit, or spirit in terms of matter,
> to make the final unity. That is the greatest attempt that ever
> failed.

In *Nature*, Emerson wrote:

> The laws of moral nature answer to those of matter as face
> to face in a glass.

> The whole of nature is a metaphor of the mind.

> Nature is the incarnation of a thought, and turns to thought
> as ice becomes water and gas.[54]

Frost's allusion to metaphor as coextensive with thought also recalls an observation by John Middleton Murry: "To attempt a funda-mental examination of metaphor would be nothing less than an inves-tigation of thought itself."[55]

In exploring the relationship of metaphor to thought, Frost cited a line from the Odyssey: "So Odysseus covered the seeds of fire in himself."[56] This passage recalls Shelley's comparison of the mind in the process of creation to a fading coal kept alive by some invisible influence—a metaphorical description of thought that Frost may have connected with Schopenhauer's "Reason is the spectacles through which the will contemplates things."[57] This approach to metaphor is somewhat similar to that of Bergson, as described by Santayana:

> We are old men trying to sing the loves of children; we
> are wingless bipeds trying to understand the gods.—Mr. Bergson
> is a most delicate and charming poet on this theme, and a

plausible psychologist; his method of accumulating and varying his metaphors, and leaving our intuition to itself under that artful stimulation, is the only judicious and persuasive method he could have employed and his knack at it is wonderful.[58]

Frost's views on the so-called experimentalists in poetry were expressed in his introduction to Edwin Arlington Robinson's *King Jasper, A Poem* (1935), in which he attacked those writers who worked

> . . . without punctuation—without capital letters—without metric frame—without any images but those to the eye—without content—without ability—without feeling or sentiment, like murder for small pay in the underworld.

As a contrast to such attitudes, he praised Robinson's satisfaction with "the old ways to be new." Frost noted further that Robinson "asserted the sacred right of poetry to lean its breast to a thorn and sing its dolefullest,"[59] as in Oscar Wilde's "The Nightingale and the Rose":

> So the Nightingale pressed closer against the thorn, and louder and louder grew her song, for she sang of the birth of passion . . . only a Nightingale's heart's-bloom can crimson the heart of a rose. (When the rose was finished, the nightingale "was lying dead in the long grass, with the thorn in her heart.")[60]

Without mentioning Georges-Louis Buffon, Frost commented on his dictum that the style is the man:

> Rather say the style is the way the man takes himself. . . .
> If it is with outer seriousness, it must be with inner humor.
> If it is with outer humor, it must be with inner seriousness.
> Neither one without the other under it will do. Robinson was thinking as much in his sonnet on Tom Hood.[61]

In particular, Frost admired Robinson's ability to "make lyric talk like drama" (in "The Mill") and his imagination for speech (in "John Gorham").

He concluded that Robinson's life "was a revel in the felicities of language," as in the following:

> . . . God forbid
> That ever I should preach, and in my zeal
> Forget that I was born an humorist;
> But now, for once, before I go away,
> I beg of you to be magnanimous
> A moment, while I speak to please myself.[62]

Who is speaking here? These lines belong to Robinson's "Captain Craig," but how much of this speech informs the tone—the voice—of Frost in "Birches"! Influence? Perhaps. Certainly this passage suggests a common bond of New England temperament in which humor and somber wit combine to form a dramatic texture.

In "The Constant Symbol" Frost repeated his statement that not only is poetry made of metaphor but "so is philosophy and science too." And he noted that "Every poem is a new metaphor inside or it is nothing. And there is a sense in which all poems are the same old metaphor always."[63]

Such views were elaborated in "The Figure a Poem Makes" (1949), which included the following observations:

> The sound is the gold in the ore.
>
> The figure a poem makes: it begins in delight and ends in wisdom. The figure is the same as for love.
>
> It is but a trick poem and no poem at all if the best of it was thought of first and saved for the last.
>
> No tears in the writer, no tears in the reader.[64]
>
> The initial surprise is in remembering something I didn't know I knew. . . . There is a glad recognition of the long lost and the rest follows. Step by step the wonder of unexpected supply keeps growing.[65]

The last statement is intimiately related to Henri Poincaré's declaration on the role of the unconscious (memory) in creativity and, of course, to Bergson's ideas on the nature and role of memory.

Frost's interest in science and his association of it with humanistic studies were recognized by the mathematician Marston Morse at a conference in honor of Frost. In his paper Morse asserted that "the basic affinity between mathematics and the arts is psychological and spiritual and not metrical or geometrical." He maintained further that in mathematics, as in the arts, the essential fact is that "discovery is not a matter of logic but rather the result of mysterious powers which no one understands." Recalling Poincaré, Morse cited Frost's "The Figure a Poem Makes," especially the observation "I tell how there may be a better wildness of logic, than of inconsequence. But the logic is backward, in retrospect after the act."

In support of this view, Morse noted that the perfect beauty of mathematics is rational, but rational in retrospect. Here Morse placed Frost beside Poincaré and Carl Friedrich Gauss, just as A. N. White-head included Shelley in his reflections on cosmology. This linking of poetry and science arises, said Morse, from the nature of the human understanding: "The urge to understand is the urge to embrace the world as a unit, to be a man of integrity in the Latin meaning of the word."[66]

Such views were reflected in Frost's assertion that mere technique cannot assure the production of a genuine poem: "Like a piece of ice on a hot stove the poem must ride on its own melting. A poem may be worked over once it is in being, but it may not be worried into being."[67] For Frost, the ontology of a poem was characterized by vocal imagery, a uniqueness of voice. His aesthetic depended on the oral-aural impact of a poem, the texture of which is essentially metaphoric. In another context, his aesthetic stemmed from images of the "pastoral self."[68] Like Virgil's and Hardy's, Frost's expression of beauty emanated from the collision of the primal self with primal forces.

Wallace Stevens (1879–1955)

Frost and Stevens, although not acquainted at the time, were fellow students at Harvard. After several subsequent meetings, Stevens expressed in his letters rather ambiguous views of Frost, such as the following: "Frost is greatly admired by many people. I do not know his work well enough to be either impressed or unimpressed."[69] Stevens's niggardly attitude often suggests in fact a jealousy of Frost.

Unlike his classmate, Stevens admired Santayana, with whom he frequently conversed and whose sonnets he praised. His doubts about and ambitions for his own future as a poet were recorded in a journal that Stevens began to keep about this time. In a manner reminiscent of Gray's "Elegy" he wrote: "Many of us deceive ourselves that we are glorious but mute [poets]." Actually, he took comfort in the thought that prosaic people did not have poetical feelings[70]—and, of course, he was not prosaic!

Stevens believed that learning was not a part of the poet's trade but was acquired because of "a need to counterbalance poetry":

> The mind cannot always live in a divine ether—There must exist—an anchorage of thought. Study gives this anchorage. . . . Study is the resting place—the poetry, the divine adventure.[71]

Concerned, like Frost, with the poetic treatment of death, Stevens found this theme in David Gray's collection of poems *In the Shadows,* of which he wrote: "There are some things in these sonnets which almost brings tears to one's eyes."[72]

After Harvard, he worked for the *Tribune* in New York. Taking refuge in his dreams, he filled his journal with all kinds of literary projects. The word "blue" began to appear: "The streets are *blue* with mists this morning" (*Journal,* January 1, 1901). "God! What a thing blue is!" Inevitably, a poem resulted, featuring the word "columbine."[73] Further, "one must have blue birds—even if one says silly and affected things about them."[74] Blue . . . blue birds—how much these images recall Novalis and the search for the blue flower, which was one of the pervasive symbols of the Edenic quest of the romantic poets and their "magic idealism."

Stevens, in pursuit of the poet within him, reported his reading of Hardy; of Matthew Arnold's notebooks with quotations within them from Sénancour's *Obermann*; of Leopardi's "Thoughts," which

Stevens likened to Pascal's "Thoughts"; and of La Rochefoucauld's "Maxims." He exclaimed: "How true they all are! I should like to have a library of such things."[75] In these words, Stevens anticipated his own "Adagia" and "A Collect of Philosophy."

Influenced by Santayana's sonnets and by the sonnet form in general, Stevens wrote in 1906, while working in a law office, that he had been "engaged—all day on a sonnet—surreptitiously."[76] To his sweetheart Elsie he quoted lines from Andrew Lang's sonnet "The Odyssey":

> As one that for a weary space has lain
> Lulled by the songs of Circe and her wine.[77]

This sonnet may have reminded Stevens of Keats's "On First Looking into Chapman's Homer" and Arnold's "Dover Beach." In any case, the figure of Ulysses dominated his later thought: "Ulysses, Symbol of the Seeker," who "crossing by night/The giant sea, read his own mind."[78]

In 1907 Stevens became a Greenwich Village sophisticate, moving to The Benedick on Washington Square, where he shared an apartment with Horace Mann. Here Stevens assumed an attitude of romantic ennui: "Life is a very, very thin affair, except for the feelings. . . . The plain truth is . . . that I like to be anything but my plain self."[79] He was struck by the lyricism of Verlaine, Housman, and Bliss Carman. He quoted Carman's version of Sappho:

> Sweet mother, I cannot weave my web,
> Broken as I am by longing.[80]

Again to Elsie, he cited a passage from Cicero that struck him "as such an admirable inscription for the façade of a library":

> O, philosophy, thou guide of life!
> O, thou that searchest out virtues and expellest vices!

Finally, he explained his penchant for "pensées," brief thoughts stored for future use: "My mind is rather full of such things, and so re-

sembles the mood that fastened me a year or so ago, so intently on
Matthew Arnold and maxims."[81] Although his own literary aesthetic
perhaps never progressed beyond the level of "pensées" and "collects,"
Stevens continued to gather such thoughts, seeking to incorporate
them into his own attitudes.

With Elsie, Stevens discussed the effect of music on the imagination, asserting that music evoked a sort of racial memory, which
illuminated the mystery of the past.[82] He also observed the effects
of light and darkness on the psyche, describing the obscurity of
twilight and night when the emotions replace intellect.[83] Here
Stevens recalls Emerson's *cognitio matutina* (morning or day knowledge) and *cognitio vesperina* (an evening or night knowledge).
Throughout this period Stevens continued to express his longing for
"an authentic and fluent speech for myself."[84]

The poetic awareness developing within Stevens at this time may
be contrasted with the work of his contemporary Edgar Lee Masters,
whose *Spoon River Anthology* was published in 1915. In this work
Masters adopted the innovative free verse of his time, "allying it
with one of the great traditions of literature through the Greek
Anthology." His subject matter confronted, as Ludwig Lewisohn
noted, "the new terrors which life had added to the old," leading
Masters to reject "a sick aesthetic and sicker ethic,"[85] in a style again
described by Lewisohn:

> Style . . . proceeds from either severity or elevation of mind
> and character. . . . Edgar Masters has that severity of mind and
> character that makes for style. . . . He can sometimes hold this
> note of style throughout a whole poem—as in that on Thomas
> Trevelyan with its admirable close:
>
> > And all of us change to singers, although it be
> > But once in our lives, or change, alas to swallows.
> > To twitter among cold winds and falling leaves.[86]

In his anthologies Masters found beauty in pain, avoiding a mannered literary flirtation with soul states, where manner obscures
content. His reflections on the conflicts of life have both emotional

and intellectual appeal, as Lewisohn remarked: "I do not in fact
know any American book in which there is more fundamental brain
work, more sharp and accurate thinking about life, than in the
'Spoon River' anthologies."[87]

By contrast Stevens seems mannered, avoiding poems of hunger,
frustration, and abortive dreams of love in favor of speculation on
the mind and "reality." Unlike Masters, Stevens was concerned with
poetry as language, rather than with language as the vehicle of the
poetry of life. Stevens, moreover, despite his wish to put "an end to
rhetoric," was rhetorical, merely mouthing an "aesthetic of evil"
while Masters communicated that aesthetic directly. Masters, no
mere "lecturer of facetious paradox," no "pessimist . . . only by word
of mouth . . . a cautious rebel" who "longed for fame," was far
removed from Stevens's "whipped creams and Blue Danube" and
"Mandolin and Liqueurs." He does not dally with things that "are
not as they are" by playing "on a blue guitar."[88]

As Stevens continued his development he occasionally expressed
misgivings about the possibility of playing the double role of poet
and businessman:

> One of the essential conditions to the writing of poetry is
> impetus. That is a reason for thinking that *to be a poet at all
> one ought to be a poet constantly* [italics added]. It was a great
> loss to poetry when people began to think that the professional
> poet was an exile.[89]

Elaborating this thought, Stevens remarked that life "means a good
deal more to us now-a-days than literature does," reversing his earlier
belief in the superior worth of literature.[90] In 1941, however, he
further developed his aesthetic in "The Noble Rider and the Sound
of Words."[91] Citing the figure of the charioteer and the pair of
winged horses from the *Phaedrus*, Stevens seems to shift his discussion of poetry from psychology to philosophy—perhaps unfortunately
in view of Plato's treatment of rhetoric as "verbal sorcery," or "spirit
raising."[92] For Stevens, nevertheless, the charioteer and the winged
horses represented the conflict of psychological opposites, although
he seems to have weakened the image in his remark that "we have

identified ourselves with the charioteer." Stevens, moreover, could not resolve the ambiguity of I. A. Richards's opposition of fancy and imagination, in which fancy is described as an exercise in selectivity from among objects supplied by association, but not of the will striving to realize itself in knowing itself.[93] Fancy, as contrasted with imagination, must in fact be the passive sensory reception of impressions, which are incorporated into a structure of appearance and illusion. Imagination is the active process of transmuting appearance and illusion into a poetic reality that, in its concreteness, transcends fancy.

Stevens's speculations were continually confused by his discussions of "reality." His remark, "In nature the imagination loses vitality as it ceases to adhere to what is real," seems obscure, unless Stevens was confusing *reality* (the nature of things as contemplated by the scientist, metaphysician, or aesthetician) with *actuality* (events as they occur in daily experience). The latter definition appears most suitable, especially because Stevens observed that Plato's figure has lost its vitality because "in it, the imagination adheres to ·vhat is unreal."[94] Stevens's own imagination was here put into ʝuestion. His concept of reality was at best that of Scottish common sense, which always held the poetic process suspect.

Such an interpretation makes questionable his thesis of the failure of the idea of nobility in art as a result of the failure in the relation between the imagination and reality. He insisted that "what has been said in respect to the figure of the charioteer illustrates this,"[95] although in fact this figure does not illustrate his proposition at all. Stevens, moreover, never clarified his concept of "nobility" in connection with poetic imagination.

Stevens also encountered difficulties in his consideration of the denotative and connotative uses of language. He indicated no authority for his statement that "Locke and Hobbes *denounced* the connotative use of words as an abuse." He followed this remark with a facile non sequitur:

> When we speak of reactions and reforms, we are speaking,
> on the one hand, of a failure of the imagination to adhere

to reality, and, on the other, of a use of language favorable to reality.[96]

Actually, the connotative and the denotative in language are never so sharply divided. For instance, the word "machine," essentially denotative, becomes connotative in the exclamatory question, "What do you take me to be, a machine!?" On this point, Philip Wheelwright, in his lecture "Poetry, Myth and Reality," admitted that no *absolute* division exists between so-called steno-language (denotative) and emotive language (connotative).[97] Even while Stevens claimed that the general movement in the arts has been toward the denotative, he was aware that this contention was disputable, that the interest in the subconscious and in surrealism revealed rather a tendency toward the imaginative and the connotative.[98]

As indicated earlier, Stevens's various reflections on poetic theory (and the ideas closely associated with it) took the form, largely, of dicta or pensées. In 1951 he expressed his regret that the only theory of poetry then possible for him was to be found in his *The Necessary Angel: Essays in Reality and the Imagination*.[99] As the title indicates, he was still preoccupied with the question of "reality" in relation to poetry: "The real is constantly being engulfed in the unreal. . . . [Poetry] is an illumination of a surface, the movement of a self in the rock.[100]

Like Frost, Stevens was an ardent reader of Bergson's *Creative Evolution*. As with Frost, moreover, William James figured in the experience. Stevens quoted from a letter addressed by the American philosopher to Bergson: "You may be amused at the comparison, but in finishing it [*Creative Evolution*] I found the same after-taste remaining as after finishing *Madame Bovary*, such a flavor of persistent euphony." Stevens himself had earlier made a reference to Flaubert, when he compared him with Stendhal.[101]

Such reading stimulated Stevens to speculate on the relationship between philosophy and poetry, perhaps mindful of Madame de Staël's comments that there are poetic philosophers as well as philosophical poets ("Our best lyric poets in France are perhaps our great writers in prose—Bossuet, Pascal, Fénélon, Buffon, Jean-Jacques

[Rousseau]"). In studying the relationship of philosophy and poetry, Stevens discovered Leon Roth's exegesis of Descartes's *Discourse on Method*. Roth referred to Descartes's dream in which he beheld two books, one containing all scientific knowledge, the other (which he valued more highly) containing all the inspired wisdom of poetry.

According to Adrien Baillet, Descartes's own interpretation of his dream was as follows: The dictionary on his table stood for sciences collectively. The other volume, a collection of poetry entitled *Corpus poetarum*, meant precisely philosophy and wisdom conjointly.[102] Roth pointed out that it was the "rationalist" Voltaire who first called attention to the "poetic" in Descartes and to the fact that his last work was a ballet. The philosopher's richness of style is also notable, even in his analysis of the "passions of the soul.[103]

Stevens labored hard to establish metaphor and analogy as the heart of poetry. For him, resemblance was one of the principal components of the structure of reality, and "poetry is a satisfying of the desire for resemblance," that is, a part of the structure of reality. Poetry and metaphor are one. When Stevens added that poetry is almost one of the effects of analogy (the analogy between the sense of our world and the sense of the poet's world),[104] he was reiterating Emerson's ideas.

Seeking to align himself with authority on all sides (to achieve "safety"), Stevens reflected:

> If we escape destruction [on the ground of the validity of poetry] at the hands of the logical positivists and if we cleanse the imagination of the taint of the romantic, we still face Freud. What would he have said of the imagination as the clue to reality and of a culture based on imagination?[105]

Here Stevens (so bent on securing poetry on the basis of reality) seems unfair both to Freud's imaginative perceptions and to the intuitive genius of Schelling and other romantics before him.

Stevens was disturbed that reason stands between imagination and reality. Reason and imagination, he said, are engaged in a struggle for reality. He felt that this conflict was a continuing struggle without a possible outcome. He turned to Pascal[106] (as he had done before) but missed the true import of Pascal's two tonalities—the spirit of finesse and the spirit of geometry.

He failed to understand that every thought and every feeling has its horizon;[107] in one instance, the emphasis on experience will manifest itself against (and in) the background of the spirit of geometry; in another, against that of the spirit of finesse. The two tonalities, however, have a common aesthetic matrix. Thus, Lucretius, in his *De rerum natura*, presented a memorable case of "passionate thought" and Henry Adams came close to combining the two tonalities in his twin poems "Prayer to the Virgin of Chartres" and "Prayer to the Dynamo."

For Stevens, *nervous sensibility* was more meaningful than plain sensibility. He divided modern poetry into two classes: modern in content and modern in form. He noted that much verse, following the example of Mallarmé's "A Throw of the Dice," resorted to the use of small letters for capitals, eccentric line endings, and erratic punctuation. Like Frost, Stevens opposed such eccentricities, but he welcomed a variety of aesthetic creeds as evidence of "exertions to find the truth."[108]

From the beginning of his career, as Samuel French Morse noted, all of Stevens's poems were "about" poetry, which "is the real subject of *Harmonium* and all the later work."[109] The theory of poetry is the substance both of "Adagia" and of "A Collect of Philosophy," which were included by Morse in *Opus Posthumous*. For Stevens, the "supreme fiction," synonymous with poetry, was life at its most satisfying—the state that resolves all oppositions.[110]

He persisted in dwelling on reality:

> thinking was a madness . . .
> feeling was a madness . . .

Both thinking and feeling were merely parts of the general fiction of the mind, and in the end there was "an end without rhetoric."[111]

In his poem "The Role of the Idea in Poetry" Stevens cited his debt to the sources from which he gathered so many of his ideas:

> One father proclaims another, the patriarch
> Of truth. They stride across and are masters of
> The chant and discourse there.[112]

In "Presence of an Eternal Master of Knowledge"[113] Stevens suggested an aesthetic in which the problems of cognition and sensitive perception (or sensibility) are mingled in an attempt at integration.

Although Stevens never achieved a systematic aesthetic, he believed that poetry is coextensive with language and with "reality," which presents itself as a tension of two pressures: from without (the world) and from within (the mind). He held further that the poet's imagination lends nobility to its material through its supreme fictions, and that poetic expression is a vital force ultimately related to the preservation of life itself.

SUMMARY VIEW OF
LITERARY AESTHETICS

No theory has as yet successfully defined the relative boundaries of aesthetics, poetics, and criticism. Within a broad philosophical framework, however, in which perception and cognition are clearly presented in their intimate relation and interaction, aesthetics takes its place as a central consideration in both experience and knowledge. Certainly, some important American thinkers, such as Dewey, Baldwin, and Pepper, have considered it in this way. The line of demarcation between aesthetics, poetics, and criticism remains blurred because the general principles of the first find their concretion in the second and their application in the third; conversely, the last two derive their values from the first.

Aestheticians, moreover, continue to encounter difficulties in their attempts to define beauty. All such definitions, from Plato through Schopenhauer and Santayana, have failed to articulate the total experience meant by the word. Edward Bullough, for example, spoke of "the Sisyphus labor of a definition of beauty."[1] The difficulty results from the complex interrelationships of the ideas involved, as in the connection of beauty and "reality."

AREAS OF AESTHETIC KNOWLEDGE

Most definitions of beauty indicate that it depends on the replacement of cacophonous tumult by musical harmony. Human
experience is enhanced by intuitive creativity, which makes possible a feeling of the total integration of a diversity of elements,
generating, through the senses and the understanding, a feeling of
exaltation and euphoria. Thus beauty is not a thing, but a process,
forever subject to Heraclitean flow. It is a transcendental form of
which each particular expression is reminiscent as shadow is of substance, as memory is of experience, and as desire itself is of fulfillment.

Hugo showed that the beautiful coexists with the ugly, as the
grotesque with the sublime. The grotesque is the ugly incorporated
in comedy. According to Hugo, the fertile union of the grotesque
with the sublime produces modern genius, which, in its complexity,
is opposed to the uniform simplicity of the genius of antiquity, thus
marking one of the major differences between classic and romantic
literature.

In ancient literature the grotesque occupied a relatively minor
place; in modern poetic thought, on the other hand, its role is immense. This role has become increasingly important from the Elizabethan period through Hugo and contemporary literature. Sganarelle
dances about Don Juan, Mephistopheles around Faust. As an element
of contrast, the grotesque is (at least in Hugo's view) the richest
source that nature can open to art. Thus in drama, which for Hugo
and others represents the summit of poetic development and of which
Shakespeare is the high point, the sublime and the grotesque inter-
link even as they do in life and creation.

If, as Sully Prudhomme suggested,[2] the genesis of rational categories finds its poetic expression in metaphysics, then poetry, and
indeed literary expression in general, becomes a fundamental statement comprising the relationship of subject and object, and as such
constitutes a universal science. This vast area of knowledge, charged
with undeniable mobility, greatly enhances the range of human

thought. Thus rhythm and metaphor fascinate the mind long before
it can grasp the full meaning of its own experience. Such an aesthetic
experience involves both a hedonistic and an evaluative response to
the thing experienced. Literary aesthetics attempts an analysis of this
experience, without providing a definite statement on the nature of
creativity.

The Aesthetic Experience

Aesthetic responses affect man's view of the world. Through the
reader's participation in artistic expression, which gives form and
shape to experience, he is enabled to confess himself and to heal his
soul. The literary aesthetic experience therefore has a cathartic value.
Both vague and definite feelings are involved. In the first instance
the feeling is directly linked with the sensuous medium; in the second
the feeling is mediated, as Parker said, "by ideas through which the
medium is given content and meaning."

Artistic expression ideally embodies both the evanescence and the
perdurability of feeling. The experience comprises, as Lipps and
Parker indicated, "aesthetic rivalry" in which such contraries as good
and evil, or beauty and ugliness, invoke each other.[3] Hugo's concept
of the grotesque illustrates this rivalry theoretically, while his novels
illustrate it in practice.[4] This conflict reflects the dialectic nature of
man's spirit and its dramatic aspect.

An integral criticism that takes this dialectic into account can act
as an energizing principle in the aesthetic experience. In this sense,
every significant literary work is a criticism of life, in which life is
not merely reported but transformed through the processes of *logo-
poeia, phanopoeia, mythopoeia,* and *melopoeia.* The first is the use
of idea and language; the second, of vision and image; the third, of
history and epic; the last, of music (melody and harmony). Together
they constitute the awesome complexity of the aesthetic experience,
which is the concern of literary aesthetics.

Aesthetics, then, deals with the dramatic transformation of sensation (passivity) into active perception, ideation, and feeling. It is

concerned with a heightened awareness of pleasure in expressive thought and feeling and with a concomitant demand for satisfactions marked by a sense of having entered the domain of beauty—a form whose manifestations are myriad but whose aspect is singular and is predominantly marked by harmony and balance. Within its presence man is afforded intimations of his highest and deepest possibilities: he finds the world desirable.

Literature and Metaphysics

Although the two primary aesthetic senses are sight and hearing, literature, in imaginatively appealing to these, adds a third sense— intellectual contemplation, in which metaphysical nostalgia and pathos play an important role. This sense reveals the familial relationship between Venus (beauty), the Lost Eden (loneliness and nostalgia), Eros (desire and love), and Thanatos (death and annihilation).

Metaphysics, as both Thomas Mann and Arthur Lovejoy indicated, may itself yield aesthetic pleasure akin to that afforded by a poem. Like art, seeking to find order in heterogeneity, it seeks to grasp the illusory and "the loveliness of the incomprehensible," as well as the awesomeness of profundity itself. Thus, "the reading of a philosophical book is usually nothing but a form of aesthetic experience, even in the case of writings which seem destitute of outward aesthetic charms."[5] For Karl Pearson, this statement is equally true of science, which he considered the "continual gratification of the aesthetic judgment which is one of the chief delights of the pursuit of pure science."[6] As Henry Adams wrote, poetry, metaphysics, and pure science are aesthetically involved in a "sensual raft in the midst of a supersensual chaos."[7]

Man's "origin, his growth, his loves and beliefs are but the outcome of accidental collocations of atoms," as one anonymous critic said. In literary aesthetics, therefore, a rigid logic and an unflinching authority are inappropriate. This study must involve a theory of perception, sense impression, and susceptibility,[8] as well as an awareness of the dramatic transformation of passive sensation into active perception, again accompanied by a sense of having entered the domain of beauty. Accordingly, the aesthetics of literature is intrinsically preoccupied with poetic essence and the extent to which that essence may be called "beauty."

THE CONCERNS OF LITERARY AESTHETICS

Literary aesthetics is not primarily concerned with technical criticism, which, while related to aesthetics, constitutes its own domain. Rather, it is occupied with literature as an energizing principle of contemplation whose objects are desire, love, birth, pain, wonderment, ambition, fulfillment, frustration, hope, despair, good and evil, beauty and ugliness, the cosmic and the tragic, the true and the false—life and death. All these factors are *aspects* of man's visions that, when articulated in artistic form, challenge the attention and study of literary aesthetics.[9]

The Study of Feeling

If the evocation of feeling and emotion is taken to be paramount in the literary process, then literary aesthetics should unconditionally include within its definition the discrimination of literary excellence in terms of the power of evocation, and the means employed would be considered excellent by that test. "Our knowledge," Pater makes his Marius say, "is limited to what we feel. But can we be sure that things are at all like our feelings?" Literature attempts to create that identity—the universe as feeling. The literary aesthetician seeks to understand the nature of this attempt.

The aesthetics of literature is affected by the possibility of a shift from the Cartesian *cogito* to the romantic "I feel." Many critics believe that a literary work may satisfy both claims—knowledge and feeling—and that both require a common metaphor whose ultimate goal would be to express a universal mathesis.[10] Some adherents of this view maintain that any sound approach to general aesthetics or to literary aesthetics in particular cannot afford to ignore the nature of intellectual activity that makes clear a certain homeostatic factor in the enjoyment or nonenjoyment of any experience. As William James wrote:

> The drainage currents and discharges of the brain are not purely physical facts. They are psychophysical facts, and the spiritual quality of them seems a codeterminant of their mechanical effectiveness. If the mechanical effectiveness in a cell, as they increase, give pleasure, they seem to increase all the more readily for that fact; if they give displeasure, the displeasure seems to damp the activities.[11]

This passage seems to provide, as a base for aesthetic experience, a principle of physical economy, not unrelated to Newton's laws of motion, comprising the principles of inertia, momentum, and acceleration.

Ontology, Dynamics, and the Poet's Domain

For Ramón Fernandez, the fundamental problem of aesthetics is "the metaphysical problem of being . . . transferred to the plane of the imagination." In his view, aesthetics must be "an imaginative ontology."[12] Those writers who see a relationship between literature and philosophy, and admit the concern of philosophy with both the denotative and connotative aspects of reality, should also be moved to see that through both symbol and figure literature achieves an articulation of the denotative as well as the connotative.

For literary aesthetics, one of the pervasive problems is the integration of the inner and outer experience through an imaginative grasp of total experiences. This process is implicit in the activity of thought, which is implemented by language. Indeed, this process is as serious for literary aesthetics as it is for science.

Both art and science are actually engaged in the same dramatic enterprise: the attempt to present the resistance called "reality" in a form that makes the resistance itself a source of fascination and pleasure. In one of its aspects, the form is called art; in another, it is known as science. Haunting both is an unseen, but none the less felt, spirit called "beauty."

In the works of Bronowski, Bachelard, and others we can see the interlocking of poetry and science in symbol and metaphor. Indeed, as Bronowski declared, "the symbol and metaphor are as necessary to science as to poetry," and the world stands as much to lose if it were emptied of feeling as it would if it were emptied of thought. From this point of view literary aesthetics is involved in the quest for a universal poetics,[13] as suggested in one of the earliest unconscious formulations of the nature of poetry, the phrase "mood-thought" from Caedmon's *Hymn*. This expression suggests a correlativity of thought and feeling in an atmosphere that was later to be called *Stimmung*.[14]

René Wellek believes that a work of art derives its ontologic status from a system of norms of ideal intersubjective concepts. These concepts change with the collective ideology of which they are a part. They are accessible only through individual mental experience, based on the sound structure of its sentences (in a literary work). Wellek avoids the problem of value and is generally opposed to "the insidious psychological relativism which must always end in scepticism and finally mental anarchy."[15]

Because the mind is, however, in William James's phrase, a theater of simultaneities, relativism remains a pervasive fact. This condition in no way makes the relativism "insidious"—except as it threatens someone's authoritarianism. Art may be a system of norms, but not necessarily of norms dependent on forensic strategy, no matter how shrewd.

Ransom differentiated one kind of poetry from another "with respect to its ontology, or the reality of its being." The issue is drawn between the poetry of things and the poetry of ideas. Plato preferred, of course, ideas to things. The imagists—and more recently such poets as Francis Ponge—have presented things in their *thingness*. "But," said Ransom, "perhaps thing versus idea does not seem to name an opposition precisely. Then we might phrase it a little differently: image versus idea."[16]

The inescapable question remains: Is an idea free of images? Is "red" merely a color, or is it also a countless number of things associated with it? Is the idea "redness" simply an abstraction, or is it, too, a countless number of things associated with it? If a work of art is a structure of values, then it ought to fill the ontological gap that is felt to exist between art and life. More than that, it ought to be part of the bridge between knowing and feeling—between what we know quantitatively and what we feel qualitatively, as Dewey suggested.

A poem is an orchestration of image, idea, and thing in a tonality of emotion that carries with it its own ontological validity. We know what it means for the heart to leap at the sight of a field of daffodils. Wordsworth's line communicates all at once the image of flower and field, the idea of surprise and promise, and the thing itself through the recovery of past sensation. Through the poem, external reality (actuality) is translated into internal ideality, and all at once everything is tipped with wingedness: we are the poem. Subject and object are melted down in one phenomenological stream of transcendence, and the ontological gap is closed.[17]

In poetry words yield more in sensation than in ideation; in prose the situation is reversed. The prose-poem combines the two tonalities —not always successfully. In prose, the reader imagines what he knows; in poetry, he knows only what he imagines. In the former, the heart of the matter (so to speak) is in the brain; in the latter, the brain is in the heart. Cognition and feeling are woven into both.

In prose the order of knowledge constitutes the horizon of feeling; in poetry the order of feeling is the horizon of knowledge. The heightened feeling of prose comes from a music of ideas; the ideas themselves create a succession of rhythms and accents. The heightened feeling of poetry comes from a music of feelings and emotions. In both cases, of course, the dominance of one or the other factor remains relative. As Oscar Wilde remarked: "If a man treats life artistically, his brain is in his heart."

On the aesthetics of poetry Guyau wrote: "Poetry will continue to be the natural language of all great and lasting emotions." For Browning, poetry was the poet's "brains beat into rhythm"; for Mill, something in the nature of a soliloquy; for Verlaine, essentially music (in contradistinction to mere "literature"); and for Baumgarten, whose work represents the fountainhead of modern aesthetics, it was "speech so charged with energy that it demands metrical expression."

Frost believed that the heart of poetry, as well as of science and philosophy, was metaphor, while the surrealists considered poetry a series of images that emerge as a result of the collision of ideas and the emotions released from a veritable logomachy in which the poet is as much an object as he is a subject of manipulation.[18]

Recent poetics has turned a highly sophisticated battery of scientific investigation on the poetic, imaginative, and emotional resonances wakened in the poet's sensorium (and in that of the recreative reader) by the elements themselves. Here Gaston Bachelard stood at the forefront. His "psychoanalysis of the elements" and the spatiotemporal categories with which we intuit them holds intimations not only of a new poetics and literary aesthetic but of an epistemology whose roots reach down into the elements themselves.[19]

Ideally, art should constitute the triumph of coherence, which is too often missing in life. The power of art to present the familiar in a new aspect is related to its ability to impose a monistic pattern on the heterogeneity of experience. A literary product can be as attractive as a musical fugue, which in itself is not a fixed form but rather a process that makes use of various forms. Thus any ideal artistic expression represents a musicalization of experience through a process in which logic is discovered after the fact. The logic of the creative artist is an equilibrium of tensions, a musical dynamism.[20]

One of the fundamental questions—How does the reader enter the domain of the poet?—has been answered variously. One answer is, of course, by the process of empathy: something in man enables him to identify both physically and psychologically with the poet's world and to partake of his emotions in a kind of symbiotic phenomenon. As Anatole France declared, all men have in themselves an exemplar of each of their poets whom no one knows and who will perish forever with all his variants when men shall no longer feel anything.

Actually, the creative artist is helpless without the creative reader —without whom, indeed, he runs the risk of remaining completely silent even when his work is in print. The work of art, then, is a partnership within the matrix of creative imagination, although the poet takes the lead in providing the occasion for the transition from passivity to activity.

THE TONALITIES OF LITERARY AESTHETICS

Within the framework of Western tradition, the conjugate categories of classicism and romanticism have a compelling and staying power. One explanation for this power was given by André Gide:

> It is important to remember that a struggle between classicism and romanticism also exists inside each mind. And it is from this very struggle that the work is born; the classic work of art relates the triumph of order and measure over an inner romanticism, and the wider the riot to be tamed, the more beautiful your work will be.[21]

Scientists report a similar struggle in their reaching out for an artistic triumph over a tumult of half-conscious ideas, as in Poincaré's adverting to a sudden illumination after long periods of resistance. The geologist M. E. Denaeyer alluded to an unforeseen moment of illumination in the process of ultimate integration, and in a passage reminiscent of Shelley he quoted Poincaré:

> *La Pensée est un éclair dans une longue nuit . . .*
> *Ah soyons tous une parcelle de cette lumière.*
>
> (Thought is a flash of lightning in a long night . . .
> Ah, let us all be a part of this light.)[22]

The universal analogy of which Baudelaire spoke so tellingly, as did Emerson before him ("Nature is a metaphor of the mind"), derives its great sustaining support from the manifest phenomenon of synesthesia. This phenomenon, in turn, suggests a conspectual totality in any significant work of art. Literary aesthetics should alert the reader to the universal aspects of art.[23]

Language and Experience

To the extent that the literary artist uses language effectively, his work of art will waken a multiplicity of experiences in the reader. The poem, the novel, the drama will constitute symbols of these reactions, and the experiences themselves will be their meaning. Northrop Frye has distinguished two senses in which words are symbols: signs, or "representations of a thing outside of the pattern of words"; and images, or units of a larger verbal pattern or structure. In signs the reader's mind is directed outward centrifugally toward the object represented; in images the mental movement is centripetal —toward the construction of the whole pattern.

Frye added a third sense—the archetype, "which regards it [the symbol] as neither image nor sign, but as the product of the two," a synthetic symbol recurring prominently in various literary works. Still a fourth conception is that of the symbol as a monad or "unit of the total poetic experience."[24] For Susanne Langer, "signs and symbols are knotted together" in a fixed reality called "fact," involving "the whole creative process of ideation, metaphor, and abstraction that makes human life an adventure in understanding."[25]

Pater's pronouncement with regard to the aspiration of all the arts to the condition of music is not to be taken as a vote for the confusion of the arts in the various means they use to express beauty. The aspiration in all cases is toward the articulation of man's desires as values beyond the forces that set these desires into motion. Thus Langer's and Albert Gehring's comments on music are true for poetry and literature in general.

Langer asserted that "music is our myth of the inner life," and Gehring declared that "in the case of measure, force, and tempo, music duplicates or photographs the mind; in the case of melody, it coincides with it." Music represents "an identification of symbol and object."[26] In the creation and in the musicalization of thought, literature and music vie in their efforts and in their effectiveness. Although the ideal of poetry as seeking the condition of music has been challenged, it has validity, especially as described by Valéry: "A poem is composed in practice of fragments of *pure poetry* embedded in the matter of a discourse."[27] The removal of this impurity is the ultimate ideal of art.

THE PREOCCUPATIONS OF AESTHETICS

The preoccupation of many critics with literary aesthetics results in part from the unconscious feeling or suspicion that the recognition of real value and beauty in works of literature somehow constitutes an opening into the secrets of the poetic or creative process itself and into its mysterious hold both on those who originate works of art and on those who appreciate them. From this belief arises the quest for a possible science of literary aesthetics latent in such disciplines as psychology, the physiology of sensation, linguistics, semantics, historical synthesis and analysis, anthropology, and philosophy in its various branches.

The first two disciplines share in the endeavor to gain an understanding of the operation of the imagination and the manner in which it transforms rudimentary sensations into images and patterned articulations of feelings and ideas. The third and fourth (often with the aid of the sixth and seventh) turn the batteries of linguistics and meaning experiences on the literary fact of which language and meaning are the factors. The fifth, preoccupied with the record, often calls on psychology to illuminate the course and destiny of literary expression. The sixth studies the literary phase of man's activity as an artifact highly charged with the nature of his culture and the crystallized image of that culture. The seventh explores the presuppositions, implications, and tendencies latent in the other fields.

A cynical, but none the less compelling, point of view would remind us that with all his posturings, including the aesthetic one,

> man has canine teeth like the dog and the fox, and like the dog and the fox he buried them at the beginning in the flesh of his fellows. His descendants slaughtered one another with stone knives for a bit of raw fish, and the equivalent still goes on under the surface of our modern conventions.[28]

This truth, representing a reality recognized by the head, is obviously abhorrent to the heart, whose instinct is to escape from such a reality into a never-never land. Taine spoke of such an escape as "creating for yourself an alibi," one form of which is aesthetic contemplation of the forms of outer nature. Another way of creating an alibi is to study history. Said Taine:

> Through this gate, you enter into revery. All opium is unhealthy; it is prudent to take it only in small doses and from time to time. Since Werther and René we have taken too much of it, we are taking it in heavier doses every day; consequently the malady of the age has been aggravated, and in music, painting, and politics a number of symptoms prove that the derangement of reason, imagination, sensibility, and nerves is on the increase. Among all the drugs that give us at our will factitious absence and forgetfulness, history is, I believe, the least dangerous.[29]

A third way of creating an alibi is by music, as in the cult of Beethoven. In a word, aesthetic experience (and reflection on it) may be regarded as a romantic reverie, an escape from reality through resort to an alibi. Taine's observations have obvious relevance for our situation now.

Inevitably, any thorough speculation on the aesthetic appreciation of a literary work leads to epistemological and metaphysical inquiry into the nature of experience and the central role of language in its three stages: prelinguistic, linguistic, and metalinguistic. Lack of exact knowledge about the emergence of consciousness and self-awareness and the origin of language frustrates the study of the first stage. The second has been studied with varying degrees of success since the days of Plato, and has reached a high level of sophistication since the emergence of comparative philology and scientific linguistics. Central to this sophistication is the study of language (hence, of literature) as symbol and metaphor in relation to semantics.[30] The third stage has been enriched by the studies of Croce, Freud, Edmund Husserl, Leone Vivante, Jean Wahl, and Bachelard, among others.

These explorations lead from the level of the instinctual, where linguistic expression is only a tool for the uncovering of processes that escape linguistic articulation, to a plane in which man negotiates the universe as language and therefore as an object of aesthetic contemplation and pleasure. On this level literary aesthetics is related to a psychoanalysis of the elements of nature themselves (earth, fire, water, air), to the absorption of the irrational in the rational, to a critique of the rational in terms of the unconscious or preconscious, and to the poetic process as a profound source of total knowledge. In this area of speculation, Valéry's *Notebooks* are beginning to yield a rich new harvest of knowledge.

To the extent that literary aesthetics is anchored in a theory of emotions and in a metaphysics of nature, it is on both counts, in its modern form, largely a product of romantic transcendentalism. Thus, Novalis is frequently mentioned in Bachelard's works.

Verbal felicity and metrical movement may account critically for a reader's response to a poem as something that creates within him a sense of beauty. A deeper analysis reveals, however, that the intensity and immediacy of response is owing to an unconscious transformation and fusion of imagery derived from a wide field of references.[31]

THE USES OF AESTHETICS

As a science, literary aesthetics seeks to provide a mutual calibration for perception and sensibility and to alert the percipient to the infinite possibilities of experience provided by the imagination as articulated in a literary work of art. Heuristically, literary aesthetics may serve to lead the human mind to realize that poetry (that is, literature) is truly, in the words of Bachelard, the *pancalist* activity of the will and that as such it not only expresses the desire for limited beauty but for a universal beauty as well.[32]

To take seriously Mallarmé's alleged admonition to Degas, that poetry is not written with ideas but with words, is to agree that literature is nothing but a glorified verbal game, which has very little to do with the life process of the mind and the emotions. An important factor here is the role of sincerity in the means the artist uses to stir the reader's emotion. Henri Peyre argued that although the element of sincerity is implicit in the literary process, no one should insist on the degree of sincerity in the literary artist.

Indeed, Peyre asserted that "the stress on sincerity would be deadly to literature if it were ever to impair the freedom which must remain the privilege of creative inspiration." Here Peyre himself was careful to point to those who are still on the side of Horace, who maintained that if the artist is to stir others, he must first have been stirred himself.[33]

Literary aesthetics, in its concern with the discrimination of means and effects, necessarily confronts the opposition between "inner" and "outer." Herbert Read, following Jung on the question of introversion and extroversion, cited Jung specifically on the activity called "phantasy":

> It is the creative activity whence issue the solutions to all unanswerable questions; it is the mother of all possibilities, in which, too, the inner and outer worlds, like all psychological antitheses, are joined in living union.

Accordingly, psychoanalysis recognized the power of art to resolve

> into one uniform flow of life all that springs from the outer mechanism of actuality—doing this, not only for the artist himself, from whose own need the phantasy is born, but also by suggestion and by symbol, for all who come to participate in his imaginative work.

In the artist two forces contend for balance: one in the direction of primitivism and the "disjointed fortuitous world of dreams," the other in the direction of the plastic and the architectonic. These contending forces "resolve themselves into some kind of unity."[34]

Literary aesthetics is normatively successful when it helps the reader to realize that a proper analysis, far from destroying the synthesis of art, helps to realize it at its fullest. At the same time it alerts the reader to the undeniable fact that vis-à-vis the materials of outer reality and of inner reality (thought and feeling), which are to be *loved* into artistic being, language is an embrace that often falls short of its mark. This failing may constitute, in part, the poet's "lover's quarrel" with the world.

For such aestheticians as Roger Fry, however, the work of art is not necessarily a daydream in which men seek, in a verbal and symbolic manner, the fulfillment of certain desires, either repressed or denied satisfaction by the rigors of daily life. Fry described a pleasure in the recognition of order and inevitability in relations. In such a view the shift is obviously from the affective zone to the intellectual.

Fry's stance can be interpreted as a leaning toward the contemplative attitude that is shared by the scientist and the poet as well as by the recreative reader.[35] If, according to psychoanalysis, the literary artist moves from neurosis closer to reality than he did before he became an artist, then the reader should be able (with the help of literary aesthetics) to follow the same rule. The notion, then, that art is an escape from reality should be replaced by the idea that if art is in any sense an escape, it is from banality, replacing flatness and mere droning with plenitude and musicality.

Through the process of allusion, literary expression is constantly kept alive and saved from being lost in the past. Thus various thinkers have shown that a first-class, original mind will absorb and digest its sources as the body absorbs and assimilates the food that nourishes and vitalizes it. The same sources will produce varying results among different minds. Originality and genius consist in the re-presentation and re-orchestration of ideas already prepared by past experience, which includes the absorption of past literature. Memory and imagination cooperate in this process.

To follow the effects of ideas as they are refracted by other minds, as light is refracted in its course through crystals, is in itself an aesthetic process. In it sensibility is sharpened and enriched by partaking in a psychodrama in which the constant collision of minds brings into view new vistas of emotional and aesthetic experience. The aesthetic of allusion, then, reveals the compounded impact of literary ideas both on those who, in their own creations, use the allusion, and on those who are exposed doubly to these incremental riches.

This subject was discussed by Ronald Christ in his *The Narrow Act: Borges' Art of Allusion*, which illustrated the magical infectiousness of the process of allusion (sometimes intricate) not only through an analysis of the work of Borges but through its magnetic involvement of many other creative artists. Thus, said Christ:

> Literature can make contemporaries of Virgil and Alexander Ross; it can raise from the dead, as in the case of Jonson and Seneca. The Immortal is Author; his immortality is Literature.[36]

In my consideration of American aestheticians, I have attempted to delineate the domain of literary aesthetics both by definition and example. It must not, in the last analysis, be understood as a "fixed subject" but rather as an adventure of the spirit among the creations of the imagination in an effort to gain some insight into its creative process that holds out the promise of an ever-renewed vision of beauty.

In such a study, one can barely escape the tenuous, for we are constantly dealing with the exquisitely fine, as in the filaments of the noiseless spider described by Whitman—the filaments men launch to explore the vast spaces of the mind's domain:

> Ever unreeling them, ever tirelessly speeding them . . .
> Ceaselessly musing, venturing, throwing, seeking the spheres to connect them,
> Till the bridge you need will be form'd, till the ductile anchor hold,
> Till the gossamer thread you fling catch somewhere, O my soul.[37]

NOTES

CHAPTER I

1. Joseph Crouch, *Puritanism in Art* (London: Cassell and Co., Ltd., 1910).
2. Ludwig Lewisohn, *The Story of American Literature* (New York: The Modern Library, 1939), p. 19.
3. John Locke, *Essay Concerning Human Understanding*, Book II, Chapter 11, A. C. Fraser, ed. (Oxford: 1894).
4. See Thomas H. Johnson, "Jonathan Edwards' Background of Reading," *Publications of the Colonial Society of Massachusetts*, (December, 1931), Vol. XXVIII, pp. 193–222; *The Works of President Jonathan Edwards*, Samuel Austin, ed. (Worcester, Mass.: 1808), 8 vols. Vol. I, p. 34.
5. Arthur Cushman McGiffert, *Jonathan Edwards* (New York: Harper and Bros., 1932), pp. 186–200.
6. *Ibid.*, p. 190 ff.
7. Edwards, *loc. cit.*; Clarence H. Faust and Thomas H. Johnson, *Jonathan Edwards: Representative Selections* (New York: American Book Co., 1935), pp. cv, cxiii–cxiv.
8. Frank Luther Mott and Chester E. Jorgenson, eds., *Benjamin Franklin: Representative Selections with Introduction, Bibliography, and Notes* (New York: American Book Co., 1936), pp. xxxiii, xl; Franklin, *Writings*, Albert H. Smyth, ed. (New York: Macmillan, 1905–07), II, pp. 230, 434–435.
9. Mott and Jorgenson, *op. cit.*, p. xlvi ff.; Franklin, *op. cit.*, Vol. I, p. ix; Vol. II, p. 24.
10. Mott and Jorgenson maintain that Franklin may have found this statement in *The Spectator* (No. 183).
11. Franklin, *op cit.*, Vol. II, p. 203; Mott and Jorgenson, *op. cit.*, p. cxxxiv.
12. Mott and Jorgenson, *op. cit.*, pp. 114–128 *passim*.
13. Gilbert Chinard, ed., *The Literary Bible of Thomas Jefferson: His Commonplace Book of Philosophers and Poets* (Baltimore: The Johns Hopkins University Press, 1928), p. 76.

14. *Ibid.*, p. 119. *Horace, Satires, Epistles, and Ars Poetica* (*Satire*, II, vii., 111–118) Translated by H. Rushton Fairclough (London: William Heinemann, The Loeb Library, 1932), pp. 234–235.

15. Adrienne Koch, *The Philosophy of Thomas Jefferson* (Gloucester, Mass.: Peter Smith, 1957; copyright Columbia University Press, 1943), p. 68.

16. Eleanor Davidson Berman, *Thomas Jefferson Among the Arts* (New York: Philosophical Library, 1947), p. 49; *The Writings of Thomas Jefferson* (Monticello Edition), Albert Ellery Bergh, managing editor, Washington, D.C., 20 vols., letter to Wirt, November 12, 1816, Vol. 8.

17. Jefferson, *Writings*, Vol. XVIII, pp. 414, 441–442; Berman, *op. cit.*, pp. 235–237.

18. Jefferson, *op. cit.* letter to Sky, 1771, Vol. III. Enrico Davila (1576–1631), famed for his *History of the Civil Wars in France*, fought under Henry IV and was wounded during the siege of Amiens (1597).

19. Edmund Burke, *The Philosophical Inquiry into the Origin of Ideas on the Sublime and Beautiful* in *The Works . . . of Edmund Burke* (London, 1854), p. 91.

20. Jefferson, *op. cit.*, letter to Charles Willson Peale, April 17, 1813, Vol. XVIII, pp. 276–279; Berman, *op. cit.*, p. 44.

21. Jefferson, *op. cit.*, letter to Maria Cosway, Paris, October 10, 1786, Vol. V, pp. 436–437, 440. For "The Head and Heart" dialogue, see pp. 431–446.

22. Lewis Leary, *That Rascal Freneau: A Study in Literary Failure* (New Brunswick, N.J.: Rutgers University Press, 1941), p. 25.

23. *Ibid.*, pp. 101, 161.

24. Fred L. Pattee, ed., *Poems of Philip Freneau, Poet of the American Revolution* (Princeton: Princeton University Press, 1907), 3 vols., Vol. I, p. 94.

25. Robert E. Spiller *et al.*, eds., *Literary History of the United States* (New York: The Macmillan Co., 1948), 3 vols., Vol. I, p. 172.

26. *Ibid.*, pp. 169–170.

27. Henry Adams, *History of the United States of America during the Administrations of Thomas Jefferson and James Madison* (New York: Charles Scribner's Sons, 1921), 9 vols., Vol. IX, pp. 175, 216–217.

28. John Quincy Adams, *Lectures on Rhetoric and Oratory*, 2 vols. (Cambridge, 1810); reprinted, with a new introduction by J. Jeffery Auer and Jerald L. Baninga (New York: Russell and Russell, 1962), Introduction.

29. ———, *A Catalogue of the Books of John Quincy Adams Deposited in the Boston Athenaeum* (Boston: Athenaeum, 1938); Charles Francis Adams, ed., *Memoirs of John Quincy Adams*

(Philadelphia: J. B. Lippincott and Co., 1874–77), 12 vols., Vol. XII, p. 286.

30. Adams, *Lectures*, Vol. II, p. 258.
31. *Ibid.*, Vol. I, p. 365.
32. Zoltan Haraszti, *John Adams and the Prophets of Progress* (Cambridge: Harvard University Press, 1952), pp. 18–19, 78, 81, 107, 235, 254.
33. For the place of associationism in eighteenth-century thought, see Ernest Lee Tuveson, *The Imagination as a Means of Grace: Locke and the Aesthetics of Romanticism* (Berkeley: University of California Press, 1960), p. 33. There he quotes from the chapter "Of the Association of Ideas" in Locke's *Essay* (4th ed., 1700, II, xxxiii, 5):

> Some of our ideas have natural correspondence and connection with one another; it is the office and excellency of our reason to trace these and hold them together in that union and correspondence which is founded in their peculiar beings. Besides this, there is another connexion of ideas wholly owing to chance or custom; ideas that, in themselves, are not all of kin, come to be so united in some men's minds, that it is very hard to separate them; they always keep in company, and the one no sooner at any time comes into the understanding, but its associate appears with it; and if they are inseparable, show themselves together.

Tuveson suggests that the theory of the unconscious implicit here took two centuries to emerge. David Hartley's physiological theory of association, developed in his *Observations on Man* (1749), supposedly influenced by Locke, held that the contact of an external object with the sensory nerves set up vibrations in the brain that were "propagated freely every way over the whole medullary substance" and resulted in sensations. Minute vibrations ("vibratiuncles") left traces in the brain that accounted for the origin of ideas (W. R. Sorley, *A History of English Philosophy*, New York: G. P. Putnam's Sons, 1921, p. 191).

34. Adams, *Lectures*, Vol. II, p. 259; Max I. Baym, *The French Education of Henry Adams* (New York: Columbia University Press, 1951), section on Adams' essay on weights and measures, which is informed by a humanistic spirit.
35. Adams, *op. cit.*, Vol. II, pp. 263–264.
36. *Ibid.*, pp. 263–264, 267,
37. *Ibid.*, p. 270.
38. *Ibid.*, p. 313.
39. *Ibid.*, p. 356.

40. Warren Ramsey, *Jules Laforgue and the Ironic Inheritance* (Oxford University Press, 1953), p. 215 ff.
41. Adams, *op. cit.*, Vol. I, p. 108.

CHAPTER 2

1. William Charvat, *The Origins of American Critical Thought, 1810–1835* (Ph.D. thesis, University of Pennsylvania, 1936); see also Harold Eby, *American Romantic Criticism, 1815–1860* (Ph.D. thesis, University of Washington, 1927).
2. Charvat, *op. cit.*, pp. 4, 63–64.
3. The French edition presumably appeared in the same month as the English translation (1813). De Staël's *Influence of Literature on Society* also appeared in an American edition in 1813.
4. Henry Adams, *History of the United States* (New York: Scribners, 1890), 9 vols., Vol. I, pp. 94, 123.
5. Emma Gertrude Jaeck, *Mme. de Staël and the Spread of German Literature* (Oxford University Press, 1915), pp. 23, 60–62.
6. *Ibid.*, pp. 76, 89.
7. *Ibid.*, pp. 108, 118.
8. *Ibid.*, p. 278.
9. *Ibid.*, pp. 332–335.
10. Ward, Preface, p. iii, translation of Goethe's *Essays on Art*.
11. *Ibid.*, pp. 12, 26, 108, 111, 135, 225–226.
12. *Ibid.*, p. 235.
13. E. W. Emerson and W. E. Forbes, eds., *The Journal of Ralph Waldo Emerson* (Boston: 1909–14), 10 vols., Vol. I (1843), p. 466.
14. Jaeck, *op. cit.*, p. 342.
15. John Weiss, Introduction, p. 10 of his translation of *The Aesthetic Letters*; G. G. Gervinus, *Geschichte der poetischen National-Literatur* (1835–58), Vol. V, p. 522.
16. Weiss, Introduction, pp. xiv–xv.
17. *Ibid.*, pp. xviii–xx.
18. *Ibid.*, pp. xxv–xxvi.
19. *Ibid.*, *Letters on the Aesthetic Education of Man* (1795), 5th letter, p. 18.
20. Charvat, *op. cit.*, pp. 62–64.
21. Daniel's translation, pp. 20–21 of the middle part of Cousin's *Du Vrai, du Beau, et du Bien.*
22. *Ibid.*, pp. 22–24.
23. *Ibid.*, p. 84.
24. *Ibid.*, p. 105.
25. *Ibid.*, pp. 125–129 *passim.*

26. *Ibid.*, pp. 158–159.
27. *Ibid.*, p. 161.
28. *Ibid.*, p. 166.
29. *Ibid.*, p. 171.
30. *Ibid.*, p. 172.
31. *Ibid.*, p. 183.
32. For the currency of the ideas of Cousin and Jouffroy in America, see Howard Mumford Jones, *America and French Culture, 1750–1848* (Chapel Hill; University of North Carolina Press, 1927); Walter L. Leighton, *French Philosophers and New England Transcendentalism* (Ph.D. thesis, University of Virginia, 1908). See further, George Ripley (chief interpreter of Cousin in New England), preface to *Specimens of Foreign Standard Literature* (Boston: 1838), Vol. I; H. G. Linberg's translation of Cousin's *Introduction à l'histoire de la philosophie* (*Introduction to the History of Philosophy*, Boston: 1837); C. S. Henry's translation of Cousin's *Éléments de la Psychologie* (Hartford: 1834). According to Ripley, Cousin had the greatest number of readers, among living philosophers, in this country. The *Dial* for October 1840 had an elaborate critical review of Cousin's *Cours d'histoire de la philosophie au dix-huitième siècle* and of the *Oeuvres complètes de Platon*.
33. Leighton, *op. cit.*, p. 24.
34. Cousin, *Introduction*, cited in Leighton, *op. cit.*, p. 32.
35. ———, preface to *Fragments Philosophiques* ("Philosophical Fragments"), cited in Leighton, *op. cit.*, p. 36.
36. ———, *Introduction*, cited in Leighton, *op. cit.*, p. 35.
37. ———, preface, cited in Leighton, *op. cit.*, p. 36.
38. *Ibid.*, p. 37.
39. *North American Review*, No. CXII, Vol. liii (July 1841), pp. 1–40, Reviews of Cousin's *Introduction to the History of Philosophy*, 1832; *Specimens of Foreign Standard Literature*, Vols. 1 and 2, containing *Philosophical Miscellanies*, translated from the French of Victor Cousin, Theodore Jouffroy, and Benjamin Constant, with introduction and critical note by George Ripley (Boston: Hilliard, Gray and Co., 1838); *Elements of Psychology*, included in *A Critical Examination of Locke's Essay on the Human Understanding*, with additional pieces by Cousin, translated from the French by Rev. C. S. Henry, D.D., 2nd ed., 1838.
40. Cousin, *The Philosophy of the Beautiful*, pp. 61, 84, 95, 97, 101, 120, 144, 146, 162, 166, 191.
41. *Ibid.*, p. 145.
42. See Daniel, *op. cit.*, p. 20 *passim*.
43. See Richmond L. Hawkins, *Mme. de Staël and the United States* (Cambridge: Harvard University Press, 1930); Max I. Baym, *The French Education of Henry Adams* (New York: Columbia Uni-

versity Press, 1951, reprinted by Kraus Reprint Co., New York, 1969); Leighton, *op. cit.*; Jaeck, *op. cit.*, William Girard, "Du Transcendentalisme considéré essentiellement dans sa définition et ses origines françaises," *University of California Publications in Modern Philology* (October 18, 1916), IV; Jones, *op. cit.*

44. Elizabeth Peabody, *Aesthetic Papers* (Boston: 1849), pp. iii, 1–4.

45. Charvat, *op. cit.*, pp. 57–58. In 1806, Lisle Bowles (1762–1850) published an edition of Pope. Bowles's severe criticism of the poet drew Byron and others into a controversy that was summed up in *The Letters and Journal of Byron* (ed. Prothero, Vol. V, 1901). See also J. J. van Rennes, *Bowles, Byron, and the Pope Controversy* (1928).

46. *Ibid.* The above three paragraphs are based, in great part, on pp. 33–35, 41–42, 46–49, 58. As for the individual and society, George H. Mead wrote more than a century later:

> Romantic philosophy pointed out that the self, while it arises in the social experience, also carried with it the very unity that makes society possible, which makes the world possible. At least from their [the romantics] point of view, it is impossible to reduce the self to the world, for the very unity of the world comes from the self. It is our thinking, our perception of the world, that gives it its unity. . . . It is the Self which organizes the world (Merritt H. Moore, ed., *Movements of Thought in the Nineteenth Century*, Chicago: The University of Chicago Press; New York: The Baker & Taylor Co., 1936, p. 125.)

47. *Ibid.*, pp. 96–97.

48. *Ibid.*, pp. 112–113.

CHAPTER 3

1. Edgar Preston Richardson, *Washington Allston: A Study of The Romantic Artist in America* (Chicago: The University of Chicago Press, 1948).

2. Earl Leslie Griggs, ed., *Unpublished Letters of Samuel Taylor Coleridge* (New Haven: Yale University Press, 1933), 2 vols., Vol. II, pp. 305–306; quoted in Richardson, *op. cit.*, p. 2.

3. Richardson, *op. cit.*, p. 5.

4. See Allston's sonnet "On a Word, Man," in Washington Allston, *Lectures on Art and Poems*, Richard Henry Dana, Jr., ed. (New York: Baker and Scribner, 1850).

5. Quoted in Richardson, *op. cit.*, p. 49.

6. *Ibid.*, pp. 4–7.

7. Allston, *op. cit.*, p. 9.

8. *Ibid.*, pp. 103, 105; Richardson, *op. cit.*, p. 70.
9. Allston, "Form" in *op. cit.*; Jared B. Flagg, *The Life and Letters of Washington Allston* (New York: 1892), p. 59.
10. Richardson, *op. cit.*, pp. 102–103.
11. *Ibid.*, p. 95.
12. William Dunlap, *A History of the Rise and Progress of the Arts of Design in the United States,* new illustrated edition with additions by Frank W. Bayle and Charles E. Goodspeed (Boston: 1918), 3 vols., Vol. II, p. 309.
13. Allston, *op. cit.*, pp. 11–12, 70–73; Richardson, *op. cit.*, pp. 160–161.
14. *Ibid.*, pp. 79, 87.
15. *Ibid.*, p. 108; Richardson, *op. cit.*, p. 163.
16. Richardson, *loc. cit.*
17. Allston, *op. cit.*, p. 163; Richardson, *op. cit.*, p. 171.
18. Richardson states (p. 173) that Allston became interested in the form of the aphorism through Fuseli's aphorisms. Actually, the form was widespread in the European literature with which Allston was familiar, as in Goethe.
19. Elizabeth Peabody, "Last Evening with Allston" in *Last Evening with Allston and Other Papers, Reprinted from Emerson's Magazine* (Boston: 1886), pp. 3–4.
20. ———, *Reminiscences of Reverend William Ellery Channing, D.D.* (Boston: 1880; copyright 1877), pp. iii, 1.
21. *Ibid.*, pp. 25, 75–76.
22. *Ibid.*, pp. 96, 98, 100.
23. *Ibid.*, pp. 268–269.
24. *Ibid.*, p. 267.
25. *Ibid.*, p. 280.
26. *Ibid.*, p. 297.
27. *Ibid.*, p. 342.
28. Margaret Fuller, *Papers on Literature and Art,* edited by her brother, Arthur B. Fuller, as *Art, Literature and Drama* (Boston: 1860).
29. *Ibid.*, pp. 13–14.
30. *Ibid.*, pp. 15–16.
31. *Ibid.*, p. 17.
32. *Ibid.*, p. 21 ff.
33. *Ibid.*, p. 83.
34. *Ibid.*, p. 98.
35. *Ibid.*, pp. 99, 109.
36. *Ibid.*, p. 111.
37. *Ibid.*, pp. 324–325.
38. *Ibid.*, p. 328.
39. *Ibid.*, p. 364.

40. *Ibid.*, pp. 225, 236.
41. *Ibid.*, pp. 248, 263, 282.
42. *Ibid.*, p. 286.
43. *Ibid.*, pp. 300–301.
44. *Ibid.*, pp. 298, 305 ff.
45. *Ibid.*, p. 326.
46. Greenough's work was reprinted by the University of California Press, (Berkeley: 1958), edited by Harold A. Small, with an introduction by A. Erle Loran. This is based on Henry T. Tuckerman's *Memorial of Horatio Greenough* (New York: Putnam, 1853).
47. Greenough, *op. cit.*, p. 71.
48. *Ibid.*, pp. 102–103. Jefferson also admired Hogarth's serpentine line. The Italian line is from Dante's *Inferno*, Canto XI, 1. 105.
49. *Ibid.*, p. 108.
50. James Moffat, *An Introduction to the Study of Aesthetics* (Cincinnati: 1856), pp. v, 9.
51. *Ibid.*, pp. 15, 21.
52. *Ibid.*, p. 139.
53. A bibliography in Moffat's book lists besides Plato, Aristotle, and Augustine, such figures as Burke, Shaftesbury, Kames, Coleridge, Winckelmann, F. Lessing, the Abbé DuBos, Le Canduls de Mezieres (*Le Génie de l'architecture ou l'analogie de cet art avec nos sensations*), Boileau (*L'Art poétique*), and Ruskin (*The Seven Lamps of Architecture*).

CHAPTER 4

1. In spite of Poe's declaration that he preferred Voltaire to Goethe and that he held Macaulay in higher esteem as a critic than the Schlegels, Albert J. Lubell has shown, with considerable acuity, the full extent of Poe's indebtedness to at least A. W. Schlegel ("Poe and A. W. Schlegel," *Journal of English and Germanic Philology*, January, 1953, Vol. LII, No. 1). See further, Mozelle Scaff Allen, "Poe's Debt to Voltaire," *University of Texas Studies in English*, No. 15; Margaret Alterton, *Origins of Poe's Critical Theory* (Iowa City: 1925); Edwin Harold Eby, *American Romantic Criticism, 1815–1860* (University of Washington Ph.D. thesis, 1927, unpublished); James A. Harrison, ed., *The Complete Works of Edgar Allan Poe*, Virginia Edition (New York: 1902), 17 vols.; A. G. Lehmann, *The Symbolist Aesthetic in France (1858–1895)* (Oxford: Basil Blackwell, 1950), *passim*.
2. Lubel, *op. cit.*, pp. 7–8. Lubell produces evidence that Poe certainly knew the 1840 edition of Schlegel's *Lectures* with R. H.

Horne's introduction. Poe's initial borrowings, however, indicate that he "knew Schlegel's *Lectures* first-hand before the 1840 edition . . ." (*ibid.*, p. 7).

3. George E. Woodberry and Edmund C. Stedman, eds., *The Works of Edgar A. Poe* (Chicago: 1894–95), 10 vols., Vol. X, p. 65.
4. See Summerfield Baldwin, "The Aesthetic Theory of Edgar Poe," *Sewanee Review*, Vol. XVI, No. 2 (April, 1918), pp. 210–221.
5. See "The Poetic Principle," *passim*, conveniently in Margaret Alterton and Hardin Craig, *Edgar Allan Poe, Representative Selections, with Introduction, Biography, and Notes* (New York: American Book Company, 1935), pp. 378–401.
6. *Ibid.*, p. 389.
7. See Marshall, below, on "algedonic representation," which unites pain and pleasure in the aesthetic experience.
8. "The Philosophy of Composition," in Alterton and Craig, *op. cit.*, p. 366.
9. "The Poetic Principle," *ibid.*, p. 378.
10. "The Philosophy of Composition," *ibid.*, pp. 366–367.
11. Baldwin, *op. cit.*, p. 220; Alterton and Craig, *op. cit.*, p. lxiv; "Marginalia" (Alterton and Craig, *op. cit.*, p. 408).
12. Alterton and Craig, *op. cit.*, pp. xvi, liii–lxiv; Charles Morice, *La littérature de tout à l'heure* (Paris: 1889), p. 203, author's translation.
13. Wallace Stevens, "Reality Is An Activity of the Most August Imagination," in *Opus Posthumous*, Samuel French Morse, ed. (New York: Alfred A. Knopf, 1952), p. 110.
14. Alterton and Craig, *op. cit.*, p. 548. Lehmann (*op. cit.*, p. 104) says that *Eureka* is a long and tedious essay in universal cosmology, not very original or assured in its speculations on nature, which appear to have been common fare since Kant's *Natural History of the Heavens* (1775), and perhaps rather obscure in its sentimental pantheism. Lehmann seems to ignore Poe's designation of *Eureka* as a prose poem.
15. Paul Valéry, *Variété*, 46th edition (Paris: Gallimard, 1924), p. 120, author's translation.
16. Thomas Stearns Eliot, "Note sur Mallarmé et Poe," *Nouvelle Revue Française*, Vol. XI, 1926, p. 525.
17. ———, *from Poe to Valéry*, a Lecture delivered at the Library of Congress, November 19, 1948 (Washington, D.C.: 1949), reprinted from the *Hudson Review*, Vol. II, No. 3 (Autumn, 1949), *passim*.
18. Alterton and Craig, *op. cit.*, pp. xxx–xxxi.
19. *Eureka* in Alterton, *op. cit.*, pp. 112–122, 132–169.
20. Lehmann, *op. cit.*, pp. 254 ff.; Baudelaire, *Curiosités esthétiques* (Paris: Michel-Levy, 1868).

21. Eliot, *From Poe to Valéry.*

22. Leo Spitzer, "A Reinterpretation of 'The Fall of the House of Usher,' " *Comparative Literature,* Vol. IV, No. 4 (Fall, 1952), pp. 351 ff.

23. *Ibid.,* p. 359 f. See Henri Peyre, *Connaissance de Baudelaire* (Paris: J. Corti, 1951), p. 111, for a discussion of the emotive and intellectual attraction between Baudelaire and Poe, and their sharing of an abstract and analytical logic rare among poets.

24. Régis Michaud, *L'Esthétique d'Emerson. La Nature, l'Art, l'Histoire* (Paris: Alcan, 1931); Vivian Hopkins, *Spires of Form: A Study of Emerson's Aesthetic Theory* (Cambridge: Harvard University Press, 1951).

25. Michaud, *op. cit.,* p. 2; Hopkins, *op. cit.,* p. 4; Kenneth W. Cameron, *Emerson the Essayist,* 2 vols. (Raleigh, N.C.: 1945), Vol. I, p. 13.

26. Cameron, *op. cit.,* Vol. I, p. 19.

27. All of the quotations from Emerson are from *Nature* (1836).

28. Quotations are from "The Poet."

29. See letters to Hedge (1836) and to Margaret Fuller (1839) on the keenness of his feeling this disparity (referred to by Hopkins, *op. cit.,* pp. 46–47).

30. Hopkins, *op. cit.,* p. 58.

31. Richard P. Adams, "Emerson and the Organic Metaphor," *Publications of the Modern Language Association of America* Vol. LXIX, No. 1 (March, 1954).

32. Stephen C. Pepper, *The Basis of Criticism in the Arts* (Cambridge: Harvard University Press, 1945), p. 45; Adams, *op. cit.,* p. 119. See also Pepper, *World Hypotheses* (Berkeley: University of California Press, 1943).

33. Adams, *op. cit.,* p. 119.

34. Hopkins, *op. cit.,* p. 130.

35. Emerson, "Spiritual Laws," *Journal,* 1831, 1867; Hopkins, *op. cit.,* pp. 176, 182, 186, 198, 204.

36. F. O. Matthiessen, *American Renaissance. Art and Expression in the Age of Emerson and Whitman* (New York: Oxford University Press, 1941), p. 73.

37. "What Music Shall We Have?"—the middle section of "The Service," rejected by *The Dial* in 1840, printed separately by Sanborn in 1902.

38. Quoted in Matthiessen, *op. cit.,* p. 84.

39. Extract from *Journal* (November 20, 1851). Convenient text: Lewis Leary, ed., *Henry David Thoreau: Selected Writings* (New York: Appleton-Century-Crofts, 1958), p. 5.

40. Matthiessen, *op. cit.,* p. 91.

41. *Ibid.,* p. 100.

42. *Ibid.*, pp. 134–135.
43. Extracts from *Journal* (February 28, 1841), quoted in Mathiessen, *op. cit.*, p. 155. Among other scientific metaphors used by Thoreau is that of the sphere as a symbol of perfection in man and his being in harmony with the celestial bodies: "Our lives will not attain to be spherical by lying on one or other side forever; but only by resigning ourselves to the law of gravity in us, will our axis become coincident with the celestial axis, and [only] by revolving incessantly through all circles shall we acquire a perfect sphericity" (*Journal*, Vol. I, pp. 142–143). "I cannot see the bottom of the sky, because I cannot see the bottom of myself. It is the symbol of my own infinity" (*ibid.*, p. 150).
44. Thoreau, "Early Spring in Massachusetts," from *Journal* in *Writings of Henry David Thoreau*, manuscript edition (Boston: Houghton Mifflin Co., 1906), p. 83.
45. John Burroughs, *Indoor Studies* (Boston and New York: 1901), p. 34.
46. Joseph J. Kwiat, *New England Quarterly* Vol. XVIII, No. 1 (March, 1945).
47. *Ibid.*, p. 56.
48. "College Essays," in F. B. Sanborn, *Life of Henry David Thoreau* (Boston & New York: Houghton Mifflin Co., 1917), p. 145; Kwiat, *op. cit.*, pp. 59, 61.
49. See Norman Foerster, *Nature in American Literature. Studies in the Modern View of Nature* (New York: Macmillan Co., 1923), p. 75.
50. See Bortholow V. Crawford, *Henry David Thoreau*, American Writers Series (New York: American Book Co., 1934), p. lii.
51. Thoreau, *op. cit.*, Vol. I, p. 400; Vol. VIII, p. 441; Crawford, *op. cit.*, p. liii.

CHAPTER 5

1. Lewis E. Gates, *Studies and Appreciations* (New York: The Macmillan Co., 1900), p. 98.
2. Gates, *op. cit.*, pp. 98–99, 105.
3. Millicent Bell, *Hawthorne's View of the Artist* (Albany: State University of New York, 1962), Chapter II, pp. 32–66.
4. F. O. Matthiessen, *American Renaissance* (New York: Oxford University Press, 1941), pp. 259–262; Malcolm Cowley, ed., *The Portable Hawthorne* (New York: The Viking Press, 1948), pp. 8–9; Bell, "The Symbolic Mirror of Art," *op. cit.*, pp. 58–59.
5. Hawthorne, "The Old Manse," *The Complete Works of Nathaniel Hawthorne*, George Parsons Lathrop, ed. (Boston and New York:

Houghton, Mifflin and Co., 1883), 15 vols., Vol. II, p. 32; *American Notebooks*, pp. 170, 148. On the role of the mirror metaphor, Bell is indebted, as are all scholars in this regard, to M. H. Abrams, *The Mirror and the Lamp* (New York: Oxford University Press, 1953); Bell, *op. cit.*, p. 60.

6. Hyatt H. Waggoner, in his *Hawthorne: A Critical Study* (Cambridge, Mass.: Harvard University Press, 1955), notes (p. 106) that in Hawthorne's playful preface to "Rappacini's Daughter," the author pretends that he is merely editing the works of an obscure French author and supplies a French title for the tale that emphasizes the centrality of Beatrice: "Beatrice, ou la Belle Empoisonneuse."

7. See Jane Lundblad, *Nathaniel Hawthorne and the Tradition of the Gothic Romance* (Upsala, Sweden: A. b. Lundequistska Bokhandelen, also Cambridge, Mass.: Harvard University Press, 1946); Leslie Fiedler, *Love and Death in the American Novel* (New York: Criterion Press, 1960; revised edition, New York: Stein & Day, 1966).

8. See "Main Street" in *The Complete Works of Nathaniel Hawthorne*, Vol. III, p. 459.

9. "You emerge from mystery, pass through a vicissitude that you can but imperfectly control, and are borne onward to another mystery" (Waggoner, *op. cit.*, p. 259).

10. Matthiessen, *op. cit.*, pp. 190–191.

11. See Max I. Baym, "The Mask of Things and the Desires of the Mind: Diderot and Baudelaire," *L'Esprit Créateur*, Vol. VIII, No. 1 (Spring, 1968), p. 25.

12. "The Chimaera" in Hawthorne, *A Wonder Book*, illustrated by Arthur Rackham (New York: Garden City Publishing Co., n.d.).

13. *Ibid.*, p. 204.

14. Jay Leyda, *The Melville Log. A Documentary Life of Herman Melville, 1819–1891* (New York: Harcourt, Brace and Co., 1951), 2 vols.

15. Melville, *Moby Dick or, The Whale*, edited with an introduction by Alfred Kazin (Boston: Houghton Mifflin Co. 1956), p. 220.

16. *Ibid.*, p. 222.

17. See Max I. Baym, "Baudelaire and Shakespeare," *Shakespeare Association Bulletin* Vol. XV, No. 3 (July, 1940), pp. 131–148; Vol. XV, No. 4 (October, 1940), pp. 195–205, especially pp. 136, 146, fn. 50.

18. Leyda, *op. cit.*, Vol. I, p. 651. In April, 1862, Melville read the second volume of Madame de Staël's *Germany* and on pp. 59–60 he underscored the following passage: "It cannot be denied that there is in Goethe's book *[Elective Affinities]* a profound knowledge of the human heart, but it is a discouraging knowledge." To this

Melville's comment was: "What inadvertence! And what an admission!—'profound knowledge' and 'discouraging knowledge.' " On p. 60 he scored and underscored: ". . . *the opinions of Goethe are much more profound, but they do not present any greater consolation to the soul*. . . . It must be agreed that to think a great deal sometimes leads to the total unsettling of our fundamental ideas." Melville admired Madame de Staël's penetration, while she possessed "so femininely emotional a nature."

19. *Moby Dick*, p. 293. Melville follows this passage with a literary reference: "As devout Eckerman lifted the linen sheet from the naked corpse of Goethe, he was overwhelmed with the massive chest of the man, that seemed as a Roman triumphal arch" (*ibid.*).
20. *Ibid.*, p. 407.
21. *Ibid.*, pp. 408–409.
22. For further images in support of this contention, see in *Mardi* the chapter called "Dreams" and *White Jacket* on the image of the world and on human evil. See also Matthiessen, *op. cit.*, pp. 388, 404f.
23. Quoted in Matthiessen, *op. cit.*, p. 415.
24. Whitman, *Leaves of Grass and Selected Prose*, introduction by Sculley Bradley (New York: Rinehart & Co., 1958), p. 2.
25. *Ibid.*, "Starting from Paumanok," p. 18; "Song of Myself," pp. 40, 73; "Crossing Brooklyn Bridge," p. 136.
26. Gaston Bachelard, *L'Intuition de l'Instant* (Paris: Editions Stock, 1932), p. 74.
27. Whitman, *op. cit.*, p. 326.
28. "A Thought on Shakespeare," *November Boughs*, (Philadelphia: D. McKay, 1888), p. 56; *Walt Whitman's Complete Verse, Selected Prose and Letters*, ed. by Emory Holloway (London: The Nonesuch Press, 1938), p. 824; Roger Asselineau, *The Evolution of Walt Whitman. The Creation of a Book* (Cambridge, Mass.: Harvard University Press, 1962), 2 vols., Vol. I, p. 13.
29. Asselineau, *op. cit.*, Vol. II, Chapter IV, pp. 91–107.
30. Whitman, "Starting from Paumanok," p. 14.
31. *Ibid.*, Preface to 1855 edition of *Leaves of Grass*, p. 466; "Starting from Paumanok," p. 18. Some of the above quotations appear in Asselineau, *op. cit.*, Vol. II, Chapter IV.
32. See Max I. Baym, "Franco-American Literary Relations," *Dictionary of French Literature*, Sidney D. Braun, ed. (New York: Philosophical Library, 1958), p. 132.
33. Whitman, "Song of Joys," pp. 151, 153.
34. "Song of Myself," pp. 33, 57; Asselineau, *op. cit.*, Vol. II, p. 357.
35. Whitman, "A Backward Glance O'er Travel's Roads," p. 478; "Democratic Vistas," p. 537.
36. *Ibid.*

37. Preface to 1855 edition of *Leaves of Grass,* p. 458.
38. "A Backward Glance," pp. 474–475; Preface to 1855 edition, p. 472; "A Backward Glance," p. 474.
39. "A Backward Glance," pp. 476, 481.
40. "Democratic Vistas," pp. 541, 544.
41. *Ibid.,* p. 537.
42. "A Backward Glance," pp. 486–487. Whitman's references here are to Taine to the effect that "All original art is self-regulated and . . . causes its own counterpoise, and does not receive it from without," and to Herder, who "taught young Goethe that really great poetry is always . . . the result of a national spirit, and not the privilege of a polish'd and select few" (*ibid.,* pp. 486–487).
43. As for Asselineau's claim that Whitman often started with prose that he elaborated later in verse, see his Vol. II, pp. 222, 224. On the differentia of prose and verse, see Max I. Baym, *In Quest of Moody Food* (Leonia, N.J.: Hilding Carlson, 1934), pp. 6–11. Whitman, "I have not so much emulated . . . ," etc.; see *Leaves of Grass,* inclusive ed., Emory Holloway, ed. (New York: Doubleday, Doran, 1927), p. 459; Asselineau, *op. cit.,* Vol. II, p. 239.
44. "Democratic Vistas," p. 539.
45. See Norman Foerster, *American Criticism: A Study of Literary Theory from Poe to the Present* (Boston and New York: Houghton Mifflin Co., 1928), p. 176. See, correlatively, Tancrède de Visan, *L'Attitude du Lyrisme Contemporain* (Paris: Mercure de France, 1911), *passim* (especially re symbolism and lyricism).
46. Matthiessen, *op. cit.,* p. 541. Matthiessen gives no reference for this quote, but it is presumably taken from Clifton J. Furness, *Walt Whitman's Workshop: A Collection of Unpublished Manuscripts* (Cambridge, Mass.: Harvard University Press, 1928).
47. Throughout this section, I am under obligation to Foerster, *op. cit.*
48. Foerster, *op. cit.,* pp. 120, 122.
49. *The Works of James Russell Lowell,* (Boston and New York: Houghton, Mifflin & Co., 1870, 1871, 1890), 10 vols., Vol. II, p. 163.
50. *Ibid.,* pp. 164–165.
51. *Ibid.,* pp. 167–168.
52. *Ibid.,* p. 174.
53. *Ibid.*
54. *Ibid.,* "Swinburne's Tragedies," p. 122.
55. *Ibid.,* "Carlyle," pp. 79, 91.
56. *Ibid.,* "Swinburne's Tragedies," p. 136.
57. *Ibid.,* "Rousseau and the Sentimentalists," pp. 240–241, 250, 259–260, 269.
58. Lowell did say:
    I would not be supposed to overlook the distinction . . . between sentimentalism and sentiment. . . . Sentiment is

intellectualized emotion, emotion precipitated, as it were, in pretty crystals by the fancy . . . the delightful staple of the poets of social life like Horace and Beranger. . . . True sentiment is emotion ripened by a slow ferment of the mind and qualified to an agreeable temperance by that taste which is the conscience of polite society. But the sentimentalist always insists on taking his emotion neat, and, as his sense gradually deadens to the stimulus, increases his dose till he ends in a kind of moral deliquium. At first the debaucher, he becomes at last the victim of his sensations ("Rousseau and the Sentimentalists," p. 252).

59. Foerster, *op. cit.*, p. 154.
60. Max I. Baym, "Henry Adams and the Critics," *The American Scholar* (Winter, 1945–46), Vol. XV, No. 1, pp. 79–89, in re irony and romanticism.
61. Foerster, *op. cit.*, pp. 133, 137.
62. Lowell, "Rousseau and the Sentimentalists," pp. 257–258.

CHAPTER 6

1. John Bascom, *Aesthetics, or The Science of Beauty* (New York: Woolworth, Ainsworth, 1872); revised and enlarged (New York: G. P. Putnam's Sons, 1891), p. iii.
2. *Ibid.*, pp. 6–8, 29, 34, 45, 59, 67, 77. Bascom's statements on the nude in art give the story of Victorian prudery in a nutshell: Human virtue is a virtue of garments and protections. The clothed races are the virtuous races. Bascom leaves no doubt where he stands with respect to the portrayal of the nude, even by such masters as Titian and Rubens. One recalls Hawthorne's prudery in this connection. For Bascom, "the human body is not simply a living body, but the soul's instrument" (*ibid.*, pp. 29, 285).
3. *Ibid.*, p. 41.
4. *Ibid.*, p. 332.
5. George Fisk Comfort, "Esthetics in Collegiate Education," *The Methodist Quarterly Review*, October, 1867, p. 581.
6. *Ibid.*, p. 582.
7. *Ibid.*, p. 585.
8. *Ibid.*, p. 588.
9. *Ibid.*, p. 589.
10. Henry Noble Day, *The Science of Aesthetics: The Nature or Kinds, Laws and Uses of Beauty* (New Haven: Chs. C. Chatfield and Co., 1872), p. iii.
11. Robert Zimmermann, *Geschichte der Aesthetik als Philosophische Wissenschaft* (1858). Other sources listed by Day are: Shaftes-

bury, Hutcheson, Burke, Alison, Washington Allston, James Moffat, John Bascom, G. W. Samson, James Jackson Jarves, Reynolds, Ruskin, William Gardner, Victor Cousin, Jouffroy (*Cours d'Esthétique*, Paris: 1845), Quatremère de Quincy, Du Fresnoy, Lotze, Winckelmann, Goethe, Schiller, Herder, Lessing, Kant, Solger, Hegel, and others discussed later in this text.

12. Day, *op. cit.*, pp. 35, 37, 45.

13. By comparison, French literature was meager in works on aesthetics. The most important were those of the Abbé Batteux, Cousin, Jouffroy, Quatremère de Quincy, and Taine, all of which were known in America.

14. Day, *op. cit.*, pp. 50–51. See Alexander Baumgarten, *Aesthetica* (Frankfurt: Kunze, 1750, 1758) Section 1: "*Aesthetics* (the theory of the liberal arts, inferior knowledge, the art of thinking beautifully, the art of the analogue of reason) is the science of sensory cognition"; *Meditationes de nonnulis ad poema pertinentibus* (Halle, "Meditations on Poetry," 1735): "*Oratio sensitiva perfecta est poema* ("The perfect language of sense is poetry. . . . I would think of philosophy and knowledge of poetic composition as often joined together in the most compatible wedlock"). See Ernst Cassirer, *The Philosophy of the Enlightenment* (Boston: Beacon Press, 1961), pp. 347–348, 350.

15. Day, *op. cit.*, pp. 423, 425.

16. *Ibid.*, p. 55; Jouffroy, *Cours d'Esthétique* (Paris: 1845).

17. *Ibid.*, p. 283; John Ruskin, *Seven Lamps of Architecture* (1849, p. 98). See also Roger B. Stein's interesting and useful *John Ruskin and Aesthetic Thought in America* (Cambridge, Mass.: Harvard University Press, 1967).

18. This work reached a sixth edition, revised and enlarged, in 1890.

19. Brother Azarias (Patrick Francis Mullany), *An Essay Contributing to a Philosophy of Literature* (New York: P. O'Shea, 45 Warren St., 1874; revised and enlarged edition, 1890).

20. *Ibid.*, pp. 70, 129, 142, 152, 188, 210, 223, 233, 245.

21. *Ibid.*, pp. 192, 206, 233.

22. William Greenough Thayer Shedd, "The True Nature of the Beautiful and Its Relation to Culture," *Literary Essays* (New York: Charles Scribner's Sons, 1878).

23. *Ibid.*, pp. 1–2. Compare Channing's similar concern.

24. *Ibid.*, p. 6.

25. *Ibid.*, p. 17.

26. *Ibid.*, p. 33.

27. *Ibid.*, pp. 3, 7, 25. The author has discussed this question at length in "Science and Poetry," *Encyclopedia of Poetry and Poetics* (Princeton: Princeton University Press, 1965), pp. 743–753; "On the Relationship Between Poetry and Science," *Yearbook of Comparative Literature*, Vol. 5 (1956), pp. 1–5; "Metaphysical Ma-

laise: Science and the Struggle for a Universal Poetics," *Bucknell Review*, Vol. IX, No. 3 (December, 1960), pp. 199–211; "Science Is Poetry," *Thought*, Vol. XLV, No. 179 (Winter, 1970), pp. 590–600.
28. G. Stanley Hall, "Is Aesthetics a Science?" *The Nation*, No. 753 (December 4, 1879), pp. 380–381, dated "Berlin, November 10."
29. A second edition of the Hegel work appeared in Chicago in 1892 as part of the Series *German Philosophical Classics*, edited for English readers by George Sylvester Morris.
30. John Steinfort Kedney, *The Beautiful and the Sublime* (New York: G. P. Putnam's Sons, 1880), p. 45.
31. *Ibid.*, pp. 54–55, 60, 63–64.
32. *Ibid.*, p. 87.
33. *Ibid.*, pp. 199–200.
34. *Ibid.*, pp. 202–203.
35. *Ibid.*, pp. 208–210. At the end of the Appendix, Kedney pays homage to Day's work, although he disagrees with Day in his definition of imagination and in his treatment of the sublime. Kedney admits that Day's acumen has rendered needless any critical work that he (Kedney) might have written (*ibid.*, pp. 213–214).
36. *Ibid.*, p. 211.
37. The second part of Hegel's *Aesthetik*, which deals with the logical and historical development of the art impulse, has been translated by William M. Bryant as *The Philosophy of Art* (New York: D. Appleton & Co., 1879).
38. Kedney, *Hegel's Aesthetics*, pp. 16, 104, 122–124. See Hegel's Part II, Chapters II–IV, on the symbolic, classic, and romantic periods.
39. *Ibid.*, pp. 126, 128.
40. Baudelaire, "Correspondances," *Les Fleurs du Mal* (Paris: Librairie Alphonse Lemerre, 1925), p. 18, author's translation.
41. Kedney, *Hegel*, p. 131.
42. *Ibid.*, pp. 171, 173–174, 179.
43. *Ibid.*, pp. 181, 221.
44. *Ibid.*, pp. 241, 249, 254, 263.
45. *Ibid.*, pp. 236–237.
46. *Ibid.*, pp. 267, 273–274.
47. *Ibid.*, pp. 301–302.
48. Henry Webster Parker, *The Spirit of Beauty: Essays Scientific and Aesthetic* (New York: J. B. Alden, 1888), p. 24. The book consists of two papers read to the Iowa Association for Scientific Research, and some other papers that elaborate and illustrate the points made in the first.
49. *Ibid.*, pp. 16, 23–24.
50. *Ibid.*, pp. 26–27.
51. *Ibid.*, p. 30.

52. See subsequent discussion of Allen and Marshall.
53. Parker finds support in James Martineau's remark that speculative science had become the slave of the metaphors "germ" and "growth" (*ibid.*, pp. 30–32), also in some of Emerson's poems and in Guyot's *The Earth and Man* (*ibid.*, p. 125).
54. *Ibid.*, pp. 152, 155. An interesting parallel exists between Parker's analogy of mind to crystals and Stendhal's notion of crystallization in his *De l'Amour*.
55. *Ibid.*, pp. 157–158.
56. *Ibid.*, p. 34. T. S. Eliot may very well have received a hint for his "objective correlative" from Spencer's remark.
57. *Ibid.*, pp. 36–37.
58. George Trumbull Ladd, *Outlines of Aesthetics* (Boston: Ginn and Co., 1886). The original copy of these dictated lectures was revised by Professor Eduard Rehnisch and published in 1884.
59. A. A. Roback's *William James: His Marginalia, Personality and Contribution* (Cambridge, Mass.: Sci-Art Publisher, 1942) is not very helpful in showing the extent of James's interest in Lotze. The present author has found in the Houghton Library that James registered his interest in Lotze through his scorings and marginalia in the text of Jones's work (mentioned above), in Lotze's *Medical Psychology*, and in his *Metaphysics* and *Logic*. James read "Hermann Lotze's Philosophy in the Last Forty Years" in the *Contemporary Review* for January, 1880 (pp. 134–155). He discussed his work in his philosophy course, as the syllabus shows. For a full treatment of the influence of Lotze on James, see Otto F. Kraushaar, "Lotze's influence on the Psychology of William James," *Psychological Review*, Vol. XLIII (1936), pp. 235–257; "What James's Philosophical Orientation Owed to Lotze," *The Philosophical Review*, Vol. XLVII (September, 1938), pp. 517–526; and "Lotze as a Factor in the Development of James's Radical Empiricism and Pluralism," *The Philosophical Review*, Vol. XLVIII, No. 5 (September, 1939), pp. 455–471; a fourth article was to appear elsewhere.
60. See *Mind*, Vol. XV, No. 58 (April, 1890), pp. 191–212, for modified abstracts of Santayana's thesis.
61. Ladd, *op. cit.*, pp. vii, 3–4.
62. *Ibid.*, p. 27.
63. *Ibid.*, p. 30.
64. *Ibid.*, pp. 33–34.
65. *Ibid.*, pp. 35, 37–40, 43–44.
66. *Ibid.*, p. 92.
67. *Ibid.*, p. 104.
68. Charles Carroll Everett, *Poetry, Comedy and Duty* (Boston and New York: Houghton, Mifflin, 1888), p. 5.

69. Gaston Bachelard has stated: "The poetic knowledge of the world precedes, as it should, the reasoned knowledge of objects. The world is beautiful before being true. The world is admired before being verified. Every primitivity is pure oneirism" (*L'Air et les Songes,* p. 192), author's translation.

70. Everett, *op. cit.,* pp. 6, 8, 25. See also Baym, "Metaphysical Malaise," pp. 209–210 (re Tyndall and imagination).

71. Everett, *op. cit.,* p. 46.

72. *Ibid.,* pp. 60, 62. Emerson, "Ode to Beauty."

73. *Ibid.,* p. 71.

74. *Ibid.,* p. 82.

75. *Ibid.,* p. 91.

76. *Ibid.,* pp. 95–98.

77. *Ibid.,* p. 100.

78. *Ibid.,* p. 102.

79. *Ibid.,* p. 104.

80. *Ibid.,* pp. 110–111.

81. *Ibid.,* pp. 115–116.

82. *Ibid.,* pp. 117, 119.

83. *Ibid.,* p. 146.

84. *Ibid.,* p. 147. See Chapter II, "Eros and Thanatos" in Herbert Marcuse, *Eros and Civilization* (Boston: The Beacon Press, 1955).

85. *Ibid.,* pp. 150–152.

86. *Ibid.,* pp. 158–159.

87. *Ibid.,* p. 160.

88. *Ibid.,* pp. 170–171.

89. *Ibid.,* pp. 176–177.

90. *Ibid.,* pp. 187–188.

91. *Ibid.,* p. 209.

92. *Ibid.,* p. 214. Everett also cites Aristotle and Spencer (*The Physiology of Laughter*).

93. Daniel Cady Eaton, "Bits of Commonplace Aesthetics," *New Englander,* Vol. 48; "Modern French Aesthetics," Vol. 49, both 1888.

94. Eaton, "Modern French Aesthetics," p. 246.

95. *Ibid.,* p. 248. See *Journal of Speculative Philosophy,* Vol. I, pp. 36, 91, 169, 221; Vol. II, pp. 39, 157; Vol. III, pp. 31, 147, 281, 317. On Benard's *Exposition of Hegel,* translated by J. A. Martling, see *Mind,* Vol. 12, p. 599.

96. Eaton, "Modern French Aesthetics," p. 248.

97. *Ibid.,* pp. 249–256.

98. "Bits of Commonplace Aesthetics," p. 20.

99. "Modern French Aesthetics," pp. 252–253. As noted, the term "aesthetics" appears for the first time in Baumgarten's doctoral dissertation, where it is used as the name of a special science.

100. *Ibid.,* p. 255.

101. *Ibid.,* pp. 260, 262.
102. "Modern French Aesthetics," p. 264.
103. "Bits of Commonplace Aesthetics," p. 34.

CHAPTER 7

1. Fred Newton Scott, *Aesthetics: Its Problems and Literature* (Ann Arbor: The Inland Press, 1890).
2. ———— and Charles Mills Gayley, *A Guide to the Literature of Aesthetics,* University of California Library Bulletins, No. 11 (Berkeley: 1890).
3. Scott, *Aesthetics: Its Problems,* p. 16. Much of Hegel in translation, including Benard's exposition, appeared in the *Journal of Speculative Philosophy.* Scott urges a reading of the entire *Aesthetik.*
4. *Ibid.,* p. 20. The situation was greatly improved in James Sully's article on aesthetics in the ninth edition of the *Encyclopedia Britannica.*
5. *Ibid.,* p. 25. Bosanquet's paper appeared in *Proceedings of the Aristotelian Society,* Vol. I, No. 2.
6. *Ibid.,* p. 30. Plotinus is said to have been the first to attempt an adequate analysis of the ugly.
7. Gayley and Scott, *An Introduction to the Methods and Materials of Literary Criticism. The Bases in Aesthetics and Poetics* (Boston: Ginn and Co., 1901), pp. iii, 2.
8. Authors cited included: Émile Deschanel, *Physiologie des écrivains et des artistes, ou essai de critique naturelle* (Paris: 1864); Edouard Droz, *La Critique littéraire et la Science* (Paris: 1893); Émile Hennequin, *La Critique scientifique* (Paris: 1888). In the background are Sainte-Beuve, Taine, and Spencer. John Addington Symonds said that Hennequin's method "may be defined as the science of the work of art regarded as a sign" (*Fortnightly,* Vol. 52, p. 774), *op. cit.,* pp. 18–21. This remark comes in the vanguard of semantics and semiotics in relation to aesthetics. Some other treatments of the relation between poetry and science mentioned by Gayley and Scott are: Woodrow Wilson, *Mere Literature, and Other Essays* (Boston and New York: Houghton, Mifflin Co., 1896); John Knight, "Poetry and Science: Their Contrasts and Affinities," *University of Chicago Record,* Vol. 3, p. 9; John Dewey, "Poetry and Philosophy," *Andover Review,* Vol. 2, p. 92; Benjamin Chapman Burt, *Some Relations Between Philosophy and Literature,* Michigan University Philosophical Papers, 1st series, No. 4 (Ann Arbor: Andrews Withersby, 1886). For an overall treatment of the subject, see Max I. Baym, "Science and Poetry,"

Encyclopedia of Poetry and Poetics, A. Preminger, ed. (Princeton: Princeton University Press, 1965), pp. 742–753.

9. Gayley and Scott, *An Introduction*, p. 76.
10. *Ibid.*, pp. 95–96; John Dewey, *Psychology* (New York: Harper and Bros., 1887), Chapter XV, "Aesthetic Feeling"; Chapter VII, "Imagination"; Chapter IX, "Intuition."
11. Charles Carroll Everett, *The Science of Thought* (Boston: 1882), especially pp. 153–163, "Propositions of Beauty," and pp. 221–223, "The Logic of Aesthetics."
12. William Knight, *The Philosophy of the Beautiful, Being Outlines of the History of Aesthetics* (New York: 1891); *The Philosophy of the Beautiful, Being a Contribution to Its Theory and to a Discussion of the Arts* (London: 1893).
13. Edward Lorraine Walter's study appeared in the University of Michigan Philosophical Papers (Series II, No. 3).
14. Gayley and Scott, *op. cit.*, pp. 332–333; George Sylvester Morris, *British Thought and Thinkers* (Chicago: 1880), pp. 80–113.
15. *Ibid.*
16. Francis Barton Gummere, "On the Origins of Poetry," Child Memorial (Boston: 1897); see also Gummere's *The Beginnings of Poetry* (London and New York: The Macmillan Co., 1901).
17. Gayley and Scott, *op. cit.*, pp. 420–422.
18. Emil DuBois-Reymond, "On the Relation of Natural Science to Art," *Annual Report of the Board of Regents of the Smithsonian Institution*, July 19, 1891, pp. 661–682.
19. *Ibid.*, p. 663.
20. See Henry Thomas Buckle, *History of Civilization in England* (New York: D. Appleton and Co. 1901), Vol. II, p. 395 f; Max I. Baym, "Science and Poetry," p. 747.
21. DuBois-Reymond, *op. cit.*, pp. 663–664.
22. *Ibid.*
23. *Ibid.*, pp. 665–666.
24. *Ibid.*, pp. 668, 676–677; John Ruskin, *The Eagle's Nest: Ten Lectures on the Relation of Natural Science to Art* (London: 1872).
25. *Ibid.*, pp. 681–682. DuBois-Reymond maintains that the transition from a literary to a scientific epoch in the intellectual development of nations is accompanied by a tendency to brilliant delineation of natural phenomena. Instances are Buffon and Bernardin de Saint-Pierre in France and Alexander von Humboldt in Germany.
26. Arthur Lincoln Frothingham, "The Philosophy of Art," *American Journal of Archaeology*, April–June, 1894, pp. 196–197.
27. *Ibid.*, p. 197. This definition attracted the attention of Gayley and Scott, *op. cit.*, p. 167 f.

28. *Ibid.*
29. *Ibid.*, pp. 200–201. Frothingham presents the ontologic foundation of beauty and deformity in primordial being and non-being in Parts I and II of *Christian Philosophy* (Baltimore: 1888), noting that these chapters are necessary to the comprehension of the ontologic basis of the philosophy of art (*ibid.*, p. 169).
30. *Ibid.*, pp. 178–179.
31. See Max I. Baym, "Baudelaire and Shakespeare," *Shakespear Association Bulletin*, Vol. XV, No. 3 (July, 1940), pp. 131–148; Vol. XV, No. 4 (October, 1940), pp. 195–205, particularly footnote 24.
32. George Lansing Raymond, *Art in Theory: An Introduction to the Study of Comparative Aesthetics* (New York: G. P. Putnam's Sons, 1894; second edition 1909). Raymond's system of comparative aesthetics included the following sections: "Art in Theory," "The Representative Significance of Form," "Poetry as a Representative Art," "Painting, Sculpture and Architecture as Representative Arts," "The Genesis of Art Form," "Rhythm and Harmony in Poetry and Music—Music as a Representative Art," "Proportion and Harmony of Line and Color in Painting, Sculpture, and Architecture."
33. *Ibid.*, pp. v–vi, viii.
34. *Ibid.*, p. xxxiv. The facile statement that science is satisfied with a single fact should be viewed skeptically. Surely Raymond was not ignorant of the inductive system, which denies the validity of the "single fact."
35. *Ibid.*, p. xxxv.
36. *Ibid.*, pp. xxxviii, xlv, l.
37. Emerson, "Language" in *Nature* (1836), *The Works of Ralph Waldo Emerson in One Volume* (New York: Walter J. Black, Inc., n.d.)
38. Raymond, *op. cit.*, pp. 77, 115–116. In *Outlines of Aesthetics* Lotze asserted: "The beautiful corresponds to so much of the idea as is actualized in us" (Ladd's translation, cited by Raymond, p. 116).
39. *Ibid.*, Chapter XII, "Beauty the Result of Harmony of Effects, Physical and Mental," and Chapter XIII, "Further Considerations Showing Beauty to Result from Mental as Well as from Physical Effects." See also Kedney, *Critical Exposition of Hegel's Aesthetics*, p. 163.
40. Raymond, *op. cit.*, p. 186.
41. Raymond, *op. cit.*, p. 248. In his *Psychology*, Dewey maintains that "a purely realistic, as a purely idealistic art, is impossible" (Raymond, *op. cit.*, p. 118).
42. Grant Allen, *Physiological Aesthetics* (London: 1877), pp. vii–viii. The title is related to Spencer's "Aestho-Physiology."
43. Allen, *op. cit.*, pp. viii–ix.

44. *Ibid.*, pp. 20–28, 47. Compare Aram Vartanian's highly instructive critical edition *La Mettrie's "L'Homme Machine": A Study in the Origins of an Idea* (Princeton: Princeton University Press, 1960).

45. *Ibid.*, pp.. 20–24, Earlier Allen used the metaphor of a steam engine. Pleasure, he says, results not from the act of coaling, watering, or oiling, but from the harmonious working of the parts (*ibid.*, p. 20 f.)

46. *Ibid.*, pp. 58–96, *passim.*

47. *Ibid.*, p. 52.

48. *Ibid.*, pp. 186–187.

49. *Ibid.*, pp. 189–191, 193. This passage anticipates Santayana's "animal faith." See Spencer's *Essay on Use and Beauty.*

50. *Ibid.*, pp. 243, 245–246.

51. *Ibid.*, pp. 265, 272, 282.

52. Henry Rutgers Marshall, *Pain, Pleasure and Aesthetics* (London and New York: The Macmillan Co., 1894), pp. vi, xi, xiii, xv–xvi, xviii. Marshall quotes from John Tyndall's "The Scientific Use of the Imagination," *Scientific Addresses* (New Haven: C. C. Chatfield and Co., 1871), p. 6: "Nourished by knowledge patiently won, bounded and conditioned by co-operant reason, Imagination becomes the mightiest instrument of the physical discoverer."

53. With regard to "feeling" (too broad a term), Marshall refers to Leon Dumont, *Théorie scientifique de la sensibilité. Le plaisir et la peine* (Paris: 1875), Joseph Rémi Delboeuf's *Théorie générale de la sensibilité* (Bruxelles: 1875), and Fracisque Cyrille Bouillier's *Du plaisir et de la douleur* (Paris: 1885), Marshall, *op. cit.*, p. 8.

54. *Ibid.*, p. 9.

55. *Ibid.*, p. 34.

56. *Ibid.*, pp. 91, 94.

57. *Ibid.*, pp. 110, 114. Marshall makes a quick survey of Plato, Aristotle, Herbart, Burke, Hogarth, Schleiermacher, Lotze, Bergman, Proudfoot Begg, and Von Hartmann (pp. 114–119).

58. *Ibid.*, p. 120.

59. *Ibid.*, pp. 142–143, 344.

60. *Ibid.*, pp. 103–104.

61. *Ibid.*, pp. 141, 144, 154. See Jean Marie Guyau, *Les Problèmes de l'esthétique contemporaine* (Paris: Alcan, 1884); *L'Art au pointe de vue sociologique* (Paris: Alcan, 1890), *passim.*

62. Edmund Gurney, *The Power of Sound* (London: 1880). See Appendix A, "On Pleasure and Pain in Relation to the Evolution of the Senses" (pp. 541–547). Gurney expresses his indebtedness to Harry Sidgwick, "Pleasure and Desire" in *The Methods of Ethics* (1874).

63. Marshall, *op. cit.*, p. 337.

64. *Ibid.*, pp. 333–334. Marshall's references here are to Sully's *Human Mind*, Chapter II, p. 128, and Lotze's *Microsmus*, Book VII, Chapter 5.

65. Marshall, *op. cit.*, pp. 246, 248. Eduard Von Hartmann, *Die deutsche Aesthetik seit Kant* (Berlin: 1886). On this complex subject, Valéry and the Symbolists come to mind.

66. Marshall, *Aesthetic Principles* (New York: The Macmillan Co., 1895, 1901), originally presented as a series of lectures at Columbia University in November and December, 1894, pp. 6, 73, 75, 79.

67. *Ibid.*, pp. 12, 14–15.

68. *Ibid.*, p. 83.

69. *Ibid.*, pp. 103–104.

70. *Ibid.*, p. 106.

71. *Ibid.*, pp. 106–110.

72. *Ibid.*, p. 148.

73. *Ibid.*, pp. 180–181, 187.

CHAPTER 8

1. Monroe C. Beardsley, *Aesthetics from Classical Greece to the Present. A Short History* (New York: The Macmillan Co., 1966), p. 329.

2. Stephen Coburn Pepper, *Aesthetic Quality; a Contextualistic Theory of Beauty* (New York: Charles Scribner's Sons, 1938), pp. 7–8:

> "There will . . . be . . . no polemical material in this book, such as fill the pages of many writings in aesthetics. For a common procedure is to begin by exhibiting the shortcomings of outstanding aesthetic theories of the day. . . . [The] implication of this procedure is that the criticisms have disposed of all rival theories, and that consequently the field is clear for the new theory which can now have the field all to itself. The method is very effective, and entirely unsound. The new theory is often not as good as the one "disposed" of. But more than that, unless the new theory is also faultless, or at least very much better than those criticized, the criticized theories will still be needed to exhibit features which the new theory probably obscures."

3. George Santayana, *The Sense of Beauty. Being the Outlines of Aesthetic Theory* (New York: Charles Scribner's Sons, 1896), Preface. See Henri Peyre, *Literature and Sincerity* (New Haven: Yale University Press, 1963), *passim*.

4. For Santayana's thesis, see Harvard University Archives and *Mind*, Vol. 15, No. 58 (April, 1890), pp. 191–212 (abstracts of the thesis). Josiah Royce actually attended Lotze's lectures. As we know now, he also exercised an influence on William James (see the studies of Kraushaar).

5. *The Sense of Beauty*, p. 57.

6. *Ibid.*, pp. 14, 39, 41, 57, 172; Beardsley, *op. cit.*, pp. 331–332. On the relation of the passion of love to aesthetics, see reference to Stendhal's *De l'Amour, passim*, p. 48 fn. 1; "Love" ("Reason in Society") in *The Life of Reason* (New York: Charles Scribner's Sons, 1924), p. 34, where Santayana links generation with love and beauty: "The machinery which serves reproduction . . . finds kindred but higher uses, as every organ does in the liberal life; and what Plato called a desire for birth in beauty may be sublimated even more, until it yearns for an ideal immortality in a transfigured world. . . ."

7. Santayana, "The Mutability of Aesthetic Categories," *Philosophical Review*, Vol. XXIV (May, 1925), p. 284 n.

8. *The Sense of Beauty*, p. 203.

9. *Ibid.*, p. 195.

10. *Ibid.*, p. 58.

11. *Ibid.*, p. 70.

12. *Ibid.*, p. 73.

13. *Ibid.*, pp. 79, 83.

14. *Ibid.*, p. 84.

15. *Ibid.*, p. 97.

16. *Ibid.*, p. 114. Like Lowell, Santayana has difficulties with the problem of sentimentalism. On romanticism, Santayana is as quixotic as Diderot is in aesthetics generally. The elusive quality of beauty is its principal attraction. The beautiful derives its fascination from the illusions it engenders.

17. *Ibid.*, p. 114.

18. *Ibid.*, p. 115. The influence of Pater is evident in Santayana's declaration that if the arts aspire to the condition of music, the sciences aspire to the condition of mathematics. In *The Last Puritan*, Pater is recalled in the remark about young Oliver's mother: "Sensations and images were what that young sensorium craved" (p. 101).

19. *Ibid.*, pp. 121–122. On unity of mind with respect to beauty, see Chapter 11, fn. 23.

20. *Ibid.*, pp. 125 n., 120.

21. *Ibid.*, pp. 127–128. In a footnote on p. 127, Santayana singles out English as "remarkable for the intensity and variety of the color of its words" and its abundance of specifically poetic terms.

22. *Ibid.*, p. 131.

23. *Ibid.*, pp. 128–129.
24. *Ibid.*, p. 132.
25. *Ibid.*, pp. 135–136.
26. *Ibid.*, pp. 140, 144.
27. *Ibid.*, p. 179.
28. *Ibid.*, p. 183. According to Santayana, the difference between the beautiful and the sublime is that in experiencing the first we sink into the object; in the second, we deny the object altogether. In experiencing the sublime, "the emotion comes not from the situation we observe, but from the powers we conceive." The imagination overwhelms the understanding (pp. 183–184).
29. *Ibid.*, p. 185.
30. *Ibid.*, pp. 187–188 *passim.*
31. Miguel de Unamuno, *Vida de Don Quijote y Sancho* (Madrid: Renacimiento, segunda edicion, n.d.) p. 64, author's translation.
32. *The Sense of Beauty*, p. 194.
33. *Ibid.*, pp. 43, 201–203.
34. *Ibid.*, pp. 199–200.
35. Santayana, *Reason in Art* (New York: Charles Scribner's Sons, 1934), pp. 8, 16–17.
36. *Ibid.*, p. 27.
37. *Ibid.*, p. 33.
38. *Ibid.*, pp. 54–55, 66.
39. *Ibid.*, p. 77.
40. *Ibid.*, p. 76.
41. *Ibid.*, pp. 80–84 *passim.*
42. *Ibid.*, p. 98.
43. *Ibid.*, pp. 98, 100.
44. *Ibid.*, pp. 103–104. See Santayana's essay on love and his interest in Stendhal's *De l'Amour.*
45. *Ibid.*, pp. 105, 113–114.
46. Santayana, *Three Philosophical Poets* (Cambridge, Mass.: Harvard University Press, 1910; New York: Doubleday Anchor Books, 1953), "Lucretius," p. 31; "Dante," p. 114.
47. *Reason in Art*, pp. 187, 193–194.
48. "What is Aesthetics?" *The Philosophical Review*, Vol. XIII, No. 3 (1904), pp. 322–324.
49. *Ibid.*, p. 327.
50. Santayana's review of Croce's *Estetica come Scienza dell' espressione e linguistica generale* (Napoli: 1902), *Journal of Comparative Literature*, Vol. I, No. 2 (April–June, 1903), pp. 191–195.
51. Benedetto Croce, *Aesthetic as Science of Expression and General Linguistic*, translated by Douglas Ainslie (London: Macmillan and Co., Ltd.,), 1922, p. 221.
52. *Ibid.* On the role of "concept" in art and aesthetics, Croce says:

> When students of Vico and Hegel understood and expounded their master's theories as emphasizing the importance of concepts in art, De Sanctis replied: "The concept does not exist in art, nature or history: the poet works unconsciously and sees no concept but only form, in which he is involved and well nigh lost. If the philosopher, by means of abstraction, can extract the concept thence and contemplate it in all its purity, he acts in a way entirely contrary to that of art, nature and history" (p. 361).

53. Santayana's review (as cited in fn. 50), pp. 194–195.
54. *Ibid.*, p. 195.
55. *Ibid.*

CHAPTER 9

1. Alexander Thomas Ormond, *Foundations of Knowledge* (New York: The Macmillan Co., 1900), pp. 518–523 *passim*, 240–241. Ormond added idealism to McCosh's strong Scottish realism.
2. *Ibid.*, pp. 71, 221, 223–224. In this work, see "The Aesthetic Categories."
3. *Ibid.*, pp. 225, 230.
4. *Ibid.*, pp. 240–241, 251.
5. *Ibid.*, p. 315.
6. Lewis Edward Gates, *Studies and Appreciations* (New York: The Macmillan Co., 1900), p. 198.
7. Hippolyte Taine, "Mérimée," *Derniers essais de critique et d'Histoire* (Paris: Hachette, 1894).
8. Francis Barton Gummere, *The Beginnings of Poetry*, p. 447. See Max I. Baym, "The Present State of the Study of Metaphor," *Books Abroad*, Vol. XXXV, No. 3, (Summer, 1961).
9. Alexander Baumgarten, *Meditationes*, in re *oratio sensitiva perfecta; Aletheophilus*, in re "poem charged with energy." Gummere, *op. cit.*, p. 38. His other references are to Gayley and Scott, *Methods and Materials*; Karl Pearson; James Baldwin; Bernard Perez, *L'Art et la poésie chez l'enfant* (Paris: Alcan, 1888); Theodule Armand Ribot, *Psychology of the Emotions* (New York: Charles Scribner's Sons, 1900); and Georg Hegel, *Vorlesungen über die Aesthetik* (Berlin: 1835; English translation by Osmaston).
10. Fred Newton Scott, "The Most Fundamental Differentia of Poetry and Prose," *Publications of the Modern Language Association of America*, Vol. XIX, No. 11 (1904), pp. 250–269.
11. *Ibid.*, pp. 253–254. See also Earle's *English Prose*, p. 151. Besides

Gummere's *Beginnings of Poetry*, Scott uses Hirn's *Origins of Art* and John Stuart Mill's *Thoughts on Poetry and Its Varieties.*

12. *Ibid.*, p. 257.
13. *Ibid.*, pp. 268–269.
14. Ethel Dench Puffer, *The Psychology of Beauty* (Boston and New York: Houghton, Mifflin and Co., 1905), p. 20. The reference is to Lewis E. Gates's paper on "Impressionism and Appreciation," in the *Atlantic Monthly*, July, 1900.
15. *Ibid.*, p. 21. See, however, Ruth Child, *The Aesthetic of Walter Pater* (New York: The Macmillan Co., 1940), Chapter IV, "Aesthetic Criticism."
16. *Ibid.*, pp. 23–26 *passim.*
17. *Ibid.*, p. 51. Reference is made to "Emotion" in Baldwin's *Dictionary of Philosophy and Psychology.*
18. Jean Marie Guyau, *Les Problèmes de l'Esthétique Contemporaine* (Paris: Alcan, 1884), p. 77; Puffer, *op. cit.*, p. 54.
19. Puffer, *op. cit.*, pp. 54–56 *passim.*
20. *Ibid.*, pp. 61–77. Puffer notes that, without using our eye muscles (even infinitesimally) we cannot think of the visual image.
21. See Paul Souriau, *La Suggestion de l'Art* (Paris: Alcan, 1893); Puffer, *op. cit.*, pp. 80, 85, 156–159, 192, 199.
22. Puffer, *op. cit.*, pp. 208, 211, 214–215.
23. It gives us pleasure, says Puffer, to have painful emotions or to contemplate other people's sorrows, *in spite* of the remains of the *"gorille féroce"* in us, to which Taine and Faguet impute this pleasure (p. 236). We should think this is *because*, not *in spite of.*
24. *Ibid.*, pp. 244, 246.
25. Charles Carroll Everett, *Poetry, Comedy and Duty* (Boston and New York: Houghton, Mifflin and Co., 1888).
26. Puffer, *op. cit.*, pp. 253–254.
27. *Ibid.*, pp. 269–270.
28. *Ibid.*, p. 277.
29. *Ibid.*, pp. 281–284.
30. Hartley Burr Alexander, *Poetry and the Individual: An Analysis of the Imaginative Life in Relation to the Creative Spirit in Man and Nature* (New York and London: G. P. Putnam's Sons, 1906), Chapter II.
31. *Ibid.*, pp. 30, 49, 92–93.
32. Theodule Armand Ribot, *L'Évolution des idées générales* (Paris: Alcan, 1897); *Essai sur l'imagination créatrice* (Paris: Alcan, 1900; English translation by Albert H. N. Baron, Chicago: The Open Court Publishing Co., 1906).
33. Alexander, *op. cit.*, pp. 117, 119. Alexander fails to discuss the aesthetic response to a scientific creation, as when scientists talk of an "elegant" solution to problems.

34. Alexander's references are to Philip Hamerton, *Imagination and Landscape Painting* (London: Seeley & Co., 1887), and Paul Souriau, *L'Imagination de l'Artiste* (Paris: Hachette, 1901), p. 46.
35. *Ibid.*, p. 125.
36. *Ibid.*, pp. 142, 147.
37. *Ibid.*, pp. 149–150.
38. *Ibid.*, pp. 151–152. See Souriau, *op. cit.*, pp. 49–51; Everett, *op. cit.*, on abstraction; Frederic Queyrat, *L'Imagination et ses variétés chez l'enfant* (Paris: Alcan, 1893, 1903); Hippolyte Taine, *The Philosophy of Art* (New York: Holt & Williams, 2nd ed., 1873), pp. 78–80.
39. *Ibid.*, pp. 160–161, 163, 168, 174.
40. *Ibid.*, p. 177.
41. *Ibid.*, pp. 195–196, 210.
42. *Ibid.*, pp. 232–233.
43. Elizabeth Kemper Adams, *The Aesthetic Experience: Its Meaning in a Functional Psychology* (doctoral dissertation, University of Chicago, 1904, published 1907), pp. 11, 17–18, section "The General Characteristics of Aesthetic Experience." Adams differs from the positions taken by Karl Groos in his *Der Aesthetische Genuss* (Giesson: 1902) and Marshall in "The Relation of Aesthetics to Psychology and Philosophy" (*Philosophical Review*, Vol. XIV, 1905), pp. 4–20, that it is necessary to distinguish rigidly between the artist and the appreciator (p. 19 f.).
44. *Ibid.*, pp. 22–23, 27–28. In the section "Previous Work in Aesthetics," Adams discusses a number of divergent points of view, from the height of German idealism, when aesthetics was in the service of metaphysics, to the advent of empiricism. During the last half of the nineteenth century, aesthetics was treated as a branch of psychology rather than of philosophy.
45. Adams, *op. cit.*, p. 35, citing Puffer, *The Psychology of Beauty*, p. 50; Santayana, *Reason in Art*, pp. 188, 193–194; Adams, *op. cit.*, p. 36.
46. Adams, *op. cit.*, p. 73, citing Henry Cecil Sturt, "Art and Personality" in *Personal Idealism* (London and New York: The Macmillan Co., 1902); Peter Koropotkin, *Mutual Aid* (New York: McClure, 1902); Charles Horton Cooley, *Human Nature and the Social Process* (New York: Charles Scribner's Sons, 1902).
47. *Ibid.*, p. 77.
48. Marshall, *Pain, Pleasure and Aesthetics*, pp. 100–104; Yrjö Hirn, *The Origins of Art: A Psychological and Sociological Inquiry* (London and New York: The Macmillan Co., 1900), p. 302; Adams, *op. cit.*, p. 80.
49. Bernhard Berenson, *The Study and Criticism of Italian Art*. First series (London: G. Bell, 1901), p. 45; Adams, *op. cit.*, p. 91; see

"Synaesthesia" in *Encyclopedia of Poetry and Poetics* (Princeton: Princeton University Press, 1965), pp. 839–840.

50. Adams, *op. cit.*, p. 102. She cites Gustav Freytag's *The Technique of the Drama*, translated from the German by E. J. McEwan (Chicago: S. C. Griggs and Co., 1895): the triangle whose left side represents the rising action; the apex, the middle of the play with its most acute conflict and crisis; and the right side, the falling action. This figure holds for every act and every scene.

51. Adams, *op. cit.*, pp. 104–105.

52. Edmund Burke, *A Philosophical Enquiry into the Origin of Our Ideas of the Sublime and the Beautiful* (1756), Part IV, Sections 1–18; Immanuel Kant, *Critique of Judgment* (1790; English translation, 1892), Part I, Book II.

53. Santayana, *The Sense of Beauty*, pp. 235–236; Adams, *op. cit.*, p. 100.

54. Adams, *op. cit.*, pp. 106–107.

55. *Ibid.*, p. 97.

56. Ormond, *Foundations of Knowledge*, p. 238; Adams, *op. cit.*, p. 109.

57. Kate Gordon, *The Psychology of Meaning* (Chicago: University of Chicago Press, 1903), pp. 62–63; Adams, *op. cit.*, p. 109.

58. Gordon, "Pragmatism in Aesthetics," in *Essays Philosophical and Psychological in Honor of William James* (New York: Longmans, Green, 1908), p. 463.

59. *Ibid.*, p. 465.

60. *Ibid.*, p. 469.

61. *Ibid.*, p. 476.

62. *Ibid.*, p. 480.

63. *Ibid.*, pp. 481–482.

64. Gordon, *Esthetics* (New York: Henry Holt & Co., 1909), p. 24; James Hayden Tufts, *On the Genesis of Esthetic Categories* (Chicago: University of Chicago Press, 1902).

65. Gordon, *op. cit.*, pp. 248–249, 269.

66. *Ibid.*, p. 275; Gertrude Buck, The Metaphor: *A Study in the Psychology of Rhetoric* (Ann Arbor: 1899); see Baym, *op. cit.*; Oliver Goldsmith, *Works* (London: G. Bell, 1885), Vol. I, p. 363. Note Meredith's remark that in drama "Passions spin the plot."

67. Gordon, *op. cit.*, pp. 269–270. This passage suggests Freud's coupling of Eros and Thanatos and the correlative pleasure-pain bond, which may explain the fascination of melancholy in poetry and music.

68. *Ibid.*, pp. 288–289.

69. *Ibid.*, p. 294.

70. Gordon's view of realism (*op. cit.*, p. 14) in relation to art seems rather naive. The artist, more than many philosophers and tech-

nicians who are often mistaken for scientists, knows that *a mere heap of stones will never constitute a house.* The phrase is that of Henri Poincaré: *"Un tas de pierres n'a jamais été une maison"* (communicated to the author by the late distinguished electrical engineer, Fernand Ernstein of Lille, in a letter dated October 25, 1964).

71. William Davis Furry, *The Aesthetic Experience: Its Nature and Function in Epistemology,* Johns Hopkins Studies in Philosophy and Psychology, No. 1 (Baltimore: Review Publishing Co., 1908), pp. v, vii, ix, xii. Furry regards James Baldwin's *Thought and Things* (London: S. Sonnenchein & Co., 1906; New York: Macmillan, 1906) as the most complete and satisfactory attempt to treat knowledge genetically (p. viii).

72. *Ibid.,* p. xiii. The term "semblant" (not clearly defined by Furry) presumably signifies the treatment of meanings by metaphoric analogies, where one set of terms is productive of another set.

73. *Ibid.,* pp. xiv–xv.

74. Furry expresses indebtedness to Baldwin both for general ideas and for details; here, to his *Thought and Things,* Vol. II, Appendix II.

75. Furry, *op. cit.,* p. 2.

76. *Ibid.,* pp. 154–155; Baldwin, *loc. cit.*

CHAPTER 10

1. Gordon, *Aesthetics,* p. 3.

2. Joel Elias Spingarn, "The New Criticism" (first published as "Literary Criticism" in *Columbia University Lectures on Literature*), *Creative Criticism: Essays on the Unity of Genius and Taste* (New York: Harcourt, Brace and Co., 1911); reprinted in *Criticism in America: Its Function and Status,* with essays by Irving Babbitt, Van Wyck Brooks, W. C. Brownell, Ernest Boyd, T. S. Eliot, H. L. Mencken, Stuart P. Sherman, and George E. Woodberry (New York: Harcourt, Brace and Co., 1924). This contains Spingarn's "The New Criticism" and "Criticism in the United States," as well as an appendix. "Criticism in the United States" is a revision of "Scholarship and Criticism," which appeared in *Civilization in the United States: An Inquiry by Thirty Americans* (New York: Harcourt, Brace and Co., 1921).

3. Spingarn, *Criticism in America,* pp. 305–307.

4. *Ibid.,* pp. 307–308.

5. *Creative Criticism,* pp. 15–20.

6. Spingarn dedicated *Creative Criticism* "To my friend Benedetto Croce, the most original of all modern thinkers on Art."

7. *Ibid.,* pp. 23 f., 29, 33, 38. Technique cannot be taught because

it is really an aspect of personality (Croce). The technique of poetry cannot be separated from its inner nature (Oscar Wilde, "The Critic as Artist"), *ibid.*, p. 38.

8. *Ibid.*, p. 44.
9. *Criticism in America*, pp. 287–288.
10. *Ibid.* (appendix to *Criticism in America*), pp. 322–324.
11. *Ibid.*, pp. 322–324.
12. *Ibid.*, pp. 291–292, 301–302.
13. *Ibid.*, pp. 293–295, 301–302.
14. Albert Mordell, *The Shifting of Literary Values* (Philadelphia: The International, 1912), p. 9.
15. *Ibid.*, p. 13.
16. *Ibid.*, p. 28.
17. *Ibid.*, p. 48. Mme. de Staël in *De la Littérature* does express belief in progress in literature (p. 49).
18. *Ibid.*, pp. 43–48 *passim*. See Baym, "Science and Poetry."
19. *Ibid.*, pp. 61–62.
20. *Ibid.*, pp. 73, 78, 84.
21. Edward Howard Griggs, *The Philosophy of Art* (New York: B. W. Huebsch, 1913). Sources cited by Griggs include Emerson, Poe, Gurney, Dwight, Stedman, Bascom, Lanier, Raymond, Puffer, Santayana, Van Dyke, Münsterberg, Babbitt, and Gummere.
22. *Ibid.*, pp. 18, 36, 39.
23. *Ibid.*, pp. 41, 44, 139.
24. *Ibid.*, pp. 225, 233, 250, 260–261.
25. *Ibid.*, pp. 267, 269, 274. See August Wilhelm Ambros, *The Boundaries of Music and Poetry. A Study in Musical Aesthetics* (Prague: 1856), translated from the German by J. H. Cornell (New York: G. Schirmer, 1893).
26. *Ibid.*, pp. 267, 269, 278–279.
27. *Ibid.*, p. 282.
28. *Ibid.*, pp. 296–297.
29. *Ibid.*, pp. 325, 329–330.
30. Havelock Ellis, *The Dance of Life* (Boston and New York: Houghton, Mifflin Co., 1923), pp. 1, 281.
31. George Edward Woodberry, "Two Phases of Criticism: Historical and Aesthetic" (The Woodberry Society, 1914), reprinted in *The Heart of Man and Other Papers* (New York: Harcourt, Brace and Co., 1920).
32. *Ibid.*, pp. 49–51.
33. *Ibid.*, p. 55.
34. *Ibid.*, pp. 61–62.
35. *Ibid.*, pp. 79–80.
36. *Ibid.*, pp. 70, 74–76.
37. *Ibid.*, pp. 82–83.

38. William Crary Brownell, *Criticism* (New York: Charles Scribner's Sons, 1914), pp. 104–107. Brownell's remarks on the historical approach may have been true in the historiography of 1914. Since then, a considerable change has occurred as a result of the progressive rapprochement between history and psychology—a development partly attributable to Freud.

39. *Ibid.*, p. 108.

40. *Ibid.*, p. 111.

41. *Ibid.*, pp. 112–113. Brownell's inclusion of Sarcey recalls Henry Adams's oblique characterization: "I am going to take Mrs. Brooks to a Conference by Sarcey, on Paul Déroulède. . . . *Est-ce assez canaille?* Sarcey is bourgeois to a point I almost respect, and Déroulède is, I believe, a sort of French Kipling. . . . His (Sarcey's) *conference* was poor enough in matter, and bourgeoisitic in appreciation of poetry." *Letters of Henry Adams, 1892–1918*, W. C. Ford, ed. (Boston and New York: Houghton, Mifflin Co., 1938), pp. 141–142.

42. Brownell, *Standards* (New York: Charles Scribner's Sons, 1925), pp. 10–11. Spontaneity of the elevated order is presumably that of great genius, while spontaneity of the elementary order is that of lesser genius that is under necessity to "reconstruct the established foundations of the splendid structure of letters and art" (pp. 11–12).

43. *Ibid.*, pp. 16–17.

44. *Ibid.*, pp. 16–22, 31.

45. *Ibid.*, p. 102.

46. *Ibid.*, pp. 83, 38, 126, 150.

47. *Ibid.*, pp. 141, 70.

48. Van Wyck Brooks, "The Critics and Young America," reprinted in *Criticism in America.*

49. *Ibid.*, pp. 118–119.

50. *Ibid.*, pp. 125–129.

51. *Ibid.*, pp. 129, 132–133.

52. *Ibid.*, pp. 142–143.

53. *Ibid.*, pp. 143–144.

54. *Ibid.*, pp. 148–151.

55. Irving Babbitt, "Genius and Taste," *The Nation*, Vol. 106, No. 2745, (February 7, 1918), pp. 138–141, reprinted in *Criticism in America.*

56. *Ibid.*, pp. 154–155.

57. *Ibid.*, pp. 157–158.

58. *Ibid.*, pp. 161–167.

59. *Ibid.*, pp. 168–170.

60. *Ibid.*, p. 170 f. The art of the child is not juxtaposed to that of Michelangelo on a comparative basis. Piaget or Melanie Klein

would have no difficulty in grasping the true meaning of Spingarn's statement: that the art of the child is a true expression of its vital energies as much as the art of Michelangelo was of his.

61. *Ibid.*, pp. 174–175.
62. T. S. Eliot, "The Perfect Critic" in *The Sacred Wood: Essays on Poetry and Criticism* (New York: Alfred A. Knopf, 1920), reprinted in *Criticism in America*.
63. *Criticism in America*, p. 199. Quotation from Rémy de Gourmont, *Le problème du style* (Paris: Mercure de France, 1902).
64. *Ibid.*, pp. 206–208.
65. *Ibid.*, p. 210.
66. *Ibid.*, pp. 214–215.
67. *Ibid.*, p. 209.
68. *Ibid.*, pp. 220–221.
69. *Ibid.*, pp. 223–224.
70. *Ibid.*, pp. 225–227.
71. Henry Louis Mencken, "Motive of the Critic," *The New Republic*, Vol. 28, No. 360 (October 26, 1921), pp. 249–251, reprinted in *Criticism in America*, p. 262.
72. *Criticism in America*, p. 265.
73. *Ibid.*, pp. 270–273.
74. *Ibid.*, pp. 276–278.
75. *Ibid.*, pp. 284–285.
76. Mencken, "Criticism of Criticism of Criticism," *New York Mail*, July 1, 1918, reprinted in *Criticism in America*.
77. *Criticism in America*, pp. 176–177.
78. *Ibid.*, pp. 178–179.
79. *Ibid.*, pp. 180–184.
80. *Ibid.*, pp. 187–188.
81. *Ibid.*, pp. 188–190.

CHAPTER I I

1. James Mark Baldwin, *Genetic Theory of Reality Being the Outcome of Genetic Logic as Issuing in the Aesthetic Theory Called Pancalism* (New York and London: The Macmillan Co., 1915). In the preface Baldwin states: "In this book the matter appears which I had intended to place in the projected fourth volume of the work *Thought and Things in Genetic Logic*." Vol. I of the latter work appeared in London and New York in 1906; Vol. II, 1908; Vol. III, 1911. The dedication in Vol. I reads: "To his friends who write in French, Janet, Flournoy, Binet and to the lamented Tarde and Marillier. . . ." Baldwin dedicated Vol. III, *Interest and Art Being Real Logic*, I.—*Genetic Epistemology* (Lon-

don: 1911), "To the Memory of William James, whose teaching was always true." The late Gaston Bachelard was among the luminaries who had a high esteem for Baldwin's work.

2. Baldwin, *Thought and Things*, Vol. III, p. x.

3. *Ibid.*, pp. 17–19. By "aesthetic experience," Baldwin (together with Furry, W. M. Mitchell, Ormond, *et al.*) meant the involvement of the self with an object in a way that did not deny its truth or its usefulness but found its proper fulfillment neither in its truth nor in its usefulness (*ibid.*, p. 13). The aesthetic treatment of a content involves (1) the "scientific" or "theoretical" imagination, which has as its end the furthering and completion of knowledge, and (2) the "practical" or "useful" imagination, which has as its end some form of appreciation or fulfillment. Without being within (1) or (2), the aesthetic treatment involves both (*ibid.*, p. 12).

4. *Ibid.*, pp. 246–247, 252–253.

5. *Ibid.*, pp. 272–273, 280. In "Appendix C: Aspects of Contemporary Thought" (Vol. III), Baldwin brings into his argument Bradley's *Appearance and Reality*, 2nd edition, 1879, and Bergson's *Les Données immédiates de la Conscience*, 6th edition, 1910 (English edition, *Time and Free Will*, 1910).

6. Baldwin, *Genetic Theory*, pp. vi, 28, 30–31, 39. Baldwin indicates that Kant intimated a synthesis of will and reason in aesthetic appreciation and that this synthesis resides in the constructive role of the aesthetic imagination. The movement toward Pancalism, Baldwin realized, received in Kant a powerful impulse. Kant suggested reasonable ground for finding the union of will and reason in feeling and for believing that this union was present in the exercise of the aesthetic judgment (Baldwin, *op. cit.*, pp. 208–211; Kant, *Critique of Judgment*, J. H. Bernard's translation, 1892, Introduction, p. 12). Baldwin found also in Schelling suggestions for his own theory. Besides the synthesis of mind and nature in art, by which the philosophical principle of identity is justified, Schelling finds in art another essential synthesis, that of knowledge and practice (Baldwin, *op. cit.*, pp. 213–214). Earlier, in *Genetic Theory*, p. 227, Baldwin states that "reality," apart from all meaning and experience, is absurdity or a mere word. See also pp. 275–277.

7. *Ibid.*, pp. 289–302 *passim*, 308.

8. *Ibid.*, pp. 309–311. Baldwin is aware that his suggestion was anticipated in Aristotle's doctrine of the imagination, reappeared in the theories of the Italian mystics and of the Renaissance generally, and was ultimately developed in Kant's doctrines of the schema and of art.

9. *Ibid.*, p. 312.

10. DeWitt Henry Parker, *The Principles of Aesthetics* (Boston and New York: Silver, Burdett and Co., 1920), pp. 51, 57, 59, 67, 72, 128, 130–131.

11. *Ibid.,* pp. 72, 81, 134–135, 146, 148. On science and poetry, see Max I. Baym, "Metaphysical Malaise: Science and the Struggle for a Universal Poetics," *Bucknell Review,* Vol. IX, No. 3 (December, 1960), p. 200, and "Science and Poetry," *Encyclopedia of Poetry and Poetics* (Princeton: Princeton University Press, 1965), *passim.*

12. *Ibid.,* Chapter VIII, "The Aesthetics of Music," pp. 135 f., 167–168.

13. *Ibid.,* p. 189. See the earlier section on Scott; Parker refers to Scott's "The Most Fundamental Differentia of Poetry and Prose."

14. *Ibid.,* pp. 191, 196.

15. *Ibid.,* pp. 223–224.

16. *Ibid.,* pp. 225–227.

17. *Ibid.,* pp. 228–230.

18. *Ibid.,* pp. 230–231, 248.

19. Herbert Sidney Langfeld, *The Aesthetic Experience* (New York: Harcourt, Brace and Co., 1920), pp. v–vi.

20. *Ibid.,* pp. 6–7.

21. John Livingston Lowes, *Convention and Revolt in Poetry* (Boston and New York: Houghton, Mifflin Co., 1919), pp. 324–326.

22. Ethel Puffer, *Psychology of Beauty* (Boston and New York: Houghton, Mifflin Co., 1905), pp. 76–79, 243; Edward Bullough, "Psychological Distance as a Factor in Art, and as Aesthetic Principle," *The British Journal of Psychology,* Vol. 5 (1912–13), pp. 87–118; Langfeld, *op. cit.,* pp. 20, 48–57, 62–63, 73.

23. On Santayana's statement of the mind's tendency to unity, see *The Sense of Beauty* (p. 121):

> The mind that perceives nature is the same that understands and enjoys her; indeed, these three functions are really elements of one process . . . the sense . . . that the whole world is made to be food for the soul; that beauty is not only its own, but all things excuse for being . . . that sense is the poetical reverberation of a psychological fact—of the fact that our mind is an organism tending to unity.

To this Santayana adds:

> The idea that nature could be governed by an aspiration towards beauty is . . . to be rejected as a confusion, but at the same time we must confess that this confusion is founded on a consciousness of the subjective relation between the perceptibility, rationality, and beauty of things (*ibid.*).

Note this expression of hesitation in relation to Baldwin's Pancalism.

24. Langfeld, *op. cit.*, pp. 169, 177, 179.
25. *Ibid.*, pp. 240–242.
26. *Ibid.*, pp. 278–280.
27. Laurence Ladd Buermeyer, *The Aesthetic Experience* (Merian, Pa.: The Barnes Foundation, 1924), pp. 12, 15; Havelock Ellis, *The Dance of Life* (Boston and New York: Houghton, Mifflin Co., 1923).
28. Buermeyer declares his chief obligations to Dewey and Santayana, and cites as his other sources of inspiration Bosanquet, Warner Fite, W. E. Hocking, as well as Ellis. He also refers to Clive Bell, whose *Art* was widely read at the time.
29. Buermeyer, *op. cit.*, pp. 71, 79, 82.
30. *Ibid.*, pp. 108–117.
31. *Ibid.*, pp. 80–84.
32. *Ibid.*, pp. 172–175.
33. *Ibid.*, pp. 179–182.
34. Munro's book was part of a series published under the general title *An Outline of Aesthetics*, Philip N. Youtz, ed. (New York: W. W. Norton Co.). Works in the series were: *The World, The Arts and the Artist* by Irwin Edman; *The Judgment of Literature* by Henry Wells; *The Mirror of the Passing World* (painting) by M. Cecil Allen; and *With Eyes of the Past* (art criticism) by Henry Ladd. In the introduction to Munro's book, Youtz states:

    > The great interest in Dr. Munro's book lies in the fact that it describes an embryo science of aesthetics which has hardly yet been born. . . . Artists and students of art will discover that scientific method in aesthetics is but another name for sanity and fresh observation in the approach to art (pp. x–xi).

35. Munro, *Scientific Method*, pp. 14–16, 19, 20–21.
36. *Ibid.*, pp. 22–23.
37. *Ibid.*, pp. 26–27, 29.
38. *Ibid.*, pp. 32, 40, 42, 45–46, 49–59.
39. *Ibid.*, pp. 61, 67–68, 70, 79.
40. *Ibid.*, pp. 91, 92. But see Henry Lanz, *Aesthetic Relativism* (Stanford: Stanford University Press, 1947).
41. *Ibid.*, p. 93.
42. *Ibid.*, p. 98. Science, says Munro, need not aim at universal mechanization. He believes, incidentally, that Croce's aesthetics is confusing in that it tries to define every concept in terms of every other, and to show the identity of science, art, criticism, expression, intuition, emphasizing points at which these concepts overlap and ignoring differences (p. 46).
43. Curt John Ducasse, *The Philosophy of Art* (New York: Lincoln McVeigh, The Dial Press, 1929), pp. 15–20 *passim.*

44. Eugène Véron, *L'Esthétique* (Paris: C. Reinwald, 1882; 1st edition, 1878), pp. 21–22.
45. Véron says that the idea he has endeavored to develop in his book is "sincerity in art by the spontaneous manifestation of the personal emotion of the artist. It alone can renew art by restoring to it the originality forbidden by the pedantry of those who exclusively admire Greek or Italian renaissance sculpture" (Véron, *op. cit.*, pp. 109, 460; Ducasse, *op. cit.*, p. 23).
46. Véron, *op. cit.*, p. 24.
47. Otto Jespersen, *Language, Its Nature, Development, and Origin* (London: George Allen and Unwin, 1922), pp. 436–437; Ducasse, *op. cit.*, p. 25.
48. John Dewey, *Experience and Nature* (Chicago and London: Open Court Publishing Co., 1925), p. 179; Ducasse, *op. cit.*, pp. 25–26.
49. Ducasse, *op. cit.*, pp. 28, 32, 35–36.
50. Lascelles Abercrombie, *Towards a Theory of Art* (London: Martin Secker, 1922), quotation from Pierre Guastalla, *Esthétique* (Paris: J. Vrin, 1925), pp. 25–26; Ducasse, *op. cit.*, p. 37.
51. Leo Tolstoi, *What Is Art?* Chapter XV; Ducasse, *op. cit.*, pp. 39–41.
52. Benedetto Croce, *Aesthetic as Science of Expression and General Linguistic*, pp. 8, 95–97; Ducasse, *op. cit.*, pp. 49–52.
53. Helen Huss Parkhurst, *Beauty, An Interpretation of Art and the Imaginative Life* (New York: Harcourt, Brace and Co., 1930), pp. 18, 22–24, 26–31 (especially p. 31). Her metaphor of the sea recalls the pervasive image of the sea as a symbol of cosmic dynamics in such authors as Melville and Victor Hugo. On the natural sources of creativity, she refers to Nietzsche's *The Will to Power*, Vol. II; Havelock Ellis's *The Dance of Life*; Yrjö Hirn, *The Origins of Art*.
54. George Santayana, *Reason in Art* pp. 56–57; Parkhurst, *op. cit.*, p. 35. But see also *The Sense of Beauty*, p. 113.
55. Parkhurst, *op. cit.*, p. 58.
56. *Ibid.*, pp. 64–67.
57. Santayana, *The Realm of Essence* (London: Constable and Co., 1928); Parkhurst, *op. cit.*, pp. 121–122.
58. Parkhurst, *op. cit.*, p. 150.
59. *Ibid.*, pp. 154–157. On the technical question of poetic rhythm in relation to music, see Sidney Lanier, *The Science of English Verse* (New York: Charles Scribner's Sons, 1880).
60. Parkhurst cites the familiar passage in Sir Thomas Browne: "Time which antiquates antiquity, and hath an art to make dust of all things, hath yet spared these minor monuments"—an example of rhythm in prose approaching rhythm in poetry (pp. 197, 201, 203).

61. *Ibid.*, pp. 205–206.
62. *Ibid.*, pp. 133–135.
63. *Ibid.*, pp. 188–197 *passim*. See Max I. Baym, *In Quest of Moody Food* (Leonia, N.J.: Hilding Carlson, 1934), pp. 7–11, in re the chief differentia of prose and poetry.
64. *Ibid.*, pp. 208–209. As for metaphor, see Philip Wheelwright, *Metaphor and Reality* (Bloomington: Indiana University Press, 1962); Colin Murray Turbayne, *The Myth of Metaphor* (New Haven: Yale University Press, 1962); "Metaphor" in *Encyclopedia of Poetry and Poetics*, Alex Preminger, ed. (Princeton: Princeton University Press, 1965); Baym, "Present State of the Study of Metaphor," *Books Abroad*, Vol. 35, No. 3 (Summer, 1961).
65. *Ibid.*, pp. 250–251. Parkhurst's own prose echoes that of Sir Thomas Browne, Gibbon, and Pater when they held forth on the transitoriness of life and the keen edge it lent to the creative imagination. Behind them is Pascal.
66. *Ibid.*, pp. 161–164.
67. *Ibid.*, pp. 302–303.

CHAPTER 1 2

1. John Dewey, *Psychology* (1887), reprinted in John Dewey, *The Early Works, 1882–1898* (Carbondale and Edwardsville: Southern Illinois University Press, 1966); "The New Psychology," *Andover Review*, Vol. II (1884), pp. 285, 287–288. See A. A. Roback, *History of American Psychology* (New York: Library Publishers, 1952), p. 101. See references in *Psychology*, pp. xxix–xlviii.
2. Dewey, *Psychology*, pp. 267–273, *passim*.
3. "Aesthetic feeling not only goes out into objects, where it takes the form of beauty, but in its connection with these objects becomes a source of interest to the mind, and hence leads to action for the satisfaction of this interest" (*ibid.*, pp. 273–274).
4. *Ibid.*, p. 279.
5. Dewey, *Experience and Nature* (New York: W. W. Norton and Co., 1925), pp. 39, 81. "Man in nature is man subjected; nature in man, recognized and used, is intelligence and art" (p. 28).
6. *Ibid.*, p. 82.
7. *Ibid.*, pp. 99, 156, 189, 204.
8. *Ibid.*, pp. 228–229. Royce's idea of the malaise of the spirit among the eternities is matched by William James's remark that one does not feel at home in infinity.
9. *Ibid.*, pp. 229–230.
10. *Ibid.*, pp. 241–245 *passim*.
11. *Ibid.*, pp. 281–282.

12. *Ibid.*, pp. 282–283.

13. *Ibid.*, p. 144.

14. *Ibid.*, p. 254.

15. *Ibid.*, pp. 331–332.

16. *Ibid.*, pp. 357–358. See Max I. Baym, "Metaphysical Malaise: Science and the Struggle for a Universal Poetics," *Bucknell Review*, Vol. IX, No. 1 (December, 1960), pp. 199–211.

17. *Ibid.*, pp. 374–377.

18. *Ibid.*, pp. 388–390.

19. *Ibid.*, p. 391.

20. *Ibid.*, p. 392.

21. Dewey, *Art as Experience* (New York: Minton, Balch and Co., 1934), p. 3.

22. *Ibid.*, pp. 22, 24, 38.

23. *Ibid.*, pp. 45–46.

24. *Ibid.*, pp. 65–67, 69–70.

25. *Ibid.*, p. 72. James's passage, which Dewey had the insight to glean for his purposes, says as much (if not more) about the act of creativity as do Arthur Koestler and Susanne Langer combined in their respective works, *The Act of Creation* (1964) and *Mind* (1967). In its essence it is worthy of Freud, who, however, admitted relative ignorance about poetic genius. Dewey's impulse to look into James for suggestive ideas on the nature of the artistic process may have come originally from his prior reading of James's *Principles of Psychology*, which contains a number of ideas relevant to aesthetics, although James deliberately omitted the separate treatment of the subject in his work.

26. *Ibid.*, pp. 73–74.

27. *Ibid.*, pp. 99, 105, 129–132.

28. *Ibid.*, p. 148.

29. *Ibid.*, pp. 150, 155, 169.

30. *Ibid.*, p. 156; George Santayana, *Interpretations of Poetry and Religion* (New York: Charles Scribner's Sons, 1900), p. 2.

31. *Ibid.*, pp. 152–153.

32. *Ibid.*, p. 194.

33. *Ibid.*, pp. 324–325. See Max Eastman, *The Literary Mind* (New York: Charles Scribner's Sons, 1931), pp. 261–262.

34. *Ibid.*, pp. 317–318.

35. *Ibid.*, pp. 318–319.

36. *Ibid.*, pp. 305–314 *passim*.

37. Dewey, aware that various meanings have been attached to his conception of knowledge as "instrumental," declares:

> Its actual content is simple: Knowledge is instrumental to the enrichment of immediate experience through the control over action that it exercises. I would not emulate

the philosophers I have criticized and force this interpretation into the ideas set forth by Wordsworth and
Shelley. But an idea similar to that I have just stated
seems to me to be the most natural translation of their
intent (*ibid.*, p. 290).

38. *Ibid.*, pp. 347, 349.
39. *Ibid.*, pp. 32–33.
40. *Ibid.*, pp. 331–332, 336–338.
41. *Ibid.*, pp. 338–339.
42. *Ibid.*, pp. 339, 342–344.
43. *Ibid.*, pp. 70–71.
44. *Ibid.*, p. 34. Dewey was familiar with Arnold's essay on Keats,
which contains the statement: "He is; he is with Shakespeare."
Dewey may also have read John Middleton Murry's *Keats and
Shakespeare*.
45. *Ibid.*, pp. 61–62, 257. Dewey maintains that the expressive act is
not an outpouring of passion: "What is sometimes called an act
of self-expression might better be termed one of self-exposure; it
discloses character to others. In itself, it is only a spewing forth."
True expression shapes materials "in the interest of embodying the
excitement . . . " for "there is no expression without excitement,
without turmoil" (*ibid.*, pp. 61–62).
46. *Ibid.*, p. 347.
47. *Ibid.*, pp. 153–154. Dewey defines the poet's rhythm as an ordered
variation of changes, also comprising variations in intensity.
48. *Ibid.*, pp. 266–268.
49. *Ibid.*, p. 322. This quotation is preceded by Dewey's introductory
statement:
> There is one problem that artist, philosopher, and critic
> alike must face: the relation between permanence and
> change. The bias in philosophy in its more orthodox
> phase throughout the ages has been toward the un-
> changing, and that bias has affected the more serious
> critics—perhaps it is this bias which generated the judi-
> cial critic. . . . [In] art—and in nature as far as we can
> judge it through the medium of art—permanence is a
> function, a consequence of changes the relations sustain
> to one another, not an antecedent principle.
50. *Ibid.*, pp. 322–323, 348.
51. *Ibid.*, p. 292.
52. *Ibid.*, pp. 321–322.
53. Dewey, "Qualitative Thought," *The Symposium* Vol. I, No. 1
(January, 1935), pp. 5–32.
54. *Ibid.*

CHAPTER 13

1. David W. Prall, *Aesthetic Analysis* (New York: Thomas Y. Crowell Co. 1936), pp. 5, 7–8.
2. *Ibid.*, pp. 9–12.
3. *Ibid.*, pp. 13–14.
4. *Ibid.*, p. 19.
5. *Ibid.*, p. 30.
6. *Ibid.*, p. 92. In this differentiation between experience and mere vague awareness, in relation to the aesthetic, Prall relies on Dewey (*ibid.*, p. 57).
7. *Ibid.*, pp. 139, 145, 147–148, 154.
8. *Ibid.*, pp. 154, 159, 163.
9. *Ibid.*, pp. 165–166, 171.
10. *Ibid.*, pp. 173–174.
11. *Ibid.*, pp. 203, 177.
12. *Ibid.*, pp. 204, 181, 193, 203 (in sequence).
13. *Ibid.*, pp. 111, 124, 163–164.
14. Stephen Coburn Pepper, *Aesthetic Quality: A Contextualistic Theory of Beauty* (New York: Charles Scribner's Sons, 1937), p. 33.
15. *Ibid.*, p. viii.
16. *Ibid.*, pp. 3, 5–6.
17. *Ibid.*, pp. 7–9.
18. *Ibid.*, pp. 10–11.
19. *Ibid.*, pp. 19, 26, 30–31.
20. *Ibid.*, pp. 32–33.
21. *Ibid.*, p. 33.
22. *Ibid.*, pp. 37–38.
23. *Ibid.*, pp. 38–41.
24. *Ibid.*, p. 42.
25. *Ibid.*, pp. 43–44.
26. *Ibid.*, pp. 46–47.
27. *Ibid.*, pp. 49–50.
28. *Ibid.*, pp. 51–52.
29. *Ibid.*, p. 53.
30. *Ibid.*, pp. 53–54.
31. *Ibid.*, pp. 54–56.
32. *Ibid.*, pp. 57–61.
33. *Ibid.*, pp. 66, 70.
34. *Ibid.*, pp. 71–72.
35. *Ibid.*, pp. 73–75.
36. *Ibid.*, pp. 86–88.

37. *Ibid.*, pp. 89–90.
38. *Ibid.*, pp. 90, 99, 106.
39. Pepper cites (p. 107) a passage from James's *Principles of Psychology* (Vol. II, p. 471) on this question of "dryness . . . paleness . . . absence of all glow, as it may exist, in a thoroughly expert critic's mind."
40. *Ibid.*, p. 109.
41. *Ibid.*, p. 115.
42. *Ibid.*, pp. 149, 160, 167.
43. *Ibid.*, pp. 180, 182.
44. *Ibid.*, pp. 187, 191–192.
45. *Ibid.*, pp. 210–211.
46. *Ibid.*, pp. 221–228 *passim.*
47. *Ibid.*, p. 229.
48. *Ibid.*, pp. 230–232.
49. *Ibid.*, pp. 235–239.
50. *Ibid.*, pp. 240–245.
51. *Ibid.*, pp. 246–247.
52. Theodore Meyer Greene, *The Arts and the Art of Criticism* (Princeton: Princeton University Press, 1940), pp. vii–viii, xiv.
53. *Ibid.*, pp. 98–107. Greene's references are to his own introduction to *The Meaning of the Humanities* (Princeton: Princeton University Press, 1938); William Empson, *Seven Types of Ambiguity* (London: Chatto and Windus, 1930).
54. *Ibid.*, pp. 100–114. Greene refers to James Bradstreet Greenough and George Lyman Kittredge, *Words and Their Ways in English Speech* (New York: The Macmillan Co., 1920).
55. *Ibid.*, pp. 185, 189, 191. See Rossetti's famous definition of the sonnet in *The House of Life*; James, *Principles of Psychology*, Vol. I, pp. 608–610.
56. *Ibid.*, pp. 351–359 *passim.*
57. *Ibid.*, p. 420. The Comparison of Spinoza and Wordsworth is in Samuel Alexander's *Beauty and Other Forms of Value* (London: Macmillan and Co., Ltd., 1933), cited in Greene, *op. cit.*, p. 420.
58. *Ibid.*, pp. 365–461.
59. *Ibid.*, p. 242.
60. *Ibid.*, pp. 248–253, 259.
61. *Ibid.*, pp. 442–443.
62. *Ibid.*, p. 401.
63. *Ibid.*, p. 392. For an analysis of vitality as a function of dynamic tension, Greene cites Kurt Riezler's *Traktat vom Schönen* (Frankfurt am Main: Klosterman, 1935) and Amanda Coomaraswamy, *The Transformation of Nature in Art* (Cambridge, Mass.: Harvard University Press, 1935).

CHAPTER 14

1. By Langer's own admission, the so-called "new key" had been struck by others "quite clearly and repeatedly" before her—for instance, by Alfred North Whitehead in his *Symbolism: Its Meaning and Effects* (New York: The Macmillan Co., 1927) and by Wilbur M. Urban in his *Language and Reality: The Philosphy of Language and the Principles of Symbolism* (London: G. Allen and Unwin, 1939). See Susanne K. Langer, *Philosophy in a New Key: A Study in the Symbolism of Reason, Rite and Art* (Cambridge, Mass.: Harvard University Press, 1942), pp. viii–ix. Langer fails to state that Santayana had already tied in suggestibility, intuition, and essence with symbol in *The Realm of Essence* (New York: Charles Scribner's Sons, 1927), especially p. 113. Outside of Whitehead, to whom her book is dedicated, she acknowledges her indebtedness to Ernst Cassirer, "that pioneer in the philosophy of Symbolism."

2. Langer, *op. cit.*, pp. 75, 83–89 *passim*.

3. James Edwin Creighton, "Reason and Feeling," *Philosophical Review*, Vol. XXX (1921), No. 5, pp. 465–581, 469–479 *passim*; Langer, *op. cit.*, pp. 99–100.

4. Langer, *op. cit.*, pp. 100–101.

5. *Ibid.*, pp. 128–132 *passim*. Donovan's essay appeared in *Mind* (1891–92), Vol. XVI (O.S.), pp. 498–506, and Vol. XVII, pp. 325–339.

6. *Ibid.*, pp. 137–139. Philip Wegener, *Untersuchungen über die Grundfragen des Sprachlebens* (Halle a/s, 1885).

7. Wegener, *op. cit.*, p. 54; Langer, *op. cit.*, p. 141. Langer refers to further studies of metaphor: Heinz Werner, *Die Ursprünge der Metapher* (Leipzig: Arbeiten zur Entwicklungspsychologie, Heft 3, 1919); Hermann Paul, *Principles of the History of Language* (London: S. Sonnenchein, 1888; German, Halle: M. Niemeyer, 1880); Alfred Biese, *Die Philosophie des Metapherischen* (Hamburg and Leipzig: L. Voss, 1893). See also Baym, "The Present State of the Study of Metaphor," *Books Abroad*, Vol. 35, No. 3 (Summer, 1961); Philip Wheelwright, *Metaphor and Reality* (Bloomington: Indiana University Press, 1962).

8. Langer, *op. cit.*, pp. 144–152 *passim*; 201–202.

9. *Ibid.*, pp. 233–235; Urban, *op. cit.*, pp. 487–488, 500.

10. *Ibid.*, pp. 260–262.

11. Langer, *Feeling and Form: A Theory of Art, Developed from "Philosophy in a New Key"* (New York: Charles Scribner's Sons, 1953). Langer regards this work as "Volume II of the study in

symbolism that began with *Philosophy in a New Key*" (Introduction, p. vii). Chapters 10, 13, and 15–19 are devoted to literature.

12. *Feeling and Form*, pp. 48–49. Frederick Clarke Prescott, *The Poetic Mind* (New York: The Macmillan Co., 1922), p. 49.

13. *Feeling and Form*, pp. 208–210, 212–213.

14. *Ibid.*, p. 230.

15. *Ibid.*, p. 237.

16. *Ibid.*, pp. 241–242. Langer says that the literature of aesthetics based on Freudian psychoanalysis belongs chiefly to the 1920s. She lists Prescott's *Poetic Mind* and *Poetry and Myth* (New York: The Macmillan Co., 1927); John MacCaig Thorburn, *Art and the Unconscious* (London: K. Paul, Trench, Trubner and Co., 1925); DeWitt Parker, *The Principles of Aesthetics* (1920) and *The Analysis of Art* (New Haven: Yale University Press, 1926) and Sigmund Freud, *Psychoanalytische Studien an Werken der Dichtung und Kunst* (Leipzig: Internationaler Psychoanalytischer Verlag, 1924). We add Frederick J. Hoffman, *Freudianism and the Literary Mind* (Baton Rouge: Louisiana State University Press, 1945), which contains a selected bibliography with many important items; Santayana, "A Long Way Round to Nirvana: or Much Ado About Dying," a review of Freud's *Beyond the Pleasure Principle* in *Dial*, Vol. LXXV (1923), pp. 435–442; Harry Slochower, "Freud and Marx in Contemporary Literature," *Sewanee Review*, Vol. XLIX (1941), pp. 315–324; Leo A. Spiegel, "The New Jargon; Psychology in Literature," *Sewanee Review*, Vol. XL (1932), pp. 476–491; Lionel Trilling, "The Legacy of Sigmund Freud: Literary and Aesthetic," *Kenyon Review*, Vol. II (1940), pp. 162–168; Eliseo Vivas, "The Legacy of Sigmund Freud: Philosophical," *Kenyon Review*, Vol. II (1940), pp. 173–185; Ludwig Marcuse, "Freud's Aesthetics," *Journal of Aesthetics and Art Criticism*; Vol. XVIII, No. 1 (September, 1958), pp. 1–21.

17. *Feeling and Form*, pp. 247–248.

18. *Ibid.*, p. 249; Prescott, *Poetry and Myth*, pp. 1, 7.

19. *Ibid.*, pp. 258, 263.

20. *Ibid.*, p. 309; for Morgan's essay, see *Essays by Divers Hands* in *Transactions of the Royal Society of Literature*, n.s., R. W. Macon, ed., Vol. 12, (1933). The essay covers pp. 61–77; see pp. 61, 70–72.

21. *Ibid.*, p. 320.

22. Eric Bentley "The Drama of Ebb," *Kenyon Review*, Vol. VII, No. 2 (Spring, 1945), pp. 169–184; Langer, *op. cit.*, p. 325.

23. Langer, *op. cit.*, p. 351, fn. 1.

24. Francis Ferguson, *The Idea of a Theater* (Garden City, New York: Doubleday and Co., 1953), p. 31. Ferguson refers to Kenneth Burke's *Philosophy of Literary Form* and *A Grammar of Motives*,

where Burke gives the three moments that constitute the shape
of a play (beginning, middle, end): poïema, pathema, mathema.

25. Langer, *op. cit.*, p. 361; Ashley Thorndike, *Tragedy* (Boston:
Houghton, Mifflin & Co., 1908), pp. 17, 19.

26. Langer, *op. cit.*, p. 376.

27. *Ibid.*, p. 378; Ernst Cassirer, *Philosophie der symbolischen Formen*
(Berlin: B. Cassirer, 1923–29, 3 vols.), translated by Ralph
Manheim as *The Philosophy of Symbolic Forms* (New Haven:
Yale University Press, 1953).

28. Langer, *op. cit.*, pp. 389–91.

29. Langer, *Mind: An Essay on Human Feeling* (Baltimore: The Johns
Hopkins University Press, 1967), Vol. I. pp. xv, 107–108.

30. *Ibid.*, p. 109.

31. *Ibid.*, pp. 114–115, 118, 149. T. S. Eliot, "The Music of Poetry,"
On Poets and Poetry (New York: Farrar, Straus and Cudahy,
1957), p. 23; *Selected Essays, 1917–1932* (New York: Harcourt,
Brace and Co., 1932), pp. 124–125. Eliot introduced the term
"objective correlative" into modern literary criticism in "Hamlet
and His Problems," *The Sacred Wood* (London: Methuen and
Co., Ltd., 1920); see *Encyclopedia of Poetry and Poetics*, Alexander Preminger, ed. (Princeton: Princeton University Press,
1965), p. 581. The term was used, however (perhaps for the first
time), in 1859 by John Fiske in a letter to his mother: "Hear my
definition of language; it is the objective correlative term to the
subjective reason or mind," in *The Letters of John Fiske*, edited
by his daughter Ethel Fisk (sic) (New York: The Macmillan Co.,
1940), p. 26. See also David J. DeLaura's interesting "Pater and
Eliot. The Origin of the Objective Correlative," *Modern Language
Quarterly*, Vol. XXVI (1965), pp. 426–431. Actually, Pater did
not use the phrase. See John Middleton Murry, *Countries of the
Mind. Essays in Literary Criticism* (London: Oxford University
Press, 1931), pp. 23–25; David Dorchester, Jr., "The Nature of
Poetic Expression," *Poet Lore*, Vol. V (1893), pp. 81–90.

32. Langer, *Feeling and Form*, p. 410. She also maintains that "Despite
all shortcomings, blind leads . . . that they may see in each other's
doctrines, . . . Fry, Bergson, Croce, Baensch, Collingwood, Cassirer
and I (not to forget . . . Barfield and Day Lewis . . .) have been
and are really engaged in one philosophical project." But see
Chapter 21 *passim*.

33. Philip Ellis Wheelwright, "Toward a Metaphysic of Literary Criticism," *The Journal of Philosophy*, Vol. XXVI, No. 9 (April 25,
1929), pp. 238–239.

34. Wheelwright, *op. cit.*, p. 237; Ramon Fernandez, "On Philosophic
Criticism," *Messages* (New York: Harcourt, Brace and Co., 1927),
p. 7.

35. Louis Grudin, "A Definition of Poetry," *A Primer of Aesthetics. Logical Approaches to a Philosophy of Art* (New York: Covici, Friede Publishers, 1930), pp. 95–101, 102–105 *passim*; Alfred North Whitehead, *Science and the Modern World* (New York: The Macmillan Co., 1925; Pelican Books, 1st Mentor edition, May, 1948), pp. 37 f. and 130 f., in re energy; Grudin, *op. cit.*, p. 107.

36. Grudin, *op. cit.*, pp. 116–120 *passim*.

37. Wheelwright, "Poetry and Logic," *The Symposium: A Critical Review*, Vol. I, No. 4 (October, 1930), pp. 445, 452–453. Wheelwright's article suffers from the logical attitudinizing of Grudin, which it reflects. What Grudin has to say, in essence—and never does say explicitly—is that a poem represents a transformation of physical energy to psychic energy (or will), and that the poem is an aesthetic entity symbolizing varying attitudes (themselves symbols) in the context of the atmosphere in which it comes to birth. Wheelwright's implicit contextualism (involving the poem and its audience) has been treated explicitly by Pepper (see discussion of Pepper above). Wheelwright's article and Grudin's book were written at a time when Richards's *Science and Poetry* was particularly influential and when some aspiring literary critics looked on symbolic logic as a sacred cow.

38. Wheelwright, "Poetry, Myth and Reality," in *The Language of Poetry*, Allen Tate, ed. (Princeton: Princeton University Press, 1942), pp. 3, 8–9.

39. *Ibid.*, pp. 8, 9–10.

40. *Ibid.*, pp., 11, 12, 18–20, 23, 27–32.

41. Wheelwright, *The Burning Fountain: A Study in the Language of Symbolism*, new and revised edition (Bloomington: Indiana University Press, 1968, originally published 1954), pp. 34, 274, fn. 3.

42. *Ibid.*, pp. 35, 37, 91, 101.

43. *Ibid.*, pp. 104–105. Martin Foss, *Symbol and Metaphor in Human Experience* (Princeton: Princeton University Press, 1949), Chapter IV, especially p. 60. Wheelwright admires this book, but not without reservations because of its leaning to semantic positivism.

44. *Ibid.*, pp. 151, 268.

45. Wheelwright, *Metaphor and Reality* (Bloomington: Indiana University Press, 1962), p. 25.

46. *Ibid.*, pp. 52, 66. Wheelwright gives the etymology of metaphor (from *phora*, "motion"; *meta*, "change," *i.e.*, semantic motion).

47. *Ibid.*, p. 178, fn. 3; p. 184, fn. 8; Wallace Stevens, *The Necessary Angel* (New York: Alfred A. Knopf, 1951), pp. 117–118; Sister Bernetta, *The Metamorphic Tradition in Modern Poetry* (New Brunswick: Rutgers University Press, 1955).

48. Wheelwright presents two kinds of complementary semantic movements in metaphor: *epiphor* and *diaphor*. The word "epiphor" he takes from Aristotle's *Poetics*, where it is said that metaphor is the "transferring" (*epiphora*, from *epi* "over into"; *phora*, "movement") of a name from that which it usually denotes to some other object. In the *diaphor* (*dia*, "through"; *phora*, "movement") the "movement is through certain particulars of experience (actual or imagined) in a fresh way, producing new meaning by juxtaposition alone" (Wheelwright, *op. cit.*, pp. 72–73, 78).

49. *Ibid.*, pp. 92, 94, 96. Thomas Carlyle, *Sartor Resartus*, Part III, Chapter III, "Symbolism."

50. *Ibid.*, p. 122.

51. Wheelwright cites Alan Watts's definition of myth: "A complex of stories—some no doubt fact, and some fantasy—which, for various reasons, human beings regard as demonstrations of the inner meaning of the universe and of human life" (*Myth and Ritual in Christianity*, New York: The Macmillan Co., 1954, p. 7); Wheelwright, *op. cit.*, pp. 129–131.

52. *Ibid.*, pp. 133–137.

53. Bernard C. Heyl, *New Bearings in Esthetics and Art Criticism, A Study in Semantics and Evaluation* (New Haven: published for Wellesley College by Yale University Press, 1943).

54. Quoted by Heyl, *op. cit.*, p. 18. The rest of the paragraph in question is: "We see it [mind] as a provisional *ad hoc* prosecuting its latest task of establishing 'values.'"

55. *Ibid.*, pp. 48–49, 86–87.

56. *Ibid.*, p. 96; "The New Failure of Nerve," *The Partisan Review* (January–February, 1943), p. 37.

57. *Ibid.*, p. 108. Theodore Meyer Greene, *The Arts and Art Criticism* (Princeton: Princeton University Press, 1940), pp. 5–6.

58. *Ibid.*, pp. 112, 118. On this point, Heyl refers to Joan Evans, *Taste and Temperament* (New York: Macmillan, 1939).

59. Dewey, "The Meaning of Value," *Journal of Philosophy*, February, 1925, p. 131; Kurt Koffka, "Problems in the Psychology of Art," *Bryn Mawr Notes and Monographs*, Vol. IX (1940), p. 202; Heyl, *op. cit.*, p. 123.

60. Heyl, *op. cit.*, pp. 154–155.

61. Bertram Morris, *The Aesthetic Process* (Evanston: Northwestern University Press, 1943), pp. vii, 7. Actually Morris borrows the suggestive designation "the theory of the satisfied imagination" from Werner Fite's *The Living Mind*, Chapter 2 (Morris, *op. cit.*, p. 53, fn. 2).

62. *Ibid.*, p. 19. Morris finds the Lipps reference in Melvin Rader's *A Modern Book of Aesthetics* (New York: Henry Holt and Co., 1935), p. 294.

63. *Ibid.*, p. 46–47, 50–51.
64. *Ibid.*, p. 53.
65. *Ibid.*, pp. 79–80.
66. *Ibid.*, p. 82.
67. *Ibid.*, p. 85.
68. *Ibid.*, pp. 85–86.
69. *Ibid.*, pp. 157, 159–160, 163.
70. *Ibid.*, pp. 92–93, 95. Morris defines a symbol as a"blueprint, which itself is not the thing referred to, but a statement of the set of conditions which a thing must satisfy in order to be a member of the class."
71. T. S. Eliot, *The Sacred Wood*, p. 101; Morris, *op. cit.*, p. 96, fn. 15.
72. Morris, *op. cit.*, p. 167.
73. *Ibid.*, pp. 168–169.
74. *Ibid.*, pp. 172, 174, 179–181.
75. *Ibid.*, pp. 183–186.
76. Morris Weitz, *Philosophy of the Arts* (Cambridge, Mass.: Harvard University Press, 1950), pp. 8–10, 18; Clive Bell, *Art* (London: Chatto and Windus, 1941), pp. 241, 292; Roger Fry, "Some Questions in Esthetics," *Transformations. Critical and Speculative Essays on Art* (London: Chatto and Windus, 1926), p. 10. See also Fry's "The Artist and Psycho-Analysis" in *The New Criticism: An Anthology of Modern Aesthetics and Literary Criticism*, ed. E. W. Burgum (New York: Prentice-Hall, 1930), p. 12, where the author points to great novels that expose the total indifference of fate to human desire and where a sense of the inexorability of fate yields a pleasure that consists of the recognition of inevitable sequences.
77. *Ibid.*, pp. 208–209.
78. *Ibid.*, pp. 49–50.
79. Cleanth Brooks and Robert Penn Warren, *Understanding Poetry* (New York: Henry Holt and Co., 1938), pp. 18–19; Weitz, *op. cit.*, pp. 55–56, 63.
80. Weitz, *op. cit.*, pp. 93, 103–107 *passim*.
81. Weitz refers to C. K. Ogden and I. A. Richards, *The Meaning of Meaning* (London: K. Paul, Trench, Trubner & Co., 1923) and to Rudolf Carnap, *The Logical Syntax of Language* (London: K. Paul, Trench, Trubner & Co., 1935).
82. Weitz, *op. cit.*, pp. 136–145 *passim*. See Theodore Meyer Greene, *The Arts and the Art of Criticism*, Chapter XXIII; Bernard C. Heyl, *New Bearings in Esthetics and Art Criticism*, Chapter III; and John Hospers, *Meaning and Truth in the Arts* (Chapel Hill: University of North Carolina Press, 1946), Chapters 5–6. Alfred Ayer, in *Language, Truth and Logic* (New York, Oxford Univer-

sity Press, 1936), denies that the language of art is emotive (Weitz, *op. cit.*, p. 142).

83. Weitz, *op. cit.*, pp. 156–157, 162–163. See I. A. Richards, *Practical Criticism: A Study of Literary Judgment* (London: K. Paul, Trench, Trubner & Co., 1929); *Principles of Literary Criticism* (New York: Harcourt, Brace & Co., 1924); *Science and Poetry* (New York: W. W. Norton Co., 1926); Cleanth Brooks, *The Well Wrought Urn* (New York: Reynal and Hitchcock, 1947), pp. 182–186, 194, 230.

84. *Ibid.*, p. 165.

85. Weitz acknowledges his deep indebtedness to Richard Stuba's paper "The Problem of Art in Freud's Writings," *The Psychoanalytic Quarterly*, Vol. IX, No. 2 (April, 1940), and declares it to be the best exposition of Freud's aesthetics (Weitz, *op. cit.*, p. 217, fn. 12). We suggest, however, that the student also consult Ludwig Marcuse's "Freud's Aesthetics," *Journal of Aesthetics and Art Criticism*, Vol. XVII, No. 1 (September, 1958), which appeared in German in the *Publications of the Modern Language Association* (June, 1957); also Herbert Read, "Psycho-analysis and the Problem of Aesthetic Value" in *The Forms of Things Unknown. Essays Towards an Aesthetic Philosophy* (New York: Horizon Press, 1960); Weitz, *op. cit.*, pp.. 196, 170–172.

86. *Ibid.*, pp. 186, 189–190.

87. Curt John Ducasse, *Art, the Critics, and You* (New York: Oskar Press, 1944), pp. 120–121; Weitz, *op. cit.*, p. 194.

88. Weitz, *op cit.*, pp. 200–201.

CHAPTER 15

1. Douglas Day, "The Background of the New Criticism," *Journal of Aesthetics and Art Criticism*, Vol. XXIV, No. 3 (Spring, 1966), pp. 430–431.

2. Rémy de Gourmont, *Le problème du Style* (Paris: Mercure de France, 1902), pp. 81, 107, 151, 153; Day, *op. cit.*, pp. 431–432.

3. Thomas Ernest Hulme, *Speculations*, Herbert Read, ed. (New York: Harcourt, Brace & Co., 1924); Hulme, *Notes on Language and Style* (Seattle: University of Washington Bookstore, 1929); Day, *op. cit.*, p. 432.

4. Hulme, "Romanticism and Classicism," *Speculations*, pp. 4–5.

5. *Ibid.*, p. 12; Day, *op. cit.*, p. 433.

6. *Ibid.*, p. 15. According to Wimsatt and Brooks, Hulme is closer here to the German romantics and Coleridge than to any neo-classical source, cited in *Literary Criticism: A Short History* (New York: Alfred Knopf, 1957), p. 662; Day, *op. cit.*, p. 433.

7. Hulme, "Bergson's Theory of Art," *Speculations*, pp. 146–148.

8. Day, *op. cit.*, p. 433.
9. See Glenn Hughes, *Imagism and the Imagists* (Stanford, California: Stanford University Press, 1931), p. 9; Frank S. Flint, "History of Imagism," *The Egoist* (London), May 1, 1915; Stanley K. Coffman, Jr., *Imagism: A Chapter for the History of Modern Poetry* (Norman: University of Oklahoma Press, 1951), p. 5; Hugh Kenner, *The Poetry of Ezra Pound* (Norfolk, Connecticut: New Directions, 1951), pp. 307–309. Day is not very complimentary to Pound (and for that matter to Hulme) as a systematic thinker. He finds Pound's prose "careless" and "hastily written," and his critical theory, such as it is, has to be "pieced together from hundreds of casual remarks" (Day, *op. cit.*, p. 434).
10. Ezra Pound, "How to Read" (1929) in *Polite Essays* (Norfolk, Connecticut: New Directions, 1939), p. 167; Day, *op. cit.*, p. 435.
11. See Preface to the 1928 edition of *The Sacred Wood*; "The Perfect Critic," *The Sacred Wood* (London: Methuen, 1920), pp. 1–16; Day, *op. cit.*, p. 435.
12. Although we have already touched on the idea of the "objective correlative" above, we repeat it here:

    The only way of expressing emotion in the form of art is by finding an "objective correlative"; in other words, a set of objects, a situation, a chain of events which shall be the formula of that *particular emotion*; and that where the external facts, which must terminate in sensory experience, are given, the emotion is immediately evoked (*The Sacred Wood*, p. 100); Day, *op. cit.*, p. 436.

13. See Murray Krieger, *The New Apologists for Poetry* (Minneapolis: University of Minnesota Press, 1956), pp. 45–56; Eliseo Vivas, "The Objective Correlative of T. S. Eliot," *The American Bookman*, Vol. I (Winter, 1944), pp. 7–18.
14. Ivor Armstrong Richards, *Principles of Literary Criticism* (New York: Harcourt, Brace & Co., 1924), pp. 249–250; Day, *op. cit.*, p. 438.
15. Day, *op. cit.*, p. 439.
16. *Ibid.*
17. John Crowe Ransom, *The New Criticism* (Norfolk, Connecticut: New Directions, 1941), p. xi. Parts of this work had appeared in *The Southern Review, The Kenyon Review*, and *HIKA*, which will be recognized as "mags" that served the proponents of the New Criticism. For the psychological aspect of literary criticism, see C. K. Ogden and Richards, *The Meaning of Meaning* (London: K. Paul, Trench, Trubner & Co., 1923); Richards, *The Principles of Literary Criticism; A Philosophy of Rhetoric* (London: Oxford University Press, 1936); Ransom, *op. cit.*, pp. 14–16.

18. For Richards's critical comment on T. S. Eliot's *The Waste Land*, see Appendix B of *The Principles of Literary Criticism*; Ransom, *op. cit.*, pp. 21–22, 41.
19. Ransom, *op. cit.*, pp. 46, 50–51.
20. *Ibid.*, pp. 52–53, 55. Richards's definition of beauty (with which he is concerned in both *The Meaning of Meaning* and in *Practical Criticism*) is that which has "properties such as self-completion in the mind."
21. Richards, *The Philosophy of Rhetoric*, p. 121; Ransom, *op. cit.*, pp. 68–69.
22. Ransom, *op. cit.*, pp. 70–72.
23. *Ibid.*, pp. 76–79.
24. J. Bronowski, *Science and Human Values* (New York: Harper and Row, 1959), pp. 48–49.
25. Our reaction is to Ransom, *op. cit.*, pp. 79–80.
26. In tragedy, Richards holds, we have a reconciliation of opposite or discordant elements. Pity, the impulse to approach, and terror, the impulse to retreat, are brought together in a single response, which is the catharsis (Richards, *Principles of Literary Criticism*, p. 245); Ransom, *op. cit.*, pp. 86–87. In a serial scheme, Ransom proposes five contexts in which poetry may be discussed: (1) the physiological, (2) the psychological, (3) the biological-psychological, (4) the biological-logical, and (5) the aesthetic (Ransom, *op. cit.*, pp. 90–91).
27. *Ibid.*, pp. 139–140; T. S. Eliot, *Selected Essays* (New York: Harcourt, Brace & Co., 1932), p. 4. See also Eliot, "Tradition and the Individual Talent," *The Sacred Wood* (London: Methuen, 1920) *passim.*
28. *Ibid.*, p. 156.
29. *Ibid.*, p. 158.
30. Ransom considers here Eliot's "The Metaphysical Poets," a review of Grierson's anthology of metaphysical verse (Ransom, *op. cit.*, pp. 175, 183, 185).
31. *Ibid.*, pp. 220–224 *passim.*
32. *Ibid.*, p. 228.
33. *Ibid.*, 249.
34. See Charles W. Morris, *Foundations of the Theory of Signs*, Vol. I, No. 2 of the *Encyclopedia of Unified Science* (Chicago: The University of Chicago Press, 1938); "Science, Art, and Technology," *The Kenyon Review* (Autumn, 1939); "Aesthetics and the Theory of Signs," *Journal of Unified Science*, Vol. VIII; Ransom, *op. cit.*, pp. 282–285, 290–293.
35. Ransom refers to Wordsworth's *Prelude*, where he finds "painful inversions" in the interest of the meter (*op. cit.*, pp. 301–305); pp. 316–317, 324–325; 330.

36. Ransom refers to Randall Jarrell's "A Note on Poetry," prefacing his own verses in *Five Young American Poets*, where are enumerated some of the qualities of typical modernist poetry: (1) great emphasis on connotation, (2) extreme intensity, (3) forced emotion (violence), (4) a good deal of obscurity, (5) emphasis on sensation, (6) preceptual nuances, (7) emphasis on details (rather than the whole), (8) external formlessness and internal disorganization, (9) lack of restraint, (10) emphasis on unconscious dream-structure, and (11) anti-scientific, anti-commonsense, anti-public attitudes (Ransom, *op. cit.*, pp. 331–332; 334–335).

37. Stanley Edgar Hyman, *The Armed Vision: A Study in the Method of Modern Literary Criticism*, revised edition, abridged by the author (New York: Random House, 1947, 1948, 1955), p. ix. The critics discussed are Winters, Eliot, Van Wyck Brooks, Constance Rourke, Maud Bodkin, Caroline Spurgeon, Blackmur, Empson, Richards, and Burke. Hyman omits F. O. Matthiessen, Ransom, Tate, Cleanth Brooks, Pound, and some others.

38. See T. S. Eliot, "The Function of Criticism" (1923) in *Selected Essays, 1917–1932* (New York: Harcourt, Brace & Co., 1932); Hyman, *op. cit.*, p. 8.

39. See Conrad Aiken, *Scepticisms* (New York: Alfred A. Knopf, 1919) and John Dewey, *Studies in Logical Theory* (Chicago: The University of Chicago Press, 1903). Aiken spoke of poetry as an organic product subject to analysis. Dewey saw a "continuity" in all experience (Hyman, *op. cit.*, pp. 16–17).

40. See Henri Peyre, *Writers and Their Critics, a Study of Misunderstanding* (Ithaca: Cornell University Press, 1944); Hyman, *op. cit.*, pp. 19–20.

41. See Edmund Wilson, *Axel's Castle, a Study in the Imaginative Literature of 1870 to 1930* (New York: Charles Scribner's Sons, 1931), p. 124; Hyman, *op. cit.*, p. 62.

42. See Eliot's "Ezra Pound," *Poetry* (September, 1946), for the role of Pound in launching *The Waste Land*; Hyman, *op. cit.*, pp. 82–84.

43. William York Tindall, *The American Scholar* (Autumn, 1947); Hyman, *op. cit.*, p. 88.

44. For a definition of "archetypes," see Carl G. Jung, "On the Relation of Analytical Psychology to Poetic Art," *Contributions to Analytical Psychology*, translated by H. G. and Cary F. Baynes (New York: Harcourt, Brace & Co., 1928); Maud Bodkin, *Archetypal Patterns in Poetry: Psychological Studies of Imagination* (London: Oxford University Press, 1934). In this, see appendix entitled "Psychological Criticism and Dramatic Conventions." Hyman, *op. cit.*, pp. 133–134, 139, 141.

45. See Freud, "The Relation of the Poet to Day-Dreaming," *The*

Interpretation of Dreams, translated by A. A. Brill (London: Allen, 1913); Hyman, *op. cit.*, p. 151.

46. Houson Peterson, *The Melody of Chaos* (New York: Longmans, Green & Co., 1931), pp. 7, 11, 18, 39, 90–95, 138–139, 157.

47. Hyman, *op. cit.*, pp. 151, 154, 178. The opening sentence of Hyman's discussion of Kenneth Burke and the criticism of symbolic action (in Chapter 10) is shrewd in observation: "If, as Kenneth Burke has sometimes insisted, a book is the indefinite expansion of one sentence, then a critical method is only the securing of material to document that sentence" (p. 327).

48. *Ibid.*, p. 351.

49. *Ibid.*, pp. 367, 373.

50. See Burke, "Demonic Trinity," *A Grammar of Motives.* The Trinity consists of the erotic, urinary, and excremental, all interrelated. Burke's use of Freudian scatalogy represents an attempt to confront the "cloacal" underlying all "transcendental activities" (Hyman, *op. cit.*, pp. 383–384).

51. Hyman, *op. cit.*, pp. 389, 400.

52. Richard Foster, *The New Romantics: A Reappraisal of the New Criticism* (Bloomington: University of Indiana Press, 1962), pp. 20–21, 25.

53. *Ibid.*, pp. 27, 29.

54. *Ibid.*, pp. 41–42. Foster cites Ransom's partial definition of romanticism as "the production of literature consciously devoted to exploiting the feelings" (*The New Criticism*, p. 15).

55. *Ibid.*, p. 57; Ivor Armstrong Richards, *Coleridge on the Imagination* (New York: Harcourt, Brace & Co., 1935), p. 47.

56. William Elton, *A Guide to the New Criticism* (Chicago: Poetry: The Modern Poetry Association, 4th printing, 1951). This work contains "A Basic Bibliography of the New Criticism," pp. 52–53.

57. *Ibid.*, p. 3.

58. *Ibid.*, pp. 42–43.

59. *Ibid.*, pp. 49–50.

60. See Ronald Salmon Crane, editor of *Critics and Criticism* (Chicago: University of Chicago Press, 1952), pp. 96, 99. I am following here the very useful article of John Holloway, "The New and Newer Critics," *Essays in Criticism*, Vol. V, No. 4, October, 1955.

61. Besides Crane and Olson, the Chicago group consisted of Richard McKeon and Norman Maclean. In Crane's book *The Languages of Criticism and the Structure of Poetry* (Toronto: University of Toronto Press, 1953), the New Critics and the myth-ritual-psychoanalysic critics (including Northrop Frye, Maud Bodkin, and Edmund Wilson) are subjected to what John Holloway calls distinctive or restrictive analysis (Holloway, *op. cit.*, p. 366).

62. Elder Olson in *Critics and Criticism*, p. 555; Holloway, *op. cit.*, p. 379.

63. James Thorpe, "The Aesthetics of Textual Criticism," *Publications of the Modern Language Association of America,* Vol. LXXX, No. 5 December, 1965), pp. 467, 479; Paul Valéry, *The Art of Poetry* (London: Routledge and Kegan Paul, 1958), pp. 144, 152.

64. *Ibid.,* p. 475.

65. *Ibid.,* pp. 481–482.

66. T. M. Gang, "Intention," *Essays in Criticism,* Vol. VII, No. 2 (April, 1957); Wimsatt and Beardsley, "The Intentional Fallacy," *Sewanee Review,* Vol. LIV (1946).

67. *Ibid.,* pp. 175–177, 181.

68. *Ibid.,* pp. 185–186.

69. All of the above is based on Carlos Baker's article on the New Criticism in *The New York Times Book Review,* Sunday, August 20, 1967. See also W. K. Wimsatt, Jr., "History and Criticism: A Problematic Relationship," *Publications of the Modern Language Association of America,* Vol. LXVI, No. 1 (February, 1951), pp. 21–31: ". . . the personal interest is not the critical—though the history of literary study shows the difference between the two to have been often rather obscurely understood. . . . 'Bardolatry' is a name which may all too well be applied to the excess of the personal to the corruption of the critical" (p. 31).

70. William Kurtz Wimsatt, "Criticism Today: A Report from America," *Essays in Criticism,* Vol. VI, No. 1 (January, 1956), p. 16.

71. Patricia Gebhard, "The New Criticism as an Aesthetic Theory," *The Western Humanities Review,* Vol. 17 (1963), pp. 155–160 *passim.*

CHAPTER 16

1. John Livingston Lowes, *Convention and Revolt in Poetry* (Boston and New York: Houghton Mifflin Co., 1919), pp. vii, 2–3, 22–23, 26, 33, 36, 44.

2. *Ibid.,* pp. 33, 46. Lowes traces the ways of convention through Chaucer, Elizabethan literature, the Orient, Symbolism, down to our present era.

3. *Ibid.,* pp. 125, 143, 145, 150, 169–170, 172.

4. *Ibid.,* p. 182, 195.

5. *Ibid.,* pp. 241–242. For Santayana's translation of Gautier's "L'Art," see Mark Van Doren, ed., *An Anthology of World Poetry* (New York: Albert and Charles Boni, 1928), pp. 755–756.

6. Lowes, *op. cit.,* pp. 308–309.

7. Max Eastman, *The Literary Mind: Its Place in an Age of Science* (New York: Charles Scribner's Sons, 1931), pp. 223, 255, 260. In this work Eastman criticizes Ogden and I. A. Richards for cutting off knowledge from life. He charges Richards with inability

to explain metaphor and calls attention, by way of contrast, to Helen Parkhurst's clear-cut declaration (in her *Beauty; an Interpretation of Art and Imaginative Life*, 1930):

> Certainly the quintessence of poetry—the pure grain of it that is left when all chaff has been winnowed away, the unalloyed gold that constitutes its substance—is little else than metaphor.

Eastman's final feeling about Richards's books is that all of them may be described as a brilliant effort to smuggle back into poetry its own essence, which he has excluded by an initial error (Eastman, *op. cit.*, pp. 301–305). But see Max I. Baym, "Science Is Poetry," *Thought*, Vol. XLV, No. 179 (Winter, 1970).

8. Lowes, *The Road to Xanadu: A Study in the Ways of the Imagination* (Boston and New York: Houghton Mifflin Co., 1927), which is actually a study of "The Rime of the Ancient Mariner" and "Kubla Khan"; Stanley Edgar Hyman, *The Armed Vision*, pp. 185–186.

9. *The Road to Xanadu*, pp. 103, 488 (fn. 50). The reference is to Lascelles Abercrombie's *The Idea of Great Poetry* (London: Martin Secker, 1925), pp. 52–58. Lowes also refers to H. W. Garrod's reference (in *Wordsworth: Lectures and Essays*, Oxford, 1923, p. 145) to "the famous, but useless, distinction . . . between the imagination and the fancy." In re fancy and imagination in Coleridge see *Biographia Literaria*, ed. with his Aesthetical Essays by J. Shawcross (Oxford: Clarendon Press, 1907), Vol. I, p. 62.

10. *Ibid.*, pp. 31, 34.

11. *Ibid.*, pp. 43, 53, 55. See *Biographia Literaria* (Shawcross ed.) Vol. II, p. 120.

12. For references to the twilight realm, Lowes cites *Letters*, ed. Ernest Hartley Coleridge, 2 vols. (London: William Heinemann, 1895), Vol. I, p. 377:

> . . . it [the twilight realm of consciousness] assumes that "in that shadowy half-being" . . . that state of nascent existence in the twilight of the imagination and just on the vestibule of consciousness ideas and images exist.

13. Henri Poincaré, *Science and Method*, translated by Francis Maitland (London: T. Nelson & Sons, 1914), pp. 56, 58, 61–63; Lowes, *op. cit.*, pp. 61–62.

14. *Works of Dryden*, ed. Scott-Saintsbury (Edinburgh: W. Paterson, 1882–1893, 18 vols), Vol. II, pp. 129–130.

15. Coleridge, *Anima Poetae*, p. 46; Lowes, *op. cit.*, p. 63.

16. Lowes, *op. cit.*, pp. 343–344, 351; Poincaré, *op. cit.*, p. 60; Coleridge, *Biographia Epistolaria*, Vol. II, p. 59.

17. Lowes, *op. cit.*, p. 400.

18. *Ibid.*, p. 401.
19. *Anima Poetae*, p. 206; Lowes, *op. cit.*, p. 403.
20. See Alfredo Niceforo, *Les Indices Numériques de la Civilisation et du Progrès* (Paris: E. Flammarion, 1921); Adolphe-Lambert Jacquis Quetelet, *Physique Sociale* (Bruxelles: C. Muquardt, 1869); Havelock Ellis, *The Dance of Life* (Boston and New York: Houghton Mifflin Co., 1923), pp. 286–289.
21. Lowes, *op. cit.*, p. 427.
22. Coleridge, *Table Talk* (Shedd ed.), Vol. VI, p. 351; John H. Muirhead, *Coleridge as Philosopher* (London: George Allen and Unwin Ltd.; New York: The Macmillan Co., 1930), p. 51.
23. Glenn Hughes, *Imagism and the Imagists. A Study in Modern Poetry* (Stanford, California: Stanford University Press, 1931), pp. vii, 9, 37. This is the most authoritative work on the subject; see also the thesis of Stanley K. Coffman, Jr., *Imagism, a Chapter for the History of Modern American Poetry* (Norman, Oklahoma: University of Oklahoma Press, 1951).
24. *Ibid.*, pp. 12–16. The reference is to Pound's preface to T. E. Hulme's five poems printed at the end of Pound's *Ripostes* (1912), where these words occur: "As for the future, *Les Imagistes*, the descendants of the forgotten school of 1909 (previously referred to as the School of Images) have that in their keeping." The school of 1909 consisted of F. S. Flint, Hulme, Joseph Campbell, Pound *et al.* Hulme was the leader. They proposed to replace poetry as then written by *vers libre*; See F. S. Flint, "The History of Imagism," *Egoist* (London) May 1, 1915.
25. *Ibid.*, p. 26.
26. *Ibid.*, p. 38.
27. *Ibid.*, pp. 39–40. In essence, these principles had already been enunciated by Hulme and Pound.
28. *Ibid.*, pp. 262–263.
29. *Ibid.*, p. 264.
30. Conrad Aiken, "The Place of Imagism," *New Republic*, May 22, 1915; Hughes, *op. cit.*, p. 51.
31. In Leonard's four articles entitled "The New Poetry—A Critique" in *The Chicago Evening Post*, September 18 to October 9, 1915. Hughes admires this critique as "the most scholarly, sarcastic and seriously considered attempt at the annihilation of imagism yet recorded." Yet he feels that it is not fair, "for it is inspired by aesthetic hatred" (Hughes, *op. cit.*, p. 54).
32. *Ibid.*, pp. 56–58.
33. *Ibid.*
34. Lowes, "An Unacknowledged Imagist," *Nation*, February 24, 1916: Joyce Kilmer's interview of Amy Lowell, published in *The New York Times*, March 26, 1916; Hughes, *op. cit.*, p. 66.

35. For Eliot's remarks, see the *New Statesman* for March 3, 1917; Hughes, *op. cit.*, p. 73.

36. *Ibid.*, p. 78.

37. *Ibid.*, pp. 80–81. For a further individual treatment of "H.D.," Fletcher, Amy Lowell, and Pound see *ibid.*, pp. 109–249.

38. Max Eastman, *op. cit.*, pp. 63–64, 73.

39. Lawrance Thompson, *Robert Frost, The Early Years, 1874–1915* (New York: Holt, Rinehart and Winston, 1966). The references are to Vol. I throughout.

40. *Ibid.*, pp. 70–71, 84, 122, 124, 136, 155, 164, 198, 236.

41. *Ibid.*, p. 238.

42. *Ibid.*, pp. 90–91, 501.

43. Rollo Walter Brown, *Harvard Yard in the Golden Age* (New York: Current Books, Inc., A. A. Wyn, 1948), pp. 105–107.

44. Robert Frost, *Complete Poems* (New York: Henry Holt and Co., 1949), p. 493.

45. Thompson, *op. cit.*, pp. 549 (fn. 4), 328, 346.

46. Nathaniel Hawthorne, *The House of the Seven Gables* (The Riverside Literature Series. Boston, New York: Houghton Mifflin Co., 1851, 1879 . . . 1904), pp. 328–329.

47. Thompson, *op. cit.*, pp. 378, 381–382. Thompson gives (p. 579, fn. 16) the passages in Bergson that represent Frost's most concentrated use of the philosopher's images and ideas in "West-running Brook." The student should examine the role James's work played in directing Frost's attention to Bergson.

48. Henri Bergson, *L'Évolution Créatrice* (Paris: Alcan, 35th ed., 1930), pp. 199–200, author's translation.

49. Jean Prevost, "Robert Frost," *La Nouvelle Revue Française*, May 1, 1939, Vol. LII.

50. Letter from England, July 4, 1913, to John Bartlett, a former student of Frost's at Pinkerton (*Selected Letters*, p. 79), quoted in Thompson, *op. cit.*, pp. 412, 418.

51. *Ibid.*, pp. 434–435, 597 (fn. 10, 11).

52. Robert Frost, "Education by Poetry: A Meditative Monologue," *Amherst Alumni Council News*, IV (March, 1931), Supplement, pp. 6–13. Reprinted from the *Amherst Graduate Quarterly*, February, 1931. Conveniently included in Robert A. Greenberg and James G. Hepburn, *Robert Frost: An Introduction* (New York: Holt, Rinehart and Winston, 1961).

53. Gaston Bachelard, *La Psychanalyse du Feu* (Paris: Gallimard, 15th ed., 1938), p. 213.

54. "Education by Poetry," p. 84 in Greenberg and Hepburn, *op. cit.*; R. W. Emerson, *Nature* (2nd series), *The Works of Ralph Waldo Emerson in One Volume*, Walter J. Black, ed. (New York: New York University Press, n.d.), pp. 537, 276; Baym, "The Present

State of the Study of Metaphor," *Books Abroad* (Summer, 1961), pp. 218–219.

55. John Middleton Murry, "Metaphor" (1927), *Countries of the Mind: Essays in Literary Criticism* (Oxford University Press, 1931), p. 2; Baym, "The Present State of the Study of Metaphor," pp. 218–219.

56. "Education by Poetry," p. 85.

57. Thompson, *op. cit.*, p. 556. Schopenhauer, *Die Welt als Wille und Vorstellung* or in *MSS fragments*, Vol. IV (Reclam edition), pp. 97–98.

58. Santayana, *Winds of Doctrine* (New York: Charles Scribner's Sons, 1913), p. 80.

59. Frost's introduction to *King Jasper* (New York: The Macmillan Co., 1935), pp. v–vi, viii.

60. Oscar Wilde, *The Poems and Fairy Tales* (New York: The Modern Library, 1932), pp. 150–151.

61. Frost's introduction to *King Jasper*, p. xiii.

62. Edwin Arlington Robinson, *Collected Poems* (New York: The Macmillan Co., 1925), p. 153.

63. Frost, "The Constant Symbol" *Atlantic Monthly*, Vol. CLXXVIII (October, 1946), and (conveniently) in Greenberg and Hepburn, *op. cit.*, pp. 87, 89, 91.

64. See John Quincy Adams's reference to Horace in Chapter 1: *Si vis me flere, dolendum est primum tibi esse* ("If you would have me weep, you must first feel grief yourself").

65. Frost, "The Figure a Poem Makes" in *Complete Poems of Robert Frost, 1949* (New York: Henry Holt and Co., 1949), pp. v–vi.

66. Marston Morse, "Mathematics in the Arts," *Yale Review*, Vol. XL (June, 1950), pp. 604–612; Max I. Baym, "Metaphysical Malaise: Science and the Struggle for a Universal Poetics," *Bucknell Review*, Vol. IX, No. 3 (December, 1960), p. 211.

67. Frost, "The Figure a Poem Makes," pp. vii–viii.

68. See Renato Poggioli, "The Pastoral Self," *Daedalus*, Vol. 68, No. 4 (1959).

69. *Letters of Wallace Stevens*, selected and edited by Holly Stevens (New York: Alfred A. Knopf, 1966), pp. 275, 278, 355 n., 422–423, 446, 571, 748, 825 (all references to Frost).

70. *Ibid.*, p. 25.

71. *Ibid.*, p. 27.

72. *Ibid.*, p. 46.

73. *Ibid.*, pp. 65–66, 71–72.

74. *Ibid.*, p. 81.

75. *Ibid.*, pp. 85–88 *passim*.

76. *Ibid.*, p. 92.

77. *Ibid.*, p. 98. His library contained *Sonnets of this Century*, edited

and arranged, with critical introduction on the sonnet by William Sharp (London and New York: Walter Scott, Ltd., n.d.); *ibid.*, p. 99.

78. Wallace Stevens, *Opus Posthumous*, edited, with an introduction, by Samuel French Morse (New York: Alfred A. Knopf, 1957), p. 99 ("The Sail of Ulysses").

79. *Letters*, pp. 105, 108–109.

80. *Ibid.*, pp. 110, 129–130. See Bliss Carman, *Sappho: One Hundred Lyrics* (London: Chatto and Windus, 1907), Lyric xiii, "Sleep thou in the bosom."

81. *Ibid.*, p. 133.

82. *Ibid.*, p. 137.

83. *Ibid.*, pp. 170–171.

84. *Ibid.*, pp. 231–232.

85. Edgar Lee Masters, *The New Spoon River* (New York: Boni and Liveright, 1924), p. 304; Ludwig Lewisohn, *The Story of American Literature* (New York: The Modern Library, 1939), pp. 489–491.

86. Lewisohn, *op. cit.*, pp. 489–491.

87. *Ibid.*, pp. 377, 379, 492–493. Lewisohn adds that the central and controlling theme of the Anthologies is sex (*ibid.*).

88. Masters, *New Spoon River*, pp. 48–49; Stevens, *Opus Posthumous*, pp. 28, 41.

89. *Letters of Wallace Stevens*, p. 274 (January, 1935). Stevens felt that to write the introduction to Dowson, he would have to "soak" himself in Dowson's poetry and that he could not do so and "at the same time be trying to do things of my own" (see pp. 272–273, December, 1934). The truth, as we see it, is that the lyrics of Dowson did not comport with his own style and temperament.

90. *Ibid.*, p. 288.

91. Allen Tate, ed., *The Language of Poetry* (Princeton: Princeton University Press, 1942), preface, p. vii. The other three lectures, incorporated in this book, were delivered by Cleanth Brooks, I. A. Richards, and Philip Wheelwright.

92. A. E. Taylor, *Plato, The Man and His Work* (New York: The Dial Press, Inc., 1936), pp. 311, 314–315.

93. Stevens, "The Noble Rider" in *The Language of Poetry*, pp. 98–100.

94. *Ibid.*, pp. 94–95.

95. *Ibid.*, pp. 95–96.

96. *Ibid.*, pp. 102–103.

97. Tate, *op. cit.*, p. 13 *passim*.

98. "The Noble Rider," p. 103. Stevens's scholarship is faulty when he attributes (pp. 103–104) the remark (at second hand) that Descartes had cut the throat of poetry to Boileau and that Freud

repeated this in his *Future of an Illusion*. This remark is to be found nowhere in Boileau but rather in the *Correspondence* of Jean Baptiste Rousseau in a letter to Brossette: *"Descartes qui a coupé la gorge à la poésie"* (Vol. I, p. 15); nor is this remark to be found in the *Future of an Illusion*.

99. Stevens, *The Necessary Angel* (New York: Alfred A. Knopf, 1951), pp. vii–viii.
100. *Ibid.*, p. viii.
101. *Ibid.*, p. 40; *Letters*, p. 505.
102. See Baym, "Metaphysical Malaise," p. 200; J. W. Smyser, "Wordsworth's Dream of Poetry and Science," *PMLA*, Vol. LXXI (March, 1956), pp. 167–178; *The Necessary Angel*, pp. 55–56.
103. *The Necessary Angel*, p. 56. See Nathan Edelman, "The Mixed Metaphor in Descartes," *Romanic Review*, Vol. XLI, No. 3 (October, 1950), *passim*.
104. *Ibid.*, pp. 71, 77, 79–82, 117–118, 122–124 *passim*.
105. *Ibid.*, p. 139.
106. *Ibid.*, p. 142.
107. See Cecil Delisle Burns, *The Horizon of Experience* (New York: W. W. Norton & Co., 1934).
108. *The Necessary Angel*, pp. 167–169.
109. *Opus Posthumous*, introduction, p. xiv. Morse notes that Stevens's theory of poetry first took formal shape in a "Memorandum" prepared in 1940 when Henry Church was considering the establishment of a chair of poetry at Princeton (*ibid.*, pp. xiv–xv).
110. *Ibid.*, pp. xvi, xxxii.
111. *Ibid.*, pp. 81, 85.
112. *Ibid.*, p. 93.
113. *Ibid.*, pp. 105–106.

CHAPTER 17

1. Edward Bullough, *Aesthetic Lectures and Essays*, Introduction by Elizabeth M. Wilkinson (Stanford: Stanford University Press, 1957), p. 35.
2. Max I. Baym, "On Mending the Broken Vase: Sully Prudhomme's Aspiration to a Unifying Aesthetics," *French Review*, Vol. XLIV, Special Issue, No. 2 (Winter, 1971), pp. 29–37 *passim*. In the present chapter, I make free use (with some emendations and additions) of my article "Literary Aesthetics," *Encyclopedia of World Literature in the 20th Century* (New York: Frederick Ungar Publishing Co., 1969), Vol. II, pp. 275–284.
3. DeWitt H. Parker, *The Principles of Aesthetics* (Boston, New York: Silver Burdett and Co., 1920), Chapters 8–10 *passim*; pp.

50, 51, 60, 85–86; Theodor Lipps, *Aesthetik* (Leipzig und Hamburg: L. Voss, 2 vols., 1914–1920), Vol. I, Chapter 3.

4. Baym, "Baudelaire and Shakespeare," *The Shakespeare Association Bulletin*, Vol. XV, No. 3 (July, 1940), pp. 195–205.

5. Thomas Mann, Introduction to *The Living Thoughts of Schopenhauer*, edited by Alfred O. Mendel (New York and Toronto: Longmans, Green and Co., 1939), p. 1; Arthur O. Lovejoy, *The Great Chain of Being* (New York: Harper and Bros. Torchbooks, 1936, 1960), p. 11.

6. Karl Pearson, *The Grammar of Science* (London: J. M. Dent and Sons, Ltd., 1937), p. 36.

7. Henry Adams, *The Education of Henry Adams* (New York: The Modern Library, 1931), p. 452.

8. Ernest Bernbaum, *Guide Through The Romantic Movement* (New York: Thomas Nelson and Sons, 1937), p. 448; Santayana, *The Sense of Beauty*, p. 14.

9. Vernon Lee, *The Beautiful: An Introduction to Psychological Aesthetics* (Cambridge: The University Press, 1913), Chapter 3, "Aspects versus Things."

10. Baym, "On the Relationship between Poetry and Science" and "Metaphysical Malaise"; J. Bronowski, *Science and Human Values* (New York: Harper and Son, 1956), pp. 48–49.

11. William James, *Principles of Psychology* (New York: Henry Holt and Co., 1891, 2 vols.), Vol. II, Chapter 26, p. 584, quoted in Leone Vivante, *Intelligence in Expression*, with *An Essay, Originality of Thought and Its Physiological Condition* (London: The C. W. Daniel Co., 1925), p. 94.

12. Ramon Fernandez, *Messages*, translated by Montgomery Belgion (New York: Harcourt, Brace and Co., 1927), p. 7; P. E. Wheelwright, "Toward a Metaphysic of Literary Criticism," *The Journal of Philosophy*, Vol. XXVI, No. 9 (1929), pp. 23–27.

13. Bronowski, *loc. cit.*; Baym, "Metaphysical Malaise," p. 199.

14. Caedmon's literary activity falls between 657 and 688 A.D. See Albert C. Baugh, *A Literary History of England* (New York: Appleton-Century-Crofts, 1948).

15. René Wellek, "The Mode of Existence of a Literary Work of Art," in Robert Wooster Stallman, ed., *Critiques and Essays in Criticism, 1920–1948* (New York: Ronald Press, 1949), p. 223 *passim*.

16. John Crowe Ransom, "Poetry: A Note on Ontology," *Critiques and Essays in Criticism*, p. 32.

17. Baym, "Metaphysical Malaise," *passim*.

18. Jean-Marie Guyau, *Les problèmes de l'esthétique Contemporaine* (Paris: Alcan, 1884), pp. 89–255 *passim*; Francis Barton Gummere, *The Beginnings of Poetry* (London and New York: The Macmillan Co., 1901), pp. 30, 38, 52; Ferdinand Alquié, *Philoso-*

phie du Surréalisme (Paris: Flammarion, 1955), *passim*; Michel Carrouges, *André Breton et les données fondamentales du surréalisme* (Paris: Gallimard, 1950), *passim*.

19. See Gaston Bachelard, *La Dialectique de la durée* (Paris: Boivin, 1936), Chapter 7, "Les Metaphores de la durée"; *La Terre et les rêveries du repos* (Paris: Corti, 1948), Chapter 3, "L'Imagination de la qualité: Rythme—analyse et tonalisation"; *The Poetics of Space*, translated by Maria Jolas, foreword by Etienne Gilson (New York: The Orion Press, 1964).

20. Igor Stravinsky, *Poétique musicale* (Cambridge: Harvard University Press, 1942), Chapter 2, "Du Phénomène musical."

21. André Gide, *Morceaux choisis* (Paris: *La Nouvelle Revue française*, 1921); Herbert Read, *Reason and Romanticism* (London: Faber and Gwyer, 1926), p. 92.

22. Marcel E. Denayer, "Science et Poesie," *Revue de l'Université de Bruxelles*, Vol. 2 (January–March, 1954), pp. 101–121 *passim*; Baym, "On the Relationship between Poetry and Science," *Yearbook of Comparative and General Literature*, Vol. V (1956), p. 24.

23. See Charles Baudelaire, "Richard Wagner et Tannhauser à Paris" (1861); Stephen Ullmann, *Language and Style* (New York: Barnes and Noble, 1964).

24. Northrop Frye, "Four Meanings of Symbolism," *Anatomy of Criticism: Four Essays* (Princeton: Princeton University Press, 1957); see also A. N. Whitehead, *Symbolism: Its Meaning and Effect* (New York: The Macmillan Co., 1927), *passim*.

25. Susanne Langer, *Philosophy in a New Key: A Study in the Symbolism of Reason, Rite, and Art* (Cambridge: Harvard University Press, 1942), p. 281.

26. Langer, *op. cit.*, p. 245; Albert Gehring, *The Basis of Musical Pleasure* (New York and London: G. P. Putnam's Sons, 1910), p. 98.

27. Jean Hytier, *The Poetics of Paul Valéry*, translated by Richard Howard (Garden City, New York: Doubleday and Co., 1953, 1966), p. 120.

28. Hippolyte A. Taine, *Vie et opinions de Thomas Graindorge* (1863–65), (Paris: Hachette, 1867), p. 267; Irving Babbitt, *The Masters of Modern French Criticism* (Boston and New York: Houghton Mifflin Co., 1912), pp. 233–234.

29. Taine, *Derniers Essais de critique et d'histoire* (1866–1889), (Paris: Hachette, 1894), p. 226.

30. Stephen Ullmann, *The Principles of Semantics: A Linguistic Approach to Meaning* (Glasgow: Jackson, Son & Co., 1951), pp. 266–272; Wilbur M. Urban, *Language and Reality: The Philosophy of Language and the Principles of Symbolism* (London:

G. Allen and Unwin, 1939), *passim*; Baym, "The Present State of the Study of Metaphor."

31. Herbert Read, *The True Voice of Feeling* (New York: Pantheon Books, 1953), *passim*.

32. See Gaston Bachelard, *L'Air et les Songes. Essai sur l'imagination du mouvement* (Paris: Corti, 1944), p. 61; also, on *pancalism*, Baldwin, above.

33. George Humphrey Wolfestan Rylands, *Words and Poetry*, with an introduction by Lytton Strachey (New York: Payson & Clarke, Ltd., 1928), p. xi; Henri Peyre, *Literature and Sincerity* (New Haven: Yale University Press, 1963), pp. 3, 339.

34. Herbert Read, *Reason and Romanticism* (London: Faber and Gwyer, 1926); Carl Jung, *Psychological Types*, translated by H. Godwin Baynes (New York: Harcourt, Brace, 1923), p. 69.

35. Roger Fry, "The Artist and Psychoanalysis," in *The New Criticism: An Anthology of Modern Aesthetics and Literary Criticism*, ed. E. W. Burgum (New York: Prentice-Hall, 1930), *passim*; Charles Mauron, *Aesthetics and Psychology* (London: L. & Virginia Woolf, 1935), *passim*.

36. Ronald Christ, *The Narrow Act: Borges' Art of Allusion* (New York: New York University Press, 1969), p. 214.

37. Walt Whitman, "A Noiseless Patient Spider," *Leaves of Grass and Selected Prose*, edited with introduction by Sculley Bradley (New York: Rinehart and Co., 1949), p. 370.

INDEX

Burke, Edmund, 8, 9, 11, 24,
31, 46, 62, 88, 111, 119,
139, 148
Burke, Kenneth, 253, 256–57,
267
Burroughs, John, 61
Bynner, Witter, 272
Byron, Lord, 7, 19, 30, 85, 93,
157

Caedmon, 296
Calderón de la Barca, Pedro, 128
Calverton, V. F., 253
Calvinism, 66, 167, 172
Campbell, Thomas, 28–29
Carlyle, Thomas, 54, 75, 159,
164, 170, 194, 234
Carman, Bliss, 282
Carnap, Rudolf, 224, 235
Carrière, Morris, 114
Cartesian cogito, 294
Cassirer, Ernst, 152, 227, 229,
230, 233
Castel, L. B., 87
Catharsis, 78, 128, 141, 143,
163, 182, 183
Cellini, Benvenuto, 86
Cervantes, Miguel de Saavedra,
157
Channing, William Ellery, 38–
40, 45, 48, 103
Chapman, George, 194, 282
Charvat, William, 16, 29–30
Chateaubriand, François René
de, 22, 85
Chiaroscuro, aesthetic experience
of the, 84
Chopin, Frédéric, 147
Christ, Ronald, 306
Cicero, Marcus Tullius, 282
Classicism: as formulated by
Mme de Staël and Schlegel,

19; and romanticism, 76,
194, 246, 249, 299
Cognition: Cognitio matutina
and vesperina, 283; and
feeling, 176, 297; and
poetry, 264; and sensibility,
289
Coleridge, Samuel Taylor, 18,
19, 30, 31, 33, 35, 36, 38,
42, 43, 47, 48, 54, 55, 66,
75, 79, 80, 86, 94, 138,
157, 168, 176, 200, 205,
219, 221, 227, 233, 246,
249, 258, 263, 267–69
Collingwood, R. G., 229
Comedy, 97, 141, 142, 147
Comfort, George Fisk, 82–83,
105
Comic, the, 101–103, 129
Conceiving, aesthetic modes of,
137
Contemplation, 39, 195, 225;
aesthetic, 175, 176, 209;
attitude of, 305; definition
of, 242; intellectual, 293;
theory of, 242
Contextualism, 212
Cooper, James Fenimore, 45, 274
Copernicus, Nicolaus, 144
Correct mean, 182
Correspondence, law of, 114
Cosmos, nature of tragedy and
the, 66
Cousin, Victor, 22–27, 29, 32,
38, 55, 84, 88
Cowley, Malcolm, 64
Crane, Ronald Salmon, 260
Creativity: the aesthetic of solitude in, 10; distinguishing
mark of, 62; and energy,
78; frustration in, 58; and
inner conflict, 187; nature
of, 23, 34, 35, 198, 201,

Poetics: recent, 298; as a subtle physics, 53

Poetry: and cognition, 264; definition of, 50, 58, 138–39, 156, 202–203, 233, 235, 286, 291, 298; and dreams, 255; experimentalism in, 278; femaleness of, 273; ideas of, 227, 296; and irony, 246; as knowledge, 52, 54; meaning and intention of, 238; and metaphor, 277, 281; and metaphysics, 51, 225; modern, 288; modernist, 252; and music, 50, 52, 78, 177, 188–89, 240, 255; New, 266; and ontology, 251, 252; and painting, 108, 158; pastoral, 274; and philosophy, 108; and preservation of life, 289; and prose, 52, 132, 138–40, 188–89, 231, 265, 272, 297; and psychoanalysis, 259; and psychology, 247; and reality, 50; and religion, 50; and science, 57, 61, 66, 86, 97, 98, 131, 132, 157, 172, 194, 203, 249, 258, 266, 280, 296, 326 n8; and sculpture, 159; as symbol of feeling, 246–47; three-stage process of, 245; and truth and illusion, 264

Poincaré, Henri, 268, 279, 280, 299

Polysemy, 234

Ponge, Francis, 296

Pope, Alexander, 76, 139

Pound, Ezra, 14, 245, 246, 252, 254, 270, 273

Pragmatism, 175

Prall, David W., 208–211, 223

Prescott, Frederick Clarke, 255, 257

Prescott, William Hickling, 16, 31, 45, 226, 227, 274

Primitivism, 166, 167, 225, 251, 305; Rousseauistic, 45

Proctor, Richard, 274, 275

Prose: maleness of, 273; organic, 159; and poetry, 297; and verse, 272, 297

Prose-poem, 297

Proust, Marcel, 241

Prudhomme, Sully, 291

Psychical distance, 179, 242

Psychoanalysis, elements of, 6, 183, 255, 298, 303–305

Psychology: and aesthetics, 94–97, 183, 254; of association, 12, 13, 29, 30; of creativity, 76, 141; and poetry, 247; as a romantic science, 7

Puffer, Ethel Dench, 4, 140–143, 146, 152, 153, 179

Puritans and aesthetic imagination, 2

Pythagoras, 3, 88

Quality: in art and science, 210; definition of, 214

Rabelais, François, 157

Racine, Jean, 132

Radcliffe, Mrs. Ann, 34

Raleigh, Sir Walter Alexander, 141

Ransom, John Crowe, 247–54, 259–60, 263, 296–97

Raphael [Raffaello Santi], 113

Rapin, René, 11

Raymond, George Lansing, 113–115, 121

Read, Herbert, 245, 304